Abercorn

THROUGH

HONI · SOIT · QUI · MAL · Y · PENSE

SOLA NOBILITAT VIRTUS

Abercorn

The Hamiltons of Barons Court

WILLIAM J. ROULSTON

ULSTER HISTORICAL FOUNDATION

2014

Dedicated to the memory
of the
4th Duke and Duchess of Abercorn

Contents

The 1st Marquess of Abercorn

Foreword

The history of any great family is a combination of individual characters and personalities and their relationship to events which are often beyond their control. The manner of that relationship tells us much of the circumstances of any one period of history but more significantly it tells of the calibre of the individual, their priorities and their personal vision. The legacy of a family through generations is most easily judged by others and through the advantage of a scrutiny of that same combination. In the pages which follow Dr William Roulston presents the reader with the fascinating story of one such family which has played a significant part in the tapestry of these islands. He has succeeded in giving us both a glimpse of the personal and the challenges of their time and how those demands were met.

I consider it a great privilege to have been invited to contribute a brief foreword for *The Hamiltons of Barons Court*. As one who has been permitted to enjoy the friendship of the 5th Duke and his wife Sacha and to have been introduced to the mystique which is Barons Court by the 4th Duke I find in this book an enthralling account which transcends a mere historic analysis to produce a picture of unique individuals who have been influential to their generation and community.

Barons Court may be the visible pin to this family story, but it is the detailed account of generations of the Hamilton family which will be welcomed. The contributions of eight Earls, a Marquess and five Dukes of Abercorn and their families to their society in peace and war, in times of civil unrest and relative peace, during years of agricultural revolution and economic hardship, in national and devolved political activity, and within the ordinary dimensions of domestic life the reader comes to appreciate the significance of the family to the beautiful estate and house at Barons Court. The story of the Hamilton family is likened to the spokes of a wheel whose hub is much more than an historic mansion set in the rolling countryside of County Tyrone; it is a fascinating account of British and Irish life through seven centuries.

The Hamiltons of Barons Court deserves a rightful place in Irish biographical history for several reasons. Perhaps the obvious affection on the part of the family for Barons Court is but only one facet of the legacy of a family which by any measure is notable and significant to their times. It is the recurring picture of Barons Court which remains central to this story. In the words of the 5th Duke of Abercorn:

> Each Duke of Abercorn has considered his tenure as a tenancy for life with the overriding responsibility of passing on the tenancy to the next generation in an improved order, both environmentally and financially …

Barons Court has responded to such affectionate and careful stewardship as a much loved family home but as these pages show there is much more to the family Hamilton story.

LORD EAMES OF ARMAGH, OM
HOUSE OF LORDS
APRIL 2014

Preface and acknowledgements

In 1830, my great-great-great-grandfather, Robert Rolleston (as the surname was then spelled), moved to the townland of Gortavea in the manor of Dunnalong to take over two holdings previously occupied by a family of Hamiltons. He thus became a tenant of the 2nd Marquess of Abercorn. Five years later he received a lease from the Marquess for his farm, the original of which is in my possession. The family remained tenants of the Abercorns until near the end of the nineteenth century when Robert's grandson, Charles Roulston, took advantage of the Irish land acts to purchase his farm outright – the farm remains in our family's ownership. As the descendant of one of the tenant-farmers on the Abercorn estate, it has been both a privilege and a pleasure to have been tasked with writing a history of the family. At the same time, it has been both daunting and challenging.

The biggest challenge has been in trying to condense the history of a family that has been involved in so many of the most significant events of the last 500 years and produced so many fascinating and intriguing characters into a single volume. Several of the title holders are worthy of full biographical studies, not least 'Don Magnifico', the 1st Marquess of Abercorn. The primary focus of this book has been on the family itself from its rise to prominence in late fifteenth-century Scotland through to its role today in Northern Ireland and beyond. This focus was further qualified by limiting the study to the main line of descent. A number of Hamiltons, whose lives could not be fitted easily into the main narrative, are looked at separately in a series of sub-chapters.

Even with clear parameters to the study, there are many aspects of the family's history that have not been dealt with as fully as they could have been. There is still considerable scope for a detailed study of the architecture of the house and estate. The incredible collection of art and artefacts at Barons Court also needs careful studying, but from someone much more qualified to do so than me. The management and development of the demesne and gardens with their flora and fauna are also worthy of a more thorough investigation. With the focus primarily on Ireland, the management of the Scottish estates has barely been mentioned, though there is a substantial volume of documentation on this in the Abercorn Papers in the Public Record Office of Northern Ireland.

In researching and writing this book, the family has been unfailingly helpful. I remember well my very first visit to Barons Court in November 2002. A rather nervous and gauche young man was quickly put at ease by the warmth of welcome from the Duke and Duchess of Abercorn. This has been the case on numerous return visits as I have carried out research and have had the opportunity to discuss the family's history with its living representatives. As my near neighbours in County Antrim, I have on many occasions enjoyed stimulating conversations with Lady Moyra and Commander Peter Campbell. With a remarkable memory, Lady Moyra has helped to clarify many matters and generously allowed me access to many of her parents' papers. I have also enjoyed the hospitality of Lord Anthony and his family and benefited from his memories of life at Barons Court just after the Second World War. The Agent at Barons Court, Robert Scott, provided me with an insight into the way in which the estate has evolved to meet the challenges of the twenty-first century and has been supportive in many other ways in the project.

I owe a tremendous debt of gratitude to Dr Anthony Malcomson, the former Director of the Public Record Office of Northern Ireland, who was exceptionally helpful in the early stages of this project in giving me the benefit of his extensive knowledge of the history of the Hamiltons and in allowing me access to his magnificent personal library. The encouragement of two other men with past associations with PRONI has been greatly appreciated. Dr Brian Trainor, formerly Director of PRONI, and my predecessor as Research Director at the Ulster Historical Foundation, transcribed many of the letters between the 8th Earl of Abercorn and his agents, in the process making them so much more accessible to researchers, and drew my attention to other sources of relevance. Dr Bill Crawford, the acknowledged authority on eighteenth-century economy and society in Ulster, added greatly to my understanding of the management of a great landed estate. Of the current PRONI staff I am especially grateful to Ian Montgomery and David Huddleston, and I cannot fail to mention the many times that the search

THE HAMILTONS OF BARONS COURT

room and reading room staff have gone the extra mile in trying to track down documents for me.

A fellow Tyrone man, Robert Corbett, has been a great source of support in recent times and kindly read through some of the later chapters and made a number of helpful comments. Others who have taken an interest in the project and with whom I have enjoyed many conversations over the years include Peter Marson and Dr Olwen Purdue whose own books on, respectively, the Lowry Corrys of Castle Coole and the 'Big House' in the north of Ireland, proved extremely valuable resources. I am especially grateful to Wendy Dunbar for undertaking the design of this book and for producing a stunningly beautiful volume. Her husband Dermott took a number of the photographs for the book including the mesmerising jacket illustration. Bryan Rutledge was responsible for photographing the portraits and family photographs at Barons Court, while Ed Winters took a number of the exterior shots as well as the photographs of the monuments at Barons Court Church. I also acknowledge the support of my colleagues at the Ulster Historical Foundation, especially the Executive Director, Fintan Mullan, who took care of the arrangements for the printing of the book.

Finally, I am thankful to my parents for their support, my brothers for their curiosity, and my wife Heather for her love and forbearance over the many years of this project.

WILLIAM ROULSTON
MAY 2014

The 7th Earl of Abercorn

JAMES
1st Lord Hamilton — m — Mary dau. of James II
d. 1479

JAMES
1st Earl of Arran — m — Janet
d. 1529 — Beatoun

JAMES
2nd Earl of Arran — m — Margaret
Duke of Châtelerault — Douglas
d. 1575

Lord Claud Hamilton

Lord John
ancestor of the Dukes of
Hamilton

Lord Claud
(of Paisley) — m — Margaret
d. 1621 — Seton

JAMES
1st Earl of Abercorn — m — Marion Boyd
1575–1618

Sir Claud
of Shawfield

Sir George
of Greenlaw — m — Mary Butler
d. c. 1654

Sir Frederick
of
Manorhamilton

James
d. c. 1658

1632 m
Catherine — JAMES
Clifton — 2nd Earl
d. 1670

Claud
Lord Strabane
d. 1638

Sir George — m — Mary
of Dunnalong — Butler
d. 1679

James
d. 1673

George
d. 1676

Anthony
d. 1719/20

Thomas
d. 1687

Richard
d. 1717

John
d. 1691

Elizabeth
d. 1708

James
Lord Paisley
d. pre-1670

GEORGE
3rd Earl
d. c. 1680

George
Lord
Strabane
d. 1668

m — Elizabeth
Fagan

1653 m
Catherine
Lenthall

JAMES
6th Earl
d. 1734

The 6th Earl of Abercorn

CLAUD
4th Earl
d. 1691

CHARLES
5th Earl — m — Elizabeth
d. 1701 — Hamilton

Elizabeth
d. 1699

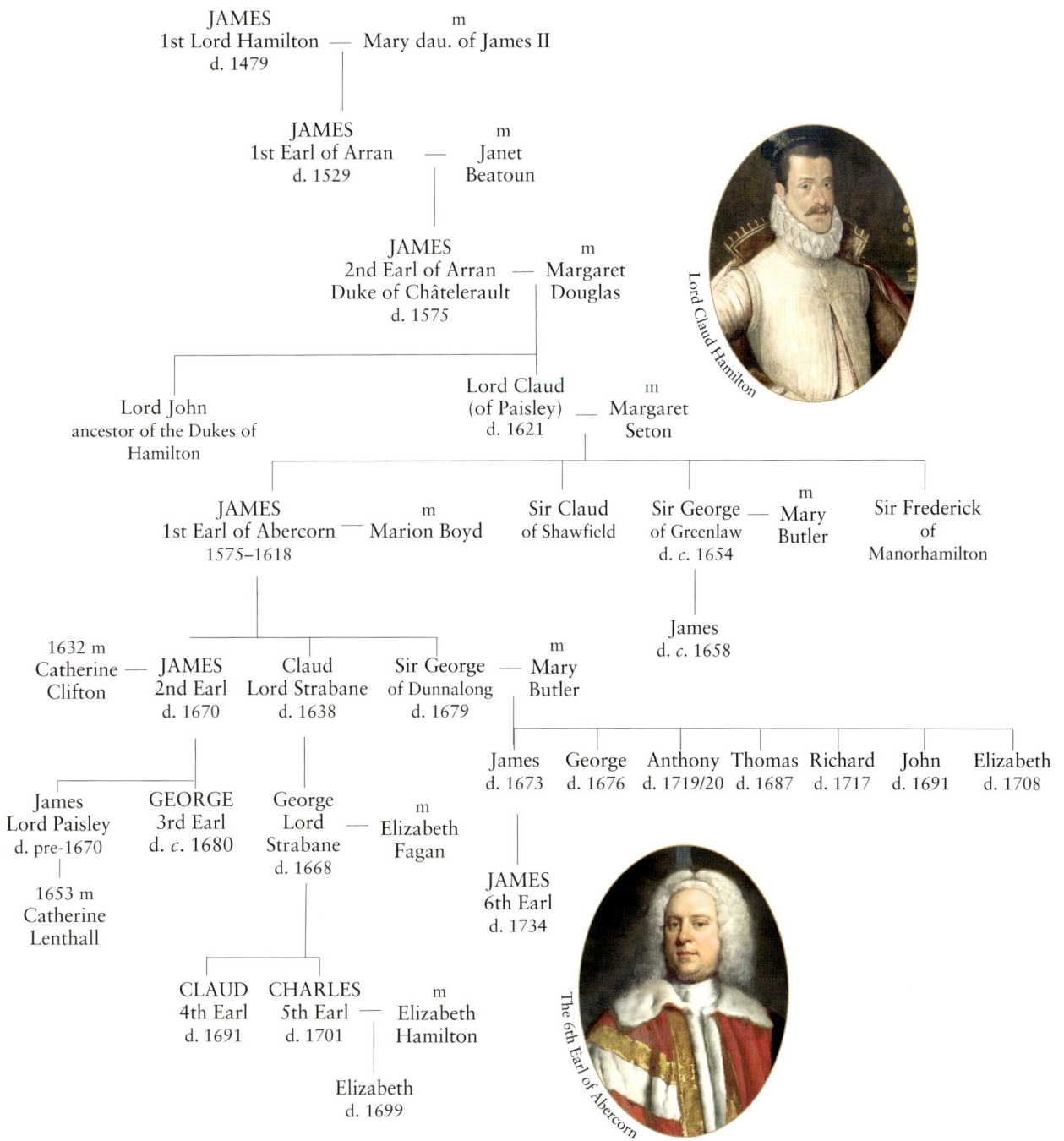

This family tree is not a complete record of all children in each generation.

JAMES
6th Earl of Abercorn — 1684 m — Elizabeth Reading
c. 1661–1734 — d. 1754

JAMES
7th Earl of Abercorn
1686–1744 — 1711 m Anne Plumer d. 1776

Charles
of Painshill
1704–86 + others

JAMES
8th Earl
1712–89

John
d. 1755 — 1749 m — Harriet Eliot (née Craggs) d. 1768

Rev. George
1718–87 + others

JOHN JAMES — 1779 m 1 Catherine Copley d. 1791 — 1792 m 2 Cecil Hamilton (issue: Frances m. Earl of Wicklow) — 1800 m 3 Anne Hatton
1st Marquess
1755–1818

JAMES
Viscount Hamilton
1786–1814 — 1809 m Harriet Douglas d. 1833

Claud
d. 1808

Harriet
d. 1803

Catherine
d. 1812
m Earl of Aberdeen

Maria
d. 1814

JAMES
1st Duke
1811–85 — 1832 m Louisa Russell 1812–1905

Claud
1813–84 — m Elizabeth Proby

Harriet
1812–84 — m William Baillie Hamilton

JAMES
2nd Duke
1838–1913

Claud
1843–1925
m
Carolina
Chandos–Pole

George
1845–1927
m
Maud Lascelles

Ronald
1849–67

Cosmo
b.+d. 1853

Frederic
1856–1928

Ernest
1858–1939
m
Pamela
Campbell

Harriet
1834–1913
m
Earl of
Lichfield

Beatrix
1835–71
m
Earl of
Durham

Louisa
1836–1912
m
Duke of
Buccleuch

Katherine
1840–74
m
Earl of
Mount
Edgcumbe

Georgiana
1841–1913
m
Earl
Winterton

Albertha
1847–1932
m
Marquess of
Blandford

Maud
1850–1932
m
Marquess of
Lansdowne

JAMES
2nd Duke of Abercorn
1838–1913

1869 m

Mary Anna Curzon-Howe
1848–1929

Arthur John
1883–1914

Claud Nigel
1889–1975
m
Violet Ashton

Gladys Mary
1880–1917
m
7th Earl of
Wicklow

Alexandra
Phyllis
1876–1918

JAMES
3rd Duke of Abercorn
1869–1953

1894 m
Rosalind
Bingham
1869–1958

Claud David
1907–68
1946 m
Genesta Heath

JAMES
4th Duke
1904–79

1928 m
Kathleen
Crichton
1905–90

Katherine
1900–85 m
Sir Reginald
Seymour

Cynthia
1897–1972 m
7th Earl
Spencer

Mary
1896–1984 m
1 Robert Kenyon-Slaney
2 Sir John Gilmour

Claud
Anthony
1939–

1982 m
Catherine
Faulkner

Anna
1983–

Alexander
1987–

JAMES
5th Duke
1934–

1966 m
Alexandra
Anastasia
Phillips

Nicholas Edward Claud
1979–
2009 m
Tatiana Kronberg

Valentina
Niva
2010–

Sophie
Alexandra
1973–
eng.
Hashem Arouzi

Caspian
2013–

Soraya
2013–

James Harold
Charles
1969–
2004 m
Tanya Nation

James Alfred
Nicholas
2005–

Claud Douglas
Harold
2007–

Moyra
Kathleen
1930–

1966 m
Commander
Peter Campbell

Michael
1970–
2003 m
Georgiana Cecil

Martha
2006–

Patrick
2009–

Rory
1967–
2001 m
Catherine Shaw

Taise
2002–

Finian
2004–

Thalia
2006–

LOUGH SWILLY

The Abercorn manors

This map shows the five manors that comprised the Abercorn estate in north-west Ulster. These manors were Cloghogall, Derrywoon, Dunnalong and Strabane in County Tyrone and Magavlin and Lismoghry in County Donegal. The consolidation of this estate occurred over the course of a century and Chapter 2 looks at this process in more detail.

LOUGH FOYLE

COUNTY LONDONDERRY

Londonderry/Derry

Cloghogall
Granted to Sir George Hamilton of Greenlaw, brother of the 1st Earl of Abercorn, in 1610.

St Johnstown

Derrywoon
Granted to George Hamilton of Binning in 1610, though in the possession of Sir George Hamilton of Greenlaw by 1613.

Letterkenny

MAGAVLIN & LISMOGHRY

DUNNALONG

Dunnamanagh

COUNTY DONEGAL

River Mourne

CLOGHOGALL

COUNTY TYRONE

Lifford

Strabane

Sion Mills

Dunnalong
Granted to the 1st Earl of Abercorn in 1610.

STRABANE

Strabane
An amalgamation of two of the original Plantation land blocks – Strabane, granted to the 1st Earl of Abercorn, and Shean, granted to Abercorn's brother-in-law, Sir Thomas Boyd, but disposed of to the 1st Earl by 1613.

Newtownstewart

Castlederg

BARONS COURT

River Strule

DERRYWOON

Magavlin and Lismoghry
Acquired by the trustees of the mother of the 6th Earl of Abercorn in 1677.

River Derg

Omagh

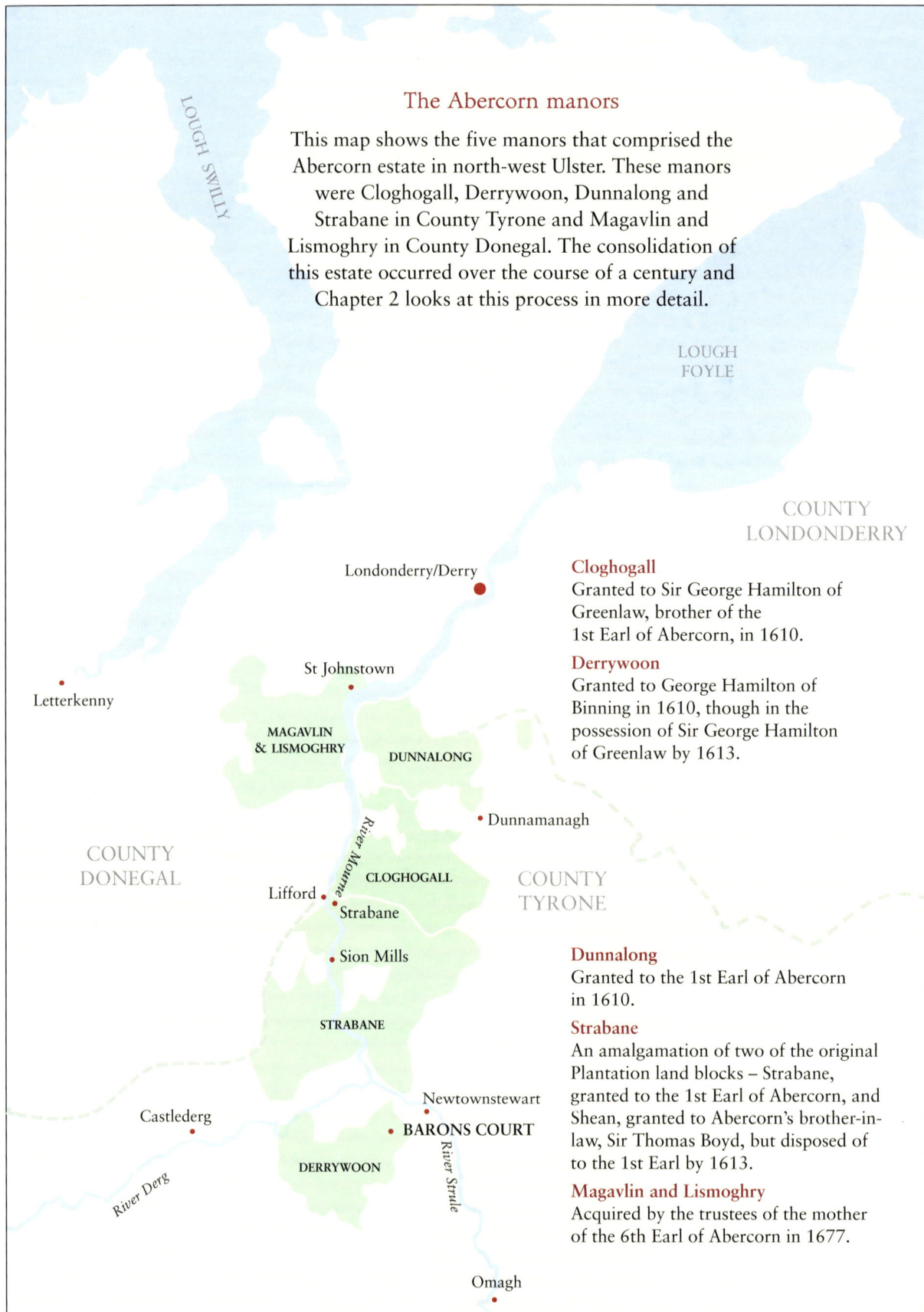

Map of the Abercorn manors

OPPOSITE: Barons Court as shown on the 1900 Ordnance Survey map

Standing
Stone

Ardstraw School

Milbrook

Mullaghamley
286

Lisnatunny

Smithy

Inn

Presbⁿ Meeting Ho.

Milltown

Mill

156

GREAT NORTH

195

Pubble Cotta

Carnkenny

Standing
Stone

Standing
Stone

Low Town

Woodbrook

Lower
Deerpark

Flax
Mill

Mill

Far
Hills

School

Wood Hill

Newto
158

Greenville

Magheracoltan

Whitehart
514

Flushtown

New Coolaghy
Br.

NEWTOWN STEWART

Deer Park

Carnkenny
Upper

Kilstrule

Lislaferty

Island McHugh Br.

Upper
Deerpark

Garch Avenᵈ
Castle

Rakelly

Meaghy
mph

482

Lough
Catherine

Semples

Oldmill
Br.

Killydart

Russell Town

Russelltown
Square

School

Holmes Br.

Lough
Fanny

Castle
castle

The
Lodge

Ballyrenan

Grouse

Bessy Bell
1387

ng Hill
324

The Home Farm

Barons Court

Upper
Beltany

Mullaghcroy
605

Lough
Mary

Cooltly

Aghasessy

Church

Nat. Smithy

Drumlegagh

Presbⁿ
Meetᵍ Ho.

P

R.C. Chapel

Legland

848

Glasmullagh

Lisnacreaght

539

Ber

Inn

Nat.
School

Legland Ho.

P

Leglands

Envagh
Lough

Tullymuck

Dunteige

Water Hill

SCOTLAND

Ardverikie

Paisley

Duddingston

NORTH
SEA

Strabane

Barons
Court

IRISH
SEA

DUBLIN

IRELAND

Nenagh

Roscrea

Beaudesert
Park

ENGLAND

WALES

Witham

Brocket Hall

Burford

Bentley Priory

LONDON

Greenlands

Eastwell

Painshill

Coates Castle

Dale Park

Map showing residences of the Hamiltons, 1550–2014

CALIDON SEA

Rona Iland

S. Rona

Iles of
rides
of Pliny
udes, of
Meuaniae

C. Wrath
or Faro head

The Swell
The Heppers
Stroma
The beyer
Sowna

Dunesbe head
Fresick cast

Caitnes

Old Weik
Ness head
Dunbeith Cast
Baridaile cast
The Ord head

Stranavern

Strath Halladail

Durness

Laxford

Ilen Handa

Gelleslung
Bailnoheglis
The Stoir of
Aſſin
Alleroct
Kikail

Skyraſſin

L. Aſſin

Rowra
Ardnaglais
Bruſs of eatha
marble of Roſse

Loch Brune

Eſbrew

Aſſin Shire

L. Gar

Skore

Offil

Slow

Zute

Mera

Claight

Feuris

Brew

Salin
Mines of Iron
Lome

Ardmanoth

Rosse

Kair

Dingwall
Beuly Abbay

The high moun:
tayns of
Ardmanoth

La Garw

Atholle

MURAY

SUTHER LAND

The marble
mountaines of
Sutherland

Strath
Leith

Ferne

Tarbart
Tarbartness

Cromarty

Loquhaber

L. Aber

Broad
Albayn

Argile

Lennos

L. Lomond

Perth

Dunkell

Dunblain

Sterling

Striueling

Edynbugh

LOUTHIANE

Cantyr

Ila
Iland

Arren

Bute

Kyle

Car

rike

Douglas da le

Anand ale

THE
IRISH

IRE LAND

Gal loway

The Mul of Gal
loway or the
Mulles nuke

Nythes dale

Liddis dale

1
The Scottish background

The seal of James, 1st Lord Hamilton, 1476

Where does one begin a study of the Hamiltons of Barons Court? The author of the entry for the Hamiltons in the *Oxford Dictionary of National Biography* admits that the family 'is of uncertain origins'. Various theories have been put forward – descent from the earls of Southampton/earls of Leicester, Northumberland roots, and so on – but it is unnecessary to rehearse these here. By the time that James Hamilton (d. 1479) was granted a royal charter in 1445, uniting his lands into a barony of Hamilton and creating him a hereditary lord of parliament with the title of Lord Hamilton, the family was already moving towards the centre of political life in Scotland. This was further confirmed by Hamilton's second marriage in 1474 to Mary Stewart, sister of James III, through which subsequent members of the family were able to claim direct descent from Scotland's royal house. An enterprising landowner, Lord Hamilton reclaimed land from the sea at Kinneil on the Firth of Forth at great expense to himself. He was also a patron of the Church. While on a visit to Rome he petitioned the pope to have the parish church of Hamilton made into a collegiate charge. He donated land to the College of Glasgow and also endowed a chapel and hospital in Shotts.

Lord Hamilton was succeeded by his son James, who in 1503 was created Earl of Arran, with a grant of the island of that name, on the occasion of James IV's marriage to Margaret Tudor. The King, Hamilton's cousin, had provided him with a wedding outfit at a cost of £76. Hamilton occupied a prominent position in the Scottish navy. In 1502, for instance, he commanded the fleet that was sent to assist the King of Denmark to put down a Swedish rebellion. Two years later he was sent to quell a rising in the Scottish Isles. In 1513, he was made commander of the naval force that was supposed to sail to France to assist the French against the English. Instead this fleet sailed round the north coast of Scotland and attacked Carrickfergus, then the chief English stronghold in Ulster; by the time the fleet reached France it was too late to make any difference. He was involved in the power struggle in Scotland during the minority of James V – he himself was third in line to the throne at this time – and for a brief period in 1517

OPPOSITE:
John Speed's map of the 'Kingdome of Scotland', 1610

1

was one of the six Regents governing Scotland. He remained close to the King after James attained his majority in 1526 and was an influential member of the Scottish Court. Hamilton died in 1529 and his title and lands passed to his son James, the elder of his two legitimate sons. He also fathered several illegitimate sons, one of whom, John, became abbot of Paisley and subsequently archbishop of St Andrews.

The 2nd Earl of Arran and Duke of Chatelherault

One of the more significant figures of mid-sixteenth-century Scottish history, the 2nd Earl of Arran has left historians puzzled as to how to evaluate his career. Described as a man of 'a gentle disposition, but vacillating in character', he was heir presumptive to the Scottish throne for much of his life and centrally involved at the highest levels of government for several decades. The lands he inherited were extensive and included properties in Lanarkshire, Linlithgowshire, Renfrewshire, Ayrshire, Kirkcudbrightshire and Roxburghshire. The family's principal power base was in the area immediately to the south of Glasgow. A boy of around 10 when his father died, Arran did not reach majority until c. 1540, by which time he was already married to the eldest daughter of the 3rd Earl of Morton. It says much for his political standing that following the death of James V in 1542 he was created governor of the realm and tutor to the infant Queen Mary.

The seal of James, Earl of Arran and Duke of Châtelherault, 1559

Early in his regency he surprised many observers by declaring his sympathy for Protestantism, removing the influential Cardinal Beaton from the post of chancellor, and adopting a more pro-English position, including support for a marriage between Mary and the heir to the English throne, Prince Edward. However, growing opposition to this resulted in Arran returning to the Catholic fold and repudiating the previous negotiations with England. The influence of his half-brother John, then abbot of Paisley, is believed to have been critical to this volte-face. Despite apparently being humiliated by this turn of events, Arran remained in power and survived a period of intense disruption through internal and external threats to his regime. For a time he entertained hopes that his eldest son James would marry the Queen, but in the aftermath of the disastrous defeat by the English at the Battle of Pinkie in September 1547 the Scots agreed to a marriage for Mary with the Dauphin of France in return for French military support. Arran himself benefited enormously from his role in facilitating this union. He was created Duke of Chatelherault, gifted a palace in Paris, and promised a French bride for his son. The arrival of French troops in Scotland did not bring about an immediate revival of the Scottish position, but eventually the English were forced to withdraw south of the border. A period of relative peace ensued and Arran, or Chatelherault as he was now known, was able to turn his

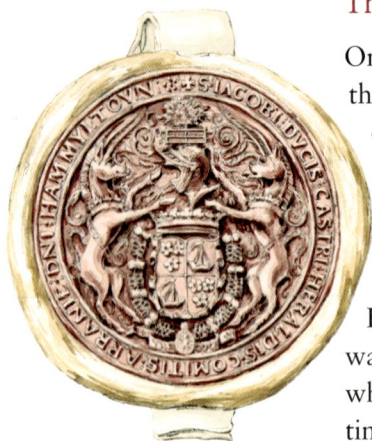

attention to his estates. In early 1554, with Mary approaching majority, he surrendered his authority to her mother, Mary of Guise, who for over a year had been working behind the scenes to have him removed. Chatelherault seems to have offered no opposition to this and was content to leave the political scene.

In the late 1550s he returned to the forefront of politics when he joined with the Protestant nobles opposed to French influence at the heart of the Scottish Court, though whether this was borne out of genuine religious conviction or a concern to ensure the continued influence of his family is open to question. Following the death of the Queen's husband in 1560 he revived hopes that his son James would marry Mary, though nothing came of this. (It was said that the failure of this marriage to go ahead resulted in James losing his reason.) Throughout the 1560s Chatelherault

the first duke of Chatelherault 1559

Portrait of James Hamilton, 2nd Earl of Arran and Duke of Châtelherault.
Once attributed to Cornelius Ketel, this is now thought to have been by Arnold Bronckhorst who painted a number of the leading figures in Scotland in the 1570s and 1580s.

continued to press his claims to the succession, though without success. Following an unsuccessful rising in opposition to the Queen's marriage to Lord Darnley in 1565, he went into exile in France for a time. He subsequently returned to Scotland where his chief sympathy lay with the now-abdicated Queen. His support for Mary's cause resulted in his forfeiting his estates in August 1571 and it was not until February 1573 that he acknowledged James VI as monarch. He retired to his home at Kinneil where he died on 22 January 1575. His wife Margaret survived him and was still alive in 1579. Due to his eldest son's insanity, it was Chatelherault's third son, John, who would inherit the ancestral estates. He was created Marquess of Hamilton in 1599 on the occasion of the baptism of the King's daughter Margaret. He died in 1604 and was succeeded by his son James. In 1643, John's grandson was created Duke of Hamilton.

Lord Claud Hamilton

Of Chatelherault's children, the one that concerns us most is Claud Hamilton, afterwards Lord Paisley. Various dates have been suggested for his year of birth, with 1543 and 1546 the most popular.[1] If the latter, then he was probably the son who was baptised in Edinburgh Castle on 9 June

The Papal Bull of 1553. The Bull of Pope Julius III granting to Lord Claud Hamilton, claimed to be fourteen years of age (actually only around seven), all the profits of the 'Abacie of Paisley to be usufructuary thereof on Resignation of John Hamilton Archbishop of St Andrews and Abbot thereof date December 9th 1553'.

1546.[2] His parents had been engaged in divorce proceedings only two years before, though presumably these were aborted. In 1553 Lord Claud was made the lay commendator of Paisley after his uncle, John Hamilton, had resigned the position of abbot to become archbishop of St Andrews. Though he never entered holy orders, in the course of time other ecclesiastical benefices were acquired by him, including dean of the College of Dunbar, canon of Glasgow and prebendary of Cambuslang. Given his family background, it is hardly surprising that Claud was heavily involved in political affairs from his late teens. In the spring of 1560, aged around 14, he was sent to England as one of the political hostages for the fulfilment of the Treaty of Berwick. He was held in Newcastle until early in 1562 when he was released, after which he returned to Scotland.

By this time Mary, a widow following the death of her husband in December 1560, had also returned to Scotland. In the summer of 1565 she married Lord Darnley, son of the Earl of Lennox. Though this union produced a son in June 1566, the future James VI, their marriage was not a happy one and in February 1567 Darnley was murdered. A few months later

Mary married the man suspected of her late husband's killing, the Earl of Bothwell. The anger against this was immense and most of the nobility were alienated from the young Queen. Bothwell fled and Mary was imprisoned in Loch Leven Castle in June 1567. The following month she was forced to abdicate and her infant son was crowned James VI. His uncle, Mary's illegitimate half-brother, the Earl of Moray, was appointed Regent. The new regime initially lacked authority and was without the support of many of the leading nobles, among them the Hamiltons. They had been opposed to Mary's marriage to Lord Darnley, seeing it as a threat to their own influence in political affairs from their Lennox rivals. In an act of defiance, they had refused to surrender the castles of Hamilton and Draffen. Subsequently they had licence under the Privy Seal to go into exile in France or elsewhere overseas, though whether Lord Claud did go abroad on this occasion is unclear.[3]

Civil war in Scotland

Following the overthrow of Mary in the summer of 1567, the Hamiltons became some of the strongest supporters of the imprisoned Queen. They were particularly angered by the fact that the head of the family, Chatelherault – a former Regent and heir presumptive to the throne – had been overlooked as Regent.[4] Moray was, however, in no way inclined to give in to their challenge and an initial encounter between his forces and those of the Hamiltons in September 1567 resulted in the latter being scattered. The dramatic escape of the Queen from Loch Leven Castle on 2 May 1568 was an event in which Lord Claud played a leading role. On the night in question he accompanied her to Niddry, the home of Lord Seton, and then on to Hamilton. Six days later on 8 May he signed the bond declaring his adherence to Mary. In the meantime the Regent began mobilising his forces and on 13 May the two sides met and fought the Battle of Langside. Lord Claud himself commanded the Queen's vanguard of 2,000 troops. Though not a particularly bloody battle, Langside resulted in a decisive defeat for Mary and her supporters.

After Langside Mary fled to Dumfries accompanied by Lord Claud, who was one of the small band that landed with her at Workington on the north-west coast of England. During the time that Mary was detained in Carlisle Castle, Lord Claud remained in the town on his own account so as to be of assistance to the Queen if the need arose. He was summoned to a parliament called by Moray after Langside, but refused to attend. In July 1568 his lands were declared forfeit and a month later they were given to his baillie, Lord Semple. In October of that year he recaptured Hamilton Castle from the Semples, but failed in his attempt to take the castle at Draffen. The following February he was once again in attendance upon the Queen, this time at

Lord Claud Hamilton. This portrait was reacquired for the 8th Earl of Abercorn in 1747 by Lord Somerville. Writing to the Earl from Holyrood House, Edinburgh, Somerville commented: 'The picture I mentioned of Lord Claud Hamilton is now in my possession and the purchase of it a very trifle, having got an obscure person to buy it. You may depend on it being an original and that it was formerly in Seaton house. It is a half length in a military dress (tho' he was a churchman). The Hamilton Arms with several historical things with interpretations, and amongst others a strong box reversed and a good deal of gold coin lying round it with Queen Mary's mark. The painting I will not say much about, it being like other old pictures of that age' (PRONI, D623/A/48/22).

Tutbury, while in August 1569 there was a rumour that Lord Claud was to marry the sister of the Regent's wife: an action, it was said, that would be akin to 'cutting the regent's throat'.[5]

The events of the following years are complex and it is not possible to reconstruct everything that Lord Claud did during this period. His fortunes, and those of his family, fluctuated considerably. He played a leading role in the conspiracy that led to the murder of the Regent, Lord Moray, at Linlithgow on 23 January 1570. The assassin, James Hamilton of Bothwellhaugh, fired the fatal shot from the house of the archbishop of St Andrews, Lord Claud's uncle, then galloped from the scene on the archbishop's horse and fled for safety to France. Almost a year later, on 17 January 1571, Lord Claud recaptured Paisley and proceeded to punish those in the surrounding districts who refused to acknowledge the Queen's authority. However, he could not hold on to Paisley for long after the town's water supply was stopped. In another blow for the Hamiltons, the archbishop of St Andrews was captured when Dumbarton Castle was surprised on 1–2 April 1571; he was executed at Stirling a few days later. Shortly after this, Lord Claud entered Edinburgh Castle and then on 4 May he and his father with 27 men took over St Giles' Church, 'breaking holes in the vaulting so they could shoot whom they pleased'.[6] The following month he had Lord Semple placed under arrest in Edinburgh Castle. On 13 June he sat in the 'Marian' parliament in Edinburgh as 'Claude Hamilton, abbot of Paisley, allowed by the Pope sixteen years past'.[7] However, he suffered a setback when his forces were defeated by the Earl of Morton's troops at Leith.

In September 1571 the Hamiltons captured the Earl of Lennox in the 'surprise of Stirling'. Lord Claud led his troops through the town shouting, 'Ane Hamilton, God and the Queen! Think on the bishop of St Andrews!' In the mêlée that followed Lennox was mortally wounded by Captain James Calder. Under torture Calder confessed that he was acting under orders from Lord Claud, while it was also alleged that Lord Claud had issued instructions that all noblemen taken prisoner should be executed as soon as they were brought outside the port of the town. On 3 July 1572 he and other Hamiltons were specifically denounced as traitors. A week later he and his supporters surprised Lord Semple, who was engaged in collecting the rents from Lord Claud's former tenants, killing 42 of his men and taking 15 of them prisoner.[8] In the Pacification of Perth the following February, which brought an end to the war between the supporters of Mary and those of her son, his forfeiture was recalled and he was restored to his possessions. His lands, however, remained in Semple's possession and it was only after some difficulty that Lord Claud recovered Paisley. In the summer of 1574, Lord Claud married Margaret, daughter of George, Lord Seton.

Banishment, reconciliation and foreign intrigue

What appeared to have been settled by the Pacification of Perth proved to be only a temporary lull in the conflict between the supporters of the young King and the Hamiltons. While Lord Claud seems to have avoided controversy during most of the regency of the Earl of Morton, he was suspected of conniving in Morton's brief fall from power in 1578. Fearing for his own position, in April 1579 Morton persuaded the privy council to take action against the Hamiltons. The council revived former acts against them, identifying their complicity in the murders of Moray and Lennox as well as other crimes as the basis of its actions. They were declared outlaws and orders were given to seize their lands. Lord Claud and his brother John were taken by surprise, but managed to escape arrest. They speedily, and with some show, garrisoned a number of their castles. This was a ruse to distract attention from their escape plans and when Paisley was captured it was discovered that 'Lord Claud was not in his strength, but had conveyed himself quietly to sic pairt as no man knows'.[9] To begin with, Lord Claud went into hiding in Scotland, later crossing into England where he was given shelter. He then made his way to London where he sought assistance from Queen Elizabeth and her ministers.

Elizabeth was sympathetic to his plight and sent one of her officials north of the border to plead his cause. The Scottish parliament ignored these entreaties and in November 1579 the Hamiltons' lands were declared forfeited. It has been suggested that Elizabeth's support for Lord Claud was partly due to the fact that his eldest brother was 'in effect the heir presumptive to the as yet childless James VI'.[10] The importance of the Hamiltons in Scottish politics was probably also a reason, and outweighed Hamilton's support for Mary. The French ambassador to Scotland, De Chastenau, also intervened on behalf of the Hamiltons, no doubt prompted to do so by Lord Claud's professed attachment to the French cause, but for the time being his master, Henry III, was reluctant to involve himself in the affair. From his banishment in 1579 to 1584 Lord Claud spent much of his time in England and in particular at Widdrington in Northumberland. He was in the somewhat anomalous position of being dependent on Elizabeth for protection while continuing to work for the cause of Mary as well as for his own restoration to his Scottish possessions. In this, he co-operated with his brother John, though they did not always agree on strategy.

In the meantime, events in Scotland had taken a new turn. Morton had again been ousted and was executed in 1581, ostensibly for his involvement in Darnley's murder. Two new figures emerged as royal favourites: Esme Stewart, Duke of Lennox, and Captain James Stewart. The latter was made Earl of Arran, a move that incensed the Hamiltons because it was a title that had been held by Lord Claud's eldest brother James, who had been declared insane. The 'Ruthven raid' of 1582, when James was captured by a group of noblemen, provided only temporary encouragement for the Hamiltons and after James escaped the following June, Arran cemented his position as royal favourite. In 1584, Elizabeth instructed Lord Claud and Lord John to go to the Scottish borders to support the former Ruthven raiders. Lord Claud ventured further into Scotland and in April of that year he was present at the capture of Stirling Castle. A setback for the anti-Arran faction resulted in his retreating to England. This time his exile was relatively brief, for in autumn 1584 he was invited back into Scotland having been promised safe conduct by James VI. Because of suspicions about his trustworthiness he was sent to live in the north of the country, where he found a temporary home with the Earl of Huntly. His period in Grampian was short, for on 6 April an Order in Council was issued banishing Lord Claud and his servants to France.

Arriving in Paris, he was warmly received by the French government, which saw in him a means by which French influence in Scotland could be revived. His sojourn in the French capital was fairly brief, and following the overthrow of Arran he was recalled to Scotland by James VI. On his return journey he carried with him a letter from Henry III for James and also a gift of 500 crowns given to him by the French King. He had an interview with James in February 1586. It was said that Lord Claud was a 'man well likit of by the King for his wit and obedience in coming and going at the King's command, and for reveling of certain interpryses of the lordis at thair being in England'.[11] A rumour that Lord Claud was to be made chancellor proved incorrect, but he was now a member of the Privy Council and 'freended' by the King who, it was said, saw in him a potential ally in forming a new faction to counter those lords who had ousted Arran.[12] On 29 July 1587, James executed a charter confirming Lord Claud's possession of the temporality of Paisley and making him a lord of parliament with the title

Lord Paisley. In 1588 he was reported to have taken the Protestant oath, though by this time his Catholicism, which previously had been cloaked in ambiguity, was well known.

Despite his apparent reconciliation with the monarch, Lord Claud continued his intrigue with foreign powers and the exiled Queen Mary. In August 1586 it was reported that Lord Claud had returned to his estates to live quietly, having left the Catholic cause to God. This was not quite the case. Only the previous month he had been considered by Mary to be her chief agent in Scotland.[13] He was regarded as one of the men most capable of reviving the fortunes of the Catholic party in Scotland, even more so than his elder brother John, and was encouraged to support the Babington plot which sought the replacement of Queen Elizabeth with Mary. It was even indirectly suggested to him that Mary wished him to be declared the heir to the Scottish throne should James die without issue. However, Mary was brought to trial in the autumn of 1586, condemned to death and executed the following February. Lord Claud had encouraged James to intervene on his mother's behalf, but the King displayed little concern for her cause.

Though the death of Mary had been a major setback, Lord Claud persisted in political intrigue and maintained a correspondence with the Duke of Parma, the governor of the Spanish Netherlands, even after the defeat of the Spanish Armada. In February 1589 copies of these letters were intercepted and passed to the Scottish government. Lord Claud's response to this was to hand himself over to the authorities, who placed him under arrest in

Lord Claud Hamilton's family home, the Place of Paisley, adjoins Paisley Abbey and was originally part of the establishment's cloistral buildings.

9

Edinburgh Castle. He remained in prison until August of that year. His presence along with that of other Catholics in Edinburgh in January 1590 aroused concerns that they were about to seize the castle by force.[14]

Later life and family

In the early 1590s Claud withdrew from national politics, his last attendance at a meeting of the Privy Council being on 24 February 1591. His retirement from public affairs was abrupt and has been ascribed to mental illness. In November 1590, Robert Bowes, the English ambassador to Scotland, noted that Lord Claud had recovered his senses after a period of illness, though in December 1591 he described Lord Claud as 'beastly mad'. Various other charges were made against him, including an accusation that he was involved in witchcraft.[15] While retiring from affairs of state, he was involved in local government in the burgh of Paisley. In July 1597 he hosted a visit to Paisley by the Queen, Anne of Denmark. The following year Lord Claud retired completely from public life and handed over the responsibility for managing his estates to his eldest son James, the Master of Paisley. In the 'Lettre of Factorie and Commissioun' he wrote: 'I haif thir sindrie yers bypast abstractit myselff for the maist pairt from the cairful gyding and administratioun of my lands … [that] I mycht be the mair abl to exerceis myself in the Service of God and in hevenlie and spirituall meditatiounis'.[16] In 1617, the King himself was entertained at Paisley, though Lord Claud was too old to take part in the festivities.[17] He died in 1621 and was almost certainly buried in St Mirren's aisle in Paisley Abbey. His wife predeceased him in February 1616. Her latter years were plagued by ill-health. Letters by her brothers refer to the 'onpleasant liffe she hes had thir manye yeares butt appeirance of recoverie'.[18]

Lord Claud and his wife had 10 children. The lives of James, George and Claud, all beneficiaries of the scheme for the Ulster Plantation, will be looked at in more detail in the next chapter. Another son, Sir Frederick, became one the leading planters in County Leitrim and a major figure in the wars in Ireland in the 1640s, while a further son, Sir John, married a daughter of one of the King of Spain's chief officials. Three of Lord Claud's children,

Monument in Paisley Abbey to three of the children of Lord Claud Hamilton. Placed in St Mirren's Aisle, this stone tablet records the deaths in infancy of Margaret (1577), Henry (1585) and Alexander (1587).

Margaret, Henry and Alexander, died in infancy and are commemorated on a monument in St Mirren's aisle in Paisley Abbey. A second daughter named Margaret married the Marquess of Douglas; the final child was Issobelle. Lord Claud also fathered two illegitimate children, James and Mary.

Opinions on Lord Claud vary considerably. *The Peerage of Scotland*, compiled in 1813, describes him as 'a brave and gallant gentleman, of steady honour, and unspotted integrity, who, by a series of virtuous actions, reflected lustre on his great ancestors, and ennobled the illustrious blood that ran in his veins'.[19] On the other hand, in 1586 he was viewed by an Englishman as 'ambitious, cruel and dissembling'. Writing in the *Oxford Dictionary of National Biography*, Peter Holmes has commented that for Lord Claud to have survived at all, 'even if at the expense of his sanity', represents a considerable personal triumph, and attributes this to his 'pliability, courage and wit'.[20] He had an instinct for survival, a trait that was to be seen during the vicissitudes of the family in the seventeenth century. This was perhaps the most important thing that later Hamiltons may have inherited from him.

PARTE OF Y BARONE OF STRABANE

(map labels include: Loughinsholin, Colrane, of Strabane, Tireconel, Tireconel, Tireconel, Tireconel, River of Loughfoyle, Parte of this Baronie, Parte of..., Mourne flu, Large flu, fiir flu)

Bodley map of the barony of Strabane, 1609 (see also overleaf).
These maps were produced as part of the plans for the Ulster Plantation scheme and show the townland distribution in Strabane barony, most of which was allocated to the three Hamilton brothers, James, the 1st Earl of Abercorn, Sir Claud and Sir George.

2
The Hamiltons in the seventeenth century

To say that the story of the Hamiltons in the seventeenth century is complex would be an understatement. It was a period of critical importance in the family's history and laid the foundations of much of what followed. At one level the story seems straightforward enough. In 1606 the Scottish earldom of Abercorn was created. A hundred years later the title was held by the 1st Earl's great-grandson, the 6th Earl; both men were named James Hamilton. However, in the intervening period the title had been transferred between three separate lines of descent from the original holder.

Furthermore, in the course of the 1600s the family's Scottish property had been lost and its landed base had shifted to Ireland. The Irish estate itself was subject to forfeiture on a number of occasions due to the family's political allegiances, but despite these threats to its very existence it was of much greater extent by the beginning of the eighteenth century than at any time in the hundred years before. This chapter attempts to unravel the vicissitudes of the family during this era.

James Hamilton, 1st Earl of Abercorn

The story of the Hamiltons and Ireland begins with James, the eldest son of Claud, Lord Paisley. Born in 1575, his earliest years were far from settled due to his father's escapades on account of his support for Mary, Queen of Scots. From his early twenties, however, and due in part to his father's withdrawal from public life, he was drawn ever more closely into the world of the Scottish Court. He was probably the James Hamilton who was elected MP of Linlithgow in 1597. In 1598, he was appointed a privy counsellor and a groom of the bedchamber by James VI, and in November 1600 he was appointed sheriff of Linlithgow. The following July he received a charter of the lands of Abercorn in Linlithgowshire and in April 1603 was created Lord of Abercorn. By this time he had married Marion, daughter of the 5th Lord Boyd. The closeness of Abercorn's relationship with James – now King of England as well as Scotland – is reflected in the fact that he was appointed a commissioner for Scotland in the ultimately unsuccessful discussions over the possibility of a political union with England. For this and for other services he was rewarded with the earldom of Abercorn on 10 July 1606. Subsequent duties undertaken by the now Earl of Abercorn included the management of the affairs of the young 2nd Marquess of Hamilton and his appointment to a commission to impose 'civilitie, oure obedyence, and trew religioun' on the Hebrides.

By this time plans were underway to officially 'plant' six of Ulster's nine counties with settlers from England and Scotland. In 1607, the leading Gaelic lords in Ulster, the Earls of Tyrone and Tyrconnell, had sailed from Rathmullan in County Donegal, hoping – unsuccessfully as it turned out – to secure support from the King of Spain for a further invasion of Ireland. The territories of these and other Ulster lords were then confiscated and for the most part parcelled out in compact estates to various categories of grantee. The most onerous obligations were placed on the new landowners of English and Scottish background (known as undertakers because they undertook to plant settlers and build on their new estates), who alone were expected to introduce families of British origin to their lands. To give encouragement and a greater sense of security to the English and Scottish grantees, it was decided to group together those of similar background by

PARTE OF THE BARONIE OF STRABANE

OMEY

OMEY

Donganon

OMEY

Parte of this Bar. of Strabane

Tirconell

_____ Map of Part of the Precinct of Strabane _____

On this Map are seen the five following Proportions:—

1. The Earl of Abercorn's Middle Proportion called Shean at the extreme right.
2. Sir George Hamilton's Small Proportion of Derriwoon, to the north of Shean.
3. Sir Robert Newcomen's Great Proportion of Lislap, to the left of Derriwoon.
4. Sir John Drummond's Small Proportion of Ballymagragh, to the north of Lislap.
5. Sir George Hamilton's Middle Proportion of Terimurnarthell, held jointly by him and Sir William Stewart, to the extreme left of the Map.

Bodley map of the barony of Strabane, 1609 (see previous page).

barony. Each barony would have a chief undertaker who was permitted to have lands totalling a nominal 3,000 acres; the lesser undertakers were allowed to have estates of no more than 2,000 acres.

Because of his position in James' inner circle, the Earl of Abercorn was drawn into the plans for the Plantation and in 1610 was made chief undertaker in the barony of Strabane in County Tyrone. It is not clear when he was first approached about becoming directly involved in the Plantation scheme, but by April 1610 he was aware that his land grant would be in Tyrone. In a letter written to the King on the 12th of that month he referred to 'that litle pairt of land you matie apperit to think fitting for me callit Strabawne'.[1] What persuaded Abercorn to accept this challenge is unknown, but it was a brave step by a man used to the lifestyle of a lowland Scottish aristocrat to forsake the comforts of his home and position at Court for what many would have regarded as the 'wilds' of west Ulster. A letter of January 1612 refers to him having been 'induced' by James to take part of the plantation as a 'countenance and strength' to others, suggesting that he had been singled out by James on account of certain qualities he possessed.

Roughly diamond in shape, the barony of Strabane occupies the north-west portion of County Tyrone. Topographically, the barony is dominated by the Sperrin mountains and their foothills and by the waterways that form part of the Foyle river basin. The most productive agricultural land is found in the river valleys, particularly the area immediately to the north and south of the town of Strabane. Abercorn's lands in Strabane barony comprised the 'great' proportion of Dunnalong (an estimated 2,000 acres) and the 'small' proportion of Strabane (an estimated 1,000 acres). In actual fact, these lands extended to nearly 24,000 statute acres. The proportion of Dunnalong occupied the 'lower part' or western part of the parish of Donagheady, while the proportion of Strabane covered the temporal lands in the parish of Camus-juxta-Mourne. Significantly, his grant included the site of the castle at Strabane that had been built by the former Irish lord Turlough Luineach O'Neill and the demesne lands around it, a reflection of the continuity of centres of power under the new dispensation.

Two of Abercorn's brothers were also granted land in Strabane barony at this time – Sir George Hamilton of Greenlaw and Sir Claud Hamilton of Shawfield. Sir George's proportion of Cloghogall lay between Abercorn's lands of Dunnalong and Strabane and roughly correlated with the parish of Leckpatrick. Sir Claud was granted the lands of Eden and Killeny, which occupied most of the eastern half of the barony and which were largely mountainous. Abercorn's brother-in-law, Sir Thomas Boyd, was a further grantee and his proportion of Shean lay immediately to the west of the proportion of Strabane in the parish of Urney. Others, not of Abercorn's choosing, also received lands in Strabane barony. The Earl was annoyed at this and claimed that he could plant twice the area that had been allocated to him. However, his attempts to prevent these nominees from receiving land grants were unsuccessful. By 1613 he had extended his property in Strabane barony by taking possession of the proportion of Shean, which had been relinquished by Boyd.

Abercorn proved one of the most active of the new Ulster landowners and took seriously the responsibilities imposed on him by the government. In this he was assisted by privileges not extended to the other Scottish grantees of lands in Ulster. For example, in 1611 he was allowed to have the assistance of

Dean Castle, Kilmarnock, the Ayrshire home of the Boyds, the in-laws of the 1st Earl of Abercorn.

25 men from the army in Ireland to help him in planting and building on his estate.[2] The following year, after he had complained about being granted land he considered insufficient for someone of his status, it was proposed to send him another 25 soldiers, though it is not known whether this occurred. In addition, Abercorn was allowed to requisition any ship on the west coast of Scotland to transport people or goods to Ireland. He was granted this right because 'ordinarie passage' boats were too vulnerable to attack by pirates. In 1613, he was consulted about the possibility of establishing a ferry service between Scotland and Ulster which would be regulated through specific ports.[3] Using a ship called *Gift of God*, Abercorn himself exported agricultural produce, including beef and oats, from Strabane to Scotland.[4] He also introduced large numbers of cattle from Scotland to manure his estate.[5]

Further evidence of favouritism shown to the Earl comes in 1616, when he was allowed the forfeiture of all bonds entered into by the undertakers of lands in Strabane barony who had not fulfilled the obligations laid down on them. It has been suggested that this may have been a settling of accounts with Abercorn, as the previous year the Scottish treasury had been unable to pay him a debt of £30,000 (Scots).[6] In 1617, his eldest son James was created Baron of Strabane in recognition of his (Abercorn's) 'services in planting a colony of brave men, professing the true religion, in Strabane barony, and many well fortified castles for the defence of Ulster'.[7] The Earl was also responsible for developing the town of Strabane, which in 1613 received its charter of incorporation and which by 1619 contained 80 houses, many of which were 'of lime and stone, very well and strongly built'.[8] Abercorn made the town of Strabane his Irish base, building a castle there as well a school-house, and starting work on a church, though this was not completed until after his death in 1618. In fact, such was his contribution to the town's early development that in 1622 the townsmen complained that since the Earl's death their settlement had 'languished and drooped'.

Castle Hamilton, Manorhamilton. This castle was built in the mid-1630s by a younger brother of the 1st Earl of Abercorn, Sir Frederick Hamilton, on his estate in County Leitrim. It was an important stronghold in the region in the 1640s.

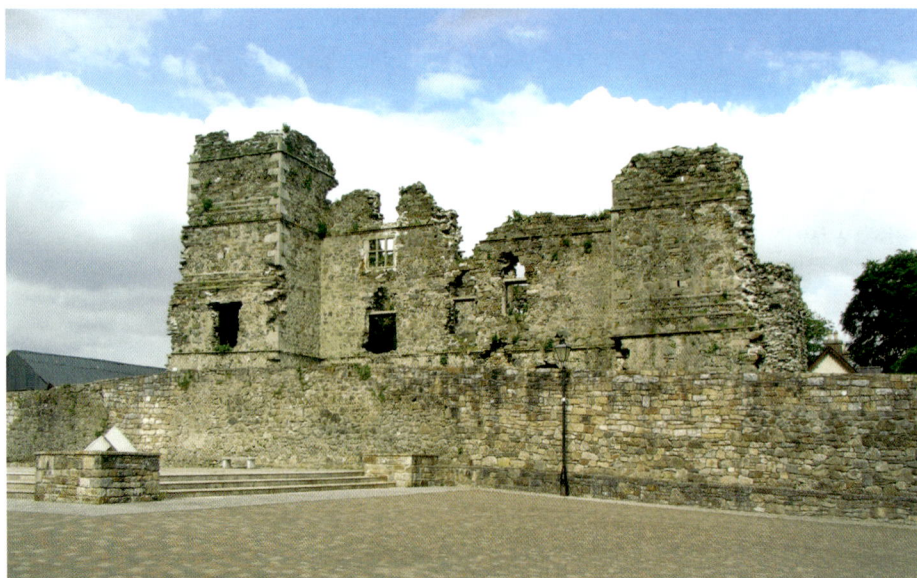

In 1614, Abercorn was appointed to arbitrate in the land disputes between Sir James Hamilton and Sir Hugh Montgomery, two Ayrshire men with vast estates in County Down. The choice of the Earl to settle the quarrels that had arisen between these east Ulster magnates is further evidence of his rank and reputation. His selection probably owed at least as much to his status and the respect that Hamilton and Montgomery would have accorded him as to his skills as a mediator. Shortly after arriving in Down in September of that year, Abercorn wrote that he had observed, while out hunting, 2,000 well-armed Scots. He was also impressed with the castle that Hamilton had built at Killyleagh, commenting that it was without equal in Ulster. Being distantly related to Hamilton, and having reported adversely on Montgomery in 1612, it is perhaps not surprising that the recommendations Abercorn made favoured the former. Montgomery protested, accusing the Earl of having wronged him, but the King, having first consulted with Abercorn, accepted his solution to the disputes.[9] The closeness of Abercorn's relationship with Hamilton is further indicated in the latter's will of 1616 in which he named the Earl as one of his executors.

Though his father may have been a Catholic and, as will be presently shown, his wife Marion and children also, Abercorn was a Protestant. He was an elder in the Kirk and a member of the General Assembly. He also inducted ministers to Paisley, such as Andrew Knox, later bishop of the Isles and then Raphoe, who were well known for the strength of their Protestantism. However, it would be going too far to agree with the characterisation of him as a committed Presbyterian. At the same time, and no doubt due to his father's espousal of Catholicism, there were those who questioned his commitment to the Reformed Church. In 1614, we find him writing to the King complaining of rumours that were being spread against him on the question of his own religion and that of 'his bed-fellows', which had reached James' ears. He requested permission from the King to withdraw for a time from the Court so that he could spend some time travelling 'for the reparation of his fortune'.[10]

On 28 September 1616, the Earl received the first of two visits from one of the foremost physicians of the day, Sir Theodore Turquet de Mayerne. The doctor's report of this visit has survived and provides a remarkable insight into Abercorn's medical history. On the day of his examination, the Earl was 41 years, one month and 13 days old. He had had smallpox at the age of three and measles aged 15. A serious illness had left him deaf in his right ear, but apart from his hearing his other senses were acute. Both of his parents were of a melancholic nature, and so was he. For seven to eight years he had been prone to dizziness and had heart palpitations. He also suffered from 'tertian ague' (a fever that recurred every other day) for three months. During this period, he lost interest in his affairs, but recovered and for the next three years was in much better health. He liked fish, but it did not agree with his digestive system. He rarely drank wine, though he did consume small quantities of ale or beer. The Earl enjoyed being at home and when unwell would never leave it. If he got his feet wet in winter he would be prone to a cold. He generally slept seven hours a night, enjoyed warm baths and took any medicine given to him.[11]

The 1st Earl of Abercorn died at Monkton in Scotland on 23 March 1618 at the age of 42. He has been described as someone of 'extraordinary accomplishments', yet he remained a man whose 'habits were simple and unostentatious'.[12] A contemporary wrote the following obituary of the Earl:

> *homme fort renommé, en tout deste isle for ses belles et virteuse qualityes; d'un esprit noble, genereux, affable, et fort aymé de tous pour ses vertues civiles et domestiques, et grandement regretté de tous ceux qui la cognoissoyent, et de tout le pays.*[13]

The inventory of Abercorn's goods and possessions compiled after his death shows that he was fairly wealthy by the standards of the time. The value of his inventory came to £23,255 10s. (Scots) and he was owed another £8,898 11s. 6d. The gross value of his 'frie gear' (free estate) was, therefore, £32,154 1s. 6d. However, his debts amounted to £23,830 15s. 1d., leaving only £8,323 6s. 5d., or about £700 sterling. Nonetheless, he was 'among Scotland's richer landlords'.[14] In comparison, fellow Scot Lord Burley, who owned an estate in County Fermanagh, left a free estate of only £60 sterling when he died in 1619.

The following extract from Abercorn's will sets out where he wished to be buried and the manner in which he was to be interred:

> I committ my saul into ye holie handis of my guid God and merciful Father, fra quhome throw ye richteous meritis of Jesus Christ, I luik to ressave it againe at ye glorious resurectione joynit wt yis same body, – qlk heir I leif to sleip and be bureit, gif it so pleis God, in ye sepulcher qr my brethir, my sisteris, and bairnis lyis; in ye iyll callit St Mirreinis Iyll, at ye south heid of ye croce churche of Paslay; trusting assuredly to rys at yt blissit resurrectione to lyf eternell. I desyre that yr be no vaine nor glorios seremonie vsit at my buriel, raying honouris, bot yt my corps be karayit to ye grave be some of my most honorabill and neriest friendis with my bairnis &c.

No monument to him survives or is known to have been erected.

The children of the 1st Earl

Though two government surveys of the Plantation, from 1618–19 and 1622, ascribe ownership of the Abercorn lands in Strabane barony to James Hamilton, the 2nd Earl, the succession was not quite as straightforward as this. Under the terms of a 'King's Letter' of 1620, one third of the estate in Strabane barony was to be enjoyed as a dower during her lifetime by the Countess of Abercorn, the 1st Earl's widow. Under the same arrangement, it was determined that the manor of Strabane (incorporating the original proportions of Strabane and Shean) would in due course devolve to Claud Hamilton, while Dunnalong would become the property of George Hamilton, respectively the second and fourth sons of the 1st Earl. The 2nd Earl was, therefore, not provided with any lands in Strabane, succeeding instead to his father's lands in Scotland, as well as those of his grandfather, Lord Claud Hamilton, who died in 1621. In addition to his heir James and sons Claud and George, about whom more will be said presently, the 1st Earl of Abercorn had two other sons, Alexander and William, and four daughters. In the summer of 1627, at the age of 14, Alexander, along with his brother George, attempted to raise troops for an expedition to Germany. By the late 1630s he was a member of the King's household. He served in the army in Ireland during the 1640s and also held the position of Engineer and Quartermaster-General to the King. He died before 4 May 1669. His son Alexander had an interesting career on the Continent, becoming a member of the Court of the Elector of Palatine and acquiring estates in Hungary and Monrovia. In 1677, he was sent as an ambassador to England by the Elector.

The remaining son of the 1st Earl, Sir William Hamilton, also found himself in an influential position on the Continent. Educated at Glasgow University, he was created a baronet in 1627 and in 1630 declared that he was going overseas to seek his fortune. It seems that he saw military service on the Continent: in 1633 he wrote from Leith to Sir John Maxwell of Pollok that he and his company were waiting 'wpon a shipe and faire winde', and in 1634 he again wrote to Maxwell, this time from Nancy in the Duchy of Lorraine, stating his confidence that by the following winter he would have sufficient expertise as a soldier to be capable of commanding Dumbarton Castle, of which Maxwell had recently been appointed governor.[15] Described as 'so noble and Catholique a gentleman', Sir William was sent to Rome in 1636 to fulfil a diplomatic role on behalf of Queen Henrietta Maria, wife of Charles I. His first audience with the Pope, Urban VIII, was reported to have been a great success: 'his Holiness … receaved him with very greate signes of joy, he is exceeding well liked of here by all and indeed I think he will give as good satisfaction as any that could have been sent from England'. Afterwards Sir William was presented with two horses for his coach by a senior cardinal.[16] In 1638, he reported back to one of the secretaries of state in London that the Pope was willing to make a financial contribution to Charles' war with the Scottish Covenanters. The King was apparently furious when he learned of this communication and threatened to have Sir William removed from his post.[17] By the spring of 1640 he had been replaced in Rome. He continued to serve the Queen during her exile on the Continent in the 1650s, reputedly spending much of his private money on her maintenance. In March 1660, in response to a petition for monies owed to Sir William, Charles II issued the following promissory note:

> Whereas a debte of foure thousande one hundred and fifty pounds sterlinge apeares to be remayning dew by the king my father to Sir W. Hamilton, brother to the Earle of Abercorne for the service done to the Queene my mother, I do hereby promis to pay ye sayde debte of £4,150 to ye sayde Sir William Hamilton his heires and assigns or to satisfie him or them to the valew thereof when it shall please God to restore me to the possession of my dominions. Given at Brussells 28 Mar. 1660.[18]

Sir William died on 24 June 1681 at South Shields, where a tombstone in St Hilda's churchyard recorded that he was 'late servant to Queen Henrietta Maria'.[19]

Lady Lucy Hamilton. Forsaken by the future Marquess of Antrim, she never married. She remained a faithful Catholic until her death making her a figure of suspicion in Edinburgh in the 1680s.

Less is known of the 1st Earl's daughters, Anne, Margaret, Isobelle and Lucy. Anne married Hugh, 5th Lord Sempill, while Margaret married Sir William Cunningham of Caprington. In 1613, Lucy was engaged to Randal, the four-year-old son of Randal McDonnell, owner of some 500 square miles in north County Antrim. As part of the arrangement Abercorn agreed to raise Randal junior should his father die young. In 1628, however, Lucy was forsaken by the now Viscount Dunluce in his ultimately unsuccessful pursuit of a daughter of the Duke of Lennox.[20] As the original contract had been broken, McDonnell was forced to pay the original 'bride price' of £3,000. She lived in Edinburgh in her later years. In 1683 she wrote to her kinsman, the Earl of Arran, asking him to help secure for her a royal pension.[21] This pension had fallen into arrears by 1687, when James II ordered the Lords of the Scottish Treasury to ensure that it was paid. During this period her Catholicism made her a figure of suspicion. In 1686, students attacked her house while the Lord Chancellor was at Mass there.[22] Two years later it was reported that her house had been attacked by a mob vandalising the homes of Catholics. She died in 1696 close to, if not already having reached, her tenth decade; Lord John Hamilton, Arran's brother, took responsibility for her burial.[23]

The Dowager Countess and the 2nd Earl of Abercorn

James, 2nd Earl of Abercorn was a minor when he succeeded to the title. He was born *c.* 1603 and in 1617 was created Baron of Strabane in the expectation that he would eventually succeed to his father's estate in County Tyrone. However, as previously discussed, the 1st Earl's untimely death in 1618 and the subsequent arrangements for the succession of the Abercorn estate in Strabane barony left him without any Irish property. At the same time, he was well provided with Scottish lands, inheriting those of both his father and his grandfather. By *c.* 1624 he had reached majority and was beginning to spend much of his time at Court in London, though he does not appear to have held any important position of state.

From the mid-1620s on, the Catholicism of the 2nd Earl and his mother frequently brought them into conflict with the Presbytery of Paisley. In 1626 Robert Boyd was appointed minister of Paisley, beginning a short but eventful pastorate. Of his relationship with the Dowager Countess, Boyd wrote: 'She is so coldly disposed toward me that I expect no friendship or courtesy on her part'. Boyd suspected her of withholding any communications to him from the 2nd Earl. Worse was to follow when he was the victim of mischief by the Master of Paisley (also known as the Master of Abercorn), the Earl's younger brother Claud. Boyd had been given a part of the Abbey for his accommodation and here made a bed and found a place for his books. However, while he was preaching one afternoon, the Master of Paisley and some others came to his living quarters and threw his books to the ground. They locked the door after them, preventing Boyd from gaining access to his lodging. The Master of Paisley subsequently appeared before the Lords of the Secret Council who were of a mind to imprison him, but for his sorrowful confession and the intervention of Boyd, who stated that he had no wish to see the young aristocrat incarcerated.

Boyd's generosity of spirit was not reciprocated by the Master of Paisley, and when he returned to the Abbey he found the locks to his quarters 'stopped with stones and other things'. He was then attacked by the 'rascally women' of the town, who verbally abused him and threw stones and dirt at him, forcing him to flee Paisley. It was only after the archbishop of Glasgow intervened that the Master of Paisley and his mother, who was suspected of being the instigator of the attacks, were summoned to appear before the Privy Council to answer for their actions. They, together with the 2nd Earl, 'being lately come from his travels', journeyed to Edinburgh 'in great pomp … accompanied with many gentlemen and friends'. Before the Council, the Earl and his brother promised not to impede Boyd in the conduct of his duties, and these assurances were accepted. Boyd, however, had had enough and he refused to return to Paisley. His successor, John Hay, was made of sterner stuff and quickly he too came into conflict with the Abercorns. He actively pursued the Catholic servants of the Dowager Countess, one of whom was denounced as 'ane enemie to the true religioune'. Among those pursued were members of the Algeo family, loyal employees of the Abercorns in both Scotland and Ireland. The Dowager Countess herself did not escape persecution, forcing her to flee for safety to, somewhat ironically, the archbishop of Glasgow. He offered her protection, forbidding the Presbytery to take any action against her without his sanction.

This state of affairs continued for some months, and might never have been taken further but for the return of the 2nd Earl to Paisley and his open avowal of Catholicism. It was reported to a meeting of Presbytery in April 1627 that Abercorn 'had made apostasie and defection from the true religion … and that he doth openly avowe himself a papist, and verie contemptuously despiseth the word of God, preached publickly or read privately, and all other public religious exercises used in the Kirk and Kingdome'. Because of this, Presbytery decided to summon Abercorn to their next meeting on 3 May, where he would be given an opportunity to repent. If he did not they would excommunicate him 'for the said apostasie and defection from the true religion'. The Earl showed his contempt for the authority of the Presbytery by refusing, on this and subsequent occasions, to appear before them. Though frustrated in their attempts to take action against the Earl, the Presbytery decided to proceed against his mother, having secured the support of the archbishop of Glasgow to do so. Hay, a man of greater determination, was ordered to 'proceed by public admonitions against her in the Kirk of Paisley'. The Dowager Countess gave illness as an excuse for not attending church services, but promised 'so soon as it should please God to give her liabilities and strength of body, she should resort to the hearing of God's Word preached'.

These delaying tactics were also adopted by the Earl. When eventually he agreed to speak with delegates appointed by the Presbytery, they reported back that 'they had conferred with his Lordship, and that he had craved continuance therein, hoping thereby he might be profited'. By such prevarications the proceedings against the Hamiltons on account of their Catholicism were stymied for several months. On one occasion Abercorn sent his brother William to the Presbytery, who claimed that the Earl would have appeared himself 'had not been occasioned by some important business'. Within the Presbytery, opinion was divided on how to deal with the Earl and his mother, with one of their number suggesting that the Earl be allowed some breathing space so that 'by their favourable dealing his Lordship might be the more easily moved to obedience and satisfaction in all points'. Eventually, however, the Presbytery had had enough, and in November 1627 it began the process of securing a warrant from the archbishop of Glasgow to have the Dowager Countess excommunicated.

This was obtained on 10 January following and pronounced 10 days later. A similar sentence would have been pronounced against the Earl, but as he had taken a journey to Court for his 'necessarie and lawful business', this was delayed on the archbishop's advice.

The relationship between the Presbytery and Abercorn continued to deteriorate in the first half of 1628. Matters came to a head in May of that year when Claud Algeo, a servant of Claud Hamilton, a younger brother of the 2nd Earl, viciously attacked an officer of the Presbytery. When Algeo told Hamilton what he had done, he 'most kyndelie and cheerefullie resaved him, allowing and approveing all that he did'. Hamilton and Algeo afterwards came 'to the streets, walked up and down a long tyme, boasting and threatning those that durst presoome to meddle with thame'. The baillies of the town were so intimidated that they allowed Algeo to escape. Again it was through the intervention of the archbishop of Glasgow that Hamilton was brought before the Privy Council, who found that he had committed 'a very great wrong' in not disciplining Algeo. Hamilton was imprisoned in Edinburgh, but released after 12 days to allow him to attend to his brother's business in Paisley.

Just over a week later the Dowager Countess' case was brought before the Privy Council. Her son William appeared on her behalf and produced a testimonial signed by the minister and vicar of Kilbarchan (a parish to the west of Paisley) and two of their elders as well as Robert Hamilton, a medical doctor, stating that illness prevented his mother from being present. She was excused on this occasion and several further occasions. Eventually the patience of the Privy Council was exhausted and, failing to appear before them yet again, she was 'put to the horn' (pronounced an outlaw for not answering a summons). Soon afterwards she was imprisoned in the Tolbooth in Edinburgh and later in the Canongate prison. The conditions in which she was kept weakened her health. Concerns for her well-being were raised with the King and it was argued that the Dowager Countess was 'being oppressed with sickness and disease of body, and requiring the benefit of a watering-place'.

The King found himself in a delicate situation, for while he had sympathy with Lady Abercorn's plight, he was reluctant to interfere in the internal affairs of the Presbytery. However, fearing 'that the lady should be brought to the extremity of losing her life for the want of the ordinary remedies', on 9 July 1629 he ordered that she be granted a licence to go to the baths 'about Bristol' on condition that she did not visit the Court and that when she was well enough she should return to Edinburgh. Probably due to her health the Dowager Countess never made the journey to Bristol, but remained imprisoned in Edinburgh for a further six months. She was then allowed to take up residence in the house of Duntarvie so long as she did not entertain Jesuits or Catholic priests.

There are differing versions of the circumstances of her death. She was apparently allowed in March 1631 to return to Paisley to attend to some important business. She agreed to return by a set day, and if she failed to do so she was liable for a fine of 5,000 merks. According to one account, she died in Paisley shortly after her arrival there. However, according to another she died in the Canongate in Edinburgh on 26 August 1632 and was buried in St Mirren's Aisle on 13 September following. Her son the 2nd Earl remained beyond the reach of the Presbytery and so the case against him was not concluded, but merely suspended.

In the early part of the same year in which his mother died, the 2nd Earl married Catherine, daughter of Lord Clifton of Leighton Bromswold. Her first husband had been the Duke of Lennox and Richmond and by royal licence she was allowed to retain her title, Duchess of Lennox. In November 1632 Alexander Hamilton informed Sir John Maxwell of Pollok, a kinsman through his mother's family, the Boyds, that his brother had married and had one of the 'fynest boyes in Ingland'. Alexander was also delighted to tell Maxwell that the Earl had dispatched to him 'sum treas of the finest kyndes in England, both apil treas, peares, peaches, abrikoks, nectarines, chiries of diweres kyndes, plums of sewerall kyndes'.[24] Throughout the 1630s Abercorn continued to make regular visits to Scotland; one of these was for the coronation of Charles I in June 1633. In April 1634, in advance of a journey north, he issued instructions for his house to be 'hansumlie drest and provyded against my homcuming'.[25] The Duchess of Lennox bore the Earl three sons: James, William and George. She died only five years into their marriage in 1637. The Earl himself fell seriously ill in late 1638 or early 1639 and, according to his sister Lucy, 'was gewen ofowr for dath by all that ded si hem'. His son George was likewise dangerously ill, but both recovered.[26]

In the period after the signing of the National Covenant in 1638, Abercorn's Catholicism again became an issue. The National Covenant was drawn up in defiance of the King and with the express purpose of binding the nation to the principles of the Reformation. As both a Catholic and a supporter of the King, Abercorn found himself in a difficult position. The inhabitants of Paisley strongly supported the cause of the Covenanters and in the summer of 1641 Henry Calvert, an Englishman who had been driven from Ireland because of the suppression of Presbyterianism there, was appointed minister of the parish. Abercorn had the right of presentation but was probably left with little choice in the matter, such was the position he found himself in. In May 1642 Calvert was sent by the Presbytery to speak to Abercorn on the matters of signing the Covenant and attendance at church. The Earl resorted to the delaying tactics that had served him well before by telling them that he had 'entered into conference with the brethren at Edinburgh' and would continue this dialogue. On being questioned on his son's upbringing, he answered that he had recommended him to a 'very religious friend and Protestant for his education'.

Abercorn's response to the Presbytery may have satisfied them to some extent on this occasion. Four years later, however, the General Assembly meeting in Edinburgh in July 1646 discussed the Earl and what was to be done about him. When he reappeared in Paisley soon afterwards, the General Assembly directed the Presbytery to speak with him and urge him to 'give his children to some Protestant friends that they may be well educated in the religion professed in this kirk'. Action was also to be taken against Abercorn for his 'obstinate continuance in Popery'. Rather than wait for the Presbytery to proceed against him, the Earl began to make preparations to leave the country. It was at this point that Abercorn's eldest son, Lord Paisley, and Lord Angus made representations to the Presbytery requesting that the Earl be allowed some time to settle his affairs properly for the good of his family. Assurances were given that the Earl's children were being given a Protestant education and that all Catholic servants had been removed from their service. The Presbytery responded by suspending its proceedings against Abercorn. The following year it was reported that the Earl's children were going to be sent to St Andrews to receive a university education because of the prevalence of the plague in Glasgow. Suspicious as ever, the General Assembly instructed the Presbytery of St Andrews to keep a close eye on the children and stop them from communicating with Catholics. Eventually, in 1649, Abercorn was excommunicated by the General Assembly and banished from the kingdom.

Abercorn's continued difficulties with the General Assembly and Presbytery coincided with increasingly strained relations between him and the town council of Paisley. It had been the custom that Abercorn chose one of the baillies elected each year and the town council chose the other. In October 1619, for example, as a young man and probably in deference to the older and more experienced members of the council, he had given them first choice in the election of the baillies. In 1624, his mother had represented him and chosen one of the baillies for the incoming year. In 1637, Abercorn chose himself as one of the baillies. The first indication of friction between the Earl and the council comes in the minutes of the meeting held in October 1647. Abercorn claimed that on the basis of earlier charters granted in 1488 and 1490 he had the right to appoint both baillies. The previous arrangement had only been a tradition that had no historical or legal basis. The council, unsure of what to do, consulted its lawyers, but seemed powerless to do anything about it. At the meeting held the following year, further concerns on the part of the townspeople were revealed. It was claimed that the Earl intended to encroach upon the town's liberties and to impede the townspeople from digging peat in the moss land. Legal advice was sought from Edinburgh at considerable expense, and the matter was resolved.

On the death of the 2nd Duke of Hamilton at the Battle of Worcester in 1651, Abercorn became the senior male representative of the house of Hamilton, though this meant very little in his present circumstances. Heavily in debt, in 1652 he sold his lands for £13,333 6s. 8d. (Scots) to the Earl of Angus, who in turn sold them on to Lord Cochrane, afterwards Earl of Dundonald. Judging by letters written by him to his sister Lucy in the 1650s, Abercorn seems to have been perpetually in debt and spent part of his time in hiding from his creditors. He was living in London in May 1660 when he wrote to the newly restored King assuring him of his loyalty and praying that Charles would show favour to the Hamiltons in the way that his forebears had done.[27] On the same day, he wrote to his brother Sir George Hamilton of Dunnalong recommending a particular individual as a useful servant to the King in Ireland.[28] At this time, Lord Paisley also wrote from London to Sir George entreating him to find him a position at Court.[29] Whether George was able to intervene on their behalf is unclear. Lord Paisley was by this time the husband of Catherine Lenthall, having married her in the Church of St Bartholomew the Less in London in April 1653. Her father, Sir John Lenthall, was the brother of William Lenthall, the Speaker of the English House of Commons during the Long Parliament. The circumstances that brought about this advantageous match are not known.

The 2nd Earl of Abercorn died *c.* 1670. By this time Lord Paisley was also dead, as was Abercorn's second son William, who had died fighting in Germany. As neither of them had left a male heir, it was the 2nd Earl's third son George who succeeded as 3rd Earl of Abercorn. Very little is known about him. He died unmarried at Padua in Italy around 1680 while on a journey to Rome. This line of the Abercorn family tree had thus come to an end. The title did not become extinct, however, for the earldom passed to the Hamilton cousins in Ireland, and it is to them that we now turn.

Lady Catherine Hamilton, wife of Lord Paisley. The daughter of Sir John Lenthall, Catherine married Lord Paisley, the eldest son of the 2nd Earl of Abercorn, in London in 1653.

The Strabane Hamiltons

To understand the events that had shaped the fortunes of the Irish branch of the family, it is necessary to go back to the period following the death of the 1st Earl in 1618. As discussed previously, it was agreed in 1620 that the Irish lands would be divided between the second and fourth sons of the 1st Earl: the manor of Strabane would devolve to Claud, while Dunnalong was to become the property of George. As they were minors when their father died, they were placed under the guardianship of their uncle, Sir George Hamilton

Begun by Sir George Hamilton of Greenlaw around 1620, Derrywoon Castle was the first Hamilton home in what is now the Barons Court demesne. It suffered in the wake of the 1641 rising and was described in the mid-1650s as 'a ruinous castle burned by the rebels'; it does not appear to have been repaired.

of Greenlaw. He was already the guardian of the sons of another of his brothers, Sir Claud Hamilton of Shawfield. Like his brother, the 1st Earl, Sir George was an enthusiastic planter. On his Cloghogall estate, he built a bawn (fortified enclosure) and founded the village of Ballymagorry. He purchased the proportion of Derrygoon (or Derrywoon) near Newtownstewart from a namesake, George Hamilton of Binning. By 1622 Sir George had 'begun to build a fair stone house, 4 storeys high, which is almost finished' at Derrygoon. When commissioners investigating the progress of the Plantation arrived at the site they found 'good store of workmen there upon it' and were informed that when it was finished Sir George intended to live there himself. The ruins of this castle stand in the present Barons Court demesne. Sir George's first wife was Isobel, daughter of James, Master of Rothes.

What made the Hamiltons stand out from most of the other settlers in Ulster in this period was their Catholicism. A central tenet of the scheme for the Plantation in Ulster had been the introduction of a Protestant settler population at all levels of society. However, while the Protestantism of the 1st Earl of Abercorn seems not to have been in doubt, the same could not be said for his brother Sir George. As early as 1614 Sir George's religious beliefs were a source of concern for the government and instructions were issued that he should either be forced to conform to Protestantism or removed from Ireland. No action was taken at this time. In 1622, Sir George was described as an 'Archpapist and a great patron of them'. He was further accused of having driven a Scottish tenant and his family out of Strabane barony

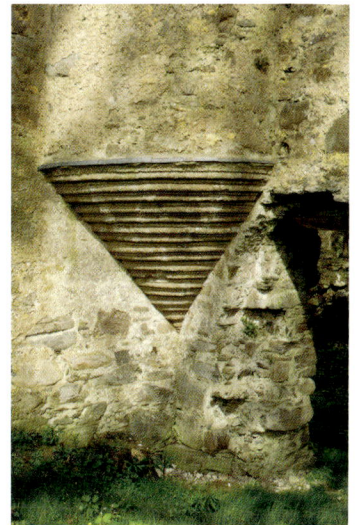

Detail of corbelling on Derrywoon Castle. Moulded corbelling is a typically Scottish feature found on many of the castles and fortified houses built by Scots in early seventeenth-century Ulster.

because they were Protestants. It was also noted that all his servants were Catholics and that he was bringing up his nephew, Sir Claud Hamilton's son and heir, 'in popery'.

In the late 1620s, when England was at war with Catholic Spain, the issue of the Hamiltons' religious beliefs was again raised. George Downham, the bishop of Derry, was concerned that the large number of Catholics he believed were living in the barony of Strabane was threatening the security of the area. In a letter of December 1629 he complained to the lord chancellor of Ireland:

> Since he got part of the Earl of Abercorn's grant of the Barony of Strabane, Sir George Hamilton [of Greenlaw] has done his best to plant Popery there and has brought over priests and Jesuits from Scotland. The Earl's second son Claude, who they call the Master of Abercorn, has now succeeded to his estates, and as Sir William has inherited the proportion of his father Sir Claude [brother of the 1st Earl] all the Hamilton lands are now in the hands of Papists.

In an interview with the Master of Abercorn, Downham advised him that if he would not 'embrace the reformed religion to keep his own religion of himself and not to poison others with the venom of Popery'. Downham was of the opinion that the Master of Abercorn 'would be a hopeful young gentleman' were it not for his Catholicism. Downham was also concerned about other members of the Abercorn family. Sir William Hamilton, third son of the 1st Earl of Abercorn, was accused of having converted his wife, a stepdaughter of Hugh Montgomery, Viscount Ards, to Catholicism.[30] While pressure may have been placed on the Hamiltons to conform, there is no evidence that direct action was taken against them on account of their religious beliefs – Sir George Hamilton of Greenlaw was an effective landlord and there were probably concerns on the authorities' part that attempting anything too drastic would have repercussions for the stability of the area. Indeed, Downham found Sir George Hamilton of Greenlaw to be a 'courteous and civil gentleman'.

Contemporary with Derrywoon castle, Mountcastle was built by the Hamiltons in their manor of Dunnalong and named after one of the titles of the 1st Earl of Abercorn. It was badly damaged in the 1641 rising and apparently not restored. It too displays the corbelling that was typical of Scottish buildings of this period.

However, it was possibly to escape some of the criticism that was being directed against him on account of his Catholicism that Sir George, having married as his second wife, Lady Mary Butler, daughter of the 11th Earl of Ormond, moved to the south of Ireland, spending most of the rest of his life at Roscrea Castle in County Tipperary.

A further Hamilton–Butler marriage alliance was formed in 1635 when the 1st Earl of Abercorn's son, Sir George Hamilton of Dunnalong, married Lady Mary Butler, granddaughter of the 11th Earl of Ormond and sister of the man who would become the 1st Duke of Ormond. Through this marriage he too relocated to County Tipperary, taking up residence in Nenagh Castle. In 1640, he and his wife were granted the manor, castle, town and lands of

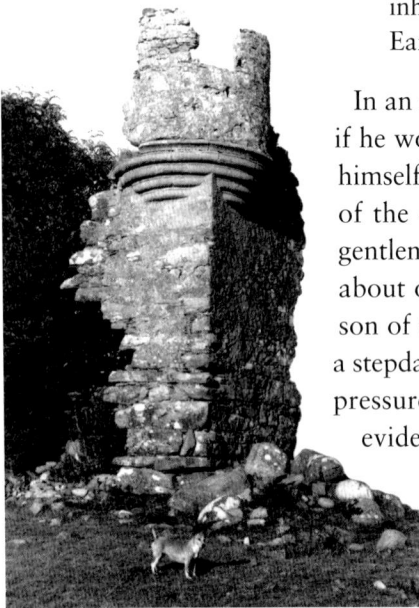

Nenagh for 31 years. Under the terms of this lease they were to 'well and truly repair the castle or manor house' as well as the orchard and garden and were also to 'impale and enclose' a park of 300 acres. Not surprisingly the presence of two Sir George Hamiltons, both married to wives named Lady Mary Butler, has been a source of confusion for historians. It is interesting to note that there is surviving evidence of fine seventeenth-century stucco work in the tower at Roscrea, to which Sir George Hamilton of Greenlaw's house adjoined, which includes elements from a crucifixion scene – overtly Catholic symbolism.

In 1633, Claud Hamilton became the 2nd Lord Strabane on the resignation of the title by his elder brother James, the 2nd Earl of Abercorn. The year before he had married Lady Jane Gordon, daughter of the Marquess of Huntly, one of the leading Catholic noblemen in Scotland. A contemporary account of this event recorded:

> Upon Wednesday the 28th of November in the afternoon the Lord of Strathbrane otherwise called the master of Abercorn was married with lady Jane Gordon the marquis youngest daughter within the kirk of Belly by an Irish minister brought with him of purpose they were honourably entertained within the Bog and within few days departed home.[31]

Though now scattered across the three kingdoms, it is clear that the Hamilton brothers acted in concert in preserving the family's interests. Claud, for example, managed the affairs of his brother James when the latter was absent from Scotland.[32] The following letter by Alexander, written from Strabane in July 1635, provides an interesting account of his travels across Ireland on behalf of his brothers.

> First at my owercuming I went to Dublin, from thence to Roscre[a], wher my brother Sir George lady wes. So my brother, Sir George, got the aixes, which continued threa weeks. So, wpon his recowery, we went to Dubline about the Earle of Antrume's bissines, wher we had not stayt tu dayes till wc had leteres of my Lord Strabane's seiknes, wpon which we both did cum to Strabane. So I stayet ten dayes at Strabane, and then I went wp to Dubline for to procur my Lord Strabane ane warrant from my Lord Deputy for to go into Skotland. So efter I had procured this I went to Roscre, my wnkill Sir George's hous, wher I foond my sister Hamilton [?Lucy]. I stayed ther ane weik till my sister wes raidy to cum ; and I hewe broght my sister home wpon the 11th of this munth. So the raisoune that I dow not cum hom with my Lord Strabane, is my brother, Sir George, being nowly to taik wp hous efter my Lord Strabane's pairting from this. So I will stay with my brother, Sir George, till he be ane fornicht or 3 weiks setilled at hom. Then he will cum with me to the Wicount Clandebue's hous,

The 'Abercorn Vault' in Old Leckpatrick Graveyard. Standing in Old Leckpatrick graveyard, near Ballymagorry, County Tyrone, this unusual building resembles a roofless burial lair found in many Scottish graveyards.

Monument in the 'Abercorn Vault'. Featuring the Hamilton coat of arms, but no inscription, this probably dates from the seventeenth century. The 2nd Lord Strabane is known to have been buried at Leckpatrick in 1638 and possibly the monument was erected in his memory.

wher I hop we shall maik ane beter agriment then Glanderstoune thinks we will; for I hewe got sum informasioune since my cuming into this cuntry that I dar mor boldly ax for my oune. So I hop that I shall giwe your worship content at meiting, for being so long of wryting. I wes in hops that Glanderstoune should hewe told my Lord my brother and your worship what hes past betuixt my Lord Clandeboy and me; bot since he hes beine so self mynded as not to speik, I am sory for it. Bot I hop at meiting to giwe your worship mor content ; so with my humble serwice to your lady, I remaine Your worship's most louing cousine and serwant.

Lord Strabane died in 1638 and was buried in Leckpatrick parish church, a few miles from the town of Strabane. He was succeeded by his eldest son James, who was a minor. His widow and their children continued to live in the castle at Strabane and Lady Strabane was responsible for extensive renovations of their home at a cost, it was said, in excess of £1,000.[33]

The 1641 Rising

In October 1641 a rising began in Ulster, plunging the province and soon the entire island into chaos. Under the leadership of a number of the Irish gentry, most notably Sir Phelim O'Neill, the insurgents captured towns and castles across Ulster and indiscriminate massacres of settlers followed. On 14 December Sir Phelim and a force of around 1,500 men arrived at Strabane. One account of events in the area at this time stated that there were 'burnings, spoilings … committed on the British inhabitants of those quarters'. However, the capture of Strabane itself seems to have been a bloodless affair. According to one report, Lady Strabane had agreed to betray the town to Sir Phelim. On the approach of the Irish a few shots were fired for the sake of appearances, but deliberately aimed wide. What prompted Lady Strabane to act in this way is not known, but it may have been simply a desire on her part to avoid bloodshed. The following spring Sir Phelim again visited Strabane and carried off Lady Strabane to his home in Charlemont, County Armagh. He asked for her hand in marriage, but she refused him, claiming that she had vowed not to marry for five years after her late husband's death. Sir Phelim then sent her with Patrick Hamill, a Franciscan friar, and a company of horseman to the Tipperary home of one of the Sir George Hamiltons – which one is not clear. By the autumn of 1643 she was back in Scotland, residing at Lesmoir, where her Catholicism was a cause for concern for the authorities. The following January it was reported that she was anxious to return to Ireland and had sent her servants to discover if it was safe for her to do so. They returned in March and 'declared hir towne to be rebuilding' after which she made immediate plans to travel there.[33] Eventually, probably towards the latter end of 1649, 'after long courting between them by letters' Lady Strabane and Sir Phelim married.[35]

On 20 July 1650 James Hamilton, 3rd Lord Strabane, joined with the forces of his stepfather that were at that time in possession of the fort at Charlemont. In August 1650 Charlemont was attacked and captured by the Parliamentarians. Hamilton fled, but was taken prisoner shortly afterwards. He then accepted a protection from the Parliamentarians. However, at the end of December 1650 Hamilton rejoined his stepfather in open rebellion. In 1653, Sir Phelim O'Neill was captured, tried for treason, and executed. Lord Strabane spent the next couple of years on the run. He died a 'roman catholick and papist recusant' at Ballyfatton, near Strabane, on 16 June 1655 – reputedly drowning in the River Mourne either while bathing or in trying to escape from government troops. An inquisition held at Strabane in 1658 found that the manor of Strabane had been 'forfeited to the Lord Protector of the Commonwealth of England' on account of the young Lord Strabane's treason. The inquisition also noted that the lands of Strabane and Shean were in the possession of Edward Roberts, the Irish auditor-general, who promised to found and maintain a school in Strabane. The 3rd Lord Strabane died unmarried and was succeeded by his brother George.

George, 4th Lord Strabane

Financial difficulties and uncertainty about his future meant that the 4th Lord Strabane was in extremely precarious circumstances when he succeeded his brother. In 1658, Sir George Rawdon wrote of him, 'I fear there is little hope for Lord Strabane, who is under age and very poor'.[36] Around this time he was banished to Connacht by the authorities, though if

George, 4th Lord Strabane, who died in 1668.

he did go there he did not remain for long: in 1659 he was living at Feltrim in Swords parish, County Dublin. His residence here can be accounted for by his marriage to Elizabeth, daughter of Christopher Fagan of Feltrim, a member of a wealthy Catholic gentry family. Lord Strabane's eldest son Claud was born in 1659 and baptised in St Audeon's Church in Dublin. The decision to baptise his son in a Protestant church was probably made for pragmatic reasons: as a Catholic living under the watchful eyes of the Cromwellians, it is likely that his actions were carefully scrutinised, even more so following his arrest during the celebration of Mass in Dublin in February 1657. With the restoration of the monarchy in 1660 Lord Strabane was among those landowners restored to their respective estates at the King's command.[37] Subsequent legislation in the form of the Acts of Settlement and Explanation ratified the new land settlement. The 4th Lord Strabane died in 1668 and was buried in Kenure Old Church, near Rush, County Dublin. The inscription on his tombstone, which also featured the family coat of arms, read as follows: 'Here under lieth the affabell, oblinginge, exemplar, wise, humble, noble, pious, devot, most charitable, most verteous and religious, the right honourable George, Lord Hamilton, Baron of Strabane, who died 14 April Anno Domn 1668'. The monument was erected by his widow Elizabeth. He was succeeded by his son Claud, who was a minor at the time of his father's death.

Claud, 5th Lord Strabane and 4th Earl of Abercorn

Following the death of the 3rd Earl of Abercorn in Italy *c.* 1680, the title passed to his cousin Claud, 5th Lord Strabane. Other than enhancing his prestige and enabling the young Lord Strabane to take his seat in the Scottish parliament, though it does not appear that he did so, it meant little because the Abercorn lands in Scotland had already been sold to cover debts owed there. Towards the end of 1682 the young Earl was reported to be in Dublin and 'in treaty' for a wife (apparently unsuccessfully); at this time he valued his estate at £6,000.[38] It was reported in 1687 that he was attempting to assert claims to the marquessate of Hamilton and dukedom of Châtelherault, putting him on a collision course with his Hamilton kinsmen, descendants of John, brother of Lord Claud of Paisley. In November of that year the Duke of Hamilton wrote to his wife Anne telling her of rumours that the Earl was 'on some new project against us', implying that an enmity already existed between the two branches of the

Claud, 4th Earl of Abercorn.

family. A few weeks later Hamilton again warned his wife of the threat that Abercorn posed to them. Stories that the Hamiltons had bribed Abercorn to drop the matter were angrily denied when they surfaced in the early eighteenth century during another period of confrontation between the two families.[39]

The 4th Earl was a leading supporter of James II. At the time of the 'Glorious Revolution' of 1688 he accompanied the King to France and returned with him to Ireland. Arriving at Derry with James in April 1689, the Earl was reputedly 'horrified' to find that so many of his kinsmen and tenantry were among the city's defenders. It was probably because of his connections with those inside the city's walls that he was sent into Derry to negotiate its surrender, though his mission proved a failure. A commemorative song of the siege includes the following stanza mocking his intervention:

> 'Twas James's plan that Lord Strabane
> Should give proud Derry warning,
> But he went off with a shot and scoff,
> His words the townsmen scorning.

Soon afterwards, in a skirmish with some of the defenders outside the walls, he was wounded and his horse killed; according to one account, he fled leaving his cloak behind. He subsequently took part in the battles of the Boyne and Aughrim, both of which ended in defeat for the Jacobites. In August 1691, the ship on which he was travelling from Limerick to France was attacked by a Dutch privateer and in the ensuing battle the Earl was killed.[40] He died without heir and the earldom passed to his English-domiciled brother Charles.

Charles, 5th Earl of Abercorn

The 5th Earl succeeded to the title, but initially not to the Irish property which had been declared forfeit on account of his brother's support for the Jacobite cause. In making the case that he was the rightful heir of these lands, the Earl revealed that he and his brother had become estranged over the former's decision to renounce his Catholicism. Charles' decision to become a Protestant had occurred soon after his marriage to his cousin Catherine Hamilton, daughter of James, Lord Paisley, and widow of William Lenthall of Burford, Oxfordshire. He later claimed that on converting to Protestantism he had 'left all of his employments (which were considerable)

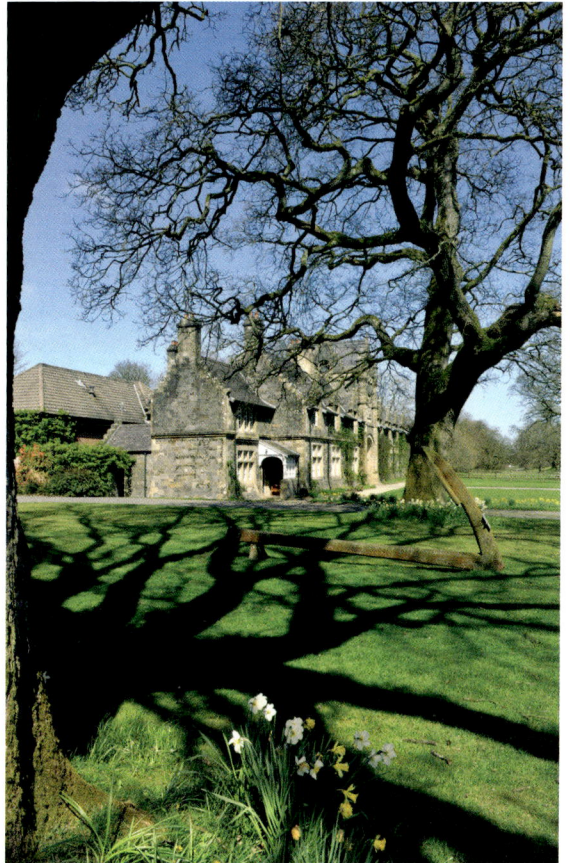

The anchor presented to the 1st Duke of Abercorn by the Waterford Harbour Commissioners. The anchor was believed to be that of the French ship *Lausun* on which James II left Ireland for France after the Battle of the Boyne.

under King James', though it has not been possible to determine what these were. As a result of his change of religious allegiance, the 4th Earl had decided to disinherit his brother and instead make his brother-in-law Gerald Dillon, husband of Abercorn's sister Mary, the heir to his property. In a further indication of his 'disgust', as Charles himself described it, the 4th Earl directed that his brother's children should be educated in a Catholic seminary 'beyond the seas', though how he imagined that this would be enforced is not clear. Aside from the distress of falling out with his brother, Charles felt aggrieved that he had run up considerable debts on his brother's behalf on being made his heir. In order to clear some of these debts his wife had sold some of her jointure lands in Oxfordshire. Eventually, on 24 May 1692, the 5th Earl was granted possession of the Irish estate on the express command of William III.[41] In addition, he succeeded to the title Lord Strabane that had also been forfeited by his brother, thus enabling him to take his seat in the Irish House of Lords, which he did in August 1695. In November of that year, he hosted the King for three days at his house in Burford.

Charles, 5th Earl of Abercorn.

The 5th Earl quickly became popular among his new tenantry and the gentry of County Tyrone. William King, the bishop of Derry, had a high opinion of him, describing him in the summer of 1697 as being of 'agreeable, easy and honourable conversation … The whole country, especially the gentry, seemed extremely taken with him and used all artifices to prevail upon him to settle on his Irish estate.'[42] King's sentiments towards the Earl probably reflect more than a little of his relief that the head of the leading aristocratic family in his diocese had conformed. Writing to the bishop of Oxford, King described Abercorn as a 'good Protestant'.[43] An action which spoke clearly of the Earl's conformity as well as his interest in Strabane was his choosing to erect a seat for himself in the south aisle of the Anglican church in the town. In addition to estate and financial matters, there were other issues preoccupying him at this time. The most serious of these concerned his sensational arrest for the murder of John Prior of Burford in April 1697. As one newspaper of the day reported: 'The Scotch Earl of Abercorn, who married a rich widow in Oxfordshire, has lately killed one Mr. Prior very basely'.[44] His trial took place in July; it lasted seven hours and ended with the Earl being acquitted due to a lack of evidence that he was the perpetrator of this crime.[45]

The ownership of the Abercorn estate was further complicated with the passing of the Act of Resumption in the English House of Commons in 1700. This act annulled all of William III's land grants, including the transfer of the manor of Strabane to the 5th Earl of Abercorn. The act did include a provision to preserve the rights of those whose interest in the forfeited lands pre-dated 13 February 1689. Such individuals were obliged to register their claims with the Trustees of the Forfeited Estates in Ireland before 10 August 1700. Having gone to considerable lengths to secure possession of the estate in the first place, the Earl was more than a little frustrated at this turn of events. Something of his annoyance comes out in a letter to the Duke of Hamilton in October 1700 in which he warned him that if ever the English parliament 'can gett the same asendant over Scotland [as over Ireland] they will not practice less tyranny'.[46] In order to prove that he was the rightful representative of the male line of the family the 5th Earl was himself forced to submit a claim to the Trustees. He would probably have reacquired his estate had he not died without heir in June 1701; his only child, Elizabeth, had died in February 1699.[47] The earldom then passed to his second cousin, Captain James Hamilton, now 6th Earl of Abercorn.

Sir George Hamilton of Dunnalong and his family

The 6th Earl will be the subject of the following chapter, but to understand who exactly this James Hamilton was and how he came to succeed to the earldom of Abercorn it is necessary to go back to the 1st Earl's fourth son, Sir George Hamilton of Dunnalong. It has already been noted that through his marriage in 1635 to a member of the Butler family he moved to Tipperary and took up residence in Nenagh Castle. Shortly after the outbreak of the 1641 rising, Sir George was detained by the mayor of Chester while on his way to Ireland on account of his Catholicism. Soon afterwards he was dismissed from his army command for the same reason. However, he was soon restored to favour and played an active role in the Royalist cause in Ireland in the 1640s. Following the final defeat of the Royalists, Sir George Hamilton of Dunnalong went into exile in France and his lands were confiscated by the Cromwellians. In August 1654 he wrote from Paris to a Mrs Taylor, whose husband had stood surety for some of Sir George's debts, lamenting that 'my present condition affords me no possibility of being able to satisfy those debts', and going on to write about the 'unhappiness of my condition'.

Lady Catherine Hamilton, wife of the 5th Earl. The daughter of Lord Paisley, the eldest son of the 2nd Earl of Abercorn, she had first married her cousin William Lenthall before becoming the wife of the 5th Earl.

At the Restoration Charles II issued a declaration which, among other things, restored a number of dispossessed to their lands immediately. Among those who were to benefit from this was Sir George Hamilton of Dunnalong.[48] A grant, 'pursuant to a certificate of the Commissioners for the Acts of Settlement', dated 24 May 1667, confirmed Sir George's ownership of the manor of Dunnalong. In addition, it granted to him the manors of Cloghogall and Derrywoon in Strabane barony previously owned by his uncle, Sir George Hamilton of Greenlaw. This Sir George had died c. 1653–4 and had been succeeded by his minor son James who died without heir some time before 27 January 1659 when his will was proved. Under the Restoration land settlement Sir George Hamilton of Dunnalong was also granted land in counties Cork, Tipperary, Limerick, Waterford, Clare, Kilkenny and Longford, though in due course all of these were disposed of. He died in 1679.

Three of the sons of Sir George Hamilton of Dunnalong were heavily involved in the Jacobite cause in Ireland in the period 1689–91. The most prominent was General Richard Hamilton, who commanded the Jacobite army at Derry for much of the siege of 1689. The following year he was captured at the Battle of the Boyne and imprisoned in the Tower of London. He was subsequently released in exchange for a prisoner held by the French. He died in poverty in France in 1717. His brother Count Anthony Hamilton, the author of the renowned *Mémoires de Grammont*, fought and was wounded at the Battle of Newtownbutler in 1689. The following year he fought at the Boyne. In 1691, he withdrew to France, where he died in 1719 or 1720. Another brother, Colonel John Hamilton, was mortally wounded at the Battle of Aughrim on 12 July 1691 and died in captivity in Dublin.

The man who was to become the 6th Earl of Abercorn was not the son of any of the above, but of his grandfather's eldest son, James Hamilton. Like the rest of his family, he had spent the 1650s in exile on the Continent; in 1655 he was with Prince Rupert at Heidelberg. In 1660, on the eve of the Restoration, he announced his intention to convert to Protestantism, much to the consternation of his mother, Lady Mary Hamilton, who attributed it to his libertine lifestyle. It coincided with his engagement to Elizabeth, daughter of Lord Culpepper, leading his mother to comment to her brother, the Duke of Ormond, 'if she be so unfortunate as to be engaged to him, I am confident she will never have much satisfaction in one that has forsaken God for her.'[49] Ormond, on the other hand, felt that his nephew was merely obeying the dictates of conscience, even if it was against his parents' wishes, adding that he had detected some indications of a change in his religious feelings as much as four years previously.[50] Hamilton was a personal favourite of Charles II and would become a well-known figure at the Restoration Court. His brother Anthony provided the following pen portrait of him in his *Mémoires de Grammont*:

The elder of the Hamiltons … was the best dressed man at Court. His person was handsome, and he had all those happy accomplishments which lead to fortune and contribute to success in love. An extremely assiduous courtier, the possessor of an unusually versatile wit, his manners were the most polite, and his attention to his master the most consistent, that it is possible to imagine. None danced better, none was so generally seductive – features which counted for something at a Court whose main existence was in merry-making and gallantry.

His enemies, however, charged him with being one of a group of men responsible for leading the King astray and envied his close friendship with Charles's sister 'Minette', the sister-in-law of Louis XIV of France. After she died suddenly and in suspicious circumstances in 1670, Hamilton represented the King at her post mortem.

Among the many honours bestowed on him, Hamilton was the ranger of Hyde Park and in 1664 was granted 55 acres adjoining the park for an orchard at a rent of £5 plus half the apples for the King's household. In the same year he was involved in an incident which started off innocuously enough, but quickly got out of hand: 'he and Mr Bernard Howard, flinging mulberries at one another in the King's presence, grew warm and fought, and James was run through the flesh under the jaw, but no great harm', though the two men spent some time in the Tower of London as a punishment. Hamilton did not long lose the favour of the King, however, and was appointed Provost-Marshall of Barbados in 1667, a position he resigned in 1670. The following year he was sent as an envoy to the Court of the Grand Duke of Tuscany at Florence. Hamilton's life was cut short when, during a naval battle with the Dutch, one of his legs was blown off by a cannon ball. Failing to receive proper medical attention, he died of his injuries on 6 June 1673 and was buried in Westminster Abbey. He and his wife had six sons, three of whom died in infancy. Of those who survived, the eldest, James, became 6th Earl of Abercorn. The younger sons were George, who was a Colonel of the 1st Guards and was killed at the Battle of Steinkirk in 1692, and William, who was the ancestor of the Hamiltons of Trebinshun in Wales.

The Hon. James Hamilton, the father of the 6th Earl of Abercorn, by Kneller.

Elizabeth Hamilton (1641–1708)

Known as 'La Belle Hamilton' or 'La Belle Anglais', Elizabeth Hamilton was the daughter of Sir George Hamilton of Dunnalong. She was probably born at Nenagh in County Tipperary, where her father had relocated following his marriage to Lady Mary Butler. She and the rest of her family went into exile on the Continent in the 1650s as a result of their support for the Royalist cause and Elizabeth was educated in Paris. The family moved to London after the Restoration and, on account of her beauty and vivacity, Elizabeth became one of the most celebrated figures of the Royal Court with numerous admirers, among them the Duke of York, the future James II. An Italian nobleman wrote that she and her sister-in-law, Frances, the wife her brother George, were 'undoubtedly the most beautiful women of this court'. She turned down several suitors from among the ranks of the British nobility before becoming engaged to the French aristocrat Philibert, Comte de Grammont, who was twenty years her senior. It seems that Grammont had second thoughts about marrying her for he

abruptly left London on his own before being intercepted at Dover by two of Elizabeth's brothers who brought him back to the capital where their marriage was solemnised in 1663. The King presented them with a jewel he had purchased for £1,260 as a wedding gift.

In the autumn of 1664, shortly after the birth of their first child, the Grammonts moved to France, though they made regular return visits to the English Court. They enjoyed a prominent position at the Court of Louis XIV and Elizabeth was made a 'dame du palais'. She enjoyed a close friendship with Louis XIV who trusted and respected her, as did a number of his ministers, though others at the French Court disliked her on account of her arrogance and pride. Her abrupt manner with even the Queen and ladies of the Court did not go unnoticed though under the spiritual guidance of Bishop Fénelon she tried to reform her ways. After James II was forced to flee England in 1688, Elizabeth found herself in an even stronger position for she was regarded as a link between the French Court and James's now exiled English Court, which included her brothers Richard and Anthony. Furthermore, she is credited with maintaining Louis XIV's interest in the Jacobite cause long after the war in Ireland had ended in defeat in 1691.

In 1707, the Comte de Grammont died. Elizabeth mourned his passing deeply, but the King would not allow her to withdraw from the French Court and live quietly. She never recovered from her husband's death and died the year after him, in June 1708. Their older daughter, Claude-Charlotte, married the 1st Earl of Stafford, though the marriage lasted less than two years, while their young daughter, Marie-Elisabeth, became abbess of Poussay in Lorraine. Her early life and courtship by Grammont is recounted in her brother Anthony's *Mémoires de Grammont*, published for the first time in 1713, which also provides an absorbing account of the Court of Charles II.

3

James Hamilton, 6th Earl of Abercorn
'An eccentric figure'[1]

In his old age the 6th Earl of Abercorn liked to reminisce on past exploits and achievements. In 1733, when he was in his early sixties, he recalled with pride that he had been 'employed by King William of glorious memory to carry arms and ammunition to Londonderry so early that my first commission to that purpose was dated by him whilst he was only Prince of Orange'.[2] On another occasion, shortly before Christmas that year, he called with the Earl of Egmont and talked to him about the time that he had been

The 6th Earl of Abercorn when he was about nine years old, by Kneller.

part of the cortege at King William's funeral. He also pointed out, with obvious satisfaction, that he had walked in processions to 'Paul's' as a Scottish earl with greater seniority than English viscounts.[3] There is no doubting that he had lived through one of the most momentous periods in British and Irish history and been involved in many of the key events of the previous half century.

Early life

The future 6th Earl of Abercorn was born *c.* 1661, the eldest son of James Hamilton and his wife Elizabeth Culpepper. He was the grandson of the prominent Royalist, Sir George Hamilton of Dunnalong, and great-grandson of the 1st Earl of Abercorn. In 1673, his father died of injuries sustained during a naval engagement. When his grandfather, Sir George, died in 1679 the young James Hamilton succeeded to the family estates. These lands were extensive and scattered across several counties in Ireland, though the most important for the future history of the family and estate were the three manors in County Tyrone: Cloghogall, Derrywoon and Dunnalong. The estate was further extended through the acquisition 'by a combination of marriage and purchase' of a large property in east County Donegal, conveniently located across the River Foyle from the manor of Dunnalong. As Malcomson explains, although the Hamilton's mother was 'technically not an heiress … [her] fortune was sufficiently large to enable her trustees to purchase, in 1677, the manors of Magavlin and Lismoghry, round St Johnstown, mainly in the parish of Taughboyne'. Half of this property was settled on Hamilton in

Mongavlin castle. This castle had been built on behalf of the Duke of Lennox in the early seventeenth century. It came into the possession of the Hamiltons in the latter part of the 1600s following their acquisition of the adjoining estate.

This stone was once at Mongavlin castle in the family's Donegal estate. The inscription reads: 'The Honble Elizabeth Hamilton, daughter of John, Lord Colepepper, widow of Coll. James Hamilton, who lost his life at sea, and in the service of his King and country, purchased this Manner, and annexed it to the opposite estate of the family, which paternal estate itself was improved by her prudent management to nere the yearly income she received thereout. She hath also setled her young son, William Hamilton, in an estate acquir'd in England, in equal value in the purchase to this, and given everyone of her numerous offspring, descended from both branches, some considerable mark of her parental care. Her eldest son, James, Earle of Abercorn, and Viscount Strabane, hath caused this inscription to be placed here for the information of her posterity, from whom she hath merited the most grateful acknowledgements and to whom she hath set so valuable an example. Anno 1704.' In the early 1800s two men picking cherries found the stone around 20–30 yards from the castle and informed the agent, Sir John James Burgoyne, who had it placed in one of the front windows (PRONI, D623/A/337A). It was probably removed to Barons Court *c.* 1903. In May of that year, it was reported that part of the castle had collapsed and another portion was so unstable that it would have to be demolished (PRONI, D623/A/334/22).

1684 and when his mother died in 1709 the rest of it merged with the Abercorn estate.[4]

Educated at Westminster School, he was still a teenager when appointed a groom of the bedchamber. In January 1684, he married Elizabeth, only daughter of Sir Robert Reading Bt, the owner of significant property in Dublin, including land and houses on St Stephen's Green.[5] Their marriage settlement made specific reference to 'a mansion-house fronting on the Green, lately built and now finishing by Sir Robert'. This house probably became the family residence in Dublin.[6] Although succeeding to his grandfather's baronetcy, Hamilton does not seem to have used this title and was often referred to as simply James Hamilton Esq. At one time he had a warrant from the King for the title of Lord Bellamont,[7] though nothing further seems to have come of this.

The siege of Derry and Williamite land settlement

The Countess of Abercorn, wife of the 6th Earl.

Like other members of the family, Hamilton enjoyed a close relationship with the Royal Family; he was one of James II's privy counsellors and commanded a regiment of horse. However, at the Glorious Revolution he deserted James and sided with William, Prince of Orange. According to one account, 'no sooner did he perceive his Majesty's intentions to introduce popery than he quitted his service'.[8] As a result of this, he was now in direct opposition to his kinsman, the 4th Earl of Abercorn, as well as several of his uncles, all of whom were prominent Jacobites. Sent on a special mission by William, he sailed into Derry on the *Deliverance* on 21 March 1689, bringing with him 8,000 muskets, 480 barrels of gunpowder and £8,595 in cash in support of the beleaguered garrison.[9] Swiftly promoted to colonel, he was a member of the 16-strong council of war in the besieged city and was instrumental in having the articles of war drawn up which regulated the conduct of the garrison. One historian of this episode has written, 'He threw himself with ardour into the all the city's preparations for defence, and no man rendered more efficient service during the long siege'.[10]

With his profile in the north-west now raised, he was elected MP for County Tyrone in 1692, serving two terms, the latter ending in 1699. He was nominated for four committees in 1692 and for 14 between 1695 and 1697. Little is known about his Commons career and he does not appear to have made a significant contribution to parliamentary debate at this time,

though it is known that he was hostile to Chancellor Porter who was accused of having Catholic sympathies.[11] From 1692 to 1700 he employed William Conolly as his agent, specifically to look after his property interests in Dublin and manage his revenue offices of king's alnager (the holder's task was to assure the quality of woollen goods) and keeper of lighthouses. These two positions had been inherited from his father-in-law in 1684 and were worth £500 a year to Hamilton; he lost them under the Jacobites, but they were restored to him in 1692.[12] Conolly would go on to become the Speaker of the Irish House of Commons and one of the wealthiest men on the island. In 1703 he loaned his former employer £4,500 and in 1708 was a trustee of an Abercorn family settlement.

On the death of his cousin, the 5th Earl of Abercorn, in June 1701 he inherited the earldom. Soon afterwards he successfully petitioned to have the title of Viscount Strabane conferred on him as well, which enabled him to sit in the Irish House of Lords.[13] He did not, however, inherit his cousin's estate, specifically the manor of Strabane, for, as previously discussed, this had been vested with the Trustees of the Forfeited Estates as a result of the Act of Resumption of 1700. On 19 June 1703 the 6th Earl purchased the manor of Strabane from the Trustees for £700, having previously been admitted as tenant of the same.[14] The 6th Earl was now the owner of lands totalling some 50,000 acres in County Tyrone, in addition to which was the Donegal property of around 20,000 acres. From this time on the ownership of the estate remained remarkably stable, with a smooth transition from one generation to the next.

With both his landed and, as shall be presently discussed, his political interests now very much focused on Ireland, Abercorn's ties with London were loosened and he lived mostly in Dublin. He had a seat in St Peter's Church, where several of his children were baptised.[15] There are occasional references to him travelling to the north of Ireland, but he seems to have been a rare visitor to his estates in the north-west. Certainly he was an absentee landowner and there is no evidence that he kept a residence on any of his Tyrone or Donegal manors. The castle in Strabane, the home of previous earls of Abercorn, was disused, while the castles built in the early seventeenth century at Derrywoon and Mountcastle continued to decay as they had been doing from the time of the 1641 rebellion. As patron of the parish of Donagheady, County Tyrone, he was offered space for a seat in the Church of Ireland church in 1701, but did not avail of this, probably because he was never likely to sit in it.[16]

Abercorn and Strabane

There are virtually no surviving records relating to the 6th Earl's management of his north-west Ulster manors. He himself thought that he had dealt with his tenants benevolently. Following the uncertainty created by the Williamite land settlement, he had respected the property rights of those who had failed to register claims for tenements in the town of Strabane with the Trustees of the Forfeited Estates so long as they 'had a mind to live therein'.[17] In 1733, he wrote to one of his agents in the north-west: 'I have endeavoured upon all occasions to be at least as indulgent a landlord as any other gentleman who resided in that part of the country'.[18] One activity that Abercorn is known to have taken an interest in was the promotion of the linen industry in the Strabane area and, based on experiences elsewhere in Ulster, his involvement is likely to have been crucial to its local development. On his journey through the north of Ireland in 1708 Thomas Molyneux described Strabane as a 'somewhat better town' than its near neighbour Lifford, and noted that here Lord Abercorn had encouraged the manufacture of linen.[19] Looking at his role retrospectively, Abercorn wrote in 1733:

> I value myself upon having soon after that happy revolution, at my own great expense, promoted the linen manufacture in that neighbourhood and which hath so far succeeded that at Strabane is now the greatest staple of linen yarn in that kingdom. There are several burgesses of that town who know that all I have herein bragged of to be matter of fact.[20]

If the evidence points to the Earl as an encourager of the linen industry in Strabane, information on how exactly he did this is not forthcoming. It is known that he was a trustee of the Linen Board and years later he pointed out to the Earl of Egmont that the success of linen manufacturing was due to his 'diligent attendance at that Board'.[21]

Most of what is known about the 6th Earl and the north-west concerns his battles to control the corporation of Strabane and with it the power to determine the parliamentary representation of the borough. In the early eighteenth century the more senior of the two MPs for Strabane, certainly as far as power and influence were concerned, was Oliver McCausland. The owner of substantial estates in the north-west as well as a resident of the town of Strabane, McCausland had first been elected MP for the borough in 1692. From the 1710s onwards the 6th Earl attempted to interfere with the selection process and in doing so created an increasingly acrimonious relationship between himself and the corporation led by McCausland. When exactly the relationship between McCausland and Abercorn began to deteriorate is not clear, though it was probably after and as a result of the Earl's switch in political affiliations from the Whig to the Tory camp in 1707–09. Certainly at one point the two men were on cordial terms. They would have fought alongside each other at the time of the siege of Derry and in the autumn of 1704 Abercorn described McCausland as a 'special, good old friend', and was prepared to honour a promise made to him of a grant of land near Strabane.[22]

After 20 years as an MP McCausland had firmly established himself as the senior representative of the borough. In advance of the 1713 election it was predicted that the members for Strabane would be McCausland 'and whoever he brings in'. By this time Abercorn was beginning to make a concerted effort to have at least one of his nominees returned for Strabane. In March 1714 he wrote to the burgesses of Strabane at a time when Queen Anne's failing health had given rise to heightened expectations that a general election was in the offing. He asked the burgesses to return one nominee of his, promising that this individual would serve the interests of the town, and granting them liberty to choose whomsoever they wished as the second nominee, provided that person was not politically opposed to the Earl. Privately Abercorn admitted that his offer to the burgesses was made on the basis that he was unlikely to be able to persuade them to leave out McCausland, 'who lives among them'.[23] In the event his suspicions were proved correct, and McCausland was re-elected. Abercorn did at least have the satisfaction of seeing his nominee, the Hon. Richard Stewart, younger brother of Lord Mountjoy, elected as the second MP for the borough. McCausland continued to serve as MP for Strabane until his death in 1723.

Irish politics

At different times in his career Abercorn played a prominent role in national politics in Ireland, though at times his behaviour was as perplexing as it was bizarre. Some contemporaries believed that he was an attention-seeker, with one writing of him 'He loves to be taken notice of'. As Viscount Strabane, the 6th Earl sat in the Irish House of Lords, where he was frequently at odds with the government. One modern historian has described him, in reference to his behaviour in 1709, as a 'determined and highly troublesome opponent to the viceroy'.[24] In the spring of 1709 Abercorn caused consternation to the committee appointed to draft the Lords' address when he proposed that some relief be given to Presbyterians in Ireland. On 7 May Joseph Addison, the secretary of state in London, wrote: 'The House of Lords have had some heats on a clause offered in their address, to encourage a toleration for the Dissenters, by my Lord Abercorn who told them, as I hear, that he did it to prevent something worse.'[25] This proposal was, however, rejected by the bishops, led by the archbishop of Dublin.

What prompted Abercorn to act in this way is unclear. He may have been conscious of the fact that the majority of his tenants in the north-west, including the greater part of the inhabitants of Strabane, were Presbyterians. A few years prior to this, in 1704, he was thanked by the Presbyterian ministers of Dublin for the 'just representation your Lordship has made of us'. However, in 1709 he may have been behaving awkwardly just to be contrary. It was felt at privy council level that Abercorn was pressing for repeal rather too forcefully, and it was surely the 6th Earl who was being described by Addison a week later as 'A noble peer who is the proposed patron of the Dissenters'.[26] Later that year Abercorn proved troublesome to the authorities in Dublin over a proposed money bill. Abercorn, who was resolutely opposed to the bill, was accused by Archbishop King of revealing the secrets of a private conversation and putting his spin on what was said. Possibly hoping to scupper the bill altogether, he make the bizarre proposal to allow the lord lieutenant and six of his favourite counsellors to tax the country in whatever way they pleased for the next three years. This was ignored and the money bill was eventually passed, though with the 6th Earl voting against it.[27]

In the autumn of 1710 Abercorn got wind of rumours that three of the commissioners of revenue were to be dismissed. Hoping to secure an appointment as one of the new commissioners, the 6th Earl began to seek support from individuals of influence. One of those he turned to was Jonathan Swift, who wrote in his *Journal to Stella*: 'I am a little soliciting for another: it is poor Lord Abercorn, but that is a secret; I mean, that I befriend him is a secret; but I believe it is too late, by his own fault and ill fortune'.[28]

The 6th Earl of Abercorn.

In the event the rumours proved false and Abercorn was frustrated in his hopes of securing an official appointment. His friendship with Swift developed, however, and the two dined together regularly. On one occasion Swift even took Lady Abercorn with him on a shopping trip for statues for the wife of the bishop of Clogher.[29]

Mention has already been made of the 6th Earl's switch in political allegiance from the Whig to the Tory camp. He was, however, in the words of Anthony Malcomson, a 'highly individualistic Tory' who was more inclined to do what he thought best at any given moment than to follow any party line.[30] For example, in the 1713 general election Abercorn supported the Tory interest in County Tyrone, but in County Donegal he backed the two Whig candidates, Sir Ralph Gore and the Hon. Frederick Hamilton. The latter was a distant relative. In his opinion the two candidates were

> gentlemen of so good sense and principles in the main, in relation to the established church and monarchy, that I have thought

fit to use my endeavours to prevent their being exposed to the mortification of disappointment.[31]

He claimed that it was his belief that a parliament was 'better constituted for consisting of Whigs and Tories; for on side being a check upon the other, neither will be suffered to run riot'.[32] Like many of the elite, Abercorn resented the interference of the clergy in parliamentary elections even though clerical interventions had usually been on behalf of the Tories. He expressed his views on this to Edward Southwell in November 1713:

> I should be very sorry to see a parliament altogether chosen by dint of implicit faith in our spiritual guides; for I fancy that we who profess bending our thoughts about temporal affairs might be allowed to understand as much thereof as those who ought to employ a great part of their time in directing us of the laity right beyond the verge of the world.[33]

This trait of outspokenness lasted with him until the end of his life and there is little evidence that he mellowed with age. To give one example, in the summer before he died he wished Sir Robert Walpole and Lord Bolingbroke 'might both be hanged together' because of the way they had treated his son and the son of Earl of Egmont.[34] He could also be extremely humorous in his descriptions of events, comparing one awkward silence during a meeting of the Dublin administration to 'one of the sorts of Quakers' meetings whence they depart without uttering any part of their meeting than what may be conjectured from sighs', and dubbing one of the participants 'Our Don Dismallo, or Knight of the Sorrowful Countenance'.[35] At other times he reveals his inability to engage in small talk. Writing to Southwell in April 1714 he admitted:

> I am so very bad at tittle tattle conversation that I avoid as much as possible what most other gentlemen are fond of, and unless my wife or daughters, who converse with those of their own sex, tell me what they happen to hear, I never know of what is chatted at tea tables until the same becomes common town talk.[36]

In the spring of 1714, at a time when certain Whigs were warning of a renewed Jacobite threat to the established order, he penned an open letter in which he condemned 'designing, intriguing men, who invent scandalous insinuations wherewith they alarm the credulous'. This was aimed at those who were, in his words, 'making a bugaboo of the Pretender'.[37]

Scottish politics

As Earl of Abercorn he was entitled to sit in the Scottish parliament, though until the issue of the union between Scotland and England came to the fore he seems to have taken little interest in the politics of his ancestral homeland. On 29 June 1706 he wrote to the Duke of Ormonde informing him that, having taken the advice of his friends, he would be attending the forthcoming parliamentary session in Edinburgh and was confident that his behaviour would be no cause for concern for those with an interest in the Hanoverian succession.[38] He also revealed that was in favour of the proposed union even though this would cause him to lose the 'only mite left him in that kingdom', probably referring to his seat in the Scottish parliament. He took his seat on 3 October 1706 and though he did not vote in the division on the first article of the treaty, he did vote in favour of ratifying the treaty on 16 January following.[39]

As far as his involvement in Scottish politics is concerned, the main area of interest lies in his proposed, though rejected, scheme for reforming the way that Scottish representative peers were elected to the House of Lords in London.[40] Following the Act of Union, the Scottish nobility was represented in the Lords by 16 peers elected by the rest of the Scottish peerage. Abercorn had contributed to the debates in the Scottish parliament, proposing that the representation would be by rotation and, when this was rejected, arguing that the election should be by balloting: this was also rejected in favour of an open election. The first of these elections, which was held in June 1708, took place against a backdrop of considerable resentment at the degree of English interference in the selection process. Abercorn himself was not present at this election, but just over a week later he wrote to the Duke of Montrose outlining his scheme for reforming the electoral process. In his view this would 'would Remoove the Umbrage, and Uneasynesse, of Courte, and Country Heere', almost certainly a reference to the politicking and party electioneering that had characterised the recent election. In the same letter, he revealed that he had similarly written to the Earl of Sutherland, though how recently he had done so is not clear.

The scheme that Abercorn proposed has been described as 'deceptively simple'. Had it been adopted, it would have removed any political interference in the election process. Peers would not have been lobbied or pressurised to vote in a particular way, as voting itself was not part of the Earl's proposal, which instead advocated a mixture of rotation and balloting as the means of selecting the representative peers. Under his scheme, Abercorn divided the 132 Scottish peers into three classes of equal size; the Earl tried as far as possible to place an equal number of each rank of the peerage into each class. Whenever there would be an election, the representative peers would be drawn from one of these classes in rotation. The top two ranks of the peerage in each class – the dukes and marquesses – would be automatically elected, while the other representative peers would be chosen by ballot. As Abercorn explained, 'let theyr Names bee promiscuously jumbled together, in a Ballotting box; and after They are sufficiently mingled, lett enough of the Lords Names bee singly drawne out thereof, to compleate the Number of Sixteen Representatives'. Montrose's response to Abercorn's scheme is not known, and there is no indication that his proposals were ever seriously considered by the Scottish peerage. He himself was never elected as a Scottish representative peer, though his grandson, the 8th Earl, was one of the more active representative peers.

The dukedom of Châtelherault

In 1712, the 6th Earl registered his claim to be considered the rightful heir to the dukedom of Châtelherault. The dukedom had originally been granted to James, 2nd Earl of Arran, by Henry II of France in 1549. In 1712, it was claimed by the 4th Duke of Hamilton through his mother, a descendant of Arran's son John. Abercorn, on the other hand, claimed it through the descent of Arran's son Claud, and as this was through the male line his claim was the stronger according to French laws of inheritance. The background to the 1712 affair was the negotiations leading up to the Treaty of Utrecht. The episode added to the tension between the two branches of the Hamilton family. At some point, though when exactly is not clear, the Duke of Hamilton was warned that Abercorn had been searching the records in Paris for documents concerning the dukedom of Châtelherault.[41] Anne, Duchess of Hamilton, mother of the 4th Duke of Hamilton, dismissed Abercorn's claim as frivolous, however.[42] In March 1712 Abercorn wrote to Swift asking him to intervene in the matter on his behalf. Swift was sympathetic to the 6th Earl's claim, writing in his *Journal to Stella*: 'I will do what I can, for his pretensions are very just'.[43] Swift was true to his word and used his influence on Abercorn's behalf. On 24 September he wrote:

> I have been mediating betwixt the Hamilton family and Lord Abercorn, to make them compound with him, and I believe they will do it. Lord Selkirk is to be here in order to go to France to make the demands; and the ministry are of the opinion that they will get some satisfaction, and they empowered me to advise the Hamilton side to agree with Abercorn, who asks a fourth part, and will go to France to spoil all if they don't yield it.[44]

Despite Swift's apparently positive assessment, the Hamiltons remained deeply suspicious of the Earl. Selkirk, who was the younger brother of the Duke of Hamilton, warned his mother that should they pay Abercorn to give up his claim to Châtelherault he might well ask for more to satisfy other claims.[45] At the same time, another brother, George, Earl of Orkney, reported that Abercorn, whom he described as 'the most headstrong positive man that ever was borne', was still demanding a quarter of what was received for Châtelherault in return for giving up his claim to the title.[46]

On New Year's Day, 1713, Swift wrote, 'yesterday Lord Abercorn was here, teasing me about his French duchy, and suspecting my partiality to the Hamilton family in such a whimsical manner that Dr Pratt, who was by, thought he was mad'. Swift was himself becoming exasperated with the whole affair, especially when, on the same day, representatives of the Hamilton family arrived and tried to persuade him to encourage Abercorn to withdraw his claim to the dukedom. In a fit of pique the dean wrote: 'Am I not purely handled between a couple of puppies'. Swift was particularly frustrated at the way the 6th Earl was now behaving: 'Abercorn vexes me more. The whelp owes to me all the kind receptions he has had from the Ministry.' The relationship between Swift and the 6th Earl became increasingly strained and later that month the dean wrote, 'Lord Abercorn plagues me to death'. Describing a visit to Court on 24 January, Swift wrote, 'it was comical to see Lord Abercorn bowing to me, but not speaking'.[47] Abercorn's desire to be recognised as the true heir of the dukedom was not realised. Article 22 of the Treaty of Utrecht, ratified in 1713, contained a promise by the King of France to 'satisfy the claims of the family of Hamilton concerning the duchy of Châtelherault'. It was to be another 150 years before the Abercorn claims to the dukedom again came to the fore.

Early in 1713 the relationship between Abercorn and Swift broke down completely. The rupture lasted for over a year, though by the spring of 1714 Abercorn was seeking a reconciliation with Swift. In April of that year Abercorn wrote to Ormonde setting out the terms on which his relationship with Swift would be restored:

> I have very lately put it in Mr Dean's power to give me a proof of his really wishing me well, which is a necessary preliminary to our friendly correspondence, though you will easily believe my suspicion being well grounded to his not thinking it to be worth his while. In case he persists in imagining it, I can be contented to take in payment such sort of excuses as he hath hitherto made.[48]

Clearly Abercorn considered himself the wounded party in the dispute – in forwarding a copy of the above letter to Southwell, he wrote: 'you may perceive, sir, how tenderly I touch upon a sore place of some who have galled me to the quick' – though the fact that he was even seeking a reconciliation with Swift is perhaps indicative of a latent guilt, or at least embarrassment, on his part. In appearing bullish to Ormonde – he even wrote that he did not at all mind if the dean saw his letter – he may well have been trying to save face, though in a letter to Southwell just a few days earlier he doubted whether he and Swift would 'ever converse with one another again upon the same foot as formerly'.

Abercorn was now seeking a grant of £6,000 from the 'Military Contingency Fund', payable in six years, to compensate for the 'disappointment I met with in the affair of Châtelherault'. He claimed that he needed the money because he had a 'numerous family of younger children to provide for, and that as my circumstances are, I must not only pinch myself, but also live longer than so crazy a man, as I now am, can reasonably hope for, to be able to do it in any decent measure, suitably to my station'.[49] When his son James had married Anne, daughter of Col. John Plumer of Blakesweare, Hertfordshire, in 1711, the 6th Earl had put him in possession of his north-west Ulster estate with an annual rental of £2,000. Abercorn was left with £4,000 in bank stock, though he had reserved to himself the power of charging his estate with £4,000 more. Three of his four daughters were still unmarried in 1714 and there were also four younger sons. One of them, John – who was to die before the end of the year, aged 20 – had already been given £2,000 'to try his fortune with'.

The scheme for the Bank of Ireland and the Georgia colony

In the summer of 1720 Abercorn, along with a number of others, including Viscount Boyne, Sir Ralph Gore and Michael Ward, drew up a petition to the King on behalf of themselves and others arguing the case for a national bank. The institution would be known as the Bank of Ireland and a fund of £500,000 would be raised. Merchants and manufacturers would be able to borrow money from the bank at 5% interest. Although the proposal was supported by Grafton and received the approval of the lords justices in January 1721, it came at a time when the Irish economy was experiencing severe difficulties.[50] The scheme was bitterly opposed by Archbishop King and ultimately the plan came to nothing. In spite of this setback Abercorn continued to take an interest in Irish fiscal matters and supported William Wood's patent to mint copper coins in Ireland. He is believed to have been the author of at least one tract on the matter.[51]

The final important venture that the 6th Earl was involved in was the establishment of a British settlement in America. Along with the Earl of Derby, the bishop of Worcester and several others, Abercorn was one of the main financiers of the Georgia colony project of the early 1730s. At a meeting of the Georgia Society in May 1733 it was announced that Abercorn had given another £100. Following his death at the end of 1734, the Earl of Egmont lamented his loss to the Georgia colony, noting that he had promised £100 a year to the project while he lived.[52] General Oglethorpe, when laying out the city of Savannah on a grid pattern, named the main street in his honour, while there was also briefly a village named Abercorn near Savannah though all traces of this settlement have long since disappeared.

Forthcoming Publication

Clergy of Limerick – Clergy of Ardfert and Aghadoe

Edited by Canon D.W.T. Crooks

This book is the fruit of Canon J.B. Leslie's unpublished Succession Lists of the Diocese of Limerick, 1936, and of his published *Ardfert and Aghadoe Clergy and Parishes*, 1940. It has been updated to include all clergy of the Dioceses since that time.

This new book will contain:

‡ Details of 3,350 clergy with genealogical notes

‡ Canon Leslie's original volume, *Ardfert and Aghadoe Clergy and Parishes*

‡ Photographs of the churches

‡ Brief historical notes on the dioceses and on some of the churches

‡ **The book will be published by Ulster Historical Foundation**

The price per copy will be €70/£60 on publication but a pre-publication subscription price of €55/£45 is offered. It is hoped that the book will be published before the end of 2014.

Suscribers names will be included in a special list in the book.

Order Form

☐ Please reserve a copy of *Clergy of Limerick, Ardfert and Aghadoe.*

NAME

ADDRESS

EMAIL

SIGNED

Payments should be sent to:

     Canon D.W.T. Crooks
     Taughboyne Rectory, Churchtown, Carrigans, Co. Donegal

Please place your name (a single line acknowledgement) as you wish it to appear in the List of Subscribers.

All subscribers will be notified of the date and venue of the book launch.

For information about Ulster Historical Foundation go to www.booksireland.org.uk

Ulster History and Genealogy Autumn School

14th–20th September 2014

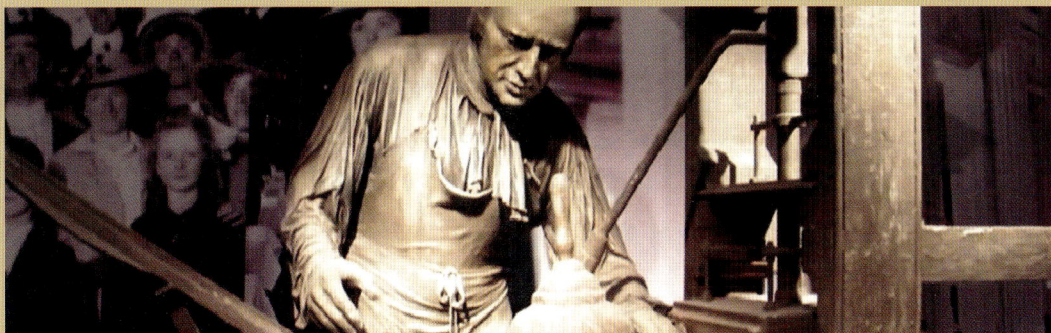

M'archibald Warwick and James M'Cullogh having finished their trials, after a suitable Exhortation, were licensed to preach

Discover your roots and Ulster's fascinating history at Ulster Historical Foundation's
Ulster History and Genealogy Autumn School

Learn about the history of Ulster and your ancestors' lives and migration experiences first-hand on excursions to some of Ulster's most historic sites. There is also time to do some research for yourself with the help of our expert genealogists and in the evenings you can relax and enjoy some entertaining and enlightening talks and discussions. If you are interested in finding out more about your Irish ancestors' lives, their experiences and the history of the Ulster, this is the perfect opportunity to do so.

Guides and speakers

Dr Allan Blackstock	Tim Smyth
Dr William Roulston	Dr Brian Lambkin
Stephen Scarth	Dr Patrick Fitzgerald

Ulster Historical Foundation
49 Malone Road, Belfast, BT9 6RY
(0)28 9066 1988   enquiry@uhf.org.uk   www.ancestryireland.com

Discover your Irish and Scots-Irish Ancestors
www.ancestryireland.com/autumn-school/

BOOKING FORM

I would like to reserve _____ places at the *Ulster History and Genealogy Autumn School*, 14th–20 September 2014.

Name_____

Address_____

_____ Email_____

Spouse/Travelling Partner's Name_____

The rates below are **per person**. To enable participants to arrange accommodation which best suits their needs, accommodation is not included in the package. UHF can advise on hotels to suit all budgets and personal requirements.

☐ **FULL RATE (EU Resident)**   £620 UK pounds (*$1,034/€754)
For those who wish to take part in all aspects of the conference, including the research days at the Public Record Office of Northern Ireland. Included in this package are: 5 evening meals; 2 lunches, transport during the event; all talks and tours; entrance fees; university fees research assistance by professional genealogists.

☐ **FULL RATE (NON-EU Resident)**   £670 UK pounds (*$1,118/€815)
Details as ABOVE. University fees, which are built in to the cost of the event, vary depending on whether or not you are resident in the European Union. EU resident delegates pay a lower rate. UHF has no control over these charges.

☐ **NON-RESEARCH**   £399 UK pounds (*$665/€485)
For those who wish to take part in the event with the exception of the genealogical research days. Ideal for travelling companions of full rate participants. Included in this package are: 5 evening meals, 2 lunches, transport during the event; all talks and tours; entrance fees.

£_____ *Total Amount Payable* (all booking fees plus any supplements). *Note all charges are made in UK pounds, dollar and Euro amounts are given for comparison only.

OUTLINE OF AUTUMN SCHOOL PROGRAMME

SUNDAY, 14TH SEPTEMBER
Informal get-together for introductions

MONDAY, 15TH SEPTEMBER
Introduction and lectures Belfast Campus of University of Ulster; visit to PRONI; Evening reception at University of Ulster

TUESDAY, 16TH SEPTEMBER
Day of assisted research at PRONI
Evening visit to Sentry Hill

WEDNESDAY, 17TH SEPTEMBER
Outing to Baron's Court, Ulster American Folk Park and the Mellon Centre for Migration Studies

THURSDAY, 18TH SEPTEMBER
Day of assisted research at PRONI

FRIDAY, 19TH SEPTEMBER
Free day; evening reception at University of Ulster

SATURDAY, 20TH SEPTEMBER
Outing to the Mourne Mountains and South Down

Payment (return with payment to address below)

☐ **Cheque** Make payable to Ulster Historical Foundation. If in a currency other than UK pounds sterling, please add an additional £3.00 (or equivalent) to cover the cost of conversion.

☐ **Credit Card** Please debit my American Express/Visa/Mastercard.

Expiry Date _____   Check Digits

Date _____   Amount £ _____

Signature _____

Return to: Ulster Historical Foundation, 49 Malone Road, Belfast, BT9 6RY **www.ancestryireland.com**

Family

The 6th Earl and his wife Elizabeth had a large family of 14 children, nine sons and five daughters, several of whom died young. The Earl's eldest son died in infancy and it was his second-born, another James, who was to succeed to the title and estate. His relationship with his eldest son was at times fraught and the two quarrelled over the terms of the latter's marriage settlement in 1711. Two of the 6th Earl's younger sons, George and Charles, became MPs, while Francis entered the Church and became rector of Dunleer in County Louth. In 1724, William King, archbishop of Dublin, wrote to Bishop Stearne of Clogher on behalf of Francis, who wished to serve as a curate in Stearne's diocese. King believed that Francis would be an excellent addition to the clergy of the diocese, and pointed out that of his own volition he had previously gone to an out of the way parish so that he would have more time to study.[53] In an age when many clergy did not display such conscientiousness, Francis Hamilton's actions speak volumes for his commitment to his calling. Another of the 6th Earl's sons, William, was lost at sea in 1721. One of his daughters died in infancy, but the other four all reached adulthood and married. Elizabeth married William Brownlow of Lurgan in 1711 and after his death Martin, Count de Kearnie. Mary married Henry Colley, MP for Castle Carberry in County Wicklow. Philippa was married first to Benjamin Pratt DD, Provost of Trinity College, Dublin, and then to Michael Connell. Finally, Jane married Lord Archibald Hamilton, son of the 3rd Duke of Hamilton, and brother of the men that Abercorn had vexed so greatly in 1712 during his pursuit of Châtelherault, though whether this represents an improvement in the relationship between the two branches of the family is not clear.

A portrait at Barons Court possibly of one of the younger sons of the 6th Earl, William, who was lost off Lizard Point in November 1721 in the *Royal Anne* galley, while travelling with Lord Belhaven to Barbados 'as a volunteer in the sea service.'

Death and burial

In his later years Abercorn was prone to bouts of ill health. In September 1730 he was said to be 'almost dead on one side from the palsy'; in the autumn of 1733 he was confined to bed for two months and was in a

Hᴼᴺ JOHN
HAMILTON.
1704.

John Hamilton in 1704.
Possibly the son of the 6th Earl
who died as a young man in
1714.

'wearing condition' when visited by Egmont.[54] The 6th Earl died on 28
November 1734 and was buried on 3 December in the Duke of Ormond's
vault in Henry VII's Chapel in Westminster Abbey. The Earl of Egmont paid
the following tribute to him in his diary entry of 3 December 1734:

> He was a man of great honour and sincerity, courage and breeding,
> and of as much public spirit as ever I was acquainted with, but
> passionate and of no great depth of understanding, yet very passable
> with mankind by reason of his virtues.[55]

He was a remarkable man who lived in an eventful age. From his London
upbringing close to the heart of the Royal Court, his involvement in the siege
of Derry, his attendance and support of the Act of Union between England
and Scotland, he had experienced first-hand some of the most important
events in British and Irish history. Through inheritance and purchase he
acquired one of the largest estates in Ireland. His impact on the fate and
fortunes of the Hamilton family cannot be overestimated, and his legacy has
lasted to the present day.

JAMES LORD
PAISLEY.
1714

4
James Hamilton, 7th Earl of Abercorn
Scientist and patron of the arts

Of those who have held the Abercorn title since the beginning of the eighteenth century, the 7th Earl is the most frequently overlooked. Whereas his father had seen active military service during the Williamite War

The 7th Earl of Abercorn

in Ireland and his grandfather had died as a result of a naval engagement, the 7th Earl of Abercorn lived in a very different era. For most of his life the 7th Earl lived in the shadow of his father. When he finally succeeded to the earldom he was in his late 40s and lived for only another 10 years. Unlike his father, he made no real impact on local or national politics. And yet, on closer inspection, the 7th Earl's life was not as uninteresting as might first appear. He was a patron of the arts, was passionate about music, wrote treatises, and conducted scientific experiments.

Early life and education

The future 7th Earl of Abercorn was born on 22 March 1686, probably in Dublin. Of his early life very little is known. In 1701, on the succession of his father to the earldom of Abercorn and viscountcy of Strabane, he was styled Lord Paisley. He received part of his education on the Continent, where his governor was a Monsieur de Choutens. For a time he was at the Academy of Leeuwarden, in northern Holland, before it closed in the summer of 1704 due to the death of the 'chief person who managed it'. His father hoped that in sending his son to this establishment he would have 'in some measure fitted himself to appear in the world'. He was then sent on to Wolfenbuttel in Lower Saxony. Not only was 6th Earl concerned about his son's education at this time, he was also anxious that in his travels through Europe he would have the opportunity to call on the Court of Hanover. Abercorn, therefore, wrote to the Secretary of State, Robert Harley, at the end of August 1704 asking him for a favour:

> The Court of Hanover being in my son's way thither, it might seem want of due respect in him to their Highnesses, and in me or due deference to the Protestant Succession as by law established, if he

A young Anne Plumer, the future Countess of Abercorn

should pass through Hanover, or reside in the territory of the Prince of that family, without behaving himself as becomes him upon that occasion. I should be glad, therefore, to have my son Paisley introduced at the Court of Hanover by Her Majesty's minister there and that you would please to honour my son with two or three lines to His Excellency.[1]

Undoubtedly these early experiences on the Continent had a strong impact on the young Lord Paisley and are likely to have contributed to the love of music, literature and learning that characterised his adult life. In the spring of 1711 Paisley married Anne Plumer, daughter of a Hertfordshire landowner, Col. John Plumer of Blakesware, who brought with her a fortune of £10,000. In 1742, Horace Walpole described her as 'a most frightful gentlewoman'. Their London residence was for many years in Queen's Square, Holborn, but later they moved to Cavendish Square. There was also a country residence at Witham in Essex which was purchased from Robert Barwell in the spring of 1720. Hamilton immediately set to work to transform the house and its grounds, as the following excerpt from Daniel Defoe's *Tour Thro' the Whole Island of Great Britain* shows:

> In the town of Witham dwells Lord Pasely, eldest son of the Earl of Abercorne in Ireland (a branch of the noble family of Hamilton in Scotland). His Lordship has a small, but a neat well built, new house, and is finishing his gardens in such a manner as few in that part of England will exceed them.[2]

In 1723, Paisley received permission to construct a vault in Witham Church with a pew over it for his family and heirs forever. As will be presently seen, he was not interred there himself. He seems to have had relatively little interest in national politics. It was not until 1738 that he was made a privy counsellor of England; in the following year he became a privy counsellor of Ireland. With regard to his official duties in relation to the Royal Family, he was a Lord of the Bedchamber.

The Countess of Abercorn

Love of science and the arts

If he was not particularly interested in politics, Paisley was enthusiastic about science and the arts. In 1715, he was elected a fellow of the prestigious Royal

Society. In 1729, following the conducting of 'several experiments very carefully made', he published *Calculations and tables relating to the attractive power of loadstones*, an account of which appeared in the *Philosophical Transactions of the Royal Society*. Music, however, seems to have been the great preoccupation of his life and he became an authority on the subject. He appears in the commonplace book of the German composer, John Sigismond Cousser, who moved to London in 1704, where he is referred to as 'My Lord Paesley, son of My Lord Abercorn'. Although the reason for the presence of his name in this volume is not made explicitly clear, it is possible that Paisley was one of Cousser's pupils or perhaps the composer performed a private concert for him.[3] Later he was a supporter of the Academy of Ancient Music and was a pupil of another German composer, the Berlin-born John Christopher Pepusch.

In 1730, the anonymous *A Treatise on Harmony, containing the Chief Rules for Composing in Two, Three or Four Parts*, based on Pepusch's teachings, appeared and its authorship has been attributed to Lord Paisley. According to John Hawkins' *General History of the Science and Practice of Music* (1776), Paisley wrote the treatise without Pepusch's consent. Another authority suggests that Paisley was able to express Pepusch's ideas in English better than the composer himself. An article in *The Universal Magazine* from 1778 states that Pepusch 'affected to speak of the publication of this book as injurious both to his character and interest; however, it did not long, if at all, interrupt the friendship between Lord Paisley and him'.[4] In 1731 a second edition of the *Treatise* appeared, which, though again anonymous, is believed to contain additions by Pepusch himself.

Through various connections Paisley had the ability to acquire copies of obscure musical works. On 27 February 1736 the Earl of Egmont went to the Thursday Vocal Academy in the Crown Tavern in London, where he heard the famous *Miserere* of Allegri. Although it was 'forbid to be copied out or communicated to any under pain of excommunication', the piece had been supplied by the now Earl of Abercorn 'whose brother contrived to obtain it'.[5] Which of Abercorn's brothers managed this remarkable feat is unclear – possibly Charles – nor is it known how he managed to do so. As an indication of the regard in which he was held as an authority on music, at a meeting of the Royal Society on 3 November 1737 he was requested to examine a treatise submitted by the famous French composer, Rameau, entitled *Génération harmonique*. The work was passed to Abercorn, who was asked to 'peruse the Treatise at his leisure'.[6]

Little is known about the 7th Earl's relationship with his Tyrone and Donegal estates. On his marriage in 1711 he was immediately put into possession of these lands – an arrangement that led to a falling out with his father – and they were managed on his behalf by a series of agents. The 6th

Earl's political interests in the borough of Strabane also seem to have been managed by his son. At this time the Abercorns did not enjoy a good relationship with the town's corporation, and Lord Paisley went so far as to disenfranchise one of the burgesses in 1733. Although on poor terms, the two men at least agreed at this time to put forward Paisley's eldest son, the Hon. James Hamilton (the future 8th Earl), as their candidate for MP of Strabane, though in the event Hamilton's candidacy did not materialise.

The 7th Earl died at Cavendish Square in London on 11 January 1744 and was buried five days later alongside his father in the Duke of Ormond's vault in Westminster Abbey. His wife survived him by 32 years, dying in 1776 at the age of 86. The 7th Earl died intestate and administration of his estate was granted to his son and heir James on 13 March 1744. He had five other sons as well as two daughters. Two sons and a daughter died young. His daughter Anne married Sir Henry Mackworth Bt and died in 1792. Two sons served in the Royal Navy and drowned in separate incidents. Lieutenant William Hamilton drowned when his ship HMS *Victory* was lost off Alderney in 1744. Captain John Hamilton, father of the future 9th Earl and 1st Marquess of Abercorn, drowned when his boat capsized off Portsmouth in 1755. The fifth son, George, entered the Church and served briefly as rector of Donagheady parish, County Tyrone; later he was canon of Windsor.

BELOW LEFT:
A graduate of the Oxford colleges of Exeter (BA 1739/40) and Merton (MA 1742), Rev. George Hamilton was presented to the parish of Donagheady by his brother, the 8th Earl, in 1753, but almost immediately exchanged this parish for Taplow in Buckinghamshire (with the rector of Taplow, Rev. George Bracegirdle, moved to Donagheady). He was appointed canon of Windsor in 1783 and died in 1787. His daughter Cecil married, as his second wife, the 1st Marquess of Abercorn.

BELOW RIGHT:
The wife of Rev. George Hamilton, Elizabeth was the daughter of Lieutenant-General Richard Onslow. She died in 1800.

The Hon. Charles Hamilton (1704–1786)

One of the most important figures in landscape gardening in the eighteenth century, Charles Hamilton was the fourteenth child – the youngest of nine sons – of the 6th Earl of Abercorn. Baptised in St Peter's Church in Dublin, he was educated at Westminster School and Christ Church, Oxford. He was MP for the borough of Strabane in the Irish parliament from 1727 to 1760, though rarely, if ever, attended.[7] In addition he was MP for Truro in the Westminster parliament in the 1740s. A number of official positions were also held, including Comptroller of the Green Cloth to the Prince of Wales (1738–47), an appointment secured through his sister Jane (usually referred to as Lady Archibald Hamilton) being the Prince's mistress. When she fell from favour Charles was dismissed. He later said that he despised the Prince so much that he could not bring himself to hang up a full-length portrait of him, presented to Charles by the Prince himself, but kept it in a storeroom. Hamilton was also Receiver General of the King's Revenue for Minorca, 1743–57, though 'a cloud of suspicion' hung over his accounts. Afterwards his close friend from their Oxford days, Henry Fox, secured for him a secret service pension of £1,200 per annum.[8]

Charles Hamilton is best remembered for his interest in horticulture and his activities at Painshill near Cobham in Surrey – 'one of the gardening glories of the eighteenth century'. He had been inspired by the landscape paintings of artists such as Poussin and Salvator Rosa while on the 'grand tour' to Rome in 1725 and returned there for a second time in 1732 when he acquired antique sculptures later to adorn Painshill. On this visit he was painted by Antonio David; his portrait shows him well dressed, holding a gun, and with hunting dogs. In the late 1730s Hamilton began to acquire land at Painshill and to remodel the landscape along the principles of the new naturalistic style. The soil was improved, new trees and shrubs were planted, as were two vineyards, and a 30-acre lake with its own island was created. In 1748, Horace Walpole commented that Hamilton had 'really made a fine place out of a most cursed hill'. A visitor in the early 1760s has left the following description of the site:

> The grounds are five miles in circumference and the soil is said to have grown nothing but heather and scrub in former times, but it has now been brought to a high state of perfection. The garden, like all of English design, is arranged according to modern ideas of an improvement on the beauty of

The Hon. Charles Hamilton. The celebrated landscape gardener is shown in this portrait holding a volume with the legend 'Views of Painshill' on its spine.

nature. ... The finest part of this Hamilton garden is the lake, very carefully made at the foot of the hill, where the water falls over large and irregularly placed rocks, and runs into a deep pool, in the middle of which is an island covered with shrubbery and walks, which lead to small bridges of artistic construction. ... it is difficult to believe how Art has been able to copy Nature to the extent done here.[9]

A biographer has written: 'By his talents, dedication, social connections, and ability to get quick and exciting results within narrow constraints of money and manpower, Hamilton devised the right model at the right moment.' His advice was eagerly sought and he corresponded with his nephew, the 8th Earl, on improvements to the demesne at Barons Court. In 1773, he was forced to sell Painshill in order to repay a loan. He moved to Bath where he built a house in Lansdowne Crescent.

Of his three wives, we know nothing about the first, though this union produced two daughters. In 1772 he married a daughter of Dr David Cockburn of Ayr, but she died later that year after bearing a daughter. His third wife was Frances Calvert whom he married in 1774. His death, on 11 September 1786, is said to have been as the result of a vigorous quarrel with his neighbour, Mr Anstey, over some acres Hamilton wished to acquire for a garden. Walpole wrote: 'Hamilton wrote a warm letter on their being refused; and Anstey, who does not hate a squabble in print, as he has more than once shown, discharged shaft upon shaft against the poor veteran [who] ... died of the volley, as even a goose-quill will do the feat at eighty-three.'[10] He was buried in Bath Abbey. After years of neglect, in 1981 the Painshill Park Trust was formed to preserve and restore the grounds which are now open to the public.

The Public Record Office of Northern Ireland holds some of Hamilton's papers, including an account book for the period 1760–1773, apparently concerning Painshill, as well as documents relating to his period as Receiver General of the King's Revenue of Minorca.[11] In addition there are letters from the Abbé Nolin, a leading French horticulturalist, to Hamilton. This correspondence interested the 4th Duke greatly and he translated the letters and deposited photocopies of them in the Natural History Museum in Paris in 1973.[12]

Mrs Charles Hamilton. The Hon. Charles Hamilton was married three times and it is not clear which of his wives this was.

THE 8th
EARLE OF ABERCORN.

5

James Hamilton, 8th Earl of Abercorn
'A man of succinctness'

The 8th Earl of Abercorn is generally regarded as the great consolidator of the family's position and property. In some ways history has not been kind to him. Despite his achievements, he has often been thought of as a rather dour, introverted individual. Horace Walpole mocked him mercilessly for his reserved nature: 'Silent as my Lord Abercorn' and 'Motionless as Lord Abercorn' being two of his less than flattering pronouncements on the Earl.[1] Gamble's comment in his *View of society and manners in the north of Ireland*[2] has often been quoted (and even more often misquoted): 'He never drank anything but water, and in consequence, as it was supposed, of a disappointment he experienced in early life, had no more relish for the society of women than of wine.' On the other hand, a later biographer wrote: 'Endowed with sound common sense, excellent judgment, and great

60

independence of character, Lord Abercorn was the most scrupulously honourable and upright of men.'[3] Anthony Malcomson acknowledges that the 8th Earl was 'a man of deeds rather than words; indeed of few of the latter', but points out that he 'emerges from his own correspondence as a man of succinctness rather than mere taciturnity'.[4] Through the many hundreds of his letters that still survive, we have an opportunity to delve into the mind of the man. His correspondence reveals him to have been someone who thought matters through, who did not act on impulse and who gave a considered response to any question put to him.

Early life and Irish estates

The future 8th Earl of Abercorn was born in Queen's Square, Holborn, London, on 22 October 1712. He was educated at Christ Church, Oxford, matriculating on 10 October 1729, just short of his seventeenth birthday.[5] Upon leaving university he went on the 'grand tour' of Continental Europe that for the sons of aristocrats was almost a prerequisite for completing their education. It was said that he had made the entire tour 'in so perpendicular a stile as to have never touched the back of the carriage'. Whether or not the theory of unrequited love referred to by Gamble accounts for his failure to marry, the 8th Earl seems to have been content with his bachelor status. He makes no complaints of loneliness or isolation in his letters, though the fact that he was a very private person would have made him reluctant to admit to such feelings even if he did have them. He was extremely close to his mother and lived with her for the first 32 years of his life. He also displayed considerable generosity towards other family members, many of whom benefited from his assistance, financial or otherwise.

The 8th Earl with the Peckwater Quadrangle of Christ Church, Oxford, in the background.

When his father died in 1744 James Hamilton succeeded not only to an earldom, but also to an estate of some 70,000 acres divided between five manors in north-west Ulster. Much of it was prime agricultural land and tenanted for the most part with the descendents of Scottish immigrants who had settled there in the seventeenth century. The town of Strabane, of which he was the lord of the soil, was one of the most important market towns in Ulster on account of its being a principal centre of the linen trade. The 8th

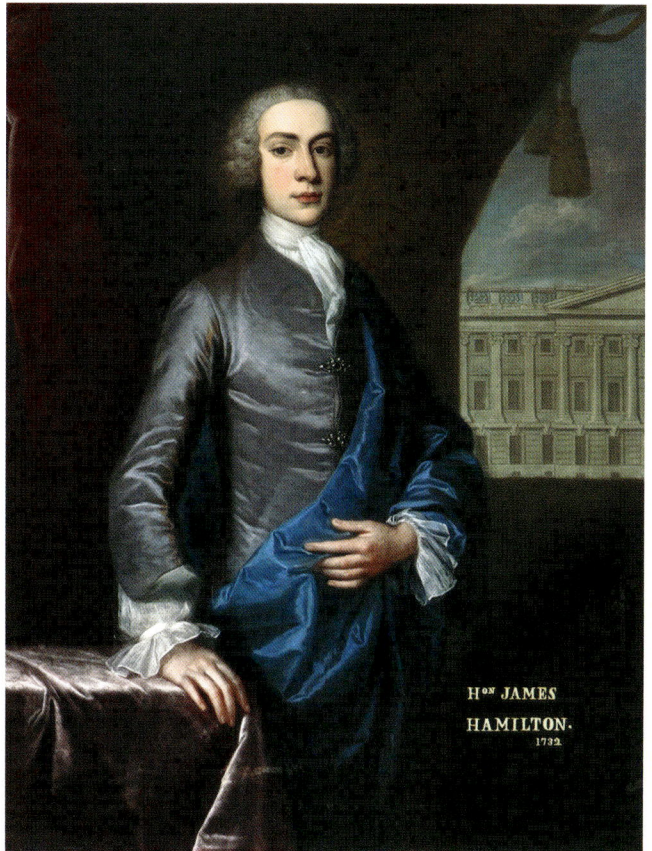

Earl, like his father and grandfather, did not live on his Irish estates. The last resident earl had been the 5th Earl, who lived in the castle in Strabane. By 1744 the castle was no longer considered suitable accommodation for the head of the family. Though a new country house was built at Barons Court, the Earl spent most of his life in England, in his London house or his estate at Witham in Essex, or at Duddingston and Paisley in Scotland. In fact he visited his Irish estates only eight times in his long life: in 1746, 1749, 1751, 1752, 1756, 1761, 1777 and 1782. In August 1745 Abercorn contemplated coming to Ireland if the 'foolish business of the Pretender's landing in Scotland should have any consequences in the north of Ireland' so that he could appear with his tenants, but in the event the troubles feared by the Earl did not materialise.[6]

Whether or not it was a factor in the infrequency of his visits to Ireland, it is clear that Abercorn did not enjoy the sea crossing. Prior to his visit to Ireland in 1749 he sought the assistance of his Dublin banker, Henry Mitchell, in finding a suitable 'full decked ship' to make the crossing between Portpatrick and Donaghadee as he did not relish travelling in an open boat. Such boats were rare on this particular route, and even the Donaghadee custom-house boat would not do for it was only half decked. In the spring of 1761 he made a similar request to Mitchell, hoping for a ship that would be 'as good and tight as may be' and capable of holding 10 horses and his chaise. On his visits to his Irish estates he met with tenants, received delegations, heard grievances, tried to sort out problems and witnessed at first hand what was happening in north-west Ulster. The statement in the *Gazetteer* of 4 October 1790 that 'though he had estates in Ireland which annually produced him 18,000 pounds, [he] never spent a shilling in that country' is absurd.

Though an absentee landowner, the frequent letters that he wrote to his agents reveal that he possessed an incredible depth of knowledge of his Irish estates. At the time of his succession as Earl, three agents in north-west Ulster were in the service of the family. John McClintock was responsible for the manors of Dunnalong in County Tyrone, and Magavlin and Lismoghry in County Donegal. Nathaniel Nisbitt looked after the manor of Strabane, while John Colhoun acted as agent for the manors of Cloghogall and Derrywoon, the latter including Barons Court. Abercorn placed considerable trust in these men. Not only were they responsible for securing and providing an accurate return of the rents in each of the manors, they were the Earl's eyes and ears in their respective localities, providing him with detailed information on what was happening on the ground. When the Earl issued instructions on a certain matter they were charged with carrying out his commands. Though a few tenants made the arduous journey to Edinburgh or London to bring their complaints to the 8th Earl directly, usually it was the agent who had to deal with various issues, such as disputes between tenants or requests to build a mill. The agents would then bring these matters to Abercorn's attention and await his directions.

Abercorn had a high regard for his agents and they had an equal respect for him. In his will John McClintock appointed Abercorn an overseer of his estate, and when McClintock died in 1751 Abercorn, who was 'much touched by the loss', dutifully accepted the responsibilities that went with that. When Colhoun died in 1755 Nisbitt was left with the responsibility for the entire estate. This proved too much for him, and in April 1757 he asked that additional agents be appointed. Those selected included brothers John, known as 'Fat Jack', and James or Jemmy Hamilton, who were distantly related to the Earl, and John Sinclair, the owner of the freehold of Holy Hill in the manor of Cloghogall. Sinclair was charged with the agency of Dunnalong, John Hamilton with Cloghogall and James Hamilton with Derrywoon. Nisbitt retained Strabane and the lands in Donegal. Though his burden was significantly lightened, the effects of Nisbitt's heavy workload may have lingered on, for in 1764 he had a mental breakdown and had to relinquish his remaining agencies with the Earl. Sinclair died in the summer of 1770, shortly after retiring as agent due to ill-health. With John Hamilton also retiring for health reasons in 1778, his brother James became Abercorn's sole agent and carried out his duties with an attention to detail that could only be matched by his master. The two men had a mutual respect, and right from the start Abercorn was impressed with his agent. In 1758, in a letter to the lord chancellor requesting that Hamilton receive a commission of the peace, Abercorn wrote, 'I have so firm an opinion of his integrity and activeness'.

Abercorn demanded that his agents be meticulous, reliable and honest in their dealings with him. In 1745, he advised one individual hoping to be taken into his service, 'Punctuality in accounts is absolutely necessary in all dealings with me'.[7] In June 1768 he told John Hamilton that he wanted his accounts prepared 'in a better hand than your clerk's', which though adequate for something unimportant was 'hardly equal to an account that there may be frequent occasion to resort to'. His instructions and advice to them were a mixture of candour and common sense. 'Growing flax is no part of the business of a linen manufacturer', he wrote to James Hamilton in the summer of 1783, 'any more than keeping sheep is the business of a woollen manufacturer'. Though his agents were to be unswerving in their loyalty to him, this did not preclude them from acting as agents on other estates. McClintock was agent to, among others, the McCauslands, while Nisbitt was agent for the Creighton and Montgomery estates in County Donegal. Abercorn did not object to this and in fact congratulated James Hamilton on his appointment as the agent on Lord Blessington's estate at

Newtownstewart in 1761. This attitude is a further reflection of the level of trust the 8th Earl had in his agents.

The 8th Earl's management of his property was both attentive and judicious. The improvement of his estates was a key element in this. In a very striking way, this was seen in the colonisation of lands that had previously been of little agricultural value. In areas such as Glenmornan, in the manor of Cloghogall, tenants were encouraged to settle on higher ground, create fields and grow crops. Various drainage schemes were implemented, particularly in the low-lying areas along the River Foyle. Tenants were also encouraged to improve their homes and farms. In 1750, to encourage improvement in his manor of Derrywoon, Abercorn introduced a series of premiums for tenants who excelled in various areas: 20 shillings for the best garden, 20 shillings for the best nursery of fruit trees and 40 shillings for the best house. He was very much opposed to granting long leases to his tenants, even if this put him at odds with his agents who advised otherwise. 'Long leases are the ruin of Ireland and of every man in it', he wrote to John Hamilton in 1774, 'and the great obstruction to improvement.' The duration of the leases he granted to his tenants was usually between seven and 21 years.

In his dealings with his tenants the 8th Earl displayed understanding and flexibility. Consider the sympathetic way he dealt with a tenant who built a mill in the manor of Dunnalong, but found his enterprise did not prove as successful as he had envisaged:

> It was very much contrary to my own inclination, entirely to gratify Mr Cary, and at your instance that I consented to the building of a corn mill at Drumgauty. I desire, however, that you will take the mill off his hands, allowing him for his expenses whatever is reasonable. And assure him there is not the least displeasure on my part, nor any reason that I know of why he should part with his farm; my wish is to accommodate him.[8]

At the same time, frustration or even anger is occasionally discernible in the 8th Earl's letters. Usually this was caused by a lack of respect for the law or the flouting of clear instructions that he had issued. In February 1761 Abercorn wrote to Sinclair in a tone of exasperation: 'I am not so much displeased at the destruction made in Menagh Hill wood as I lament the thievery and villainy by which that unfortunate country is distinguished from the rest of the world.'[9] However, he was not vindictive in dealing with those who had committed minor crimes on his estate. In April of that year he pardoned John Leslie for stealing timber provided he paid 40 shillings to the local rector within a fortnight for the use of the poor. He was less forgiving with those who were believed to have been stealing timber in 1781, giving Hamilton clear instructions on how he was to deal with them:

> The tenants upon whom you report to me as suspected of cutting sticks, will laugh at us if we fine them four times the value. Fine each of them two months' rent. There is no inequality in this, for the offence is greater in proportion as the tenant pays the larger rent, and the size of the stick hardly makes a difference.[10]

In this instance Abercorn was concerned that his reputation was at stake if he did not effectively discipline the offenders. Requests from tenants to subdivide their farms to provide for a son or other family member could also provoke his ire. In 1778, he wrote to James Hamilton: 'Samuel Smith of Ballymagorry can upon no account split his farm. This is, I hope, the last time you will give me occasion to write upon this sort of subject.'[11] At the same time, he could be flexible when the circumstances dictated it. By 1787 he was able to advise Hamilton, 'Where farms are large you may admit splitting a little more freely than we used to do'.[12]

As with many landlords, improvement was not restricted to land and buildings, but was something to be encouraged in the manners and habits of his tenants. A particular area of concern was the level of consumption of alcoholic beverages, particularly of whiskey. One solution to the problems associated with whiskey was to encourage the drinking of beer or ale, which was not as strong. He felt that his fellow landlords should set an example in this, reflecting in 1779, 'If the nobility and gentry would drink their own beer, instead of French claret, it would be of great use'. In his pronouncements on this subject the 8th Earl's dry wit comes through on occasion. In November 1780 he wrote to James Hamilton, 'There is no danger that barley will not find its value: the failure of the distillery is one of the blessings that Ireland can never hope to obtain.' On a perceived change in the drinking habits of some of the inhabitants of his manors he wrote in 1783, 'I am glad the poor people here at last found out they were starving in consequence of drinking their barley instead of eating it'.

The Earl was also desirous that the inhabitants of his estate should have a strong work ethic, especially the cottiers or undertenants, as this would determine whether they merited assistance in times of need. His views on this are clearly set out in a letter to Colhoun in November 1747:

> I apprehend the people are disposed to be very idle now meal is so cheap. I would therefore have you appoint three of the principal tenants to go round the manor of Derrygoon [Derrywoon] and take an account of all the cotters and poorer tenants distinguishing which of them are industrious and which not, either in their own persons or in neglecting to send their children out to service for reasonable wages, that I may the better judge which deserve to be employed when they stand in need of it.[13]

Every so often the cottiers on his estate either vexed him or aroused his sympathy. In 1761, on one of his trips to Ireland, and passing through Ballymagorry, Abercorn 'found great complaints of trespass committed by cottiers of Woodend who live there in great numbers upon the lands under long leases and bring their turf through Ballymagorry from Woodend bog'. The Earl instructed his agents to put an immediate stop to this. One of Abercorn's principal objections to cottiers was the pressure they were putting on natural resources such as turf, which was becoming increasingly scarce as more and more land was reclaimed. In a dispute over turf rights in Gortavea in 1761, Abercorn demanded that the cottiers living under Thomas Hamilton were to be removed or else the advanced rent mentioned in the lease would have to be paid. The Earl was at this time keeping a list of cottiers on his estate, and only those that were on this list were permitted. In 1775 he wrote to James Hamilton: 'I am sensible of the want of turf about Burndennet. It is owing in great measure to a number of cottiers harboured about the mill whom I took great pains to get rid of.'

Although he considered cottiers to be something of a nuisance, there were occasions when Abercorn sympathised with their plight. In 1769, a case involving cottiers living on a farm in the manor of Dunnalong was brought to his attention. The difficulties arose when a new tenant came into possession of the farm and wished to get rid of the cottiers living on his holding. Abercorn instructed his agent to 'give the new tenant to understand that his own possession will not be safe till he gives ample security to these poor people'. In the right circumstances he did believe that cottiers were an important part of the rural economy, as a letter of 1776 reveals: 'I always think it right that the tenants should not be discouraged from keeping labouring servants in distinct tenements, provided the greatest part of their labour be employed in the service of the tenants.' The small farmers and cottiers were the first to suffer during difficult times such as those brought on by poor harvests and the consequent food shortages, and on occasion Abercorn provided for those facing the prospect of starvation. In January 1776, during a period of particularly bad weather, he directed that £10 be given to the poor in each of his Tyrone manors and £20 to those in his Donegal lands. In May 1783 he instructed James Hamilton to distribute £300 among the poor on his estates, especially those in the more remote parts.

Abercorn and the churches

Voluminous though Abercorn's letters were, they reveal very little of his personal attitude to faith and religion. Whatever his thoughts on this subject were, he kept them to himself. Though a member of the Anglican establishment, Abercorn was sympathetic to those of a different religious background. One of the simplest ways in which he could demonstrate his tolerance of other denominations was in allowing them to build places of public worship on his lands. In the early 1740s, following a split in the Presbyterian congregation of Donagheady due to a disagreement over the choice of a new minister, he granted permission to build a new meeting house in the townland of Sandville. In 1765, a Covenanter or Reformed Presbyterian congregation was formed in the Foyle Valley and in 1771 some of its members petitioned Abercorn to be allowed to build a meeting house at Bready. This Abercorn readily consented to, and in 1778 he defended the congregation from those seeking to encroach upon the site of its church.[14] Neither was he opposed to the lifting of some of the measures introduced through the Penal Laws. Writing to Dean Barnard in the summer of 1778, ahead of the passing of the Catholic Relief Act, he commented, 'As a friend to liberty, I cannot help wishing the relief of the Roman Catholics in the hope and confidence that their great sufferings will be a warning to them not to abuse the indulgences that may be shown them.' He granted permission to the Catholics of Leckpatrick parish to build a chapel at Cloughcor in 1784, and later another in Glenmornan.

The Earl was concerned that clergy should be resident in their parishes. When the parish of Taughboyne in east Donegal fell vacant in 1782, he emphasised to the bishop of Raphoe the 'propriety of residence, both in a spiritual and in a temporal view'. He had already seen the repercussions of non-residence on the fortunes of the family of a recently deceased rector of a parish of which he was patron. In 1753, Rev. George Bracegirdle had been appointed rector of Donagheady in a straight swap with Abercorn's younger brother, Rev. George Hamilton, who moved to Bracegirdle's former parish of Taplow in Buckinghamshire. Bracegirdle refused to live in Donagheady, preferring the urban comforts of Strabane, and was not prepared to erect a parsonage in the parish despite the various encouragements to build contained in a series of acts of parliament. Had he done so his family would have been compensated a substantial part of the outlay on the house by his successor. When he died in 1768 his widow and children were left impoverished. In a latter to the dean of Raphoe on the family's difficulties, Abercorn was 'forced to reflect how happy it would have been for Mr Bracegirdle's family if they could have prevailed upon him to have built upon his glebe'. In Scotland Abercorn enjoyed the right of presentation to Paisley Abbey. He had little interest in its ministers, however. In 1773, he wrote to James Blair, the factor of his estate at Paisley, telling him that he had no wish to be involved in the issuing of a call to a prospective new minister and if Blair attended the ceremony it was to be in his own capacity and not as Abercorn's representative.[15]

Abercorn also found himself having to deal with disputes over tithes. The payment of tithes for the support of the Church of Ireland clergy was deeply resented by both Catholics and Presbyterians. If the clergy found it difficult to collect tithes from parishioners who also happened to be tenants on the Abercorn estate, they would often write to the Earl asking for assistance. For example, when the newly appointed rector of Ardstraw parish found it difficult to collect tithes he sought Abercorn's intervention. The 8th Earl's reply is very interesting, for in it he encouraged him to

> be cautious of believing complaints and suggestions that may be made to you until you have examined them. In such a number of people you must expect to find some that will be wrong-headed and absurd. But you will see that kind usage will operate strongly upon the majority; and the more because they are little accustomed to it … Whenever I have said anything to my tenants about their tithes, my advice has always been such as I think best calculated to preserve peace and quiet, and extremely simple. It is this: to agree for their tithes, when they can do it to advantage; when they can not, to set them out in the fairest manner.[16]

Rather than giving his outright support for the rector, he encouraged him to take a more balanced view and give some consideration to the consequences of his actions. One historian has commented: 'There is no hint of condescension in this letter which Abercorn injected with just the right amount of gravity.'[17]

Abercorn and Strabane corporation

Unlike many of his contemporaries – and in stark contrast to his successor – the 8th Earl of Abercorn had little interest in political intrigue and lacked personal political ambition. He did not move in political or aristocratic circles in Ireland, and once remarked that he would not even recognise Lord Donegall, another of Ireland's leading titled landowners, if he saw him. However, given his family background and landed interests, it was impossible for him to avoid politics altogether. In 1733, at a time when his father and grandfather were attempting to regain control over the corporation of Strabane, he, as the Hon. James Hamilton, was proposed as a candidate to represent the borough in the Irish House of Commons. In the event his candidature did not materialise. In 1736, in his 24th year, he was summoned to the Irish House of Lords as Baron Mountcastle. He did not, however, play an active role in parliamentary life in Ireland and his involvement in Irish politics was principally in relation to his struggles for control of the corporation of Strabane. These tussles have been skilfully charted by Anthony Malcomson, who has identified several phases in the attempts of the 8th Earl to regain control of the borough.[18] His main opponents were Oliver McCausland, grandson of the Oliver McCausland who had served as

MP for Strabane between 1692 and 1723, and William Hamilton of Dunnamanagh, one of the two sitting MPs for the town. McCausland and Hamilton were on poor terms by the early 1750s and both men were in serious financial difficulties.

The first phase began in the early 1750s when Abercorn began to make cautious approaches to various individuals either on the corporation or with influence over burgesses in an effort to discover who he could win over. His relatively regular visits to Strabane during this period – four times between 1746 and 1752 – allowed him to get personally acquainted with the situation. He was also at pains to point out that it was not his intention to dominate the parliamentary representation of the town. As he directed in a letter to his agent, Nathaniel Nisbitt, in 1751, anyone who suggested otherwise was to receive a swift rebuke: 'I have no desire to have two of my family chosen for it, nor even one that would not attend in parliament, but that I stand up for the freedom of the town against all persons.' He also indicated that he was prepared to promote the economy of the town, which was mainly based on the linen industry. In a letter to William Hamilton of Dunnamanagh in 1752, Abercorn wrote: 'Every scheme is agreeable to me that carries an appearance of benefiting the linen trade, which my family has always been so zealous to promote from the smallest beginnings.' Drawing on the way in which his forebears had acted in the interests of the town was to be characteristic of many of the Earl's attempts to reassert his authority in Strabane. Abercorn's interventions on this occasion had little effect. His statement that he did not wish to have a family member who would not attend parliament lacked credibility when his own uncle, the Hon. Charles Hamilton, the other MP for Strabane at this time, had not set foot in the Irish House of Commons since his election in 1727.

After this failure of the first phase of the 8th Earl's attempt to regain his influence over the corporation, he adopted a more proactive approach. In 1755, by which time McCausland and William Hamilton had patched up their differences, Abercorn began legal proceedings designed to prove that various acts of the corporation were illegal and, therefore, invalidated all subsequent acts of the corporation and all elections to it. Highlighted in particular was the disenfranchisement of the burgess George McGhee in 1733, which, it was argued, had been unlawful. There was a not a little irony in this claim, given that McGhee's disqualification had been the doing of the Abercorns themselves. Abercorn's action was strongly opposed, with the provost and town clerk doing their best to prevent Abercorn's lawyers from gaining access to the corporation books. The 8th Earl was, however, confident that he would be successful in winning the first stage of the litigation at the Court of the King's Bench. It must have been something of a shock to him, therefore, when his action fell at the first hurdle. The judges of the King's Bench decided that too much time had elapsed since the supposed transgressions had taken place and that to intervene now would set a precedent that could have ramifications for many other corporations in Ireland. Like the first, the second phase in the 8th Earl's dealings with the corporation of Strabane had ended in failure.

In the third phase, Abercorn resorted to litigation once more, focusing on the attempts by the corporation to exact tolls and impose its authority on those parts of parish of Urney directly across the River Mourne from Strabane, where some limited urban development had spilled over by the middle of the eighteenth century. Similarly, on the north side of Strabane the corporation was attempting to exercise its authority in the adjoining manor of Cloghogall. As early as March 1747 Abercorn issued instructions to Nisbitt on these matters: 'You may tell James McAlpen that I shall protect his tenants in Urney from all demands of the corporation. And if they exercise any jurisdiction on that side of the water you will acquaint me.'[19] Now, 10 years on, Abercorn saw in these matters a way of reasserting his own authority over the corporation. In arguing that the corporation was unwarranted in attempting to raise revenue in areas outside its jurisdiction he was on surer ground. In addition, the financial difficulties of Hamilton and John McCausland (son of Oliver who had died in 1756) meant that they were not in a strong position to bear the expense of fighting their cause in the courts. McCausland did receive a financial boost in 1761 when he sold his seat for Strabane to Robert Lowry of Millberry, County Tyrone, ahead of the 1761 general election. With William Hamilton of Dunnamanagh holding the other seat – and therefore not benefiting financially from the deal with Lowry – it meant that for the first time in 34 years an Abercorn family member or nominee did not represent the borough in parliament.

William Hamilton died in 1763 and was succeeded as MP by his son John Stewart Hamilton. Soon he and McCausland were on poor terms and the effects of the litigation were beginning to have an effect on both. McCausland saw that their only recourse was to reach an agreement with Abercorn. In return for his support on the corporation, McCausland asked Abercorn for £2,000 in cash, an indemnity against the legal costs still outstanding, and a promise that he would have the right to nominate the next MP for Strabane. These demands were considerable, but in the end Abercorn agreed to them except that the sum of money was reduced to £1,000 and was to be in the form of a loan to McCausland rather than an outright payment. Malcomson has commented that in accepting this arrangement Abercorn was displaying 'magnanimity and common sense'. He was aware that Lowry was seriously ill and if McCausland was able to sell a seat for the second time in three years, his financial position would be strengthened and this might enable him to hold out against Abercorn for several more years. The Earl's wisdom was soon justified, for Lowry died in August 1764, shortly after the agreement with McCausland had been completed. Abercorn also reached an agreement with John Stewart Hamilton, lending him £500 and declaring that he could remain an MP for Strabane for as long as he wished. In return Hamilton was to consider himself Abercorn's nominee and act as the Earl directed him to do so in parliament. Abercorn's generosity towards both men was further reflected in his continuation of both as burgesses and his support of McCausland as provost of Strabane in 1765.

The inhabitants of Strabane themselves presented a petition to Abercorn at the time of these negotiations, avowing their loyalty to him and asking for his continued patronage:

> With hearts overflowing with joy, to return to your Lordship our hearty and unfeigned thanks for taking us into your favour and protection. Your noble ancestors set up, supported and established ours without a rival in trade, and they gave birth and maturity to the linen manufacture, our staple commodity, now falling into a languishing state, and tis not to be doubted but that your Lordship would have continued the like favours to us had we been truly represented to you. We beg leave to assure your Lordship from the most profound sincerity of heart that we always did, do and ever will truly love, esteem and regard your Lordship, your noble family and interest. We therefore most humbly beseech your Lordship to take us into favourable consideration and to lend your hand to trade, now tottering in our streets, by which it will revive, we shall flourish, and your Lordship rejoice to see it.[20]

For the inhabitants of Strabane, it was to their advantage that they had the patronage of a wealthy and influential aristocrat such as Abercorn rather than two provincial and impecunious gentlemen like McCausland and Hamilton. Now in control of the corporation, Abercorn considered it ripe for reform. In May 1765, he recommended a number of changes: an annual payment of £40 to the provost, the election of a treasurer, and consideration to be given to replacing of the current town clerk. Other matters to be dealt with included the wages of town sergeants, the repair of the market house and street lighting. Abercorn also believed that the restrictions on 'strangers' settling in the town should not be overly harsh. It had taken 20 years, but now the 8th Earl's authority over Strabane corporation had been secured. Malcomson has written:

> Throughout the three phases of his counter-attack, Abercorn had shown that he wanted merely to be restored to what he considered to be his own and not to revenge himself on his dispossessors. In this he

displayed a restraint remarkable among borough patrons in an age when boroughs were regarded as a species of private property and opposition to the patron an invasion of property rights.[21]

Furthermore, the manner of his conduct in re-establishing the family's authority over the corporation had won over the townspeople. His agent noted that the 'revolution' had given the people of Strabane 'universal pleasure'. The agreements of 1764 more or less settled matters as far as the parliamentary representation of Strabane was concerned. Henceforth those who sat for the borough were Abercorn's nominees. In the general election of 1768 John Stewart Hamilton, as he had been promised, was returned for the borough; he continued to sit for Strabane until 1797. The other seat was filled by Claud Hamilton of Beltrim, a distant relative of the Earl and brother-in-law of his agent, James Hamilton. Prior to the election of 1776 Abercorn decided to drop Claud Hamilton and bring in Arthur Pomeroy, a great-grandson of the 6th Earl of Abercorn. Pomeroy was again Abercorn's nominee at the 1783 general election.

The Earl remained in touch with political developments in the town through his agent, James Hamilton, and other correspondents. In the autumn of 1779 he also asked for the local newspaper, the *Strabane Journal*, to be sent to him to read for himself how local events were reported. By this time the Volunteer movement was gaining strength, with several units being raised in the Strabane area alone. This movement had initially emerged in response to fears of a French invasion of Ireland while the regular army was taking part in the American War of Independence. Soon, however, it became a major political force with the support of the 'patriots' in the Irish parliament and began to espouse various popular causes. The Earl was not overly concerned with these developments and, almost whimsically, put forward his own claim to patriotism at a time when the Volunteers were campaigning for free trade with Britain:

> The first time I was at Strabane, I made up a suit of cloaths of the cloth of the neighbourhood; it was dressed at a tuck mill that was then, I think, at Sian. But nobody at Strabane followed my example. So I may reckon myself the oldest patriot, though I was then a very young one, and the last time I was in Ireland I certainly drank no liquor but Irish.[22]

Improvements at Strabane

During the eighteenth century many of the landowners invested heavily in the development of a town or village on their estate. The results of their efforts, in the form of architecturally distinguished buildings such as market, court and alms houses, or well laid out street plans, can still be seen in many places today. For a variety of reasons, however, the 8th Earl of Abercorn did not effect significant and lasting changes to the infrastructure of Strabane. In the early years, a contributory factor was undoubtedly his dispute with the corporation, which would have made him cautious about making a significant investment in the town. He was still asked for advice on various matters in relation to the town, such as when he was consulted on the proposed new market house in February 1751. On being sent the plans of the market house, he replied at length to the provost of Strabane on the principles of architecture which, in his opinion, were not being followed in this rather amateurish attempt at designing a public building. Commenting on the fact that there were five arches on the ground floor but six on the first floor, he observed that 'every rule, as well of strength as of duty, demands that the openings of one storey should be over those of the other'.[23] A few months later he indicated that he was willing to offer 40 guineas towards the costs of the building work, while his mother was ready to give 20 guineas.[24] By 1765, when he was firmly in control of the corporation, he was playing a much more active role in the plans for a new market house in the town, going so far as to have his Scottish architect, William Chambers, then busy with his new house at Duddingston, Edinburgh, prepare plans for the building.

In 1755, the Earl instructed the architect, Michael Priestley, whose other buildings included the court house in Lifford and Prehen House, to draw up plans for him for a new development in the Irish Street area of Strabane. The scheme that Priestley came up with included the construction of 300 new houses. The new lots were to be let for 21 years and three lives. This marked a departure from the family's leasing policy in the seventeenth and early eighteenth centuries, when most of the tenements in Strabane were leased in fee-farm, that is in perpetuity. The new arrangements were much more in line with the urban patronage policies of landlords in other parts of Ireland. The fact that most of the property in Strabane was held in perpetuity limited Abercorn's ability to effect significant changes to the infrastructure and layout of the town. To have done so would have required buying out many of the fee-farmers, a protracted and costly business. This explains why the new development was to be on the edge of the existing town in the manor of Cloghogall. Abercorn was concerned with the appearance of the new development, and issued instructions that only one house was to be built on each of the new lots. These houses were to be not less than 12 feet high in the side walls next the street, and both the houses and out-houses were to be slated. In 1757, Priestley received a further commission from Abercorn, this time to draw up plans for a housing development alongside a proposed canal through the bog into Strabane.

It is not known how many new houses were built at this time, but it is doubtful if it was anywhere near as extensive as originally envisaged. There were further plans to build houses in the Irish Street area in the mid-1760s. In 1765, Abercorn wrote to his agent, John Hamilton, to tell him he approved the plan for houses beyond the Church of Ireland church in Strabane. These lots were to be for 31 years and three lives, and again the Earl was concerned that houses to his liking would be built: 'I shall not like a new set of cabbins there.' Another even more ambitious proposal was considered in 1768. In July of that year Abercorn wrote to John Hamilton:

> I have long been of the opinion that the Mourne may be easily made navigable into the middle of the county of Tyrone, and that it is an object well deserving the attention of the public, as thereby a communication would be opened to an extensive and fruitful country, which now lies under the disadvantage of an expensive land carriage.[25]

While willing to contribute to this proposal, the Earl expressed his concern as to whether it would be of any great benefit to Strabane. Furthermore, it could result in trade shifting from Strabane to Newtownstewart and Omagh. What he would support was a canal from the River Foyle to Strabane and no further, and this was something to which he had been giving some consideration. A fortnight later Abercorn wrote to his cousin, William Brownlow of Lurgan, on his proposed navigation scheme, soliciting the latter's assistance in finding a suitable engineer. Nothing further seems to have happened at this time, but at the beginning of 1774 Abercorn announced that he was prepared to subscribe £12,000 towards a navigation of the River Mourne and believed that the Italian Davis Ducart, then working on various projects in Ireland, would be a 'proper skilful engineer' to survey the river as far as Omagh. Again nothing came of this proposal, and it was not until his nephew succeeded to the title and estate that a canal to Strabane was completed.

Relationship with other landowners

Though an absentee, Abercorn was conscious of his position as the leading magnate in west Tyrone and east Donegal and of the expectations that went with it. In 1767, he readily consented to give £20 per annum to the county hospital proposed for Omagh. When it was settled that the new hospital for County Donegal would be at Lifford rather than Letterkenny as initially proposed, Abercorn willingly gave a £10 annual subscription. In 1776, he offered £100 towards the new spire that Bishop Hervey had commissioned for St Columb's cathedral in Derry. Although he was rarely in the position of being able to extend personal hospitality to visitors to Barons Court, he presented gifts in various forms to the neighbouring gentry and clergy. For example, in the summer of 1767 he directed James Hamilton to kill six bucks from the park at Barons Court and send one to the provost of Strabane.

Other suitable persons to whom gifts of venison could be sent included the bishop and dean of Raphoe, Claud Hamilton, Stewart of Killymoon, and Dr Pelissier, rector of Ardstraw. He also alerted Hamilton to the fact that 'sometimes a stranger of great distinction comes into the neighbourhood of Barons Court that it may be right to make a compliment to'. Hamilton was to ensure that Arthur, possibly the gamekeeper, was to 'shoot them well, and dress them clean'. Arthur was allowed to keep the shoulders and hides for his own use. Two years later Abercorn was happy to comply with the bishop of Clogher's request for some of his deer. Hamilton was instructed to give the bishop a two-year-old buck and a few younger deer of each sex.

The Earl also made representations on behalf of members of the gentry seeking commissions in the army or other favours. In 1761, he wrote to the Earl of Halifax asking for a captain's commission for one of the regiments then being raised in Ireland. This was to be given to the eldest son of William Hamilton of Dunnamanagh. Abercorn justified this favour on the grounds that: 'Though he must in time succeed to a good estate, his father's indiscretions (to give them no harder appellation) leave him little other resources at present than his lieutenancy, and, I hope, his integrity … his influence in the neighbourhood will facilitate the raising [of] his company expeditiously.' That Abercorn was prepared to do this on behalf of a family with which he was at odds indicates an ability to act without prejudice in dealing with his opponents. He also assisted his tenants in securing opportunities for their sons. In 1768, he loaned Robert Porter £150 to enable one of his sons to go to the East Indies.

Activities in England and Scotland

Though making little use of his seat in the Irish House of Lords, in 1761 the 8th Earl was chosen as one of the 16 Scottish representative peers at Westminster. Why he should have accepted this position, given his lack of political ambition, is not clear, but it was probably related to his desire to restore the standing of the family in Scotland at a time when he was, as will be presently shown, reacquiring the ancestral lands in Scotland. Attendance at the sessions of the House of Lords would have suited him, as London was his usual residence. In the Lords he opposed the American Stamp Act in 1766 and voted for the rejection of Fox's India bill in 1783. In 1776, the Earl was one of the peers in attendance at the trial of Elizabeth Chudleigh, Duchess of Kingston, for bigamy. She was found guilty and as a punishment she was to be burned with an iron on the right hand. Claiming the privilege of peerage, which exempted her from corporal punishment, she was let off with the simple requirement to pay her fees. The trial had engrossed London society, but after more than five days of proceedings Horace Walpole was beginning to tire of it. As ever, he left the last word to the 8th Earl: 'Yes, I will tell you what the droll, caustic Lord Abercorn said. Somebody hoped his Lordship had not suffered by the trial; he replied, "Nobody suffered by it".[26] Abercorn continued to sit as one of the Scottish representative peers until 1786, when he was created a peer of Great Britain with the title of Viscount Hamilton of Leicester with remainder to his nephew, John James Hamilton.

When in London, Abercorn's usual residence was in the family home in Cavendish Square. In the 1770s he moved to a house in Grosvenor Square. He also owned a country estate at Witham which he had inherited from his father. Members of the Royal Family were frequent visitors to Witham, especially if they were travelling to or from the port of Harwich. George II occasionally stayed with Abercorn at Witham, and it was reputedly on Abercorn's advice that the King began to use the banking firm of Coutts, an association that has lasted to the present day.[27] In 1761, Queen Charlotte stayed at Witham following her arrival in England as the bride of George III. Abercorn was not there, for the visit was unplanned; the Queen should have landed at Greenwich, but contrary winds drove the ship to Harwich. She was, however, suitably entertained and spent the night in what Horace Walpole witheringly called the 'palace of silence' in reference to her absent host's reserved nature, to which dismissive remark he added, 'she must have thought she was coming to reign in the realm of

The 8th Earl of Abercorn.

taciturnity'.[28] In 1764, Witham hosted Princess Augusta, sister of the King, and her newly married husband, 'His Serene Highness, the Hereditary Prince of Brunswick'. Walpole wrote to the Earl of Hertford on 22 January 1764 with an account of the visit, 'They lie tonight at Lord Abercorn's at Witham, who does not step from his pedestal to meet them. Lady Strafford said to him, "Soh! My lord! I hear your house is to be royally filled on Wednesday." "And serenely", he replied, and closed his mouth till next day.'[29]

The 8th Earl placed a high premium on the family's honour, and the importance he attached to his lineage is shown in the care he took in having an account of his family history prepared for Robert Douglas, who was editing a volume of pedigrees in the late 1750s. Abercorn was able to draw on a range of documentation, including a pedigree copied from the Lyon or Herald Office in Edinburgh in 1683. Almost certainly he included information from the inscription on the memorial to the 4th Lord Strabane at Rush in County Dublin, which he had had copied for him several years

before. He had a good knowledge of the vicissitudes of the family in the late seventeenth century and understood how it was that the estate had been acquired by his grandfather, the 6th Earl. It was with some disappointment then that he read the account of his family sent to him by Douglas in May 1758. Rather than using the information that Abercorn had supplied to correct the mistakes in the family history that had appeared in previous accounts, Douglas had repeated these errors. The Earl asked that his name be removed from the references in the margins as he was 'afraid it should be understood that I acquiesce in the truth of others, which I know to be false'. Later he would write to a relative 'I am the last person (according to the ideas of this country) that should promulge a pedigree with pompous titles'.[30]

In 1745, he took the first steps in recovering the family's status in Scotland by purchasing from the 3rd Duke of Argyll the barony of Easter and Wester Duddingston near Edinburgh.[31] He then set about reorganising farming practices on the estate. Previously the tenants had possessed their land in run-rig or rundale. Abercorn abolished this system and introduced leases, usually for 19 years. The *Annals of Duddingston* note that the change was remarkable as farms were enlarged, roads made and hedges planted. In 1750, James Robertson was sent down to lay out the grounds. A large park of *c.* 200 acres was fenced off for pleasure grounds and artificial lakes created

Duddingston House with Arthur's Seat in the background.
Admired by contemporaries as 'one of the finest houses in Scotland', Duddingston, built for the 8th Earl, is still regarded as one of the best houses of its date anywhere in the British Isles.

with grottos, temples and statues. He introduced a herd of deer which was 'of a breed supposed to be as fine as any in Europe'.[32] The property included the additional resources of saltworks and coal mines. Abercorn also purchased the barony of Brunstan from the Fletchers.[33] In the summer of 1760 he summoned his Irish surveyor, William McCrea, to Duddingston to devise a plan for dividing *c.* 1,000 acres into small parcels. McCrea would be paid 30 guineas to cover his time and travelling expenses, and he would be lodged in the home of one of the chief tenants on the estate. Abercorn himself would be present to advise and direct him. In the early 1760s Abercorn commissioned the famous architect William Chambers, whose work *Treatise of Civil Architecture* had recently been published, to design a house for Duddingston. The house Chambers designed was on the villa plan, with the main focus being on the portico and main entrance hall.[34] The house and offices were finished in 1768.

In 1764, the 8th Earl purchased what remained of the Paisley estate from the 8th Earl of Dundonald for £10,000.[35] He also reacquired the Place of Paisley, the home of his ancestors. In 1770, he began to restore St Mirren's Aisle, Paisley Abbey, the historic place of burial of the Hamiltons. He placed in the aisle the memorial of his ancestor Margory, daughter of Robert Bruce, wife of Walter Steward and mother of Robert II, the first of the Stuart kings of Scotland. She had been killed in a fall from a horse while hunting near Paisley. Her monument had been removed from the aisle at the time of the Reformation and had lain for many years in the ruined cloister court.[36] He had ambitious plans for the town of Paisley, and had a scheme drawn up for the 'New Town'. In 1778, what remained of the park and gardens of the abbey was divided up into regular lots which were feued out for building purposes. Within three years, 83 houses had been built and the new streets laid out – among them, Gauze Street, Lawn Street, Thread Street and Silk Street – were named after the different branches of the weaving trade in the town.[37] Abercorn also had plans for a marketplace and an inn, and in March 1780 instructed his factor Walter Scott, father of Sir Walter, to begin the latter immediately. The Earl was concerned that the building should be an edifice of distinction and so asked his architect, George Steuart, then working on the new house at Barons Court, to spare one of his men to oversee the work. The inn, with stabling for 28 horses, was in New Abbey Street and was described as 'one of the largest, most commodious and most elegant inns in Scotland'.[38]

The 8th Earl and Barons Court

In the early seventeenth century, one branch of the Hamiltons built a castle in what is now the Barons Court demesne. It was abandoned after the 1641 rebellion and has remained a ruin ever since. In 1739, during one of his few visits to Ireland, the 7th Earl of Abercorn seems to have visited a number of sites on his estate hoping to find a suitable location for a country residence, and settled on Barons Court as the best of these. Certainly from late 1739 there was some activity at Barons Court and discussions took place over the possibility of renovating the small medieval castle on Island MacHugh in Lough Catherine. Andrew Kinnear was commissioned to conduct a survey of the structure and provided a rather damning report to Abercorn's agent, John Colhoun, in February 1740:

> I have examined the old castle of Island MacHugh, and do not believe the walls are capable of carrying a roof with safety, considering the many shakes [?] that's in the walls, and it's therefore my opinion, a new house could be built there, from the ground some[what] cheaper and with a great deal more room than to repair those old walls.

This advice was followed, and soon afterwards the house usually referred to as the 'Agent's House' was started. Its builder was James Martin, who was also responsible for the new Church of Ireland cathedral at Clogher. With the death of the 7th Earl in 1744, it was left to his son and heir to complete the new house. In April 1744, Colhoun was able to report that the work was progressing, notwithstanding the recent storms that had 'rusled' several parts of the roofs. Colhoun added: 'the stairs are almost finished, all the rooms in the offices are floored and cieled, and most part of the upper rooms of the house with lime'. Martin himself wrote to Abercorn at the end of August to tell him that he hoped the work would soon be finished. Some

The 'Agent's House' at Barons Court. Started by his father, this house was completed by the 8th Earl, but proved far from satisfactory. It was originally two storeys.

aspects of the interior of the house remained outstanding when Abercorn wrote to Colhoun in January 1745 complaining that he had not received a reply to his last letter to Martin, and expressing his concern that some chimney pieces, 'bespoke in Dublin', had been lost in a recent shipwreck. He was anxious to have the house 'completely finished' and further instructions on the house were to be passed to Martin. Although he had previously considered iron rails for the stairs, Abercorn was now content with 'some slight plain ones, such as are commonly used for back stairs'. He was also concerned with security and asked for bars to be put on the shutters and locks on the doors. Lastly he wanted the house to be 'thoroughly painted', with the doors to be of 'chocolate colour'.

The architectural historian Alistair Rowan has described the house as a 'charming little essay in rustic Palladianism' and asserted that it is 'one of the most interesting small Classical houses in Ulster, one of the more ambitious and one of the earliest'.[39] Although now only single storey, the references to stairs indicate that it was originally a two-storey house. The removal of the second storey may have taken place at the beginning of the 1780s. In 1781 it was reported that George Steuart had drawn up plans 'for converting the late house … into conveniences for stabling, farming etc., still retaining, however, a look of the house as it was'. Two years later the old house was described as 'completely fitted up'. As it now stands the house is of three bays with a central Tuscan portico. The walls are of brick, the elaborate eaves cornice of stone, and the roof is slated. While certain elements of the house are resonant of the work of the English architect James Gibbs, author of the famous *Book of Architecture* (1728), Rowan sees a source closer to hand in the house designed by Edward Lovett Pearce known as Bellamont Forest at Cootehill, County Cavan.

Other work was also going on at Barons Court at this time. The aforementioned Andrew Kinnear was responsible for building a granary between 1740 and 1744. In January 1745 Abercorn announced that he intended to convert the granary into a stable that summer. He also instructed his agent to have the ditch of Barons Court park repaired, but warned him not to expend too much money on it as he hoped to have it walled in a 'year or two'. The following month Abercorn issued instructions to Colhoun for work to be carried out on widening the canal between the two lower loughs, a scheme he envisaged would provide work for the poor. With typical common sense he stipulated that if the canal was 40 feet wide at the top it was not to be more than 25 feet wide at the bottom, to prevent the sides from falling in.[40] Further instructions were given to Colhoun in March 1745 to make preparations for the building of the garden wall. He also gave directions for the planting of trees in the vicinity of the house: 'I will have ten clumps of trees planted in the park where you think proper, at a distance from the house, about 100 or 150 in each clump, and the trees above five feet from each other. These must be mixed: half chestnuts and the rest birch and "liburnums".'[41] At the beginning of January 1749 Abercorn announced his plan to build a brewhouse that summer.[42]

Like his uncle, Charles Hamilton, the 8th Earl was interested in gardening. While he did not achieve at Barons Court what Charles accomplished at Painshill, he was concerned that the gardens should be laid out appropriately. In the summer of 1747, in between discussing fruit trees for Barons Court, he lamented to Colhoun that 'the garden is very ill-stocked in other respects'. To try to improve his garden he did what other landowners did, and turned to fellow enthusiasts for advice and assistance. For example, a request was sent to John Folliott MP to forward to the Earl a catalogue of the plants in his garden near Dublin. A number of men were employed to maintain the gardens at Barons Court. On 13 February 1746 Abercorn announced that he had hired James Broomfield to be the gardener. He instructed Colhoun to pay Broomfield five guineas on his arrival from London to cover his travelling expenses and time on the road, and four English shillings a week thereafter. Broomfield received regular directions from Abercorn regarding tasks he was to fulfil in the grounds of Barons Court. For example, in October 1747 the Earl directed him to 'remove so many of the little beeches and firs behind the house, as will make an opening over against the salon window 26 feet wide, answering to the width of the "turrit"'.[43] Broomfield, however, did not have a long and successful career at Barons Court.

In 1748, it was brought to Abercorn's attention that Broomfield was neglecting his duties, had undesirable drinking companions and had been married according to the rites of the Roman Catholic Church. The Earl exhorted his gardener to forsake his 'bad company' and marry again in a Church of Ireland ceremony. He refused to allow Broomfield to bring his wife to live at Barons Court, but would permit her to live in a house nearby 'where she may occasion less hindrance to his business'. Some time after this Broomfield left Abercorn's service and went to Scotland; though it is not clear if he was dismissed, this seems the most likely explanation for his departure.[44] Problems with the staff at Barons Court persisted when the new gardener, one Allen, fell out with one of the housemaids. Abercorn reasoned that he could 'get another maid with much less trouble than another gardener' and told Colhoun to instruct the maid to behave herself.

In advance of his visits, Barons Court was the scene of frenetic activity as the Earl's very precise instructions were carried out prior to his arrival. In 1746, his asked his agent, Colhoun, to ensure the house was sufficiently habitable for him on his arrival. The required work included fitting up the kitchen and offices with 'shelves and dressers and necessaries of that sort'. Two maidservants were to be hired, one to assist the cook and the other to clean the house. Colhoun was also instructed to make sure the road from Newtownstewart to Barons Court was passable for the Earl's coach and to have the stables ready for his horses. In preparation for the Earl's visit in 1749 Colhoun was instructed to have the plaster walls and cornice in the salon painted. Around a month before his expected arrival Abercorn stipulated that fires were to be lit in the salon and his bedchamber every day until he appeared. Two cows and poultry of 'all sorts' were to be acquired and fattened to provide sustenance for the Earl during his stay.

The 8th Earl also introduced a herd of deer to Barons Court. In the spring of 1767 he was satisfied that the park was 'fully stocked' and that a select number of deer could be shot each year for venison.[45] Capturing a deer in the park at Barons Court was not easy, as Abercorn revealed in a letter to the bishop of Clogher in 1769: 'The difficulty of catching a full grown deer is much increased by there being, at one end of the park, no fence, but water which several of them have taken without much provocation.' When instructing James Hamilton to capture some of the deer in the park for the bishop he advised him to 'line the end next the lough with people to prevent the deer from taking the water'. Such an event would have sparked a great deal of local interest, but Abercorn wished to avoid a public spectacle, telling Hamilton to 'take them as privately as possible' so that it would not be 'a hunting match for the neighbourhood'.

In the mid-1770s Abercorn turned his attention to a major new building project at Barons Court – the construction of a new mansion to replace the earlier house. He was prompted to do by the continuing costs of maintaining the existing house with its numerous problems. At the same time, he was in his mid-60s and would have been considered rather old to be starting out on such a project. That he was conscious of this is reflected in a letter to Arthur Pomeroy in which he wrote, 'At my time of life, it is perhaps necessary to find excuses for engagements of this sort. Mine, must be, that it sets very many people to work, who would otherwise be idle.'[46] A site on lower ground closer to Lough Fanny having been chosen, preliminary work began on 12 July 1776. This included digging out the ground for the cellars and building sheds for carpenters to work on site. Two days later 44 tons of cut stone arrived. Other materials were brought from further afield. Wheels for the carts were brought from Liverpool, while timber was imported from Norway. On 20 July the foundation stone was laid by agent James Hamilton. This was marked with the appropriate festivities. However, there then followed a lengthy delay. There were various reasons for this: bad weather had held up the making of bricks, while the stonemasons found that the stone from the quarries was not easy to work with.

The architect Abercorn hired to prepare plans for the new house was George Steuart, a Gaelic-speaking Scotsman, whose other major projects include Attingham Park in Shropshire, a mansion that bears some similarities to the house he designed for Abercorn.[47] Very little of Steuart's work at Barons Court survives, the result of subsequent fires and remodellings. What can be said is that it was of three storeys, with the tallest windows on the ground floor and those on the second story much lower. In the summer of 1778 Abercorn commissioned Steuart to 'take a view of Barons Court, and to consider how the house may be most conveniently improved'. It is not absolutely clear whether Abercorn was referring to improvements to the existing house or to the scheme for the projected one. It is likely that Steuart considered both in preparing his report.

The Scotsman enjoyed his time at Barons Court and appreciated the 'civilities' extended to him by James Hamilton and others. When he returned to London he submitted his ideas to Abercorn, who was left somewhat mystified by them, as he admitted to his agent: 'His various schemes perplex; perhaps the present house at Barons Court may last my time.' Despite these concerns, the Earl kept faith with Steuart and sent him back to Barons Court at the beginning of the following year. By this time Abercorn seems to have set his mind on a new house. He had also determined that the project would not be a burden on his tenantry, telling Hamilton that he would not call on his tenants to provide carriage for building materials except in special circumstances. On 8 June 1779 Steuart arrived at Barons Court and took the project in hand. He sought out a better local source for stone. For the columns and window dressings he tried Clyde stone, which, though not as pleasing in colour as Portland stone, was the best he could get. He identified stone from Liverpool as suitable for stairs and pavements.

Two elevations and a ground floor plan of Barons Court:
South elevation of house (below)
East and west elevations of house (p. 84)
Plan of the ground – or 'Principal' – floor (p. 85)
These survey drawings of Steuart's house at Barons Court were prepared in March 1791 in advance of the changes that would be introduced by Sir John Soane. The elevations show a south front of seven bays with a central pediment at the level of the eaves and a forestanding portico of paired Tuscan columns. The wings to the rear were of two storeys. The ground floor plan shows that in the main block there were the following rooms: 'Eating Parlor', 'Saloon', 'Withdrawing Room', 'Dressing Room', 'Great Stairs', 'Back Stairs' and 'Ante Room'.
COURTESY OF THE TRUSTEES OF SIR JOHN SOANE'S MUSEUM
Photo Ardon Bar Hama

Elevation. South.

The Marquess of Abercorn. — Barons court

March 1791

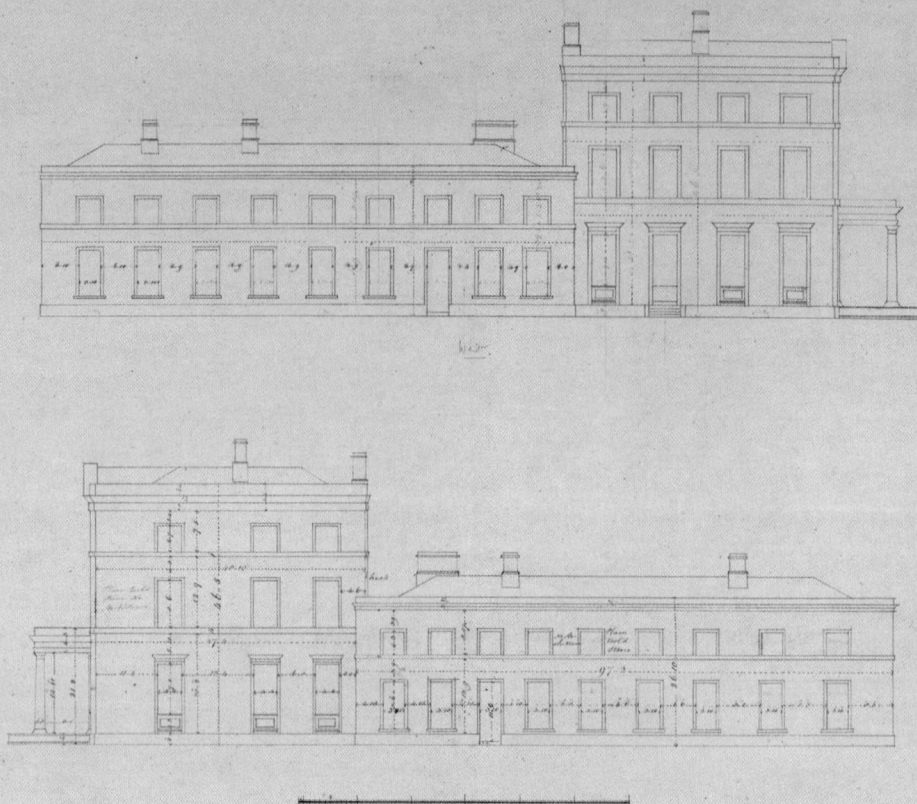

The Marquiss of Abercorn. Barons Court. Elevation of East Front

Copy March 23ᵈ 1791

The construction of a new house at Barons Court excited much interest, and news of its building spread throughout Ireland. In answer to Arthur Pomeroy's enquiry as to whether it was true that Abercorn was building at Barons Court, the Earl was able to confirm that this was indeed the case and he hoped that one day he would be able to entertain Pomeroy there. 'The people seem so much amused with the novelty of it', he wrote, 'that I hear no mention of their intention to pull it down'. He was in a rather different mood the following month when he wrote to James Hamilton. 'The melancholick prospect of Irish affairs', as he described recent political events, led him to fear that he would never see Barons Court. However, he was determined 'of going on with the house, as it is so far advanced, and take my chance for what is to happen'.

Work on the house began in earnest on 20 March 1780. Only six 'wallers' were initially on site because a large quantity of stone had already been prepared. By the beginning of April, however, the number of workmen had increased significantly, with 10 bricklayers and 41 stone-cutters at work as

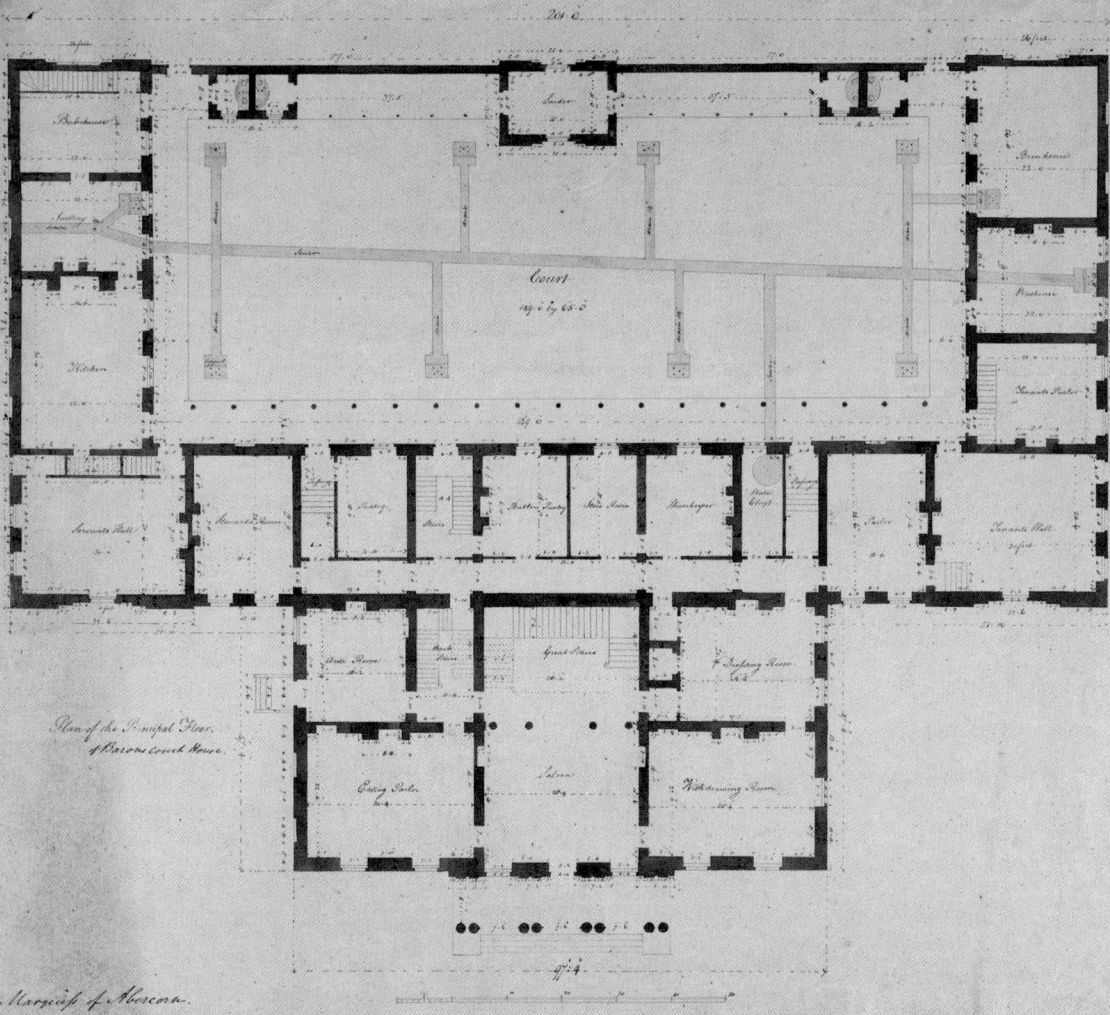

well as carpenters and joiners. James Hamilton was able to report to Abercorn on 23 June that the work was 'going on exceedingly well and that it will be noble indeed'. By 9 July the wings had been built and ready for the roof. However, further progress was being checked because a ship bringing timber from Riga had not arrived in Derry. The ship had still not docked by 29 August, when the house had reached the attic storey, and there were serious concerns that the roof would not be completed before beginning of winter. As an interim measure the walls were covered in straw to act as a protective coating for the masonry. Eventually on 19 December the ship from Riga arrived in Derry.

Early in 1782 Abercorn began to make preparations for a visit to Barons Court to see his new house. The usual arrangements were made: the planning of the journey, the commissioning of a ship to Ireland and the dispatch of household items needed during the stay. At Barons Court there was also a rush of activity to make things ready for the Earl's arrival. At the beginning of April James Hamilton wrote to Abercorn, 'The old house, as it is called,

85

is perfectly well aired for your Lordship's coming; the beds in it are all made up, and a bed for your Lordship and other beds in the new house. Mr Hawkshaw thinks there is no danger in your Lordship's sleeping there.' Abercorn arrived at Barons Court a short time afterwards and spent the next four months there. It would have been an opportunity for him to see for himself the result of the massive project of building that had been going on for several years. He would have advised on the tasks required to complete the house and no doubt would have suggested appropriate furnishings for each room.

However, just short of his seventieth birthday, he was conscious of his age. He wrote to Lord Welles on 30 June 1782, 'it is highly probable that I am now here for the last time in my life'. He was to be proved correct. When he left Barons Court a few weeks later, it was to be for the final time. There were rumours that he planned to return permanently to Barons Court. *The Public Advertiser* of July 1783 announced, 'The Earl of Abercorn is building a mansion in Ireland; his lordship's purpose being, we understand, to finish his days in that country'. However, these stories proved false. The house and demesne caught the attention of travellers to north-west Ulster. Daniel Beaufort wrote in 1787: 'Through hills at the foot of Bessy Bell … we come to Baronscourt, Lord Abercorn's magnificent seat … the great number of fine oaks and three long narrow lakes which ornament this place give it an air of great grandeur.' The Duke of Rutland in his 'Journal of a tour in the north of Ireland. July 1787' wrote of Strabane: 'It belongs to Lord Abercorn, who has built a large and handsome mansion house in its neighbourhood, where he never resides.' By the time it was finished, the house had cost £8,015 8s. 7½d.[48]

Monument to the 8th Earl in Paisley Abbey. It is interesting to note that the inscription states that the 8th Earl was additionally Duke of Châtelherault even though there is little evidence that he pressed his claims to this latter title. The only mention of it identified in his correspondence dates from 1778 when he wrote to a Mrs Cameron, 'I am much obliged to you, for what you say respecting the Duchy of Châtelherault. I did not know, that any person thought of setting up a pretension to that title in a female line …' (PRONI D623/A/23/23).

Death and legacy

In the autumn of 1789 the 8th Earl of Abercorn left Duddingston to return to London. He was seriously ill, having been suffering from paralysis for some time, and had been advised to defer his journey until he was fitter.[49] He made it as far as Boroughbridge, near Ripon in Yorkshire, where he died on 9 October, three days short of his seventy-seventh birthday. A fortnight later his remains were removed from Boroughbridge to Duddingston, where he lay in state for a couple of day before being brought to Paisley Abbey for burial in St Mirren's Aisle.[50] He was the first head of the family to be buried here for over a hundred years. He was styled 'Duc de Châtelherault' on the plate on his coffin and on the marble tablet in Paisley Abbey: like his

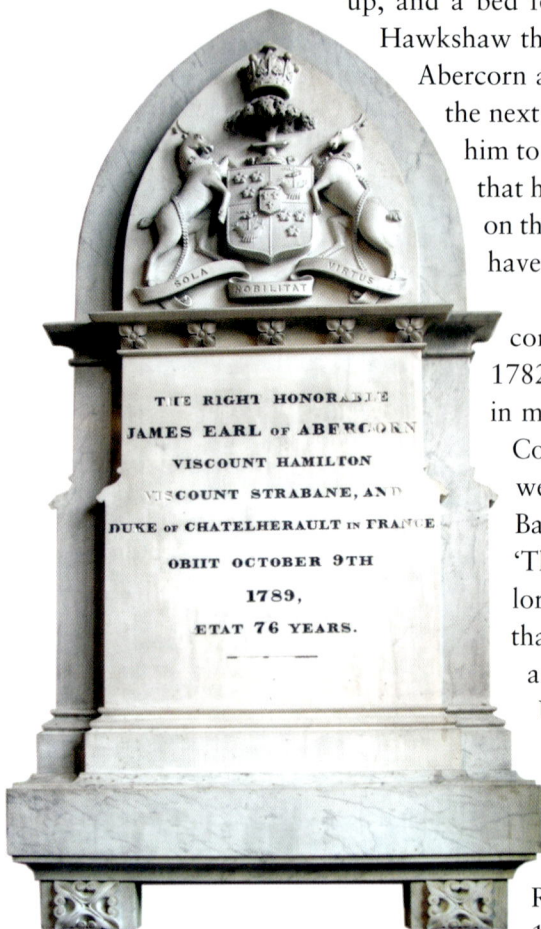

predecessors he claimed this French dukedom, though he does not seem to have made any effort to assert his right to it. Francis Grose, in his *Antiquities of Scotland* (1797), has the following to say about St Mirren's Aisle:

> The Earl of Abercorn's burial place here, is said to be famous for a remarkable echo; not having heard of it I did not visit it. It is thus described by Mr. Pennant. "The Earl of Abercorn's burial place is by much the greatest curiosity in Paisley; it is an old Gothic chapel, without pulpit or pew, or any ornament whatever; but it has the finest echo perhaps in the world, when the end door, the only one it has, is shut; the noise is equal to a loud, and not very distant clap of thunder: if you strike a single note of music you hear the sound gradually ascending, till it dies away, as if at an immense distance, and all the while diffusing itself through the circumambient air. If a good voice sings, or a musical instrument is well played upon, the effect is inexpressibly agreeable."

Shortly after his death an obituary appeared in the *Gentleman's Magazine* which, though paying tribute to his generosity to his family and the way he judiciously managed his estates, referred to his lack of sociability and 'Castilian pomp'. One particular story related in the obituary was the Earl's curt reply to an uninvited guest who remarked that the trees in his park at Duddingston were doing well: 'They have nothing else to do.' In a subsequent issue of the periodical this tale was refuted as a 'story ill-told' and the same writer asked his readers to remember the Earl for his character rather than for his personal eccentricities: 'Any little peculiarities of his manners ought, on account of his honour and integrity, to have been overlooked.'[51] A number of contrasting views of the Earl have been highlighted at the beginning of this chapter, from Walpole's ridicule for his reserved nature to Mary Bailie Hamilton's lauding of his character and integrity. Certainly he was a shy, quiet man, to the point of rudeness in the minds of some. Yet at the same time, he was generous to his family and friends and sympathetic to the needs of his tenants. What comes across very strongly from his correspondence is that the 8th Earl of Abercorn attached a great deal of importance to upholding the family's good name. In purchasing Paisley, the 8th Earl was more than simply investing in property in Scotland. In recovering this estate, he was restoring the family's honour in Scotland. The same may be said for his struggles with the corporation of Strabane. These had less to do with politics than with reasserting the family's position in the town that his ancestor had founded.[52] A better summing up of the 8th Earl's character cannot be found than that in the *Statistical account of Scotland*, in which he was described as a 'nobleman whose character was but little known, or rather but little understood, but who possessed singular vigour of mind, integrity of conduct and patriotic views'.[53]

Captain the Hon. John Hamilton (1714–55)

The father of the 1st Marquess of Abercorn, John Hamilton was the second son of the 7th Earl. As a young man, and following in the footsteps of several other members of the family, he joined the Royal Navy. In December 1736, his ship, *Louisa*, was wrecked while escorting George II from Hanover,

> when a violent storm arising, wherein all the fleet narrowly escaped being lost, his ship was wreck'd; and boats being sent to their relief, he bravely refused to go into them before the sailors saying, *In that common calamity he would claim no precedency*; and was the last that quitted the ship. On going ashore he was presented to the King, who graciously received him.[54]

Captain John Hamilton was the subject of one of Sir Joshua Reynolds's finest portraits – in fact, the painting that launched the artist's career. Painted around 1746, it shows Hamilton posing in the uniform of a Hungarian Hussar, on top of which he is wearing a fur coat. His portrayal is very much that of an adventurer. The background of a stormy sea is possibly an allusion to the shipwreck of 1736.

He served on a number of other ships before being appointed captain of the *Deal Castle* in February 1741. Other commands followed and he spent much of the 1740s off the south coast of Ireland protecting trading vessels. In 1749, he married Harriet, daughter of James Craggs, a diplomat and politician, and widow of Richard Eliot of Port Eliot, Cornwall. Around a year later a daughter, Anne, was born.

He is described in the *Dictionary of National Biography* as 'a man of rare humour, which bubbles up in an amusing way in his official letters to the Admiralty'. These contain much outspoken comment on naval administration as the following extract from the *DNB* reveals:

> He had, for instance, while in the *Augusta*, to complain of the marines' clothing, and begged their lordships to 'examine the enclosed pattern which, with great management, I have contrived to cut off, fresh and entire, as they see it;' then after further details he added, 'they (the marines) are miserably accoutred, and, properly speaking, miserably fleeced … they really put me in mind hourly of Sir John Falstaff's recruits' (2 Oct. 1743). On another occasion, complaining of some men who had been sent on board the Kinsale, one, he wrote, 'is by employment a limeburner, which

has affected his sight with the infirmity our opticians call the Gutta Serena, to that degree that a gnat appears to him of the size of a lark;' another 'is a little old cobbler of fifty-six, taken out of his stall rather, it should seem, for pastime than service' (14 April 1742); and again, complaining that he could not get the necessary stores for the *Lancaster* from the dockyard, he added, 'I humbly conceive his majesty's ship *Lancaster* is no alien; very sure I am that she has a true English heart in her' (7 June 1755). His official correspondence is full of most instructive remarks on the faults and abuses of our naval organisation in the middle of last century, which none but him ventured to expose so fully and unsparingly.

In February 1755, he was placed in command of the *Lancaster* which patrolled the Channel and Bay of Biscay. On 18 December, while anchored off Spithead, Hamilton was making his way ashore when the tail of his boat hit what became known as the Hamilton Shoal. It overturned and Hamilton and most of the crew were drowned. It was reported at the time that 'He swam twenty minutes about the boat, exhorting the men to resignation in case they were not saved, and at the same time encouraging them to exert their strength to preserve their lives'.[55] Another account of his death derives from the first Lord Eliot, Captain Hamilton's stepson.

> This Captain Hamilton was a very uncommon character, very obstinate, very whimsical, very pious; a rigid disciplinarian, yet very kind to his men. He lost his life as he was proceeding from his ship to land at Plymouth [*recte* Portsmouth]. The wind and sea were extremely high, and his officers remonstrated against the imprudence of venturing in a boat where danger seemed imminent. But he was impatient to see his wife, and would not be persuaded. In a few minutes after he left the ship the boat upset and turned keel upward. The Captain, being a good swimmer, trusted to his skill, and would not accept of a place on the keel, in order to make room for others. Unluckily he had kept on his great coat. At length, seeming exhausted, those on the keel exhorted him to take a place with them, and he attempted to throw off the coat, but finding his strength fail, told the men he must yield to his fate, and soon afterwards sank while *singing a psalm.*[56]

His wife, awaiting his arrival on the shore, is said to have witnessed his death. His body does not appear to have been recovered. Seven months after his death Harriet gave birth to a son – John James Hamilton, the future 1st Marquess. His widow survived him by thirteen years, dying in January 1769 while on a visit to Port Eliot. Their daughter Anne died in 1764.

A studious John James Hamilton.

6

John James Hamilton, 1st Marquess of Abercorn

'Don Magnifico'

There was no member of the family quite like the 1st Marquess before him, nor has there been one since. Anthony Malcomson, in the only recent essay that considers him in any detail, believed him to be 'perhaps a fitter subject for fiction than biography'.[1] Elsewhere he has described him as 'that truly proud northern leviathan'.[2] The Marquess' great-grandson, Lord Ernest Hamilton, who devoted a chapter to him in his book *Old Days and New*, wrote that while he 'could not, strictly speaking, lay claim to be reckoned, on all points, an exemplary character, he was, beyond question, an interesting one'.[3] A contemporary, the novelist Lady Morgan, wrote, 'he was so organised to be the man he was that no education or example could have made him otherwise. Had he occupied the throne of his ancestors[4] he would have been the justest despot that ever reigned.'[5] The society hostess Lady Holland observed, 'He is haughty and capricious, with enough of vanity to make him do a generous action, and with a dash of madness to make him do a lively one.' Many of those who have commented on him have focused on his eccentricities or behaviour arising from his undoubted pride – stories that he insisted his maidservants wore white gloves when changing the bed sheets or that he wore his Garter while out shooting. However, by concentrating on such trivia the real man is lost. His friend Sir Walter Scott called him 'much misrepresented'. The Marquess' conduct at times may well have earned him the epithet 'Don Magnifico', but there was much more to this complex man than has often been acknowledged.

Early life

John James Hamilton was born in London in July 1756 and baptised in St George's Church, Hanover Square. He was the son of John Hamilton, younger brother of the 8th Earl of Abercorn, a captain in the Royal Navy, who had drowned off Portsmouth a few months before his son was born. His mother was Harriet, natural daughter of the Right Hon. James Craggs, Secretary of State, and widow of Richard Eliot of Port Eliot. He probably spent his childhood in Highgate, where his widowed mother had made her home. He had only one sibling, an older sister, Anne, who died young in 1764. His mother died in 1769 when he was only 13. He received his initial education at a small private school in Paddington before going to Harrow in 1767. The earliest surviving letter from his uncle and guardian, the 8th Earl, was written to him while he was there. In it the Earl admonished him to avoid the company of 'idle, dirty boys and tell-tales and proud fellows' and encouraged him to continue his interest in the theatre. When he came of age he was allowed £4,000 a year by his uncle.[6] Relatively little is known of the relationship between the two, though it would appear that John James held his uncle in high regard. Following the death of the 8th Earl in 1789, he described him as 'the wisest and most accurate man it has ever fallen to my share to know'.

From Harrow he went up to Cambridge, matriculating at Pembroke Hall on 30 July 1773. It was here that his friendship with William Pitt the younger was forged. The relationship between the two was to be one of the most significant in Abercorn's life. Another close companion was Philip Yorke, later 3rd Earl of Hardwicke, whom Abercorn described as his 'best and earliest friend'. In a letter of March 1773 he commiserated with Yorke for having been sent to 'infinitely the worst college that the banks of Cam afford', his particular objection to it being 'its full quantum of drinking, stupid and noisy companions'. To cap it all, it possessed 'no atonement that

I know of in the largeness of its society'.[7] In the early 1780s he undertook a Grand Tour of the Continent. His comments confirmed the view that some held of him as conceited. 'Dresden', he opined, 'is a place for gentlemen to live in and, as far as I can judge, is actually inhabited by gentlemen.' On this trip, or possibly on another, he styled himself 'D'Hamilton, Comte Hereditaire d'Abercorn' to ensure his aristocratic pedigree would not go unnoticed. By this time he had married the first of his three wives. His bride was Catherine Copley, daughter of Sir Joseph Copley, a Yorkshire baronet, whom he married in St Marylebone Church, London, on 20 June 1779. They lived for a time at Petersham Lodge in Surrey.

Entry into politics

Lord Ernest Hamilton was wrong when he attributed his great-grandfather's passing from public imagination to his lack of interest in politics. Lady Mary Baillie Hamilton too was incorrect in writing that the 1st Marquess 'had no inclination for political life'.[8] Far from being apathetic, the 1st Marquess was obsessed with politics and devoted much of his life to the pursuit of political advantage. He entered the House of Commons in 1783 as MP for East Looe; the following year he was returned MP for St Germans. Both of these constituencies were in Cornwall and Abercorn's entrée to parliament was through the influence of both his Eliot and his Copley relatives.[9] He was a strong supporter of Pitt the younger, but not slavishly so. His maiden speech was made on 8 December 1783, less than a week after entering the Commons, during the third reading of the East India Bill. This measure had been introduced by Charles Fox and was for 'vesting the affairs of the East India Company in the hands of certain commissioners for the benefit of the proprietors and the public'. Opponents of the bill saw in it an attempt by Fox to place an immense amount of patronage in the hands of his followers. Pitt described it as 'the boldest and most unconstitutional measure ever attempted'.

In addressing the Commons, Abercorn spoke of his abhorrence of the measure, which he believed had been introduced under false pretences. Fox came in for particular criticism, with Abercorn describing his conduct as 'tyranny, contempt of decency, law and the security of the people'.[10] Fox responded angrily, viewing Abercorn's contribution to the debate as an act of impudence for a young member. At this time new MPs were expected to familiarise themselves with parliamentary procedures and customs before rising to speak. The 1st Marquess, however, had exhibited an 'arrogant solemnity of manner' that was considered unbecoming of his 27 years. Horace Walpole, in providing an overview of the various contributions to the debate, wrote: 'Mr Hamilton, Lord Abercorn's heir, but by no means so laconic, had more success. Though his first essay, it was not at all dashed by bashfulness; and though he might have blushed for discovering so much rancour to Mr Fox, he seemed rather impatient to discharge it.'[11] The Lords threw out the bill, which brought down the government. Pitt then assumed the premiership and formed a new administration.

An indication of the confidence Pitt had in Abercorn and of the strength of their friendship at this time is the fact that he entrusted to him the task of moving the address at the opening of the 1784 session of parliament. Abercorn's manner, bearing and physical appearance all contributed to his impact on the political stage, as the political commentator Nicholas Wraxall in recounting this occasion noted:

> Tall, erect and muscular in his figure; thin, yet not meagre; with an air of grace and dignity over his whole person, he could not be mistaken for an ordinary man ... Of a dark complexion, with very intelligent and regular features, he resembled more a Spaniard than a native of Britain; and his arrogant solemnity of manner, augmented by the peculiarities of his demeanour, obtained for him from Sheridan the name of "Don Whiskerandos".[12]

In moving the address, his speech was marked by his partiality towards Pitt and his intense aversion to Fox. This was 'manifested ... in a manner scarcely compatible with the rules of debate and the forms of decorum'. He had, without doubt, impressive rhetorical skills. Pitt described one of his speeches as 'admirable' and is supposed to have said to William Wilberforce that, as a speaker, Abercorn 'would have beaten us all'. During the impeachment proceedings against Warren Hastings for alleged misconduct while in India, Abercorn felt compelled to intervene on behalf of the accused man when it seemed that the process was being prolonged unnecessarily. This put him at odds with Pitt, who had exhibited a lack of purpose during the proceedings. In moving a vote designed to hasten the process, and looking directly at Pitt, Abercorn declared, 'I entertain little doubt that I find myself this evening in a minority. Nevertheless I will divide the House on my motion.' The motion was lost by 69 votes. His Commons career ended, as it had been expected to, with the death of his uncle in October 1789 and his elevation to the earldom of Abercorn.

Portrait of the 1st Marquess by Thomas Lawrence.

A year later he was created 1st Marquess of Abercorn in the British peerage. The earldom of Abercorn was a Scottish title that did not automatically entitle its holder to sit in the British House of Lords. The 8th Earl did sit in the Lords between 1761 and 1786, but this was by virtue of being an elected Scottish representative peer. In 1786, through John James' relationship with Pitt, a British viscountcy had been conferred on the 8th Earl, giving him an automatic right to sit in the Lords, with remainder to his nephew. A viscountcy would not suffice, however, for man of considerable political ambition. In fact, when Abercorn had approached Pitt on the subject of aristocratic promotion in the summer or early autumn of 1790, it was not a marquessate he was after, but a dukedom. This was a promotion too far too soon. Almost apologetically, Pitt wrote to Abercorn to explain the situation:

> I really see insuperable difficulties in the way of the immediate completion of your wishes … If you are willing to begin with a marquessate, there could of course be no hesitation on that point, and it might smooth the way to the other under more favourable circumstances.[13]

The Marquess of Abercorn by Romney. This was commissioned by Abercorn in the aftermath of his wife Catherine's death in 1791. It depicts a very different Marquess from the one shown in Thomas Lawrence's portraits. In his right hand he holds 'An Epitaph', composed by him on his wife's passing.

Naturally there were those who resented the favouritism shown to Abercorn and ascribed it to Pitt's 'pecuniary embarrassments' and his need for the Marquess' cash.[14] However, these 'concealed causes' for Abercorn's promotion were dismissed as being without foundation.[15] One mutual friend later told Lord Aberdeen, 'It is well he did not wish to be Emperor of Germany, for Pitt would certainly have done his best to make him so.'[16] For a time, he seems also to have been keen to press his claims to an older title that his ancestors had also sought. George Selwyn wrote to Lady Carlisle, 'He will himself be Duc de Chatellerault, to which I know that he has no more pretensions than I should have to an estate that an ancestor of mine had sold a century ago.' However, he does not seem to have actively pursued this, the revolutionary situation in France probably dissuading him from doing so.

On 13 September 1791 his first wife died at Bentley Priory at the age of 32. Her constitution had never been strong, and from early in 1791 her health began to decline noticeably. In August she had been advised to travel to the south of France so long as she could cope with the voyage, but this never occurred. Abercorn was genuinely grieved by her death, being moved to write 'An Epitaph' and commissioning a painting by Romney showing him holding a manuscript of this poem.[17] He regularly referred to her as 'The Angel'. A monument was erected in the church at Stanmore, Middlesex, that the Abercorns attended when in residence at Bentley Priory. The following extract from its lengthy inscription testifies to the Marquess' sense of loss at his young wife's passing:

> She was for twelve years the affectionate and as she testified in her last moments, the happy wife of a husband, who to his many faults and follies, did not add insensibility to those merits of which, unless it be the will of God that he should survive his faculties, he will not survive the remembrance! whose most ardent and anxious hope it is, that the five children she was so loath to leave, though deprived of the blessing of her example and her care, may throughout their lives prove themselves inheritors of her mind and disposition.[18]

Irish politics

Following his succession to the earldom, Abercorn became actively involved in politics in Ireland. Malcomson has written of him, 'Abercorn had the ambition and most of the qualities needed to break the mould of Anglo-Irish politics in the last decade of the eighteenth century'.[19] His main ambition was to secure the lord lieutenancy of Ireland. This was one position which, in spite of changes taking place in the political arena, was unquestionably the preserve of the aristocracy. In order for him to be considered a serious contender for this position, he had to build a solid political power bloc. In February 1790, a mere four months after succeeding to the title, Abercorn signalled his intentions to one of his supporters, writing that he 'meant to omit no honourable mode of increasing my parliamentary strength in the greatest possible degree'.[20] What these were will be discussed presently, but here it may be observed that right from the start he drew on his political connections in England to reinforce the seriousness of his intentions in Ireland. This may be seen in the letter he wrote to Lord Westmorland, the Lord Lieutenant of Ireland, in advance of the general election of June and July 1790 in which he expressed his total support for and devotion to Pitt:

> It would be wasting words to talk of my good wishes to the present government. Pitt I have loved, and lived with in private life as a friend and brother; in public as the man in whom the fate of Britain is involved, and … the only man breathing under whose banners I would fight as a partisan. Talking, therefore, of my interest, is talking in other words of his.[21]

As much as anything, Abercorn wished to leave Westmorland in no doubt as to who had the ear of the Prime Minister.

With regard to the political assets he had inherited, Abercorn controlled the parliamentary representation of the borough of Strabane thanks to the steady efforts of his uncle. However, whereas for the 8th Earl exercising sway over the representation of Strabane had been the extent of his political ambitions in Ireland, and more to do with restoring family pride than anything else, for the 1st Marquess Strabane was just one piece in a much larger political game. When Abercorn succeeded his uncle the two sitting MPs for Strabane were Sir John Stewart Hamilton and Henry Pomeroy, both of whom were re-elected in 1790. Abercorn attempted to increase his political influence through purchasing additional boroughs, but this strategy produced mixed results. Of the four boroughs he sought, he was successful in acquiring only one – Augher in County Tyrone, which cost him (Ir) £11,500. Those he failed to purchase were Philipstown in King's County and the two County Donegal boroughs of Donegal Town and St Johnstown. The last was actually on the Abercorn estate, but control of the corporation had been lost to the family in the 1730s. By the late eighteenth century it was controlled by the Lord Wicklow. Abercorn was particularly keen to restore it to the family's political stable. Writing to Pomeroy in February 1790, he confided, 'I cannot bear not to recover that family borough if possible'. Here we see something of the sense of honour that pervaded his uncle's political interventions, that desire to restore the Abercorn patrimony that had been lost by previous generations. However, the Wicklows were equally keen to hold on to St Johnstown, and Abercorn failed in his attempts to recover it.

When it came to county politics, the extent of his estates in Donegal and Tyrone ought to have given Abercorn a decisive role in determining the parliamentary representation in both. However, Abercorn's first foray into county politics produced mixed results. At this time membership of the county electorate rested on the possession of a freehold, and specifically a freehold worth at least 40 shillings after the rent and other fees had been paid. For electoral purposes a freehold was defined as property either owned outright or held by a lease for lives.[22] The 8th Earl, having no interest in creating a political power base in Ireland, was content to issue leases for a determinate number of years. His tenants, therefore, were unable to vote in parliamentary elections. His nephew realised that if he were to challenge for political supremacy in north-west Ulster he had to create a substantial electorate from among his own tenantry. Shortly after succeeding his uncle, Abercorn wrote to the Chief Secretary claiming that 'With more time before me, I should have very little doubt of securing the election of a friend of my own in each of the counties of Tyrone and Donegal.' At that moment he was executing new leases which would enable him to make freeholders of hundreds of his tenants. The difficulty was that the general election was expected to take place before these freeholds had taken effect.

As far as electoral politics in Donegal was concerned, he was also naïve and so his tactics were hopelessly wrong. A strong independent spirit existed among the electors in Donegal, many of them substantial Presbyterian farmers in the east of the county, which created a suspicion of outsiders interfering in their affairs. Abercorn did not appreciate this, and his attempt to put forward two moderate landlord candidates at the 1790 election failed miserably. Overtures to him from Lord Erne, owner of the Lifford estate, suggesting an alliance were also rejected unless Erne was ready to accept secondary status. In the event the two sitting MPs were returned unopposed. Abercorn's first foray into Donegal politics, therefore, proved an abject and humiliating failure. His first venture into Tyrone politics, however, displayed slightly more tactical awareness. Here his principal rival was Lord Belmore. On this occasion Abercorn did not openly challenge the political status quo and one of the sitting MPs, the popular James Stewart of Killymoon, was returned along with Thomas Knox, son of Lord Welles (soon to become Viscount Northland) of Dungannon. The election of Knox was something of a triumph for Abercorn, for though the MP was nominally Belmore's man, he was one of those young MPs of talent and ambition that Abercorn was beginning to form a strong political faction around. His brother George, MP for Dungannon, was another, as was Edmund Pery, MP for Limerick. Abercorn wished, however, for his 'strength to be more in certainty and respectability than in reputed numbers'. Even so, he was building a powerful grouping in the Irish House of Commons.

Abercorn and the Catholic Question

On the wider political front, moves to grant Catholics political and other rights were gathering pace in the early 1790s. The 1792 Catholic Relief Act fell short of expectations, not only for Irish Catholics but also for Pitt, who needed their support if he were to embark on a major European war. Of the outstanding issues, one of the most important was the right to vote. There was a clear divergence of opinion between Pitt and his Irish administration, headed by Lord Westmorland, which was reluctant to grant any further concessions. At this time Abercorn occupied a position somewhere in between. He was a supporter of Catholic rights as far as arms and the army were concerned, but he was not yet in favour of extending the franchise. More than that, he was firmly against Catholics taking matters into their own hands. In January 1792 he wrote to Thomas Knox that 'if the Catholics join any particular interest or party, or endeavour to gain their ends by fomenting or abetting political dissensions, we [the Abercorn party] shall resist them forever'.[23] However, it may have been his greater flexibility on the Catholic Question that made some within the Catholic community see him as a possible champion of their cause.

In the autumn of 1792 John Keogh, the leading figure on the General Committee of the Catholics of Ireland, instructed its Secretary, Theobald Wolfe Tone, to write to George Knox and suggest to him that Abercorn 'take up the cause of the Catholics and assume the lieutenancy of Ireland'. This, Keogh argued, would make the Marquess 'the most popular lord lieutenant that ever was in Ireland'. Keogh clearly saw in Abercorn a champion of the rights of Irish Catholics. However, he was somewhat naïve in his thinking. For one thing, Abercorn was in no position to 'assume' the lord lieutenancy, a position filled at the discretion of Pitt himself. In any case, Abercorn disapproved of the activities of the Catholic Committee and flatly rejected Keogh's scheme. On being shown a memo or abstract of the Marquess' response to the plan, Tone wrote, 'Lord Abercorn quite wild; his idea is that the Catholics should renounce their present system for the chance of what he would do for them. Damned kind!'[24] In other words, Abercorn insisted that the Catholic Committee put their trust entirely in him. Keogh was left despondent and the Catholic Committee looked to Westmorland to further their cause.

In December representatives of the Catholic Convention travelled to London to present their petition to George III. Through the Knox brothers, it was arranged that a private meeting should also take place with Abercorn. George Knox proposed a meeting at his own lodgings. This Abercorn objected to as he did not want anything that might have the 'appearance of clandestine proceeding on my part'. Instead he insisted that 'it must be perfectly understood that it is their desire to see me, not mine to see them'. On 21 December the delegates called at his London home. The meeting that took place was a complete failure. Marianne Elliott sums up the proceedings:

> What passed threatened to reduce the Catholics to the position of servile supplicants ... Abercorn represented them as having eagerly sought him out both in Ireland and England, attributed to them certain principles which they rejected, criticised them for not applying to the government in Ireland and sent them away without any promise of support.[25]

Tone was left fuming and complained to George Knox, who in turn blamed Abercorn for what happened. The lack of respect that had been afforded to the delegates was a particular source of frustration, and contact with the Marquess was not maintained.

Nonetheless, when Pitt's Catholic Relief Bill was brought before the Irish House of Commons in February 1793, it was with Abercorn's agreement that George Knox proposed an amendment to it whereby Catholics would be entitled to seats in parliament as well as the vote. This was the first ever proposal in parliament for complete Catholic emancipation. For Abercorn to have backed it was clearly an attempt on his part to 'steal the thunder of the British government, and to out-Pitt Pitt'.[26] The amendment failed. Pitt was by now infuriated by Abercorn's interventions. For the Prime Minister it was essential that Irish Catholics should feel that they owed their new-found status to the British government. The Marquess' actions were endangering this. There was also considerable anger within the Irish administration at Abercorn's interference, especially from Fitzgibbon, the Lord Chancellor. Pitt could not have made his feelings clearer than when, on the death of the next Knight of the Garter in May 1793, Abercorn was snubbed. That the honour was given to Westmorland was even more galling. 'We see things in too different a light for discussion to be worthwhile', the Marquess wrote to Pitt, 'So, God bless you, and may you find all your new friends as good ones as your old friend.'

In spite of this estrangement from Pitt, an Abercorn lord lieutenancy remained a serious possibility, prompting, in September 1793, a vitriolic attack on Abercorn by someone calling himself 'Mentor' which appeared in *The Morning Post or Dublin Courant*. The author was probably a member of the Irish administration who resented Abercorn's pretensions to the viceroyalty.

> Your affected intimacy, my lord, with Mr Pitt is a mere *ignis fatuus* that constantly leads you astray. He has too much discernment ever to distinguish by any employment of trust a man whom he can gratify with the bauble of a title for the grossest prostitution of principle and character. You wish my lord to be the chief governor of this country … [and boast] that no aristocrat in the kingdom would outdo you in venal parliamentary influence. This gave you irresistible claims upon the minister [Pitt], that hypocritical pretender to reform. But the virtue of the sovereign saved the country. He put his negative upon the appointment of a man whose private enormities he considered an earnest of public vices.[27]

The letter suggests that the King himself had intervened to prevent Abercorn from becoming lord lieutenant, an assertion that cannot be substantiated. Rumours persisted that Abercorn was to realise his chief political ambition. One from November 1793 suggested that he was 'immediately to be lord lieutenant'. Early the following year the incoming chief secretary wrote to Pitt on whether there was any substance to these stories. Pitt's response had more than a tone of exasperation. Rejecting his lord lieutenancy as 'out of the question', he declared:

> He would be the most unfit person in the world. His pride is carried to such an excess as to be quite ridiculous. I had a great acquaintance with him at Cambridge. He has been very kind and friendly to me, and is a man of very considerable talents. But his pretensions are so great as to be intolerable.[28]

What especially infuriated Pitt was the fact that Abercorn 'talked as if he knew my opinions and intentions better than Lord Westmorland does, and I have found it necessary to take pains to prevent that impression'. Abercorn's pride and presumptuousness were serious character flaws and much commented on at the time. In June 1797, Lord Castlereagh remarked to his wife that he had seen Abercorn at a military revue 'in his most magnificent manner – stands always in an attitude'.[29] In 1799, the Earl of Mornington wrote to Grenville, 'to talk like Lord Abercorn, you will gain much credit by conferring some high and brilliant honour upon me immediately'.[30] A London hostess remarked in 1800: 'He was always supposed to be a little cracked, and his pride is beyond belief ... his language is so *outré* from the manners of common life that it would appear caricatured.' The story is told that in response to being asked whether he based his livery on that of younger branches of the Royal Family he exclaimed, 'My family took it from them? No!! It was the livery of the Hamiltons before the House of Brunswick had a servant to put it on.'[31]

Abercorn's own 'squadron' of MPs was weakened when in May 1794 his relationship with his political manager Thomas Knox, already uneasy, broke down completely and irreconcilably. Knox had given up hope of ever seeing an Abercorn lord lieutenancy and was offended by the Marquess' preference for his younger brother George. Abercorn was also frustrated at the lack of support from some of his MPs. His Strabane MP, Sir John Stewart Hamilton, contributed little to the Abercorn grouping. Hamilton, 'a man of small fortune and large stature, possessing a most liberal appetite for both solids and fluid, much wit, more humour and indefatigable cheerfulness', was considered the leader of a group of MPs who spent their time 'in high conviviality' until called upon to vote at the ring of the division bell. Abercorn demanded more of his MPs than this, and Hamilton's 'services' were dispensed with prior to the general election of 1797, leading to a complete breakdown in the relationship between the two. When, as a result of the Act of Union, Strabane was disenfranchised, £15,000 in compensation was paid to the Marquess, despite the best attempts of Sir John Stewart Hamilton to secure an amount for himself. The commissioners for compensation dismissed Hamilton's application as the 'effusion of a disordered brain'; Abercorn reacted with more hostility, accusing Hamilton of 'baseness and ingratitude'.

The 1797 general election and the events leading up to it highlighted again Abercorn's electoral weakness at county level. Prior to the 1790 general election, Belmore and Lord Welles had agreed that if Welles' son Thomas contested that election for Tyrone, the next would be contested by Belmore's son, and each family would support the other. This was no secret, and Abercorn would certainly have known of it through his relationship with the

Knoxes. By the mid-1790s Abercorn's rivalry with Belmore was more heated than ever. Much of this arose from their falling out over the Tyrone Militia. Abercorn was the 'figurehead commander' of the Tyrone Militia following the passing of the Militia Act in 1793. When Belmore sought a commission for his son Lord Corry in the Militia, Abercorn felt he could not refuse, but was unwilling to give him too high a rank – 'I certainly will not consent to Lord Belmore's son as being more than captain.'[32] This insulted Belmore to the extent that he refused to have anything more to do with the Militia. Abercorn viewed Lord Corry's candidature as a serious threat. However, early in 1795 questions were asked on whether Lord Corry was actually old enough to contest an election. Sir John Stewart, MP for Augher and Abercorn's new political manager, investigated the matter in Dublin until he found the relevant baptismal register and was forced to admit that the young candidate was in fact eligible to stand should there have been an election.

In the summer of 1795 Thomas Knox returned to the Belmore camp, and though Abercorn underestimated the significance of this move and other developments, it was clear to others that the tide was turning against him. For one thing the Militia was unpopular among Tyrone Presbyterians, and Abercorn's unwavering support for it put him at odds with much of the electorate. In 1796, Abercorn's candidate for Tyrone, Nathaniel Montgomery-Moore, withdrew (but was subsequently elected for the borough of Strabane) and the Marquess was forced to accept that he would have to wait for another opportunity to impose his will on that county's electorate. In Donegal, however, Abercorn was determined to have his candidates elected in 1797. Unfortunately for him, he had not learned the lessons of 1790. His approach to the independent-minded electors of Donegal remained the same and he was unwilling to accept advice on how to win them over. He also had a disdainful attitude towards local patronage which he could have exercised to his advantage in the run-up to the election. For these reasons and others his candidates were defeated.

Portrait of the 1st Marquess in robes by Thomas Lawrence.

Abercorn reacted with fury to yet another rejection by the electorate, threatening to withdraw from Irish politics rather than waste his time with a people who failed to appreciate all he had to offer them. Malcomson attributes his political failings to the fact that he 'lacked the common touch which was essential to success in an open constituency even in the days of the unreformed electoral system'.[33] In September 1797, Abercorn put the borough of Augher up for sale. He hoped to receive 16,000 guineas for it, the exorbitant price probably to deter Belmore from thinking of buying it, but there were no takers.

Remarriage, divorce and remarriage again

Abercorn's withdrawal, temporarily as it would turn out, from the Irish political scene coincided with difficulties in his personal life. Following the death of his first wife, he had married on 4 March 1792 his first cousin Cecil, the daughter of his uncle George Hamilton, canon of Windsor. A month before the ceremony he wrote to Thomas Knox to explain, in a remarkably candid way, why he was about to do so:

> I will announce to you an event that may or may not surprise you. It was determined upon the day before yesterday. With the event you shall have my reasons … That my great object should be to give my children a kind and careful mother and protectress, and that I could no-where else be so sure of the attainment of that object, requires no explanation. But why I should by an appearance of precipitancy give a handle against myself to all those whose universal passion (even without real malevolence of heart) is to think and speak as ill as possible of friends and neighbours, to censure me for impropriety or want of respect to the memory of one for whom my sentiments (whether tomorrow or fifty years hence) will go unimpaired with me to my grave, you might not be aware without an explanation.
>
> The fact is that, except my house, Lady Cecil has no home. The character and conduct of her mother are such as to render any communication impossible to me, or any that belong to me. It was my intention to have had (as we hitherto have) either Lady Watson or Mrs Buller (who are aunt and sister to Miss Copley) in the house, till my term of mourning should expire. Of both those resources within a few days, untoward and unforeseen accidents have deprived us, and it would remain for us to be months in the house together without a protectress, and consequently subject to disreputable insinuations, which might attach upon Lady Cecil if I did not prefer to draw censure upon myself alone, by the determination I am come to.
>
> I confess, the alternative is a very unpleasant one for me, but I do what I think every man ought to do: balance the good and bad on both sides, and then act as right as I can, to the best of my judgment. I am not apt to care a farthing about the tittle-tattle of the world. Perhaps this is exactly the only subject upon which I mind it, and I have at least the comfort of knowing that, not only all the near

relations of – but all who really know me, do me justice. You are one of the first persons anywhere, the very first in Ireland, to whom I talk upon this topic. You will also be the last with whom I enter into any discussion of it, for it is very painful to me. As yet you may as well not mention it to anyone (unless Mrs Knox) till you hear it mentioned. Then you may say what you please.[34]

Abercorn and Cecil were married by a special licence at the Marquess' house in Grosvenor Square; Pitt gave the bride away. Over two years before this, on 27 October 1789, and in the lifetime of the Marquess's first wife, she had been raised to the precedence of an earl's daughter by royal warrant. As the *Complete Peerage* put it, 'This was certainly a most unusual proceeding.'[35] Her father was dead by this time, while her four older sisters were passed over. The move excited 'no inconsiderable conversation in politic circles' with one observer commenting, 'Mr Hamilton now Lord Hamilton, but *toujours magnifico*, will have one of his cousins a lady as if she had been an earl's daughter, and no other of her sisters.' According to Wraxall, the honour was not conferred 'without strong marks of repugnance being evinced by their Majesties'.[36] It was also alleged that Abercorn had used his influence with Pitt to obtain the honour. Why Abercorn should have pressed for this designation for his cousin is unclear. Cecil had lived in the same household as a 'kind of mistress of the robes to the first Lady Abercorn' and there were rumours that she was his mistress. There were also stories that he wished to marry Cecil, but was not prepared to do so if she was a mere commoner. However, as noted above, the Marquess mourned his first wife deeply and, as he later confided to Lord Aberdeen, at the time of Cecil's preferment he had not the slightest intention of marrying her and he regretted his action in seeking it.[37]

The marriage to Cecil Hamilton was neither happy nor long-lasting. It was said that the couple had been pressurised into marrying, with Cecil's family particularly anxious for the union to take place.[38] Initially they seemed content, and entertained regularly at Bentley Priory. One notice reported on a ball given by Lady Abercorn 'which was very numerously attended by a fashionable circle'. At another, or perhaps the same one, 'there were twelve ladies in the garb of statues; one of those posing as a statue was asked 'whether she really was as naked as she appeared to be, and said she really was very near'.[39] Abercorn and his second wife had only one child, a daughter named Frances who was born in July 1795. During this period Abercorn spent much of his time in Ireland, gradually becoming estranged from Cecil.

In 1798, an affair between Cecil and Captain Joseph Copley was revealed. The *Morning Post* of 10 November announced, 'The attentions of the captain and the dispositions of the Marchioness have for some time been known to the *beau monde*.' Copley was in fact the brother of the first Lady Abercorn and a man of notorious character. The affair emerged after Cecil fell pregnant by Copley; as she and the Marquess were no longer sleeping together it was clear that he could not have been the father. With little option than to tell him the truth and fall on his mercy, she went to Abercorn and told him the full story. It was said that he 'took it very coolly, though with great surprise, and behaved with sufficient temper and liberality … She meant to return to her hack chaise, but Lord Abercorn insisted on her going like the marchioness of Abercorn and taking his coach and servants.'[40] The calmness with which Abercorn handled the situation was, according to Lady Holland, who detested the Marquess, 'a disappointment, as people had hoped his pride would be so galled that he would afford some sport to the wags, but he wisely enough seems of the opinion of La Fontaine, "*Quand on l'ignore, ce n'est rien, et quand on le scait, c'est peu de chose*". His absurd vanity has made him more conspicuous than he would have been otherwise.'[41] The following April they were divorced by act of parliament. Several weeks later, on 21 May, Copley and Cecil married in London.[42]

His two eldest daughters were now coming of age, and in the spring of 1800 hosted their first ball at the family's London home. The *Morning Post* of 8 March provided the following account of the event:

> On Friday night Ladies Harriet and Catherine Hamilton, the amiable daughters of the Marquess of Abercorn, gave a grand entertainment at the family residence in Grosvenor Square … Three hundred cards only were given out, the party being select, to avoid confusion in the ballroom … [His daughters] inherit all the innate dignity which characterises their noble father. Good humour and festivity marked the hour; and the Marquess, who is the patron of literature as well as the supporter of that refined gallantry which the illustrious Burke lamented as No More, is also one of the most tasteful leaders of splendid hospitality.

Two hundred guests sat down to dinner, but flour in any form was not part of the meal. This was at a time when flour was scarce and consequently very expensive. Abercorn set an example by prohibiting its use in his household, substituting rice and potatoes (from which pastry was made). Two weeks later a further extravagant gathering was organised at his London home. Prior to this event, someone – invariably described as a 'malicious person' or a 'good-natured friend of the Marquess' – had sent out a number of bogus invitations. On learning this, the Marquess had the following notice inserted in the press:

> As some foolish person has issued false cards of invitation to the Marquess of Abercorn's house this evening, this notice is given that

none may have the trouble of coming to the door who were not either personally invited, or received a card brought by a livery servant of the family. The type of the forged cards is different from the real.

Just to make sure that no-one gained access to the ball who should not have been there, Abercorn summoned Townsend, one of the Bow-Street Runners, to check the invitations of those who arrived at his house. Only a few individuals did turn up with sham invitations and of these the only one to gain admittance was a 'foreign Count … [who] would not understand the remonstrances of Townsend'. It was later revealed that the forgery was the work of a 'certain lady, who invited every person the Marquess disliked, except herself'.

One cannot help but imagine that the Marquess' parties at this time were a statement that he was back to his usual self after the difficulties of the previous two years. Further evidence of this comes with his marriage on 3 April 1800 to Lady Anne Jane Hatton, widow of Henry Hatton of Great Clonard, County Wexford, and daughter of Arthur Saunders Gore, 2nd Earl of Arran. Their courtship was brief, for Lady Anne had only recently broken off her relationship with Lord Morpeth, and it caught most people by surprise. The wedding took place at the London home of Lord Sudley, Lady Anne's brother. Present were the Marquess' daughters Harriet and Catherine and Miss Copley, the younger sister of Abercorn's first wife, who was responsible for looking after the Marquess' children. In describing the new Lady Abercorn, Lady Holland wrote in her journal, 'She is 36, her appearance is so youthful that no one guesses her to be above 24, if so much. Her figure is light, airy, and graceful.' On the other hand there were those who, while acknowledging that she possessed 'a sort of vivacity that raises your expectations', thought that 'what she says is so flat that it damps curiosity'.

Shortly after their wedding the Abercorns hosted a celebratory ball at their London residence which was attended by the Prince of Wales and the Duchesses of Gloucester and Cumberland as well as a number of other members of the aristocracy. Concerns were raised about Lady Anne's suitability as a bride, even, so it was said, from within the Royal Family. The Queen is supposed to have summoned Miss Copley and encouraged her to forgo her desire to leave the Abercorn household and to remain with her nieces – which she did. However, any suggestions that this union would result in the Marquess being shunned by London society proved unfounded. Lady Anne proved a devoted companion, especially during those years in which he experienced much personal sorrow; as will be discussed in more detail below, between 1803 and 1814 all five of his children by his first wife died, among them his son and heir.

Frances Hawkins

Content though he appeared to be with his third wife, Abercorn continued to conduct an affair with Frances Augusta Hawkins. Her background is shrouded in some mystery. She was born into a respectable Scottish family; her brother or half-brother was General Sir Fitzroy Maclean Bt, though her own birth is absent from the family genealogies.[43] When exactly she became Abercorn's mistress is not known. Years later her counsel in a matrimonial lawsuit stated, 'This lady, who is most highly respectable by birth and connexions, had unfortunately by a most singular and deplorable combination of unfortunate circumstances, fallen in early youth. She had fallen, however, into generous hands … a Nobleman now no more.' Abercorn provided her with a London house in Beaumont Street, Piccadilly, and another close to Bentley Priory. She seems to have been accepted by the Marquess' third wife, and there is some evidence that a degree of cordiality existed between them, though it is doubtful if, as was said, the latter conveyed Abercorn to his mistress' door. To Frances, the Marquess was 'dearest J.J.', an informality of address that would have astonished those who knew him only as the haughty and distant Lord Abercorn.

In 1804–05, Abercorn commissioned Thomas Lawrence to paint a portrait of Frances and their oldest child, John James. On a number of occasions Lawrence sought the opinion of Joseph Farington, an important member of the Royal Academy, on the painting. Farington first saw it on 12 February 1805, when he entered in his diary, 'Went to Lawrence as he wished to have my opinion upon the circular picture which he was painting of Mrs Hawkins and John James Hamilton, son of Lord Abercorn'. At the end of April Farington recorded in his diary the views of the Swiss-born artist Henry Fuseli on the painting. A picture like it 'had not been painted in 100 years', Fuseli opined. 'Sir Joshua Reynolds could not have done it … it was singly worth all the pictures Gainsborough had ever painted.' The painting was displayed in public for the first time at the Academy's 1806 exhibition – when it was given the title 'A Fancy Group' – but it did not meet with universal approval. Another member of the Royal Academy, James Northcote, was particularly critical. Farington, who accompanied Northcote to the exhibition in May of that year, recorded his views on the painting: 'The woman looks like a Whore, which was not necessary as she might have been made to look jocund without it.' Northcote also took the view that the boy John James had been given an expression which, 'for his age, was unnatural', adding, 'He looked as if he had been bred among the vices of an impure house.'[44] It has been suggested that the painting 'should be regarded as an expression of that extravagance and theatrical creativity that appears to have been such part of Abercorn's public persona and life at Bentley Priory'.[45]

Around this time Frances moved to Barons Court. This had first been mooted at the end of the previous summer and was rumoured to have been to 'remove a cause of jealousy in Abercorn's family'. It was not her first visit to County Tyrone, for in 1803 she had accompanied the Marquess and his family to Barons Court, where she was accommodated in the Lodge. This time she was on her own and, as one writer has put it, 'was quite at ease as chatelaine of the place', living extravagantly and charming every man who came into contact with her.[46] The Marquess' agent James Hamilton junior, who had fallen under Frances' spell during her previous visit, became a regular visitor to Barons Court. Through an anonymous letter, Abercorn got wind of this and Hamilton was forced to admit that he had dined with Frances 'perhaps 4 or 5 times or maybe oftener'. In May 1807, a year after arriving in Tyrone, she was heavily pregnant, exciting much gossip among the local populace. The father was not, however, the Marquess' agent, but almost certainly Abercorn himself, who had visited Barons Court nine months before.

If Frances' pregnancy had set tongues wagging, what was revealed in the coming weeks left everyone flummoxed. On 1 June James Hamilton junior reported to Abercorn that he had met Captain Constantine Maguire at Barons Court, who informed him that he was the husband of Frances, their marriage having 'long since taken place, and privately'. However, Maguire, who sprang from one of the oldest families in County Fermanagh, wished to have the marriage solemnised for a second time by Stewart, Hamilton's brother, who was the Church of Ireland rector in Strabane. This was done secretly with only the agent and one other individual witnessing the ceremony. That very night Frances gave birth to a son. Maguire had possibly first encountered Frances when he spent the previous Christmas at Barons Court while recovering from illness.

Aside from her charms, Maguire would have been attracted by the substantial annuity – initially £200 and later doubled to £400 – that Abercorn had settled on her (and which was to be paid to her for the rest of her life). It was later alleged that this annuity 'formed no trifling ingredient' in Maguire's pursuit of her, though the captain would have been disappointed to find that this money was solely for the use of the recipient. Abercorn himself seems to have been highly satisfied with this turn of events for his ardour for Frances had long since cooled, notwithstanding their liaison the previous autumn. Frances' marriage to Maguire was not a happy one. While living in Dublin, Maguire began an affair with one of his wife's friends. In 1816, he attempted to have his marriage annulled on the grounds that it had taken place at Barons Court in 1807 had never been officially registered. He was thwarted, however, when Abercorn, to whom Frances had appealed for help, intervened on her behalf.

Their son John James had died in April 1808 and was buried in the family vault in Stanmore. A memorial was erected in The Priory grounds; the following is an excerpt from the inscription: 'In the garden which, having been a scene of amusement to six other beloved children, had just been dedicated to the amusement of John James Hamilton, this stone is dedicated to his memory. He was a sweet and promising child.'[47] Frances is known to have borne two other sons and a daughter to the Marquess. One son was drowned in 1842 with his wife and family, while the other, Col. Arthur FitzJames, who commanded the Middlesex Militia, lived until 1887.

Politics after the Act of Union

Abercorn was an enthusiastic supporter of the Act of Union, which came into force on 1 January 1801. However, on that very day he was in a mood of despondency. He confided to Lord Darnley:

> As to politics, whether apathy or patience be the word, I certainly as much as possible avoid thinking of them. Whatever were my opinions of some of the measures of the government and some of the members, it would not be likely to have much weight with a public which has witnessed with acquiescence and approbation the subversion of the aristocracy, the overthrow of the Militia and an income tax clause of which, letter and spirit, is a degradation of individuals and extinction of the constitution. Least of all do I conceive that my eloquence would have any great effect upon a House of Lords, the majority of whose titles and faces I have not yet had an opportunity of getting acquainted with. Till new appearances present themselves, my plan is to eat, drink, be as merry and think as little as I can.[48]

Abercorn's sense of hopelessness at this time is hard to fathom. Certainly he was disappointed with the turn of events in relation to the Militia, from which he had resigned, but just a few months earlier he had had the satisfaction of seeing his brother-in-law, Viscount Sudley, elected MP for County Donegal in a by-election. Furthermore, Belmore's strong opposition to the Act of Union had made him unpopular with the government. The resignation of Pitt from the premiership later that year added to Abercorn's sense of woe, but he was a supporter of the administration of Pitt's successor, Henry Addington. When he discovered that Belmore had approached Addington looking for political favour in return for parliamentary support, he angrily reminded the Prime Minister that Belmore was that 'violent opposer of the Union' and that he and Addington were old friends. Furthermore, the Marquess had as many seats in parliament as Belmore, 'though I do not job them'. The irony of this statement was probably not lost on Addington, but he dismissed Belmore's propositions.

The passing of the Act of Union reduced Abercorn's political influence considerably. The boroughs of Strabane and Augher were disenfranchised, thus removing four MPs from the Abercorn group. The Marquess continued to enjoy a good relationship with Lord Northland and his son George Knox, and because of this he could count on the support of the representative for the borough of Dungannon – one of the few Ulster boroughs to survive the cull of 1800. In 1805, he had the satisfaction of seeing his eldest son James, Viscount Hamilton, returned to Westminster as MP for Dungannon. James held the seat for two years before becoming MP for Liskeard in England, and was replaced in Dungannon by his younger brother Claud. George Knox himself sat for Dublin University, mainly through Abercorn's influence. However, Abercorn's interest in electoral politics was now firmly fixed on the county constituencies of Donegal and Tyrone. Belmore's grip on Tyrone politics remained apparently unassailable, and early in 1802 Abercorn almost gave up hope of ever usurping his dominance. He wrote to Sir John Stewart on 2 February:

> I see there are so many different interests in the county to be managed and canvassed and courted, so much of the trouble which I hate most, and am most unfit for, and so much uncertainty at last, while Lord Belmore makes electioneering the sole object of his life, that if my son sees things as I do, he will think representing the county, unless with more quietness and unanimity, very little worth his while.[49]

This letter reveals much that helps to explain Abercorn's previous electoral failures. He was simply unwilling to apply himself to the business of winning an election by the accepted methods of the day. Belmore, on the other hand, was, though it was also somewhat disingenuous of Abercorn to accuse his rival of making 'electioneering the sole object of his life'. The supreme irony was that on the very day that Abercorn had apparently relinquished, for the time being at least, his political ambitions in Tyrone, Belmore died at his lodgings in Brock Street, Bath, where he had gone for the sake of his health.

Abercorn immediately saw how this changed the political landscape in the county – 'Lord Belmore's death puts an end to all our doubts and difficulties'. The succession of Lord Corry to the earldom necessitated a by-election in Tyrone in which Sir John Stewart was returned unopposed. Abercorn seemed to have learned from past mistakes, for instead of brushing aside the new Earl of Belmore he offered him the hand of friendship and the prospect of a political alliance. On the basis that 'we do not seem to have anything to quarrel about now', he wrote to Castlereagh, who was acting as an intermediary, 'we might as well be on friendly terms'. Attractive though Abercorn's propositions were, Belmore was being pressurised by his father's anti-Union associates to side with them against the Marquess, and was unable to come to a decision on where his political future lay. Abercorn was generous enough with his putative protégé to write to Addington requesting an English peerage for him. He was rebuffed, though one wonders just how hard he pressed Belmore's claims, especially as the latter had still to accept Abercorn's offers.[50] It was only a matter of time before Abercorn gave up trying to reach an agreement with the young Belmore, and the rivalry that characterised the Marquess' relationship with the 1st Earl was continued with the 2nd Earl. However, the Belmore stranglehold on Tyrone politics had been broken and at the general election of 1802 Sir John Stewart was again returned, while in Donegal Abercorn had the satisfaction of seeing his candidate, Sir James Stewart, returned.

In 1804, Abercorn became embroiled in a controversy with Mr Justice Luke Fox. The former MP had, at the Donegal assizes, accused Abercorn of neglecting the responsibilities of a major landowner and of failing to show sufficient respect to the judiciary on circuit. Abercorn was furious and had Sir James Stewart present a petition complaining of the judge's behaviour. The affair became a matter of national concern, and at the beginning of November 1804 Baron Redesdale, the Lord Chancellor of Ireland, wrote to Spencer Perceval, the British Attorney General:

> What you state to me of the resolution with respect to Mr Justice Fox, whatever the [?matter] to Lord Abercorn, surprises me much. A formal complaint has been made by the lord lieutenant to the secretary of state that a judge on the bench has grossly attacked him and his government in a charge to a grand jury, and Lord Abercorn is thought the fit person to vindicate the honour of the lord lieutenant. The resolution in effect tells the judges they may abuse the lord lieutenant as they please: unless he can find a Lord Abercorn to take up his quarrel, government will not.[51]

Several times Abercorn attempted to institute impeachment proceedings, but these were systematically delayed by the House of Lords. Exasperated, Abercorn forced a vote, but was defeated.[52]

Despite the Fox imbroglio, Abercorn looked like he had now firmly established himself on the local political scene. Frustratingly for him, however, events conspired to destroy his new-found political hegemony. It largely came down to the terms on which his tenants held their leases. Whereas on some estates leases for three lives were commonplace, on the Abercorn estate the leases were for only one life. This was a risk, for if the named life died the leases would no longer be valid and therefore the tenants would not be able to vote. Furthermore, freeholders had to be registered at least six months before an election. The life inserted in the leases granted to Abercorn's tenants was that of his uncle's old and faithful agent, James Hamilton. At the beginning of 1806, when he would have been approaching 90, Hamilton suffered a near fatal accident when he fell downstairs. He managed to recover from this, but shortly before the election of that year he died, thus extinguishing the freeholder status of the Abercorn tenantry. Compounding the situation was the fact that this election was followed by another five months later, leaving Abercorn not enough time to issue new leases.[53] As a result Sir John Stewart lost out in Tyrone in 1806, being replaced by Abercorn's erstwhile ally Thomas Knox. He considered standing in the 1807 election, but when it became obvious that he would not have sufficient support he withdrew. In Donegal Viscount Sudley, with whom Abercorn had fallen out for a variety of reasons, including the handling of the Justice Fox affair, did not seek re-election. There was little comfort to be drawn in the return of Sir James Stewart in both 1806 and 1807, for he had defected to Lord Conyngham. The year 1807 effectively marked the end of Abercorn's involvement in Irish politics.

Knight of the Garter

In the early years of the nineteenth century Abercorn gradually healed his rift with Pitt. By the summer of 1804 Pitt was again a visitor to Bentley Priory, the English country home of the Abercorns, and a guest in their box at Covent Garden. Thomas Lawrence related to Farington an account of a curious exchange between Abercorn and Pitt in November 1804:

> Lord Abercorn said, while the subject was upon the human figure and where it was to be found in the greatest perfection, that it was not among the labouring class of people, who were exposed, ill-fed and hard-worked; that on looking around the House of Lords, he had remarked what a fine body of men the nobility were, and that there might be found a superiority. 'That' said Mr Pitt 'may be owing to the new nobility' – very sarcastic to Lord Abercorn who would attach everything to his ancestry.[54]

Malcomson raises the issue of whether Lawrence or the person to whom he related this story fully understood the nature of the interplay between the Marquess and Pitt. The latter may indeed have been sarcastic, but then again he may have been laughing at himself, for it was Pitt who had promoted many commoners to the Lords. Either way no damage was done to the relationship between the two. In December 1804 Pitt asked Abercorn to move the address in the House of Lords, a request that harked back to the occasion fully two decades earlier when he asked the then John James

Du Très-Noble et Puiſsant Prince, JEAN-JAQUES, Marquis
D'ABERCORN, et Vicomte *HAMILTON*, en la Grande
Bretagne: Comte d'*ABERCORN*, Baron de *PAISLEY*,
d'*ABERCORN*, de *HAMILTON* et de *KILPATRICK*, en
Ecofse: Vicomte et Baron de *STRABANE*, et Baron de
MOUNT-CASTLE en Irlande ; et Chevalier du très-
-noble Ordre de la *JARRETIERE*: Inſtallé au
Chateau de Windsor le XXIII Jour d'Avril MDCCCV.

The Abercorn coat of arms. The inscription refers to Abercorn having been installed as a Knight of the Garter at Windsor on 23 April 1805.

Hamilton to do the same in the House of Commons. Early in the New Year Abercorn received an honour that had long eluded him when he learned he was to be made a Knight of the Garter. On first hearing of this, Abercorn wrote to Pitt, 'I received with the very greatest pleasure the proof of a friendship which will last our lives.'[55] It was given to him by Pitt for personal rather than political reasons, a fact demonstrated by the reaction of the Marquess of Stafford, a much more politically influential individual than Abercorn, who angrily went into opposition.

Much has been made of Abercorn's penchant for wearing the Garter excessively or on what seemed to some inappropriate occasions. Lady Morgan wrote of him: 'He is always dressed *en grande tenue* and never sits down to table except in his blue ribbon with the Star and Garter.'[56] He was even said to have gone out shooting in it. Pitt's niece, Lady Hester Stanhope, later famous for her travels in the Levant, mockingly asked the Marquess if he used the Garter to tie up his broken leg.[57] This may have been in reference to an injury sustained by the Marquess while driving his wife and daughter in a two-horse phaeton at The Priory. Both his legs were broken and, while he made a good recovery, thereafter he walked with a limp.

Pitt died in January 1806. Abercorn was a pall bearer at his funeral, an honour he considered his 'last ostensible tribute of admiration, gratitude and affection'. Pitt's passing meant Abercorn no longer had a friend and supporter at the heart of government. For Pitt's political heirs the Marquess was 'one of the more burdensome features of their inheritance'.[58] He demanded much, but delivered little in return. The Chief Secretary, Sir Arthur Wellesley (the future Duke of Wellington), wrote in January 1809 that 'the support of his influence in Ireland, from which the government derives no strength, costs us more than can be imagined'. In spite of his lack of political clout, Abercorn was still coming forward to 'claim from government the first vacancy in the representative peerage and the first bishopric, for persons certainly not the most fit to be preferred to either situation'.[59]

Barons Court

A little over a year after succeeding his uncle, Abercorn began to plan a radical overhaul of Barons Court. Part of this seems to have been driven by necessity, though the desire to leave his own stamp on the house was undoubtedly a factor. In mid-January 1791 Abercorn wrote to George Steuart telling him that 'the house which you built a few years ago for my late uncle appears to be giving way in more places than one' and asking him to furnish John Soane with 'plans, elevations and documents upon the subject' so that the necessary reparations and alterations could be devised.[60] The Marquess had his own ideas on the changes to the house he wished to see implemented, but wanted his architect to view Barons Court for himself. Accordingly, in May of that year Soane travelled across to Ireland, enduring a thoroughly unpleasant crossing of the Irish Sea. Upon arriving he quickly set to work and the agent, James Hamilton junior, provided the Marquess with an account of Soane's imaginative recasting of the house:

> I have just returned from Barons Court where I went to meet Mr Soan[e], who arrived there last night. Before I left him he had nearly completed the plan for the intended additions and alterations at Barons Court, which seemed so wonderful that I cannot describe how I felt. The additions your Lordship spoke of when here, I was prepared for, but the alterations Mr Sloan [sic] proposes astonishes me not a little. He just reverses the house; what was the backside is to be the entrance and the front part the rear. The drawing room parlour and as far of the hall as to the pillars is to be thrown into one great gallery and the two walls that necessarily must come down, are to be supported by two pillars each ... The entrance is to be exactly in the centre of the colonnade, where the portico is to be removed.[61]

Hamilton's letter was hurriedly written on the night of Saturday, 14 May and the following day Soane made significant amendments to his initial scheme (none of which overturned any of the proposals outlined in the above extract), all of which the agent considered 'in every instance for the better':

> From the hall, you go directly through where the store is under the stairs to the billiard room, which will stand directly under the skylight and consequently be effectually lighted. The stairs are to be entirely removed and the back stairs made to answer in their room. There are to be four entrances to the great gallery, one as it stands at present from the library to the drawing room, another at the opposite end, where the false door to the parlour stood, and the other two are to be from the billiard room. It will be a most magnificent room; the only things I think to be feared would be lest the ceiling should appear too low for its prodigious length and whether the four pillars would be sufficient to support the two walls, which are principal ones.[62]

Determined not to endure another long sea journey, Soane set out for Donaghadee for the 'short sea' crossing, allowing him the opportunity to visit the Earl Bishop's houses at Downhill and Ballyscullion. Before leaving Barons Court he also left instructions about the required building materials and craftsmen. The Marquess was evidently pleased with Soane's proposals and preparatory work started soon afterwards. In September Soane sent his assistant Robert Woodgate over to Ireland with a team of craftsmen. It was under Woodgate's direction over the next four years that the work was completed.

The new plan and elevations are shown in Soane's own *Sketches in Architecture* (1793). As noted above, the principal change under Soane's direction was to reverse the house so that the north side now became its front. On this side of the house curving screen walls masked, among other rooms, schoolrooms and a doctor's surgery on the left, and a servants' hall and cook's room on the right. The top storey on Steuart's original entrance front – now the back of the house – was removed, and the design of the ground floor windows altered. By the end of January 1792 the dismantling of the original portico was underway and James Hamilton junior believed that it would make this side of the house have a substantially 'lighter and more cheerful appearance'. Internally, Soane created a gallery running the full width along the south side of Steuart's house. At 88 feet long it was the longest room in a private house in Ireland. Another innovation introduced by Soane was the removal of the main stairs and the creation of a round billiard room in the vacated space. Presumably this was where the billiard table ('12 by 6 feet inside the cushions') that Abercorn had ordered in December 1789 was placed.

The works had only just been completed when a disastrous fire caused enormous damage on 14 December 1796. The following day James Galbraith wrote to Abercorn with an account of what had occurred:

> It is with the deepest concern I sit down to address you a letter from this place, now almost a ruin. About 7 o'clock yesterday morning a fire broke out in one of the upper bed chambers in the centre building, the corner over the lake, which is supposed to have been occasioned by some coals falling out of the grate, all the rooms having had fires to keep them aired since the frost commenced. The flames had gained so much strength in the room before there was daylight to observe it that after daylight their progress was so rapid that the great pillars in the gallery fell and the dome of course fell in before ten [o'clock]. Most fortunately Mr Woodgate was at Strabane and came to the house with such expedition as to be on the spot as the flames were beginning to communicate to the wings but by his uncommon coolness and great exertions in getting the doors from the centre to the wings built up with immense quantities of wet sods the

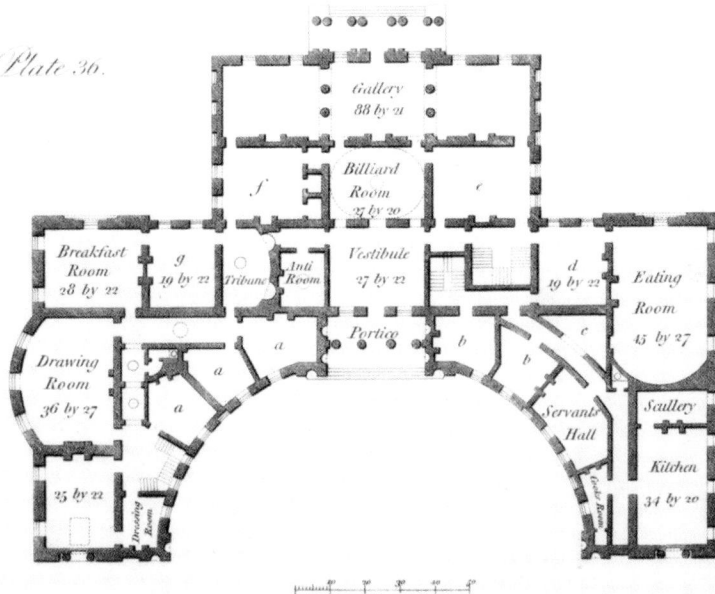

PLATE XXXVII.

Plan to Plate 36.

Gallery
88 by 21

Billiard
Room
27 by 20

Breakfast
Room
28 by 22

g
19 by 22

Tribune

Anti
Room

Vestibule
27 by 22

d
19 by 22

Eating
Room
45 by 27

Drawing
Room
36 by 27

Portico

Servants
Hall

Scullery

Kitchen
34 by 20

25 by 22

Dressing
Room

Published by J. & J. Taylor, High Holborn, London, Jan.ʳʸ 1ˢᵗ 1793.

Soane's elevation and ground plan of Barons Court. Published in Soane's *Sketches in architecture* of 1793, the text accompanying these drawings reads: 'Elevation of a Villa near Strabane in Ireland belonging to the Marquis of Abercorn. The house and offices were built for the late Marquis [Earl] by Mr Charles [George] Steuart The fronts have been considerably altered as well as the whole of the interior arrangement'; and 'Contains the plan of the principal floor with its improvements The portico in the front of the gallery formed a part of the original plan but has been taken away to make the centre part of the gallery more cheerful.'

innumerable hands were enabled to make their labours tell to the greatest advantage so that about 8 o'clock at night both wings were completely out of danger.[63]

It was thanks to Woodgate's quick thinking that the entire house was not razed, but the centre block had, with the exception of one cross wall and the stone staircase, been left a 'vacant square'. Due to the assistance of innumerable volunteers the contents of the house, with 'very few and inconsiderable exceptions', were saved, including the billiard table, the books, and the carpets, and thankfully no-one was injured.[64] Even with the unsettled state of the country, there was no doubting that the fire was purely accidental. James Hamilton junior suspected that it had been the result of a 'practice of putting dry turf under the grates at night, in order to insure kindling in the morning' which in one room had spread beyond the fireplace. Nonetheless, rumours that the fire had been as a result of an arson attack were 'infamously and maliciously reported'.

Abercorn was philosophical about the incident, writing to John Stewart, in response to one of the many letters reporting the fire:

> The report was by no means exaggerated, as letters from the spot accompanying yours yesterday proved. But it requires no great strength of mind in one who has always been aware that he is to have his share of the rubs and accidents of life, as well as others, to submit without murmuring to a piece of bad luck which he could neither foresee nor prevent, and which is unattended with any loss of character, friends or fortune.[65]

Coloured drawing of Barons Court prepared for an exhibition at the Royal Academy, 1793. This drawing is more elaborate than the published elevation for it shows statues in niches and standing figures on the roof.
COURTESY OF THE TRUSTEES OF SIR JOHN SOANE'S MUSEUM

·BARONSCOVRT·
·A·SEAT·OF·THE·MARQVISS·OF·ABERCORN·

There was further damage to the house the following February when, as a result of strong winds, 'a great part of the front of that part of the house that was burnt fell in'. Nearly a year and a half was to pass before any works were carried out to the house. In July 1798 Woodgate began alterations to the structure; these seem to have been to the part of the house unaffected by the fire. In August 1800 Lord Cornwallis stayed at Barons Court for several days and slept in Abercorn's bedroom, the Marquess being absent from the house. In 1803, creepers were planted against the walls of the burnt-out part of the house, but otherwise it remained untouched for several more years.

In May 1808 his agent John James Burgoyne urged Abercorn to authorise some remedial work to the burnt-out portion. He was particularly concerned that the arches of the cellars in the damaged part, having been exposed to the elements for so long, were about to collapse. Burgoyne investigated what was required for both repairs and restorative work, and by the autumn an estimate of £2,461 had been received from a mason named Turner for 'finishing the gallery and passage hall', repairs to the arches being additional to this. Burgoyne had also attended an auction and purchased 42 tons of timber. The Marquess was somewhat more cautious, writing to Burgoyne in December of that year:

> We must come to a determination upon the subject of building. I certainly will not go on with the house while I am at Barons Court, if I cannot inhabit it till June twelvemonth. In that case, what must be considered and ascertained is, for what sum, and by what time, I can just build up and cover in just enough to prevent injury by weather, and then remove rubbish, and defer doing anything whatever to the inside for a year or two. If, with the timber we have, this can be done under £1,000, I think we may do it. If not, we may as well sell our timber to advantage, and defer the whole business. Get an accurate estimate from Turner, and till we can determine, do not let the timber get further then Strabane.[66]

Work progressed slowly, not a little due to Turner's addiction to alcohol. On one occasion he was so drunk that the agent believed 'he was incapable of understanding any directions about the building'. In August 1810 he and Burgoyne had a long conversation about the building work and the former said that if the structure were to be ready for its roof by November he required '12 stone cutters, 13 masons, 6 sawyers and 24 labourers'. Burgoyne was anxious to have the roof erected before the winter set in and so provided him with this assistance. The agent was also confident that, notwithstanding the mason's personal problems, 'the whole building will be perfectly strong and well bound together'.[67]

By the end of February 1811 the roof had been completed and Burgoyne had issued instructions for completing the gallery and billiard room. Turner

BARONSCOURT.

NORTH or ENTRANCE

FRONT

Two drawings by the architect William Farrell of Barons Court as it looked in 1835. These show the house as it had been reconstructed by the 1st Marquess in the years after the disastrous fire of 1796.

also carried out works to the entrance to the house and these were to Burgoyne's satisfaction, for in April of that year he wrote to Abercorn, 'The front of the new building is very beautiful'.[68] The Marquess himself returned to Barons Court shortly afterwards and was able to see for himself the works that had been carried out, though his thoughts on them have not survived. A glimpse of life in the restored Barons Court is provided in a letter to his son-in-law, Lord Aberdeen, written on Christmas Eve 1813: 'I am now sitting quite established in my new library, having first indulged Lady A. in her taste of papering, painting and gilding, and since broken her heart by putting none but old chairs, tables and desks in it.'[69]

Bentley Priory

Abercorn's home for most of his adult life was Bentley Priory, which he purchased in 1788. A medieval monastery had stood on or near the site of the later mansion. The monastery having been dissolved at the time of the Henrician Reformation, the property came into lay possession. The owner previous to Abercorn, James Duberly, bought Bentley Priory c. 1776 and rebuilt the house, removing in the process a remaining vestige of the medieval structure.[70] In 1797, Abercorn described it as 'a large house, [run] at great

BARONSCOURT.

SOUTH FRONT

expense, without what deserves the name of property around it'. Even so, the adjoining estate was probably the largest property in England that the family ever owned, certainly since the 5th Earl had sold the estate he possessed through his wife in Oxfordshire.

The house impressed visitors with its scale and grandeur. In 1805, it was described as 'this magnificent chateau, which has been denominated the Court of Pleasure'. Another account from the following year reported that the Priory contained no fewer than 11 reception rooms and 58 bedrooms. The novelist Lady Morgan wrote:

> No words can give an idea of the extent or splendour of this princely palace. The house is not a house at all, for it looks like a little town, which you will believe when I tell you that 120 persons slept under the roof during the Christmas holidays, without including the underservants, and that the Marquis and Lord Hamilton have between them nine apartments *en suite* and Lady Abercorn four. The Queen's Chamberlain told me indeed that there is nothing like the whole establishment in England and perhaps – for a subject – in Europe.[71]

In 1816, the interior of the house was described as comprising 'a suite of very spacious apartments', but its principal interest lay in the works of art it contained. These included 'several antique busts, of great beauty and value; and a tasteful collection of pictures by the old masters, together with some fine portraits'. The paintings included a portrait of Charles I by Van Dyck, two by Kneller of the 6th Earl and his father, and a portrait of the 8th Earl by Gainsborough. There was also a painting of the Marquess's father by Sir Joshua Reynolds as well as a full-length portrait of the Marquess himself by Sir Thomas Lawrence. Of some interest were the works of the renowned Italian artist Paolo Panini.[72] Lawrence was a long-time friend of Abercorn and was responsible for at least five portraits of the Marquess. Abercorn does not appear, however, to have been the most patient of sitters. In 1813, he complained to Lord Aberdeen, 'I am posing for my picture more to Lawrence's pleasure than mine. The contest between garter robes and everyday coat seems decided in favour of Black and Blue.'[73] The grounds of the house also provided opportunities for amusement, while the Serpentine Lake was used for rowing and fishing. Abercorn entertained regally at Bentley Priory and accounts of

This portrait of the Marquess of Abercorn by Lawrence dominates one end of the present family room at Barons Court.

parties thrown by the Marquess occupied many column inches in the newspapers and magazines of the day. According to one account from 1805, following breakfast, guests would be given four opportunities to consume lunch, with dinner served at 8 o'clock and supper at midnight. The evening entertainments could include a ball, concert or card party. The Marquess' daughters took their turns at entertaining guests by playing the organ, harp or piano.

Those entertained at The Priory included major politicians, artists, actors, and members of the Royal Family. Abercorn was particularly fond of amateur theatricals, and these were part of many an evening's entertainment at Bentley Priory. Discussions and debate over a wide range of subjects also took place, and Sir Walter Scott, who called the Priory 'the resort of the most distinguished part of the fashionable world', wrote that evenings there 'resemble a Greek symposium for learning and literature'. Scott also acknowledged, contrary to other accounts, the welcome offered to guests by their host: 'the stateliness of which the late Marquis of Abercorn was accused, drew no barrier between the Marquis of Abercorn and those who shared his hospitality'.

Among the guests in the winter of 1800–01 were Sir William and Lady Hamilton. Sir William, who had recently retired from his longstanding position as the British ambassador to the court of Naples, was related to the Marquess – he was a grandson of the 6th Earl of Abercorn – and the two were close friends. It is doubtful, therefore, if Abercorn was particularly amused by the following letter written from Naples by an M. O'Byrne in December 1789:

There is a Sir W. H[amilton] here that says he is your relation, which I don't believe, though I won't contradict it. I called him Sir W. Miserable. He lives all the winter in the country, to keep out of our way, and he has taken a whore to exempt him from receiving the English ladies who are here in the summer.[74]

When in 1791 Sir William married Emma Hart, much to the annoyance of his immediate family, Abercorn was present at the ceremony and in fact gave the bride away. After Sir William's sister, the Dowager Lady Warwick, learned of the marriage and the role that Abercorn was to play, she is reputed to have said that 'it was a disgrace to the family, but if done by any of them

This painting by Lawrence shows the novelist Lady Charlotte Bury, a distant relative of the Hamiltons. The painting was once in the dining room at The Priory. It is now in the entrance hall at Barons Court.

the deed was fitted to the one who had the blot in his escutcheon and a crack in his skull'. Despite the reservations expressed about the suitability of Sir William's bride, Abercorn took a liking to Emma and commissioned Thomas Lawrence to produce a portrait of her. The Marquess was one of Lawrence's early patrons, and the painter was later to write that Abercorn had been 'particularly kind to me in real services and very gratifying distinctions'. The connoisseur and collector, Richard Payne Knight, wrote to Sir William in October 1791 that it would 'be one of the finest portraits ever painted'. The portrait shows Emma Hamilton as La Penserosa and caused much excitement when it was exhibited at the Royal Academy the following year.[75]

Sir William was a noted antiquarian and assisted the Marquess in securing works of art from Italy. For instance, in December 1791, on Abercorn's behalf, Sir William bought a painting by Parmigiano at a cost of £1,500 (shipping and insurance cost a further £90).[76] His expenditure on this and other paintings, coupled with his building projects at this time, prompted him to jokingly ask Thomas Knox, 'Does not this … make it appear as if the fool and his money were parting rather too quick?'[77]

While this study has attempted to avoid reducing Abercorn to a caricature, there is no doubting that his personal foibles fascinated contemporaries and filled the pages of the society magazines of the day and in the decades after his death. One of the stories related about him concerned his fixation with punctuality, and related to a dinner to which the Marquess had invited a large number of guests and which was to start promptly at 5pm. The Percy brothers take up the story:

Lady Emma Hamilton, the wife of Abercorn's kinsman, Sir William Hamilton.

> On that hour arriving, his lordship found himself attended by a single gentleman; he, however, sat down to dinner, and partook of the first course. About 6 his visitors began to drop in; his lordship was at dinner. No apology was made; they seated themselves in awkward confusion, looked at their watches, and took dinner. The still more polite part of the assembly arrived about seven, and instead of dinner, they were served with coffee![78]

Presumably his guests grasped the message for their next dinner invitation. His impatience is also shown in the stories that are told of him curtailing lengthy sermons in Stanmore church with a dismissive wave of his hand to bring the discourse to a summary conclusion.[79]

His London house was in Grosvenor Square. The *Morning Post* of 8 March 1800 provides a description of its layout and furnishings:

> His Lordship's house is spacious extending many paces into Brook Street, the staircase is adorned with many noble paintings by Rubens and Van Dyke; the two drawing-rooms, the ball room, etc. have recently been ornamented with a beautiful yellow satin paper, and in lieu of a paper border, gold is substituted. The apartments are well illuminated by a number of chandeliers and cut glass lustres. The dining-room engrossed the most attention, and indeed claimed the admiration of all the company, from the extreme beauty and novelty of the design; it was hung with a paper executed under the Marquess' own direction. The subject is the hop-grounds on his estate when in their full growth and luxuriance. The appearance, on entering the room, has all the rich and strong colouring of nature.

Lady Harriet Hamilton

Lady Harriet Hamilton. On the eve of her wedding to the Marquess of Waterford, Harriet died after a short illness on 30 April 1803. 'Possessed of every requisite to render her beloved by the noble lord to whom she was betrothed; her person was beautiful, but her mental qualifications were even superior; endowed with a good understanding, she had devoted her time to continued acts of benevolence' (*The Annual Register*, 1803, p. 506).

Contemporary accounts give the impression of an aristocratic family enjoying life to the full, and in the first few years of the nineteenth century this was undoubtedly true. Abercorn comes across as a devoted family man. In 1803, Thomas Lawrence wrote of him, 'Whatever character of pride the world may have given to Lord Abercorn, he is just as pleasant and kind and gentle with his family and friends as a man may be.'[80] In addition, the Marquess' third wife Lady Anne enjoyed a good relationship with her stepdaughters. However, there was also much sadness, as all five of his children by his first wife predeceased him. The first to die was Harriet, his eldest daughter, who passed away at Easter 1803, shortly before her intended marriage to the Marquess of Waterford. She was 19. The cause of her death was the same illness that brought her mother's life to a premature end – consumption. However, this could not be accepted by Abercorn. It was, after all, a disease of the lower classes, and any notion that the daughter of a marquess had succumbed to it was to be dispelled. Abercorn summoned five

Lord Claud Hamilton

eminent doctors and surgeons and instructed them to compose and sign a letter to be sent to the *Morning Post* disclaiming the cause of Harriet's death as it was reported in the press.

Lord Claud Hamilton, the Marquess' second son, also suffered from respiratory problems that eventually led to his death. From late December 1807 there were a number of reports in the press about him being ill, and at the end of January following it was announced that he had 'left town yesterday for the Brazils. His Lordship's health is such as to require immediate change of climate.' He sailed on the *Eclipse* accompanied by Dr Pemberton and a surgeon named de Bruyn. Towards the end of the year the sad news reached The Priory that he had died at Madeira. 'Our poor departed friend', wrote Scott, 'was the delight of all who knew him. Several of his fellow students were in Edinburgh last winter and used to talk of him in terms which I now recollect with fruitless sorrow.' A story related to Mary Baillie Hamilton by Admiral Baillie Hamilton was that while at Oxford Lord Claud was so determined to prove wrong those of his friends who, because of his slender physique, thought him incapable of bearing pain that he held his finger over a lighted candle until it was burnt to the bone.

In 1812, the Marquess' second daughter, Lady Catherine, also died of consumption. She had been married in 1805 to George, 4th Earl of Aberdeen. Two years later in 1814 the final two children of his marriage to Catherine Copley, Lady Maria and Viscount Hamilton, succumbed to the disease. The death of his heir and only surviving son was a devastating blow to Abercorn. Lord Hamilton had stood down as MP of Liskeard in 1812, the state of his health being the major factor. Abercorn's hopes of building a powerful political faction through his sons had been ended. His only surviving daughter, Frances, the lone child of his marriage to Lady Cecil Hamilton, married the son and

Lady Catherine Hamilton

James, Viscount Hamilton, depicted as an angel by Thomas Lawrence.
In 1808, Spencer Perceval, then Chancellor of the Exchequer, described him to George III as a 'young man of very great ability'.

Either Lady Maria Hamilton, who died unmarried in 1814, or Lady Catherine Hamilton, who married the 4th Earl of Aberdeen, and died in 1812.

heir of the 3rd Earl of Wicklow in 1816. Originally her marriage portion amounted to £10,000, but this was increased to £15,000 with the additional £5,000 to be paid at the Marquess's death.[81]

Death and burial

In 1817, Abercorn's own health began to fail, and it had deteriorated significantly by November of that year, when news began to filter through that all was not well with the marquess. One news report put it down to the 'effects of a severe cold', but in reality his illness was much more serious than this. Christmas was celebrated at Bentley Priory in the usual fashion, but Abercorn was by now visibly worsening. Thomas Lawrence wrote: 'I looked for Lord Abercorn in his arm chair and could not see him, he was so shrunk'. The Marquess knew himself that the end was near, admitting to his wife shortly before he died, 'You think I am quite well, but I tell you I am not – I am dying.' The 1st Marquess of Abercorn passed away on 27 January 1818, still only 61. The *Morning Post* carried the following announcement:

> At Bentley Priory, Stanmore, on Tuesday last, died John James Hamilton, the Most Noble, the Marquis of Abercorn, Knight of the Garter. It is some weeks since we noticed in our Paper the lamented indisposition of this highly respected and benevolent peer. So anxious was his Lordship to prevent the anxieties of his friends, that he forbade his domestics ever alluding to his illness in the slightest way. To prevent the parade of physicians attending him at his country seat, he constantly came to town, to meet them in Stratford-Place three times a week. The fatal complaint existed in the stomach, said to be attended by an enlargement of the liver. Appearances during the previous week became still more alarming. Dr Pemberton and other members of the Faculty were then summoned to attend their patient at the Priory. The Noble Lord suffered much previous to his demise … By the death of this Nobleman, the poor have sustained an incalculable loss.

His funeral took place over a week later at Stanmore. Those in attendance included his sons-in-law, the Earl of Aberdeen and Lord Clonmore, the bishop of London, Sir George Hill and Major Humphreys. The *Gentleman's*

Magazine recorded: 'An immense concourse of persons of the neighbourhood paid their respectful attendance on the occasion; among whom were considerable numbers of the labouring class, who for many years had owed their chief support to the benevolence of the Marquis.' His third wife survived him by nine years, dying at Naples on 8 May 1827; she was brought back to Stanmore for burial on 14 August following.

The final summing up of this extraordinary man's life may be left to his friend Sir Walter Scott:

> Those who saw him at a distance accused him of pride and haughtiness. That he had a sufficient feeling of the dignity of his situation and maintained it with perhaps an unusual degree of state and expense may readily be granted. But that expense, however large, was fully supported by an ample fortune wisely administered and in the management of which the interests of the tenant were always considered as well as those of the landlord. He racked no rents to maintain the expenses of his establishment nor did he diminish his charities which were in many cases princely for the sake of the outward state, the maintenance of which he thought not unjustly a duty incumbent on his situation.[82]

The 1st Duke as a young man. 'Such a noble handsome-looking man', observed Queen Victoria, while for G. W. E. Russell he was 'one of the handsomest men of his generation'.

7

James Hamilton, 1st Duke of Abercorn
'Old Splendid'

'Old Splendid', as he was known, took the family to new heights. He succeeded where his grandfather had failed in that he was both appointed lord lieutenant of Ireland and elevated to a dukedom. He also re-established an intimacy between the Hamiltons and the Royal Family that had not existed since the late seventeenth century. Yet what is remarkable about the 1st Duke is that for the first 55 years of his life he had a relatively low political profile, certainly in comparison with the heights he was to reach in the second half of the 1860s. By the end of his long life, however, he had become a highly respected figure within the Irish establishment. He was beloved by his family and held in high regard by his tenants. Even today, his descendants refer to him as 'Daddy Duke'.

Early life

James Hamilton, the future 1st Duke of Abercorn, was born on 21 January 1811 at Seamore Place, Mayfair, London, the son of James, Viscount

Hamilton, and Harriet, daughter of the Hon. John Douglas, son of the 14th Earl of Morton. Viscount Hamilton had been central to his father's political ambitions, but his parliamentary career was cut short by ill-health. In reply to an offer from his relative Lord Eliot, in September 1812, to once again return Hamilton for the Cornish borough of Liskeard, the 1st Marquess was forced to accept that his son was no longer capable of discharging the responsibilities of an MP. Replying to Eliot, he wrote:

> When you brought Lord Hamilton into Parliament, I was the father of two sons who seemed to promise everything that a father could wish. Their abilities, dispositions and acquirements must have ensured advantage to their country and distinction to their family and themselves. The loss of one, and the long-continued situation of the other on the brink of the grave, have extinguished all my worldly prospects and ambition, and I have only to feel and say, '*occidit, occidit, spes omnis et fortuna nostri nominis*'! I have long thought it unfair, both towards you and towards the Government which we support, that in such trying times, a seat should be occupied by one who, however zealous, has been utterly incapable of assisting his friends with a single vote. The last vote that he gave (in support of the Duke of York), I believe cost him very dear. With these sentiments, my answer to your most kind and friendly offer would be obvious. But as I could not bear to give an answer on such grounds as mine without my son's knowledge, consideration and concurrence, the hour, which has elapsed, has been passed in conversation with him upon the subject. He entirely concurs in my sentiments and feelings. He feels your kindness as he ought, but he will not avail himself of it unfairly. He is convinced that it must be long before he could venture upon the fatigue and danger of hot and late Houses, and he only hopes that returning health may one day enable him to avail himself of your kindness upon some future occasion.[1]

Harriet, Viscountess Hamilton. After Lord Hamilton's death, she married the 4th Earl of Aberdeen.

Viscount Hamilton lived for only a little over a year and a half after this, dying in Mayfair in May 1814. He left three young children: James, Harriet and Claud.

James was only three when his father died and only seven when his grandfather passed away and he succeeded to the marquessate. His guardian was the 4th Earl of Aberdeen, who had married his widowed mother in July 1815 and with whom he enjoyed a close relationship until Aberdeen's death in 1860. Abercorn's earliest surviving letter is one written to his grandfather, the 1st Marquess, in December 1817, when he would have been a few weeks short of his seventh birthday. In large, neat handwriting he begins, 'My dear

Grandpapa, I hope you will not be displeased if I write to you' and closes with 'Your affectionate grandson, Hamilton'.[2] When he began his schooling at Harrow he would walk the six miles there and back from The Priory 'attired in tight green trousers with brass chains under his shoes', though later he and his brother Claud stayed at the house next to 'the Park' at Harrow.[3] It was said of him that while he was a pupil there he was a 'conspicuous dandy' and someone with 'excellent abilities'.[4]

One of Abercorn's passions was cricket. He played it as a youth at Harrow and was to continue playing the game until he was well into his 60s. The *Times* of 5 September 1828 carried a report of a match that had been organised by the young Marquess at Bentley Priory a few days previously. He had formed a team comprising himself, his brother Claud, several of his aristocratic friends who were visiting with him, and six of his menservants. The opposition was made up of the most talented cricketers among the tradesmen of the nearby towns of Stanmore and Edgeware; it was led by a butcher from Edgeware, locally considered to be a 'crack cricketer'. On the day of the match the grounds of Bentley Priory had been opened to all-comers, who were liberally supplied with food and drink throughout the day. The game began at noon, but to much disappointment the Marquess was bowled out early on. The contest continued into the early evening, to the consternation of those who were kept waiting for dinner in The Priory. Eventually the light faded to the extent that play was no longer possible and the match had to be abandoned as a draw.

Following in the family tradition, the Marquess continued his education at Christ Church, Oxford, matriculating on 2 July 1829. Shortly after he began his studies there, Lord Aberdeen wrote to him with fatherly advice. He hoped that when the 'first novelty of your College life is passed by you will apply yourself more seriously to the purpose for which you are [at] Oxford'. This was 'not to ride over the country and give dinners', but of course to gain a degree. He had, his stepfather pointed out, the next 50 years to enjoy life, 'so pray be wise and do not follow frivolous examples'. In Aberdeen's view 'the set of noblemen at Oxford now are very second rate as to solidity and talents'. Abercorn was encouraged to 'stand forward as an exception and a sufficiently brilliant example to invite others to follow your course'.[5]

Coming of age and early political activity

On 21 January 1832 the Marquess officially reached adulthood. A month later, at the King's first Levee Court of the season, held on 22 February, he was presented to William IV by Lord Aberdeen.[6] Having reached majority, Abercorn took his seat in the House of Lords, where one of his earliest acts was to vote against the Reform Bill. He did not, however, play an active part in parliament in the 1830s and it was to be 1842 before he made his maiden speech, when he moved the address to the Queen. However, now that he was officially an adult, Abercorn began to take a much more active role in social occasions in his own right. In March 1833, for example, he chaired the 50th anniversary celebration of the Benevolent Society of St Patrick. It was the first time that the Marquess had attended one of the meetings of the Society and he subscribed £105, matching that of the King and superseding everyone else.[7] The following year he was appointed a governor of Harrow, a position he held until his death.

The first major political demonstration in which Abercorn played a leading role was a meeting held in Dungannon on 19 December 1834. This was the 'great Tory demonstration' attended by the gentry and freeholders of County Tyrone in their thousands. This gathering took place against a backdrop of intense political excitement following the dismissal of the Whig administration by William IV and the recall to office of Wellington and Peel. In what was a remarkable spectacle, the Marquess and his brother Claud rode to Dungannon with 1,100 of their tenants marching behind them. Abercorn spoke at the meeting and impressed those in attendance with what he had to say.

Because he had succeeded to the marquessate as a child, Abercorn never had an opportunity to serve as an MP – unlike, for example, his father and grandfather. On the other hand, it was widely anticipated that his brother Claud would pursue a career in the Commons, most probably as one of the two MPs representing County Tyrone. This was apparent not just to those within the family circle, but to other landowners with strong interests in the parliamentary representation of the county. These included the Earl of Belmore, one of the principal political brokers in Tyrone, who, in November 1829, wrote from Jamaica, where he was governor, to the Duke of Wellington on the likelihood of Lord Claud's candidature for Tyrone materialising at some point in the near future and the ramifications of this.[8] The 1835 general election provided the first opportunity for Lord Claud to stand as an MP. His campaign was based around defending the place of the Bible in the National Education system and protecting the Orange Order at a time when the institution was under threat of prorogation. He secured 1,057 votes, well ahead of Belmore's brother, Henry Lowry-Corry (627), and the Earl of Caledon's son, Lord Alexander (510). Electioneering was expensive and on 19 January 1835, when it was clear who the victors would be, one observer wrote to J. G. Beresford, the archbishop of Armagh, 'I fear the two lords [Abercorn and Belmore] have fooled away a large sum of money.'[9]

Though he did not actively engage in politics at a national level in this period, Abercorn continued to make occasional political interventions in the local arena. In early January 1837, for example, the Marquess presided over a meeting, which was held in the courthouse in Omagh, to establish a County Conservative Association.[10] In his speech on this occasion Abercorn robustly defended the House of Lords and its Conservative character. On reading a report of this meeting, his stepfather wrote to congratulate the young Marquess on his performance, adding, 'not that I care a straw about a Conservative meeting ... but the manner in which you appear to have conducted your part of the business was excellent'. Aberdeen went on to encourage Abercorn to think seriously about politics and his involvement in it, for he felt it would result in 'much more interest than in the pursuits with which you have been chiefly occupied'.[11] Abercorn's participation in such events raised his profile both locally and nationally, gaining him the praise of his supporters and opprobrium of his political enemies. He was verbally attacked by Daniel O'Connell, who is supposed to have said of him, 'I tell him that as a man, he is contemptible, as a human being he is ludicrous; and as a peer he derives his title and his estates from the commission of the foulest crimes that can by possibility disgrace human nature.'[12]

Lord Claud's initial foray into parliamentary politics was not a success. By the time of the 1837 general election he had made himself deeply unpopular with the Tyrone electorate and it seemed unlikely that he would be re-elected. Despite this, he was initially determined to stand and on 15 July issued a lengthy statement setting out his views on a number of issues, most of them in some way connected to religion and the Church. He strongly defended the position of the Church of Ireland, making clear his opposition to any attempt to interfere with its landed endowment 'and to break down the power of an institution with which the best interests of society are interwoven'. He also emphatically opposed the annual grant to Maynooth College, claiming that in its current set-up it was 'the nursery of political incendiaries, not of pastors devoted to the pure and peaceful preaching of the Gospel'. A further source of concern for him was the National Education system, which he regarded as 'totally repugnant' and 'a vitiated medium of conveying instruction to the poor'.[13] Upon learning that Lord Claud was intending to stand, the Earl of Caledon, whose son, the defeated candidate in the 1835 election, was hoping to replace him as MP, wrote to Belmore, 'the only motive I can attribute this conduct to, is his desire to put the other candidates to trouble and expense'.[14] In the end, with his support collapsing, Lord Claud withdrew from the contest and Lord Alexander was returned in his stead.

His absence from the Commons was to be brief, however, for with the death of the Earl of Caledon in April 1839, and the elevation of his son to the title, it was necessary to call a by-election in Tyrone. This provided Lord Claud with an opportunity to return to parliament, and Abercorn immediately began to canvass support for his brother's candidature.[15] The

The 6th Duke of Bedford

other candidates were Major Humphreys, Abercorn's agent, who apparently stood so that his second votes could go to Lord Claud, and James Alexander Boyle of Drumquin. Boyle declared himself a liberal and in favour of the political independence of Tyrone from Conservative landlord control, but managed to secure a solitary vote. A rumour that a son of Sir James Stronge would stand with the support of Lord Belmore did not come to pass. Lord Claud won comfortably, therefore, and so began an uninterrupted period of over 30 years in the Commons.

Marriage and family

On 25 October 1832, at Fochabers Episcopal Church, Elgin, the Marquess of Abercorn married Lady Louisa Jane Russell, daughter of the 6th Duke of Bedford. It was said that they had first met at a children's party given by the Prince Regent at Carlton House when they were, respectively, seven and six years old. When courtship began is not known, but we do have an undated letter in which Abercorn reveals his feelings for Louisa to his prospective mother-in-law, the Duchess of Bedford, telling her, 'I like Ly L. more than any other girl.'[16] This union brought Abercorn into close contact with one of the leading families in England, and one at the heart of parliamentary politics. It did not, however, change his own political outlook for while the Bedfords were Whigs, the Marquess remained a lifelong Tory.

The Abercorns had a large family – seven sons and seven daughters. The youngest child was born when the Marchioness was 46; in fact, she bore three children after the age of 40. All of Abercorn's daughters reached adulthood and all married into the upper ranks of the aristocracy.[17] Two of the sons died before they reached majority. Cosmo died on the same day he was born, 16 April 1853; Ronald died at the age of 18 on 6 November 1867 at Bangor in north Wales. His death was a source of great sadness for the family.

The early years of their marriage were spent at The Priory, and it was possibly to nearby Stanmore that their son Lord Frederic was referring when he wrote that his mother, from the start of her married life, made a practice of '"visiting" in the village twice a week', looking out

Georgiana, Duchess of Bedford

131

The Marchioness of Abercorn by Landseer. 'My mother's character,' wrote Lord Frederic, 'was a blend of extreme simplicity and great dignity, with a limitless gift of sympathy for others. … throughout her life, she succeeded in winning the deep love of all those who were brought into constant contact with her.'

for the needs of its inhabitants. According to Frederic, she concocted what could be described as a tonic for the local people:

> With the help of her maid, my mother used to compound a cordial, bottles of which she distributed amongst the cottagers, a cordial which gained an immense local reputation. The ingredients of this panacea were one part of strong iron-water to five parts of old whisky, to which sal-volatile, red lavender, cardamoms, ginger and other warming drugs were added. "Her Grace's bottle," as it was invariably termed, achieved astonishing popularity, and the most marvellous cures were ascribed to it. I have sometimes wondered whether its vogue would have been as great had the whisky been eliminated from its composition.[18]

The Priory was not, however, to remain their English home. According to the Marquess' youngest son, Lord Ernest, its convenience to London placed it within easy reach of his father's many friends, who found the house 'so pleasant to stay in, and so difficult to say goodbye to' that for reasons of 'self-preservation' the Marquess was forced to give it up and find a home elsewhere.[19] He did not sell it immediately, but rather let it to the Dowager Queen Adelaide, the widow of William IV. After leaving The Priory, the family led something of a nomadic life, moving from country house to

Two of the daughters of the 1st Duke – Beatrix (in the cot) and Harriet. This painting by Landseer was exhibited at the Royal Academy in 1836 and was afterwards engraved.

country house, but never settling down permanently in any of them. For a time they lived at Dale Park, a property near the south coast of England, about which more will be said presently. They also spent time abroad, sojourning in Italy for several months in 1853.[20] In the late 1850s the family was in residence at Brocket Hall, a property rented from Lord Palmerston. In 1863, the Abercorns moved to Beaudesert Park, a house of Lord Anglesey's. By this time, the London residence of the family was Chesterfield House. Lord Ernest remembered a high degree of formality about the dinner parties hosted there – 'footmen were dressed up in gorgeous pink uniforms with silver epaulettes, heavy silver aiguillettes, white stockings and powdered hair'. The younger Abercorns would watch furtively from behind the banisters on the large marble staircase as the dinner guests arrived, but none excited their attention as much as the footmen did.[21]

In contemporary accounts of him, Abercorn never comes across as anything other than the devoted family man, beloved by his wife and children. It is somewhat surprising, therefore, to find among the family papers an anonymous letter of 1862 addressed to the 'Marcus of Abrecawn' warning him against going about the country 'looking and winking at our sisthers and our swatehearts'. The writer warned him that if he continued to act in this way, he would 'not be long in the land of the living'. The letter is appropriately illustrated with sketches of a skull and crossbones, coffin and daggers.[22] It is doubtful if it is a genuine attack on Abercorn's alleged philandering. The style and especially the spelling seem a little too fake and it is more likely that the letter was intended as a joke (the very fact that it was kept rather than being discarded lends support to this supposition), though its author remains a mystery.

It was said of the Marchioness that she possessed a 'strong strain of Evangelical religion, which had reached her in early life indirectly from Charles Simeon'.[23] This remained with her for the rest of her life. She was later described as having been 'curiously aloof from the excitements, the ostentation, and the moral pliability of what was then called the "Beau Monde"'.[24] The Marquess too was a man of religious piety. Every morning and every Sunday evening he read family prayers. Lord Frederic remembered Sunday being strictly observed as a day of rest when he and his siblings were growing up.[25] Their toys and books were packed away on a Saturday night and only a few select volumes were permitted to be read on the Sabbath. Sporting activities were banned, and no-one dared suggest that cards be played. In 1875, Frederic spent some time in Brunswick and on one occasion attended an opera performance on a Sunday. His mother was deeply concerned at this, and wrote to her husband asking him to give Frederic some advice on the matter. 'These Germans are rationalists', she wrote, 'and our boy will never prosper if he forgets God.'[26] The couple did not dine out on a Sunday, nor did they invite people to dinner so as to give those in their employment a day of rest. When in London, the Abercorns attended the Scottish Presbyterian Church in Crown Court, close to Drury Lane Theatre, where the minister, Dr Cumming, enjoyed a good reputation with his congregation. The pew in front belonged to Lord Aberdeen and was regularly occupied by his brother, Admiral Gordon.[27]

The Duchess of Abercorn portrayed as a cottage girl by Landseer, *c.* 1835.

The reconstruction of Barons Court

Barons Court had hardly been used in the 1820s and upon reaching majority the Marquess gave little indication that he was prepared to make it his permanent home, preferring to spend most of his time at The Priory. He did, however, have grand ideas for the house and demesne and his intentions were well known. In his statistical account of the parish of Ardstraw, drafted in February 1834, Lieutenant Lancey wrote in reference to Barons Court, 'Considerable alterations and improvements are about to be made to it immediately.'[28] Lancey was somewhat premature in his timescale, but Abercorn was committed to making his own mark on his Irish home and

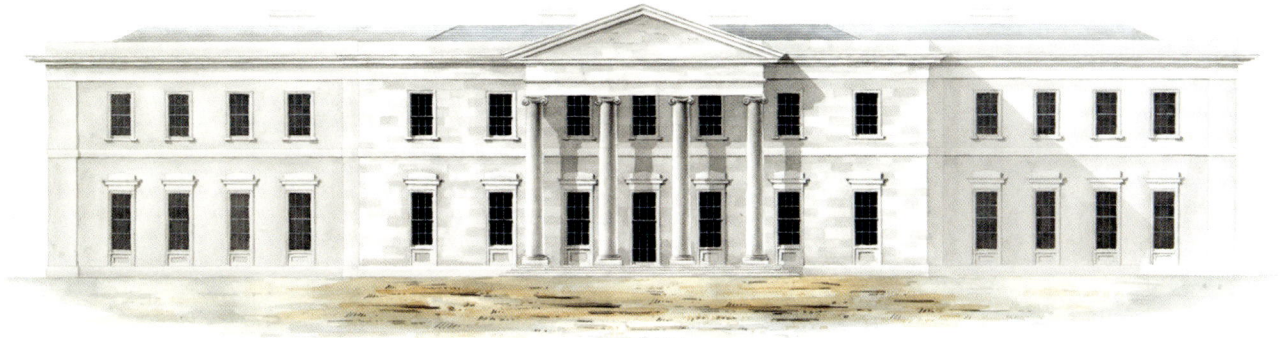

Drawings by William Farrell of his proposed modifications to Barons Court.

before the end of that year would purchase a copy of J. C. Loudon's *Architecture*, possibly to glean helpful ideas. In 1835, the architect William Farrell, who worked on a number of important buildings in the north-west of Ireland, among them Colebrooke in County Fermanagh, prepared plans for enlarging Barons Court, though his proposals went no further than the drawing board.

The man whom Abercorn eventually commissioned to redesign Barons Court was the celebrated architect William Vitruvius Morrison, who, in April 1835, was paid 10 guineas by the Marquess for 'inspecting the House'. In the previous decade Morrison and his father Richard had established a successful architectural practice. Their principal achievements were the houses at Killruddery, County Wicklow, and Ballyfin, County Laois. The designs for Barons Court having been accepted, the Dublin contractor James Pettigrew was employed to oversee the building work. His tender of £19,728 14s 9d. had been accepted, but through various changes being made to the original plans, the final cost exceeded this. Pettigrew approached his task with energy and drive. He opened 25 quarries either on the estate or in its vicinity looking for suitable building stone, and in the process provided employment to local people, but failing to find appropriate local stone was forced to look to Scotland for it.

William Vitruvius Morrison and Pettigrew did not have a good working relationship and quarrelled on a number of points. The latter was critical of the architect for adding a number of extras for which he was never paid. He

135

Proposed elevation of Barons Court by William Vitruvius Morrison.

also poured scorn on Morrison for 'want of foresight in making the Portico higher than the polygonal building' which necessitated making 'two large panels to show the effect of raising the parapet.' Morrison, whose health had been deteriorating for a number of years, did not live to see the building finished, dying in 1838, and it was his father Richard who saw it through to completion. Pettigrew also fell out with Morrison senior, calling him 'that old villain' after the contractor was asked to carry out work not in the original contract. If the architects and contractor were frequently at loggerheads, the same can be said about the relationship between Pettigrew and the agent, Major Humphreys. Eventually in the spring of 1839, with the work well advanced, their disagreements resulted in Pettigrew and his men being ordered to leave the site. At this time Pettigrew was employing 37 tradesmen and 13 labourers and had over the previous two years expended over £4,603 on wages. It would be an understatement to say that Pettigrew felt aggrieved at his treatment. Years later he was to write to Abercorn that 'in the building annals … a contractor was never worse used'. Various attempts to seek redress for what had happened to him, which continued for nearly 40 years, were unsuccessful. By the time that he ceased to be involved

A view of the north front of Barons Court showing the full extent of the Morrisons' changes on this side of the house.

The north front today

at Barons Court the work was nearing completion, and it was finished
shortly after this.[29]

It was as a result of this remodelling that Barons Court reached its zenith
in terms of scale and splendour. The architectural historian Gervase Jackson-
Stops provided a marvellous overview of the changes introduced by the
Morrisons.[30] Soane's reversal of the original house so that the front was on
its north side was retained by William Vitruvius Morrison. His *porte-cochère*
'with its crisply carved Ionic capitals, based on the famous Erechtheion order,
and its frieze decorated with chaste wreaths in the French Empire style'
provides a hugely impressive entrance to the house. The family arms in the
pediment were the work of the Dublin sculptor Terence Farrell. In 1838 he
was paid £30 for these, and the same for the arms in the pediment on the

The coat of arms in
the pediment of the
porte-cochère.

The entrance hall with the portraits of Lady Charlotte Bury (left) and Lady Emma Hamilton (right) on either side of the door through to the rotunda.

The bay window at Barons Court

garden front. Jackson-Stops provided the following description of the way in which the Morrisons had transformed the entrance hall:

> Once inside the front door the full extent of the Morrisons' remodelling is immediately apparent. The Hall, which basically occupies the same space as Soane's entrance 'vestibule', provides an austere Greek Revival prelude to the sequence of rich neo-Classical rooms beyond … it is closely based on the Hall at Ballyfin, with the same pilasters and coffered ceiling – an intentionally restrained scheme so as to heighten the drama of what is to follow. The chimneypiece is curiously Palladian in appearance, apart from the neo-Classical scrolls at each side.

The west and east wings were largely rebuilt at this time. The former was to contain the Marchioness' apartments. On its west side is a bay window, the original design for which was drafted by Richard Morrison, but he was overruled by his son, providing Pettigrew with a further gripe. The east wing contained the dining room, a vast double cube. The plasterwork is remarkable for its quality, 'far richer and more accomplished than anything to be found in England at this time' in the opinion of Jackson-Stops who further believed that 'William Vitruvius Morrison's responsibility for much of the decorative ornament is beyond dispute', even if there is some uncertainty as to who actually executed the work. A story that has come down through the family relates that when

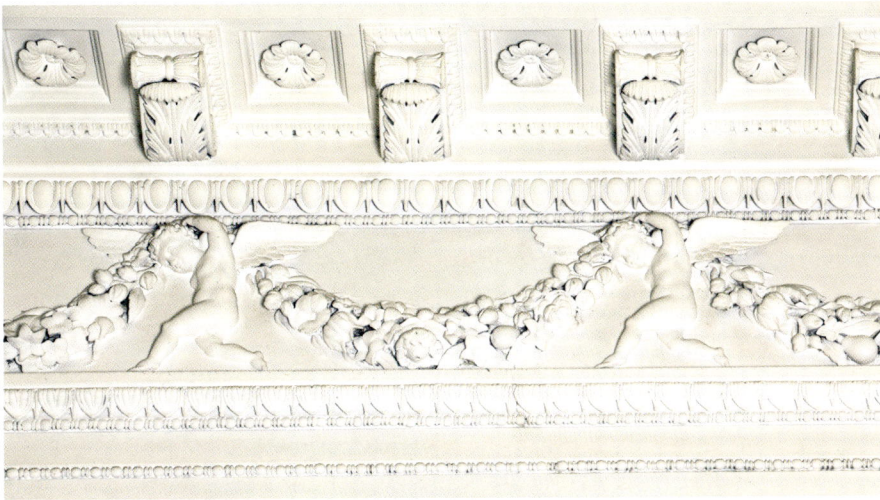

Plasterwork in the ceiling of the old dining room (now the family room).

the future 2nd Duke was a small boy and curious to find out what was happening in the house during this period of upheaval, he came upon the craftsmen at work and was shocked to find them stripped naked, clearly more concerned to preserve their clothes than their skins.

Renovations to the house were accompanied by improvements to the gardens and demesne. Lancey, in his aforementioned account, noted that Abercorn had given directions that any arable land lying between the demesne and the roads should be planted with trees. A Scottish visitor to Barons Court in October 1836 has left the following description of the demesne:

> There is a succession of pretty lakes, long and narrow in the low ground, and wooded banks all along and round them. It is on the whole a rather dull place – perhaps owing to the uniformity in the management of the wood which looks as if it was all of one growth, and affords little or no variety in size or apparent age: but probably still more from the natural swampy character of the low ground.[31]

The writer, however, noted that Abercorn was 'doing a great deal … about the grounds' and was reported to have planted 5,000 acres in the past year.

The lower parterre beside Lough Fanny, probably by Broderick Thomas.

It is believed that the man employed by the Marquess to oversee the enlarging and remodelling of the parkland at this time was the well-known landscape gardener James Frazer. With regard to the formal gardens, the Marquess' mother-in-law, the Duchess of Bedford, is said to have given advice and it is likely that the Morrisons were also consulted. However, it appears that the lower parterre between the house and lake was designed by Broderick Thomas and created in the late 1840s; it was removed in the early 1900s.

At the same time that Barons Court was being remodelled, the Marquess was avidly collecting works of art. Receipts from the late 1830s show that he was spending extravagantly, employing an agent, Andrew Wilson, to source appropriate items on his behalf in Italy. The precise instructions that Wilson was given are not known, but he was kept busy procuring paintings, sculptures and other *objets d'art* from Rome, Naples, Leghorn, Florence, Genoa, Venice and Bologna. One listing of expenditure from August 1839 totals over £4,150, with over £2,000 being spent on six paintings from the famous Zambeccari collection in Bologna. Another £450 was spent on a Murillo purchased in Genoa and £128 on two paintings by Canaletto.[32] These were not necessarily intended for the reconstructed Barons Court for the Marquess had several houses at this time, but their acquisition does draw attention to Abercorn's ambition to be recognised as a connoisseur of fine art.

The dome of the rotunda with its octagonal coffering is supported on eight freestanding Ionic columns with a frieze decorated with panthers and female heads supporting baskets of fruit.

Though Abercorn and his family may have been infrequent visitors to Barons Court, when they did entertain there it was on a lavish scale. A County Tyrone landowner, John Ynyr Burges of Parkanaur, provided the following account of a visit to Barons Court in January 1844:

> Paid a visit to Barons Court. Lord and Lady Abercorn were there with a large party of friends in the house, Lord and Lady Moreton, Lord Aberdour [*sic* – Aberdeen?], Mrs Balfour and Miss Balfour, Lord Grimston, Mr Ellice, etc, etc. The establishment was in the zenith of its splendour, a house steward who lived with George IV, a most distinguished major domo excellently got up, a first-rate cook, and remarkable lords-in-waiting dressed in crimson and silver. No livery could look richer. The dining room was everything it ought to be. A colossal shield of arms enriched the wall where the mighty sideboard rested, glittering with plate. The tables were covered with ornaments. In the centre was the far-famed Warwick vase, which always looks better in silver, and viands of every kind. The manners and deportment of the noble host and hostess were kind, graceful and dignified. You felt at home in a moment, and they so gently and pleasingly wished you to be so. The evening passed too quick away, and both left an impression on my mind of the nicest persons I ever met, which I never have had reason to change.[33]

The Hamiltons and the Royal Family

In the decade that followed his coming of age, the Marquess formed an increasingly close attachment to members of the Royal Family. It has been said of him, 'As one of the most eminent members of the British aristocracy, a fluent socialite, and a skilled cricketer, he was regarded as an appropriate companion' for royalty.[34] In 1844, like his grandfather before him, he was made a Knight of the Garter, filling a vacancy that had been created through the death of the Duke of Dorset. In the same year he was made lord lieutenant of County Donegal. Two years later in 1846 he was appointed Groom of the Stole to Prince Albert, 'whose particular protégé he was',[35] though this carried little real responsibility. The position had apparently been refused by the Marquess of Worcester on the grounds that he did not wish to compromise himself politically. Some thought Abercorn's appointment was a calculated political move designed to encourage his brother Claud to vote in favour of the ministry.[36] Leaving aside such speculation, Abercorn's new role showed just how close the Royal Family and his own family had become.

In the mid-1830s, at a time when it was becoming increasingly fashionable for the aristocracy to holiday in the Highlands where they could pursue the

Lord Claud shooting at Ardverikie by Landseer.

The Duke in Highland costume by Landseer.

sport of deer hunting, Abercorn leased a large stretch of forest and moorland at Ardverikie near Loch Laggan in the Scottish Highlands. The Marquess' in-laws, the Bedfords, had already taken out a lease of nearby Glenfeshie. In 1837, it was reported that Abercorn was planning to build a 'magnificent chateau' in the Highlands. In the event, the shooting lodge constructed in 1840 was a more modest affair, but it provided a convenient and comfortable base for hunting parties. Among his regular guests at Ardverikie was the renowned artist Edwin Landseer who, though a poor shot, expected to be allowed the best beats as much as anyone else. The landscape around Ardverikie provided inspiration for Landseer, and many of his most famous paintings derive from his time here. Landseer was also responsible for the frescoes that adorned the walls of Ardverikie. What prompted him to create them was the fact that the whitewash on the dining-room walls hurt his eyes and so, as Lord Frederic later recounted:

without saying a word to any one, he one day produced his colours, mounted a pair of steps, and proceeded to rough-in a design in charcoal on the white walls. He worked away until he had completely covered the walls with frescoes in colour. The originals of some of his best-known engravings, 'The Sanctuary,' 'The Challenge,' 'The Monarch of the Glen,' made their first appearance on the walls of the dining-room at Ardverikie.[37]

Unfortunately, the shooting lodge was destroyed in a fire in 1871 and with it were lost Landseer's wall paintings.

In late summer 1847 Abercorn invited the Queen and Prince Albert and their family to stay at Ardverikie. Arriving on 21 August, Victoria noted in her journal:

We saw Lord Abercorn's house of Ardverikie long before we came to it ... It is quite close to the lake, and the view from the windows, as I now write, though obscured by rain, is very beautiful, and extremely wild. There is not a village, house, or cottage within four or five miles: one can only get to it by the ferry, or by rowing across the lake. The house is a comfortable shooting-lodge, built of stone, with many nice rooms in it. Stags' horns are placed along the outside and in the passages; and the walls of the drawing-room and ante-room are ornamented with beautiful drawings of stags, by Landseer.[38]

The Queen was impressed with Landseer's skill as an artist and while at Ardverikie she decided to commission him to paint a picture that would serve as a reminder of the Royal Family's Highland holiday. Abercorn was asked to use his influence with Landseer and impress on him a sense of urgency in the matter, for the Queen was anxious to present it to Prince Albert that Christmas. Landseer accepted and fulfilled his commission on time; the resulting painting, *Queen Victoria sketching at Loch Laggan*, is now one of the best-known works of art in the Royal Collection.

For the young Hamilton children the Royal Family's visit to Ardverikie was remembered for the fact that they were forced to give up their nurseries in favour of the Royal children and provided with rather cramped accommodation on the adjoining farm. On the day after Victoria's arrival the Marchioness took her children, dressed in their best clothes, with the boys in kilts, to be presented to the Queen. All went well until Lord Claud was asked to make his bow. This provided an opportunity for the impish four-year-old to show his resentment at being forced out of his nursery rather than respectfully bow before the Queen, as his older brother had done, he stood on his head. Her Majesty was not amused. Having been severely chastised, he was brought back to the Queen later in the day to make his apologies, whereupon he did exactly the same. For the rest of the Royal visit he remained in disgrace.[39]

Landseer and the Duke of Abercorn return from a shoot.

These childish indiscretions did not, of course, impair the close relationship between the Abercorns and the Royal Family. The Marquess deeply mourned the passing of Prince Albert in December 1861. In writing to the Queen early in 1863, Abercorn admitted that he still grieved for the Prince, for whom 'for so many years it was my pride and happiness to serve', adding, 'May Providence in his soothing mercy grant such comfort and consolation as can be given to our beloved Sovereign.'[40] Victoria's prolonged period of mourning for her husband is well known. Lord Frederic admitted that he was left with a feeling of disappointment on being presented to the Queen for the first time. Rather than a 'dazzling apparition arrayed in sumptuous robes, seated on a gold throne', he encountered a middle-aged lady, simply dressed in her widow's clothes and seated in an ordinary arm-chair.[41] Nonetheless, he, along with the rest of his family, had a deep respect for the Queen. The Marchioness enjoyed a close friendship with Victoria for over half a century, and kept up a regular correspondence with her.

Estate and financial affairs

In many ways it was fortunate for the estate that Abercorn was a minor when he succeeded his grandfather. As a result of the post-Napoleonic economic depression the value of the estate rental fell dramatically, from £37,000 per annum in 1815 to £26,000 in 1832. During the Marquess' minority the

estate was managed by trustees, the most important of whom was Abercorn's stepfather, Lord Aberdeen. Years later, in attempting to explain his father's 'natural indolence and extraordinary shyness' which made him too reliant on others, the Marquess's son George suggested that these were the result of being surrounded in his earliest years by those who took care to ensure that 'his expenditure and amusements were not to their disadvantage'.[42] We know less about the management of the property during his tenure as head of the family than during the period of the 8th Earl and 1st Marquess, for the voluminous estate correspondence that exists for most of the eighteenth century and the early part of the nineteenth is absent for most of the rest of the 1800s. Nonetheless, although the detail might be absent, enough can be recovered to provide a broad outline of the management of the estate during the Marquess' tenure.

From the early 1830s Major John Humphreys, father of the hymn-writer Cecil Frances Alexander, was the chief agent of the Irish property. Of Norfolk origins, he had served in the Royal Marines and had fought at the Battle of Copenhagen in 1801. Prior to entering Abercorn's service in 1833, when he succeeded Sir John James Burgoyne, Humphreys had been agent to the Earl of Wicklow – the Marquess' uncle. Burgoyne had been an effective administrator, but towards the end of his tenure the management of the estate seems to have slipped somewhat. When Humphreys arrived as agent he found that the 'tenants were all greatly in arrears, and not one could show a clear receipt for several years past'. The approach adopted by the Major to recover these debts was through promising not to dispossess any tenant who would pay three half years' rents annually until his arrears had been cleared.

Though Humphreys' assiduous management resulted in an improvement to the rental income and the recovery of much of the arrears that had built up during his predecessor's time, the Marquess' extravagant living was an increasing cause for concern. In January 1841 Humphreys wrote to Abercorn setting out in stark terms the parlous condition of the family's finances and advising the Marquess that he would have to consider changing his lifestyle:

> I hope you will give serious attention to the following statements and I earnestly beg of your lordship not to deceive yourself by considering the income greater than is here set down, or that your expenses can ever be brought to meet it without a general revision of the expenditure of the entire establishment. If this is judiciously done, by discarding superfluous and extravagant expenses, your lordship will find that the splendour which ought to accompany your high rank and great fortune, will be fully and amply supported.[43]

Humphreys went on provide a summary of the family's income and expenditure. The Irish rental, after deducting the tithe rent-charge, came to £28,479, on top of which were £327 from the Ardstraw churchlands leased from the bishop of Derry, and £1,000 for 'slates, canal and turf'. The Scottish rental was £8,000, while the English rental brought in £2,749. Other incidentals brought the total income up to £41,675. As far as expenditure was concerned, interest charges on a capital debt of £177,200 came to £7,490, while a further £1,765 went on annuities. House, household, travelling and incidental expenses came to £22,500. This figure broke down as follows: £3,500 on The Priory, £2,500 on Barons Court, £1,500 on Scotland, and £2,000 on Dudley House, the family's then London home. Finally, there were interest payments totalling £800 on various 'outstanding bills'. All of these expenses left a disposable income of £7,190. Humphreys was not afraid to express his views to Abercorn in such blunt terms, and he clearly recognised the seriousness of the situation and the need to take action to preserve the family's fortunes. How Abercorn responded to this bleak assessment of his financial position is not known, but it does not appear that he curbed his expenditure to any great extent.

Largely under Humphreys' management the Tyrone estate had been extended through the acquisition of additional properties, for the most part townlands that adjoined the existing manors. There were various reasons for the purchase of these lands. In the case of Lisdivin Lower, in the manor of Dunnalong, for which £3,264 was paid in 1832, a townland that had been granted in fee farm by the 1st Earl of Abercorn in 1615 was restored to the estate. Other townlands were in the immediate vicinity of Barons Court and could be added to its demesne. The sum of £5,368 was expended on Legland, which was then 'fenced, drained and planted by Lord Abercorn' so that it added 'much to the beauty of the place'. In the case of the Ardstraw churchlands, held by lease from the bishop of Derry, there was political advantage in acquiring these townlands, for among the tenants there were 172 men eligible to vote. When they came up for sale the Earl of Belmore offered £7,000 for them. Unable to stomach the prospect of his chief political rival in Tyrone acquiring both the lands and the electors, Abercorn offered £7,200 for the lease of the churchlands, which was accepted. In all some £29,300 was spent on adding to the Tyrone estate between the 1830s and the early 1850s. This figure, though not insignificant, was dwarfed by the

The memorial to Major Humphreys at Barons Court Church. Major John Humphreys died on 12 June 1872. His wife Elizabeth Frances died the next day.

145

sums expended by the Marquess in extending his landed base in England. The most important of these purchases was that of Dale Park, near Arundel in Sussex, for which he paid John Abel Smith, the MP for Chichester, nearly £100,000 in the summer of 1848.[44] In his pursuit of English estates Abercorn greatly overextended his financial resources and quickly found himself in a situation where he had accumulated debts in excess of £340,000. By this stage the Marquess had five houses to maintain – Barons Court, The Priory, Dale Park, Chesterfield House in London, and his shooting lodge at Ardverikie.

The bleakness of the situation was apparent to Abercorn's solicitor, Froggatt, who presented a blunt assessment of the estate's finances to Humphreys in the summer of 1849. He highlighted in particular the 'unfortunate purchase' of Dale Park, of which he was not made aware until the sale had been agreed. In a tone of self-congratulation, Froggatt was pleased to tell Humphreys, 'Happily neither you nor I had anything to do with it – both would no doubt have advised, had we been consulted, against it.' In lamenting Abercorn's extravagant spending, Froggatt observed, 'Year after year, the Marquess has gone on borrowing 'till we have only £10,000 left to be borrowed on the Irish estates ... Coutts & Co. are tired of our incessant applications.' The interest payments on the borrowed money came to around £14,500, while £140,000 had been borrowed on the Irish estates alone. 'I am sure it will be impossible for the Marquess to go on as he has done', opined Abercorn's solicitor, adding, 'There is a word, perhaps a most unpalatable one, which would answer the question – Retrenchment.' For the Marquess' own sake something had to be done to 'rescue him from his present state of embarrassment, and preserve his credit, which does not hold the proud position in which it once stood.'[45] (This letter was later used by Froggatt's clerk, Patrick Duffy, in an unsuccessful attempt to blackmail Abercorn.)

Humphreys himself admitted to Aberdeen and the other trustees of the Abercorn family settlement in July 1850 that the purchase of Dale Park had been 'contrary to my earnest advice'. He also realised that there was a serious flaw in the sale in that the property – it was subject to a mortgage of £70,000 and under the terms of the purchase agreement Abercorn was to pay 5% interest on this. It transpired that 'Lord Abercorn had not his attention particularly directed to this part of the agreement', and though he subsequently complained about it there was little that could be done. Abercorn was fortunate in that he had generally competent men around him, chief among them Humphreys, even if their counsel was frequently ignored. More than once the wily agent resolved a potentially damaging situation. On one occasion, when John Abel Smith was pressing Abercorn for a cash instalment arising from his sale of Dale Park, it was only through

Humphreys' intervention and personal connections with Lords Manners and Aberdeen and the Duke of Devonshire – who were persuaded by Humphreys to forgo their claims on a mortgage with the Marquess – that this money could be found.[46]

Despite his undoubted ability there were some who questioned Humphreys' management of the Abercorn estates. In 1850, the trustees of the Abercorn family settlement directed Henry Harrison to carry out an inspection of estate accounts. Harrison reported favourably on Humphreys' management of the estate, stating that the system he used in collecting the rents was an 'admirable one'.[47] Humphreys, however, was concerned that the very fact that an inspection was authorised called his integrity into question. Referring to the 'very disagreeable reports that have been circulated respecting the object of your visit here', he implored Harrison to make clear that his conduct had been above reproach.[48]

Though one occasionally gets the impression that Abercorn himself was blithely unaware of the gravity of the situation regarding his financial position and the implications of his reckless spending, by 1850 even he recognised that drastic measures were needed if he was to remain solvent. In April of that year he acknowledged to his brother-in-law, Captain W. A. Baillie Hamilton, that the 'establishment required for a London house and Barons Court as a winter residence would be very much smaller than one required where the Priory is kept. … The establishment I have been required to keep for the Priory is inconveniently large.' He also realised that he would have to relinquish ownership of one of his English properties: 'If Dale Park can be sold to satisfaction, it will be an enormous relief.'[49] From letters between Baillie Hamilton, who was one of Abercorn's trustees, and W. M. Coulthurst of Coutts, we have further evidence that those responsible for managing the Marquess' financial affairs were frequently exasperated with him. In November 1850 Baillie Hamilton wrote to Coulthurst, 'I am really anxious for Lord Abercorn's sake that he should practically understand that of the two ways of doing business the simplest and most straightforward is the best.' Baillie Hamilton felt that Abercorn lacked the 'subtleties of business' and was 'wont to prefer a course which shall keep a business furthest from completion'.[50] On another occasion, in February 1854, Coulthurst expressed his wish for a five-minute conversation with the Marquess so that he could 'prove to him that his reasoning is founded upon a misapprehension of the facts of the case; for my part I cannot discover a mode of eating one's cake and still having it'.[51] One wonders whether it was with feelings of satisfaction or frustration that Baillie Hamilton read 'any directions given by the trustees are always acquiesced in by me with pleasure, and more than pleasure – with thanks for the very great trouble they take in my behalf' in a letter from the Marquess of February 1853.[52]

Mounting debts at last forced the Marquess to sell the Bentley Priory estate and other lands at Stanmore, as well as Dale Park. In the summer of 1852 the sale of Bentley Priory to John Kelk was concluded.[53] This, together with the sale of other agricultural land in 1852–54, raised in all around £90,000. In April 1853 a sale of the contents of the house was advertised.[54] While a number of the most precious objects in the house had been removed by the family, it is clear that among the items offered there was still much of value. The auctioneers were keen to emphasise the royal connection, drawing attention to the fact that the sale would include the furniture in the rooms occupied by the late Dowager Queen Adelaide. Humphreys, who seems to have been opposed to the sale of any property that had been in the family's possession from before the Marquess reached majority, lamented the sale of The Priory. He knew that expressing this view would not make him popular, but he could not forget 'its bygone splendour' or the considerable sums that he had spent on the property on Abercorn's behalf.[55] Coulthurst too regretted that 'Lord Abercorn has no hereditary fondness for the place', but was forced to admit that the family 'entertained a positive dislike to the Priory'.[56]

If the disposal of English estates was one thing for Abercorn's trustees and agent, the sale of property in Ireland that had been in the family's possession for generations was quite another. In the spring of 1852 Abercorn considered selling the manor of Magavlin and Lismoghry in County Donegal. Humphreys was not impressed at the prospect of disposing of the 'most improvable and improving' part of the estate, writing to Aberdeen that the Marquess did not 'hold his Irish property in very high estimation'. Though opposed to the sale, the Major did as he was instructed as he wished to avoid another row with his employer: 'I am fearful he has not forgiven the decided opinion I gave respecting the sale of Baronscourt', a clear indication that this was not the first time that Abercorn had contemplated selling part of his Irish patrimony. The Marquess instructed Humphreys to contact John Stewart, uncle and sole trustee of Mr Stewart of Ards, near Dunfanaghy, and offer to him the Donegal property for 20 years' purchase of its net income. Humphreys thought these terms far too generous and, unsurprisingly, the Stewarts readily accepted the offer. For reasons that are not altogether clear, the sale did not go through.

In a further attempt to raise funds, in the summer of 1854 Abercorn declared his intention to sell a portion of his Irish estate up to a value of £50,000. Since the Tyrone lands were an integral part of a family settlement, the disposal of any part of them required lands of equal value to be brought under the terms of that settlement. Because of the additions to the estate in the previous 20 years the possibility was explored of introducing these recently acquired lands to the settlement in exchange for those to be sold. Although, as noted above, the total price paid for these lands was just over

£29,000, Humphreys for one was convinced that they were worth a great deal more than this. In June 1854 he wrote, 'without the purchased property the family could never be secure in the enjoyment of the splendid family residence of Barons Court, besides the political influence it gives in the county'. He firmly believed that the 'value of the purchased property to the family was of infinitely greater importance than the lands to be given in exchange'.[57] After some deliberation, eight townlands in the manor of Dunnalong and two in the Donegal portion of the estate were identified as suitable for disposal. They were valued at £50,000 and were to be offered at 24 years' purchase.

Humphreys, as ever, was alive to the political implications of the sale of any part of the estate. Unless they were bought by a political supporter of the family, the sale of these 10 townlands would mean the loss of 58 votes. By this stage Humphreys had given up trying to caution the Marquess against disposing of part of his patrimony and had a new-found confidence in him. Writing to Coulthurst about the proposed sale, he commented, 'I have only to carry out his lordship's wishes, and as he now takes an interest in his own affairs, and is so capable of judging what is best to be done, I feel less [concern] on the subject than I otherwise should do.'[58] In the end nothing came of this, and the townlands in question remained part of the Abercorn estate. The precise reasons for this are not clear, but may have been to do with the implications the sale would have had for the existing family settlement and the failure to reach an agreement with the trustees on the best way to proceed.

Despite the failure to dispose of part of the Irish estate, the sale of properties in England, raising in all around £200,000, had gone a long way towards alleviating Abercorn's financial problems. Early in January 1856 Abercorn had another offer for part of his estate which was of much greater significance. On 14 January he wrote to his brother-in-law, the 7th Duke of Bedford:

> Louisa has already prepared you for the asking of your advice in a matter of considerable moment to us. I have had an offer for the whole of my Irish estates, at the rate of twenty-five years purchase on the gross rental. This, in round figures, may come to about a million. Were I at liberty to act for myself, I should not hesitate to accept it, looking to the discomforts of Irish residence and property; but unfortunately it is necessary to have the consent of my eldest son, and it is with this view that I ask you to give him your advice upon it, and urge him to see the expediency of accepting the offer.
>
> The advantages in a money point of view should be obvious, as the purchaser would be settled with all the expenses, outgoings, agencies, etc and the keeping up of Barons Court – amounting to at least £7,000 a year – which would be a clear gain to the family. The object would

be to wash one's hands of the whole Irish concern, and to invest, say £300,000 in a suitable English residential property, keeping the remainder probably as a first charge upon the whole capital estate at 4 per cent.

This, backed up by the original estates of the family in Scotland would, I think, make a far more desirable position than that of a resident of Ireland, which the possessor of Barons Court, whoever he is, must essentially be.

It seems rather strange that Abercorn would not have been in a position to influence his son James directly, who, after all, would have been only 17 at the time: perhaps it suggests that even at this stage the heir had a certain independence of mind. The letter also reveals the Marquess' continuing desire to establish an English landed base, even if that meant relinquishing all connection with Ireland. In the event Abercorn did not part with his Irish estates, on the advice, so it is believed, of his stepfather Lord Aberdeen, who persuaded him that he could not possibly sever the link with Ireland. For this timely intervention the Marquess' descendants have been immensely grateful.

The dukedom of Châtelherault

In the early 1860s Abercorn began to actively assert his right to the dukedom of Châtelherault. So far as is known, this claim had not been formally made since the time of the 6th Earl. Though he was styled 'Duke of Châtelherault in France' on his monument in Paisley Abbey, there is no evidence that the 8th Earl pursued the title with any enthusiasm. The same can be said for his nephew, the 1st Marquess. In the 1820s, Lord Aberdeen had investigated the matter on behalf of his stepson, but with little success. What brought the issue to the fore in the 1860s was the attempt by the Dukes of Hamilton, rival claimants to the title, to solicit the support of Napoleon III, a relative by marriage, to have the dukedom conferred on them. The Dukes of Hamilton descended from the third son of the Earl of Arran (who in 1548 had been created Duke of Châtelherault), whereas the Marquess of Abercorn descended from Arran's fourth son Claud. However, in 1651 the 2nd Duke of Hamilton died without male issue. His daughter married a Douglas, who changed his name to Hamilton, thus allowing the title to continue. However, the Dukes of Hamilton could no longer claim to be in the direct male Hamilton line, whereas Abercorn could.

In an attempt to outmanoeuvre his distant kinsmen, in January 1862 Abercorn went through the legal process of being declared the heir male of the body of the 1st Duke of Châtelherault by the Sheriff of Chancery in Scotland. However, on 20 April 1864 the French Emperor issued a decree confirming the 12th Duke of Hamilton as the rightful heir to the hereditary dukedom of Chatelherault. Furious at this, Abercorn challenged the decision through an appeal to the Conseil d'Etat. The basis of his argument was that if the dukedom was indeed hereditary as Napoleon III's ruling had maintained, then it belonged to him.[59] He believed that the Hamiltons had obtained the ruling in 'an underhand way', and secured the support of a number of influential individuals in his campaign to have the Emperor's decision overturned.[60] The French jurist, Monsieur Dufaure, was in favour of Abercorn's claims to the title, stating, 'I am of the opinion that if the Dukedom of Chatelherault is to be revived in favour of a descendant of the Earl of Arran, the Marquess of Abercorn has incontestably the best claim to have the title conferred on him.'[61] Others, however, were somewhat scathing of the dispute and to some he was known as the 'French Frog' for pursuing his claims to this dukedom.[62]

The matter seems to have lapsed in the late 1860s, but was revived in the early 1870s following the overthrow of Napoleon III. In October 1872 Sir Bernard Burke, the Ulster King of Arms, travelled to Paris to investigate the matter, meeting with various individuals as he sought to establish the basis of the 1864 ruling. His findings were not conclusive, though he informed Abercorn that he would be giving a full account of the case in the next edition of the *Peerage*. However, upon returning to Dublin and having had time to review the matter, he advised the Duke to postpone any further action 'until more propitious times'. Burke argued that with the overthrow of the monarchy there was no sovereign power in France and so no way to prove Abercorn's right to the dukedom. He warned against going before the courts of common law, where a ruling could be issued denying the very existence of the dukedom of Chatelherault. Burke himself had no doubts as to the rightful possessor of the title, declaring, 'This is certain – if the dukedom of Chatelherault be not extinct, you are its duke.'[63] And there the matter seems to have rested.

Lord lieutenant of Ireland

Early in 1866 a new Tory government came to power with the Earl of Derby at its head. The main concern of the administration in Ireland at this time was with countering the Fenian movement. Its rise had caused considerable alarm and a number of measures had been introduced to deal with it, including the creation of a Special Commission and the suspension of habeas corpus. In early February 1866 Abercorn, in what was up to that point one of his few contributions to debate in the Lords, commended those who had been involved in the judicial process in relation to the Fenian conspiracy; their behaviour, he argued, 'all tended to increase the dignity of the law in Ireland'. He was, however, critical of the way in which the late government had dealt with the conspiracy, believing it to have lacked sufficient determination to take on the conspirators, something he believed the Fenians could have interpreted as weakness. Nonetheless, Abercorn was 'satisfied that there is in that country an amount of loyalty by which the evil will be successfully combated'. It is doubtful that the Marquess imagined that a few months later he would be appointed to the lord lieutenancy of Ireland and charged with confronting the threat posed by the movement.

The position of lord lieutenant of Ireland was one that the 1st Marquess of Abercorn had actively sought for himself, but failed to secure. The lack of political ambition displayed by his grandson in the 30 years since reaching majority did not make him an obvious choice for this position. In fact it is clear that he was not the first choice of the new administration. Initial attempts to persuade Lord John Manners to accept the appointment failed. Instead the position was offered to Abercorn, who accepted. He had not quite been plucked from obscurity to fill the office, but he certainly had no previous experience of holding such a responsible position. His appointment did meet with the approval of the Queen, and possibly it was her sanctioning of his appointment that ultimately persuaded him to accept it.[64] There was also a feeling that the position of lord lieutenant had in recent years lost some of its status from a social perspective, and that it required an Irish aristocrat with a reputation for lavish spending to restore some of the prestige associated with the office. Abercorn, it was felt, fulfilled these criteria. As it turned out, the Marquess was a remarkably successful lord lieutenant. His son George was later to reflect that 'he astonished his old associates and his new political colleagues by his ability, powers of speech and rapid appreciation of a difficult or serious task'.[65]

From the time of his appointment in the summer of 1866, Abercorn was involved in developing a strategy to tackle the Fenian movement and in particular to deal with an expected armed uprising. Troops were quartered in various parts of Ireland in November and measures were taken to improve defences in Dublin. He worked with Lord Strathnairn, the commander of the army in Ireland, to improve security across the island, though the two of them were not always in full agreement on certain issues. Abercorn, for example, did not want to make the defensive measures appear too conspicuous and so draw attention to government alarm at the situation. By early December there was considerable tension in Dublin and around the country and an expectation that something was about to happen. One of the so-called prophecies of Columbkille in circulation was that Abercorn would be the last English governor of Ireland and that he would be assassinated near Dublin. Concerns that the viceregal lodge, where Abercorn and his family were spending much of their time during the closing weeks of 1866, was in an exposed location led to a series of measures being taken to provide extra security. Windows were barred and bolted and an alarm bell had been erected. Fears that the so-called 'Fenian liquid-fire' would be used during an incendiary attack resulted in the construction of an enlarged water main to the building and the placement of buckets filled with water in many of the rooms. In addition, the lodge was patrolled throughout the night. In the garden four light field-guns were positioned, while a row of gas-lamps was installed. In the event, Christmas passed peacefully at the viceregal lodge, but at the beginning of the following year the family moved to the greater security of Dublin Castle.

It was not until the beginning of the spring of 1867 that the long-anticipated Fenian insurrection began. The rising commenced on 5 March, but it proved disastrous for the Fenian movement. Within the organisation's ranks there were many informants, while it also faced the hostility of the Catholic Church. For these and other reasons the rising was quelled with relative ease. How the viceroy reacted to the news that some of those arrested gave as their name and address, 'James Abercorn, Vice-regal Lodge', is not recorded. On the eve of the rising three of the younger Abercorns, having contracted measles, were confined to the viceregal lodge. Concerns that the lodge would be captured and the children held as hostages resulted in their being brought to Dublin Castle under armed escort as soon as advance warning of the rising was received. One of the children, Lord Frederic, later recalled walking among the prisoners paraded in the yard at Dublin Castle following their capture by troops led by Straithnairn, describing them as 'very forlorn and miserable'. That afternoon Abercorn and his wife were driven slowly and without an escort through the poorest districts in Dublin in order to show that they were not afraid. This experience was gruelling, especially for the Marchioness, but she was lauded afterwards for undertaking it.[66] In his congratulatory address following the suppression of the rising Abercorn inadvertently managed to offend Strathnairn by failing to highlight sufficiently the part played by the commander of the armed forces in quelling the disturbances.

In the aftermath of the rising the lord lieutenant found himself having to deal with some delicate, and potentially inflammatory, situations. One of the most serious of these followed the conviction for treason and sentencing to death on 1 May 1867 of the leading Fenian, Thomas Burke, known as General Burke. A campaign for clemency began, and quickly gained momentum and widespread support. On 24 May Abercorn received a delegation led by the lord mayor of Dublin seeking a commutation of Burke's sentence. Others were insisting that the execution be carried out. However, the sheer volume of the pleas for clemency which had been received by the government resulted in a volte-face, and on 27 May Abercorn announced that Burke's sentence would be commuted to penal servitude for life. In writing to the lord mayor, the viceroy expressed his hope that this act of mercy would result in Burke's sympathisers determining to 'live for the future in loyalty to the Queen and in peace with Her Majesty's faithful subjects'.[67]

Among those who had visited the lord lieutenant seeking clemency for Burke was the leader of the Catholic Church in Ireland, Cardinal Paul Cullen. Abercorn had already gone to considerable lengths to reach out to the Catholic community, and in particular to Cullen. After a banquet given by Abercorn early in 1867, where Cullen had been given second place at the table after the viceroy, the Cardinal wrote that the Marquess had been 'most polite' to him. Soon afterwards Abercorn wrote to Cullen 'expressing his great desire to do anything in his power to please our bishops'. Cullen, however, was cautious in his dealings with Abercorn. He distrusted him on account of the Marquess's prominent position within the Freemasons. Nonetheless, Abercorn afforded Cullen great respect and this was appreciated by the Cardinal. After the announcement had been made of the commutation of Burke's sentence, Cullen wrote to the viceroy, 'I beg to thank most sincerely your Excellency for your kindness in acquainting me with the merciful resolution of Her Majesty's Cabinet in regard to the convict Burke. I am confident that this happy resolution will prevent much evil and be productive of much good.'[68] Periodically the Fenian movement continued to trouble the government during the remainder of 1867, though not to the same degree as it had in the early months of that year. In December 1867 the viceroy allowed a mock-funeral organised by those in Cork protesting against the execution of the 'Manchester martyrs' to go ahead. On the other hand, he was annoyed when his chief secretary sanctioned a similar march to proceed through the centre of Dublin.

Early in 1868 Benjamin Disraeli replaced Lord Derby as Prime Minister. So far as was possible Disraeli wished to retain in the government the men who had served under Derby. With regard to the Irish lord lieutenancy, however, it was more than simply continuity that prompted him to appeal to Abercorn to remain in post. Writing to the viceroy on 28 February, Disraeli set out his reasons: 'I wish to secure in that country the presence of a Viceroy, whose admirable ability in every respect, has already vindicated Her Majesty's authority under almost unprecedented difficulties, and in whose wisdom and resource, will be found the best means for the improvement and welfare of the country.'[69] It seems to have been with little reluctance that Abercorn accepted Disraeli's offer to serve in his administration.

The visit of the Prince of Wales to Dublin

Though Ireland had not descended into the widespread disorder that many feared, the Fenian disturbances had brought home to the government the need to broaden popular support for its Irish administration. Disraeli believed that the presence of members of the Royal Family in Ireland would contribute to the 'tranquillisation' of the island. Abercorn shared this view, believing that the residence of a royal in Ireland for at least part of the year would be an effective focus for expressions of support for the Crown and arguing that it was important to steer 'the Irish National feeling into direct sentiments of loyalty to the Royal Family'.[70] As a first step towards achieving this aim, Abercorn, with a willing ally in his chief secretary, Lord Mayo, conceived of the idea of a visit of the Prince and Princess of Wales to Ireland attended with as much pageantry and ceremony as possible. At the same time, they were aware that the matter would have to be handled sensitively if the Queen was to be won over to the idea.

In early March 1868 the viceroy sent Mayo to London to visit the Prince and tentatively explore the possibility of his visiting Ireland that spring. On 4 March Mayo reported to Abercorn on his visit:

> I went to see the Prince of Wales last night and had a long talk with him – he appears to be perfectly willing to go to Ireland at Easter. I spoke to him very strongly indeed on the good that it would do. He said that it could not be finally settled until the Queen's consent was obtained, that he thought that if Disraeli as Prime Minister pressed on Her Majesty, she would probably acquiesce … I spoke to him about the Patrick Ribbon and the function in the Cathedral. He seemed quite pleased with the idea and said he had not got the [Order of St] Patrick, and would like to have it … I have little doubt therefore that if Disraeli speaks strongly to the Queen the thing is done.[71]

Two days later Mayo provided an update to Abercorn: 'Disraeli saw the Prince last night and it was settled that it would be desirable that HRH should in the first instance speak to the Queen himself when she comes to town tomorrow, which D. will then follow up as strongly as he can. I think it will do.'[72] As Abercorn and Mayo had suspected, the Queen was initially opposed to the idea of a visit by her son to Ireland, and was upset by the lord lieutenant and chief secretary's promotion of it without first consulting her. In the end, however, and chiefly thanks to Disraeli's intervention, she was persuaded of its benefits, though willing to sanction only a short trip, fearing that every part of the Empire would now expect a royal visit. On 9 March Disraeli wrote to Derby informing him that 'The Lords Abercorn and Mayo are pardoned.'

In advance of the visit there was some doubt as to whether the Princess of Wales would be well enough to travel to Ireland. The Prince wrote to Abercorn's son, Lord Hamilton, on 19 March: 'I think I am now able to tell you confidentially that if the Princess continues strong and well, she will be able to accompany me to Ireland (although I don't think the Queen quite likes the idea).' The Prince also gave his views on the activities planned:

> I should be quite ready to hold a Levee soon after our arrival on the Wednesday. I think the arrival should be a semi-state one, i.e. in plain clothes as on former occasions. Thursday and Friday should, I think be kept free for the races – as I am sure the people would wish me to go both days. I quite agree about the carriages and horses and it will be done as Lord Abercorn wishes. There will be no difficulty I hear about the Treasury defraying the expenses. The Lord Mayor's Ball cannot of course be avoided.[73]

The royal visit took place from 15 to 20 April, generating huge interest from all sections of the population. Abercorn claimed that as many as 100,000 people had seen the couple at Punchestown on their first visit to the races, while it was reckoned that 150,000 had turned out to see them in Phoenix Park. The Prince's second visit to the races aroused the ire of the Queen, forcing the viceroy to defend the conduct of the heir to the throne. While in Ireland the Prince also received an honorary degree from Trinity College, and, in a wise move, visited the Catholic University where he met with senior clergy.

The centrepiece of the royal visit to Ireland was the installation of the Prince of Wales as a Knight of the Order of St Patrick. This was intended to be much more than simply a spectacle, but rather a great national event, drawing together people from the whole of the island, irrespective of creed or political allegiance. The installation took place in St Patrick's Cathedral on 18 April. Only a few years before the royal visit the cathedral had been carefully restored, largely at the expense of Sir Benjamin Guinness, as Ireland's 'National Cathedral'. The preparations for the installation were carefully directed by Sir Bernard Burke. In the days leading up to the ceremony there was considerable disruption to the cathedral's normal routine. Even on Easter Sunday the celebration of Holy Communion was limited to one 8am service. Galleries were erected in the choir and nave, and the cathedral's west doors were replaced by a scarlet curtain.[74] A proposal to sell tickets for the ceremony was vetoed by Abercorn. The installation ceremony itself was a magnificent spectacle. Lord Frederic, who was one of the pages at the installation, vividly recalled the proceedings:

> The ceremony was very gorgeous and imposing, and as the pages were all the while in attendance on the two principal persons concerned, we got an admirable view of it. My father as Grand Master of the Order invested the Prince and gave him the *accolade*, after which he and the Archbishop of Dublin placed the new Knight in his proper stall amidst a great blare of trumpets. I remember being immensely impressed when the procession of Knights of St Patrick swept in from the Lady-Chapel in their flowing sky-blue satin mantles, and Sir Bernard Burke, the Ulster King-of-Arms, filled me with joy for in his

heraldic tabard he looked exactly like the King in a pack of cards …
Everyone was amazed at the beauty of the music, sung from the
triforium by the combined choirs of St Patrick's and Christ Church
Cathedrals, and of the Chapel Royal, with that wonderful musician,
Sir Robert Stewart, at the organ.[75]

The Marquess had attempted to make the installation a cross-
denominational event and had invited representatives of the other churches
in Ireland to it. Cardinal Cullen, however, was not prepared to attend the
installation in St Patrick's Cathedral, though he did accept Abercorn's
invitation to the subsequent dinner at the Castle where he would have an
opportunity to meet the Prince. Describing the event, Cullen wrote:

> The Prince of Wales sat opposite the Lord Lieutenant. The Prince of
> Saxe Weimar sat next to the Prince and then I came next. The Princess
> of Wales sat next the Lord Lieutenant, the Duke of Cambridge next
> here, and Prince Teck who was opposite me. I suppose I got my proper
> place as a cardinal.[76]

Afterwards Cullen chatted to the Marchioness of Abercorn about Rome
and other matters.

The Irish administration considered the royal visit a great triumph.
Abercorn went so far as to write to the Queen informing her that even former
Fenians had cheered the Prince and Princess of Wales 'with real cordiality'
during their visit.[77] He argued that a 'foundation has been laid by which the
loyalty of the Irish people, and their strong natural attachment to Your
Majesty's person, and to the Royal Family, has been aroused to a point that
may easily be kept up and even augmented by any further similar
occurrences.' For him, the Royal Family could be a powerful unifying force
in Ireland, overcoming divisions based on nationalism and class.[78] Full of
enthusiasm, Lord Mayo wrote to the viceroy on the need to act quickly to
build on the success of the visit: 'Now that the great event of our
administration is so well over, we must really take advantage of it at once
and endeavour to secure to Ireland that on which she has set her heart, i.e.
provision for the residence of the Prince of Wales in the country for a certain
portion of the year.'[79] After the conclusion of the Royal visit, the Queen
wrote to the Marchioness to thank her for the care she had shown towards
the Princess of Wales and also to express her gratitude to the Marquess for
the 'most admirable way' in which he had looked after every aspect of the
visit.[80] Abercorn was, however, to be disappointed in his wish to see a royal
residence established in Ireland, for the Queen remained strongly opposed
to the idea.

The 1st Duke in the Garter Riband.

The Dukedom

Even before the successful royal visit, stories were circulating in the London press that Abercorn was to be made a duke.[81] Whether there was any substance to these rumours is unclear, and certainly there was no announcement following the return of the Prince and Princess of Wales to London. Instead Abercorn found himself once again preoccupied with the frequently mundane work of the lord lieutenancy. By the summer, however, it was clear from behind the scenes discussions that Abercorn was indeed to be given a dukedom. When Disraeli wrote to Abercorn on 26 July 1868 to inform him of his promotion, he emphasised the role of the Queen in initiating this. According to Disraeli, his elevation was due to the Queen's 'entire satisfaction with the manner in which, in difficult and dangerous times, Your Excellency has represented Her Majesty in that part of the dominions' as well as the 'dignity, ability and wisdom' Abercorn had shown 'on all and trying occasions'.[82] Reporting back to the Queen on 28 July, Disraeli wrote: 'Mr Disraeli assured His Grace that altho' Mr Disraeli was personally gratified by the great distinction he had achieved, he wished His Grace to understand the truth, that the act as not only the cheerful, but also the spontaneous act of Y[ou]r Majesty – and this he greatly appreciated.' Disraeli wrote that Abercorn, on being informed of his elevation to the dukedom, 'really looked six inches taller, and he was really moved to enthusiasm etc. wh[ich] seems foreign to his character'.

To begin with it was not clear what precisely the title would be. Disraeli wrote to the Earl of Derby on 31 July 1868:

> Lord Abercorn is to be an Irish Duke … What the Irish title is to be I can't tell you. The Prince of Wales wants it to be Ulster, of which he is an earl,[83] but as I would not countenance this, HRH is to go the Queen tomorrow anent. I should think that the regal brow should be clouded, and that our friend must be content with being Duke of Abercorn.[84]

Therefore, by patent dated 10 August 1868 he was created Duke of Abercorn, the last marquess but one to be promoted for political reasons. At a personal level his elevation to a dukedom was the high point of what had been considered a successful lord lieutenancy. His son George wrote that 'by the power of his speech and administration, by the equipment of his establishment and the selection of his staff, he placed that office upon a higher plane than it had occupied for many years past'. The Duke of Cambridge is supposed to have remarked that Abercorn's establishment as viceroy was 'the best organised and most comfortable that he had ever known'.[85] There is no doubt that Abercorn was personally generous when it came to his official duties. During a debate in the Commons in July 1868 on whether or not to increase the lord lieutenant's allowance, it was argued that this was essential as no future viceroy 'would be likely to maintain the dignity of the office with the splendour with which it has been maintained by Lord Abercorn on the sum now allowed'. In response, Disraeli said that parliament 'should not contemplate anything so distressing' as Abercorn's retirement. And yet, a few months later Abercorn did stand down as lord lieutenant following the fall of the Conservative government.

It must be acknowledged that despite the acclaim he received, Abercorn was not universally popular as lord lieutenant. He has been described as 'haughty in demeanour' and overly concerned to maintain the proper trappings of Court.[86] He was accused of being 'very fond of effect' and mocked on account of his reputed practice of combing and scenting his beard prior to important functions.[87] Percy Fitzgerald, author of *Recollections of Dublin Castle and of Dublin Society*, wrote of the contrast between an earlier viceroy, the Earl of Carlisle, and the Duke as viewed by two Irishmen:

VANITY FAIR.   Sept. 25, 1869.

STATESMEN, No. 32.

The Duke as featured in *Vanity Fair* on 25 September 1869.

Ah sure, I'm for Abercorn any day. Now Carlisle, you see, would receive you in the most cordial way, and talk and be delighted to see you; ask how you were and all that. But give me Abercorn. Shure, there he stood, without a word, looking down with the utmost contempt on you, just as if you were the very dirt of his shoe.[88]

It was widely believed that Abercorn's vanities provided the inspiration for the character of the duke in Disraeli's novel *Lothair*, first published in 1870. Certainly his friends and acquaintances could not have failed to recognise Abercorn from the opening description of the duke in this novel:

The duke, though still young, and naturally of a gay and joyous temperament, had a high sense of duty, and strong domestic feelings. He was never wanting in his public place, and he was fond of his wife and his children; still more, proud of them. Every day when he looked into the glass, and gave the last touch to his consummate toilet, he offered his grateful thanks to Providence that his family was not unworthy of him.

Abercorn was probably charmed rather than offended by this, and he and Disraeli remained close. In declining a dinner invitation in May 1873 on the basis that he was 'living in seclusion so far as general society is concerned', Disraeli wrote to the Duchess, 'Your "boys" deserve kindness and encouragement because they are clever and, above all, industrious, and perhaps, also, because they inherit the agreeable qualities of their parents.'[89]

The disestablishment of the Church of Ireland

Throughout his adult life, and notwithstanding his attendance for a time at a Presbyterian Church in London, Abercorn showed a strong commitment to the Anglican Church, whether that was the Church of England or the Church of Ireland. At Argyll House in October 1829 he had been confirmed in the Church of England by the archbishop of Canterbury in the presence of numerous relatives.[90] As noted later in this chapter, he was instrumental in the construction of a Church of Ireland church at Barons Court in the mid-1850s. While lord lieutenant he had been responsible for appointing churchmen to vacant bishoprics. One of his appointments was William Alexander, dean of Emly, to the bishopric of Derry. In his letter to Alexander of 20 July 1867, Abercorn showed an awareness of the prevailing theological sensitivities in the diocese, warning Alexander that 'even a moderate amount of High Churchism would be more out of place in the diocese of Derry amongst the somewhat severe and rugged people than perhaps in any other diocese in the kingdom'.[91]

When in the late 1860s Gladstone outlined his plans to disestablish the Church of Ireland, Abercorn was at the forefront of the opposition to the proposal. In the debate in the Lords in June 1869 he argued that the changes proposed by the disestablishment bill amounted 'to nothing less than a severance of the connexion between the Church and the State' in Ireland and warned that it would only be a matter of time before such changes were implemented in England as well. Contrasting the rapidity with which the measure was being pursued with the years of discussion that had led up to the passing of the Emancipation Act in 1829, he further argued that the changes proposed by the bill were 'not only dangerous in the extreme, but they are novelties among our political expedients'. The Duke also argued that, contrary to what might have been expected, the Catholic laity was indifferent to disestablishment, while the Presbyterians opposed it. In closing he called on the Lords to 'reject a measure so full of injustice to Ireland, and so fraught with danger to the religion, the property, and the peace of the United Kingdom'. Not everyone, of course, agreed with Abercorn's analysis of the effects of disestablishment or of his assessment of the mood in Ireland regarding the bill. In the ensuing debate, the Duke was forced on one occasion to rebut an accusation that that he had implied that the Catholics of Ireland were disloyal. Others thought that his contributions to the debate lacked substance. Earl Granville, in a letter to the Queen, summed up his speeches as, 'voice and manner perfect, matter middling'.[92] Abercorn's successor as lord lieutenant, Lord Spencer, had similar reservations, writing to the Lord Chancellor, Thomas O'Hagan, 'My predecessor made many envious of his voice, manner and delivery, but not of his [?matter] or good sense. *The Times* criticism is sarcastic, but eminently true.'[93] O'Hagan shared Spencer's doubts about Abercorn, describing him as 'complacent and useless', and adding, 'It is odd that people who appear so good and kindly, as he and his, should make themselves so servilely the tools of faction.'[94]

Following the passing of the Irish Church Act, the Church of Ireland now had to find a way to structure itself for a post-disestablishment era. Here too Abercorn played an important role. His most significant contribution was in proposing a compromise solution – which secured overwhelming backing – to a complex issue concerning the position of the bishops in the councils of the Church.[95] Referring to the compromise proposed by Abercorn, James Spaight afterwards wrote to the Duke, 'It is now generally admitted by the great body of the Convention that it was the only wise and prudent course to adopt … It never would have been carried without the advantage of your Grace's influence with the bishops and popularity among the laity.' To many Abercorn was the 'Preserver of the Irish Church in the supreme moment of her imminent danger'.[96] In his 'Recollections', Edward Tipping reflected, 'If it were not for some moderate men, the work would hardly have been completed. Chief among these was the late Duke of Abercorn. His influence was very great and he always at the critical moment came forward as a peacemaker.'[97]

Abercorn's attachment to the established church, whether in England or Ireland, was also reflected in his belief that the governors of Harrow School should be members of the Church of England. In May 1871 he had unsuccessfully argued in the Lords for the inclusion of a religious test in the school's new statutes then being drafted. The Privy Council had made clear its opposition to this move, but for unknown reasons the religious qualification for governors had slipped through. The historian of Harrow has suggested that this occurred through the collusion of the clerk, Waring Young, with Lord Verulam, the chairman of the board of governors, and Abercorn.[98] Only in 1974, during discussions to revise the school's statutes, was it revealed that the requirement that governors be members of the Church of England should never have been enforced. The Duke was an active member of the board of governors of the school and in June 1871 chaired the celebration of the tercentenary of Harrow.[99]

After leaving the viceregal lodge in 1868 Abercorn found a new home in Eastwell, the former house of Lord Winchilsea. The younger sons loved it, Lord Ernest remembering with fondness the 'vastness of the Park, the solitude and silence of its giant beech-woods, and the wonderful variety of its scenery.' For the grown-ups, however, it was its extent that was 'its condemnation' and there were few regrets when it was given up after five years.[100] In 1869, the family found a new London home when the Duke acquired the leasehold of Hampden House in Green Street.[101]

Arisaig, on the west coast of Scotland, proved a popular holiday destination on a number of occasions in the early 1870s. In 1873, in order to avoid a journey of nearly 100 miles by road from Kingussie, the Duke bought a 50-ton steam yacht, the *Neireid*, so that he could sail to Arisaig from Greenock. Over 50 years later Lord Ernest looked back on the excitement he experienced in sailing on her. He described the *Neireid* as 'a comfortable and confidential little boat, but as crazy as Bedlam among anything but Lilliputian waves'.[102] Though the Duke had doubted her seaworthiness when he bought the yacht, he was determined to attempt a voyage across the Minch from Arisaig to the Hebrides. All went well until, about halfway across, they were met by a strong north-westerly gale which buffeted the boat with some force. Lord Ernest takes up the story:

> For some little while after the bursting of the storm all went well, or, at any rate, nothing went very badly. Then, suddenly, to our horror, we saw the skipper, who had so far been at the wheel, fling himself down on his knees on the deck and commence an impassioned appeal to the Virgin, leaving the wheel to take care of itself and the nose of the vessel to do as it would. The *Nereid* was a small boat and it took my father but three strides to reach the derelict wheel and seize the spokes. For half a minute or so I believe it was touch and go with us, for the boat's bow had fallen perceptibly away from the waves and the lee gunwale was very near under water; but after a few desperate and nerve-racking plunges, she came back to her true course and the imminence of the danger was past. The situation, however, was still sufficiently terrifying, for the *Nereid* had to stand almost on end to climb the giant waves that raced down on her, and when her nose plunged down on the far side, it seemed as though the next wave must inevitably overwhelm her.[103]

In the midst of this chaotic and potentially fatal experience Lord Ernest looked with pride on his father 'as he stood with quivering nostril and flashing eye, gripping in his muscular grasp the controlling spokes, the correct handling of which meant life or death to us'. Eventually the ship made it safely to harbour.

Politics in Tyrone

In the early 1870s Abercorn continued to be a major figure in Conservative politics in Ireland, chairing the informal meetings of Irish peers. He also found himself involved in parliamentary politics in County Tyrone more deeply than at any time since the 1830s. At the beginning of this decade relations between landlords and tenants in County Tyrone were reasonably good. The tenant right movement of the early 1850s had made little impact on the county. The historian R. W. Kirkpatrick has noted that the 'liberality [of the Duke of Abercorn] as a landlord was legendary'.[104] On occasion Abercorn hosted dinners for a selection of his tenants. For example, shortly before Christmas 1855 he invited over 50 of his tenantry to share a meal with him at Barons Court. In his speech Abercorn referred to the centuries old bonds that linked his family and the tenants on the estate.[105] Politically, the landed class seemed secure in its control of local parliamentary representation. In the general election of 1868 Lord Claud Hamilton and Henry Lowry-Corry, by now hugely experienced parliamentarians, had been returned unopposed (as they had been in every election but one since 1839).[106] By this time Lord Claud was known within the family as 'The Dowager' on account of there being a younger Claud, the Duke's second son. He was remembered by his nephew Lord Frederic for his peculiar style of dress: 'He wore an old-fashioned black-satin stock right up to his chin, with white "gills" above, and was invariably seen in a blue coat with brass buttons, and a buff waistcoat.'[107]

The first serious challenge to landlord-dominated politics in Tyrone came in the by-election of 1873 caused by the death on 6 March of Lowry-Corry. A week after this, at a meeting in Killyman, the Tyrone County Grand Orange Lodge selected the barrister J. W. Ellison Macartney as its favoured candidate in the forthcoming election.[108] There was immediate alarm from the landlord party at this alliance between Orangemen and a man rumoured to be sympathetic to the tenant right issue. In a confidential letter to the Earl of Belmore, Abercorn indicated his willingness to give his full support to the candidate chosen by the Conservatives in the county:

> As regards myself, the gentlemen of the county have behaved so handsomely to me during the last 35 years that I am entirely in their hands as to any candidate that they may generally elect to support. If either your brother [H. W. Lowry-Corry] or Monty Corry should be the person they decide on, I shall be most happy to give every assistance and support in my power, and I shall be very glad to hear they have done so.[109]

Abercorn regarded Ellison Macartney as a 'very troublesome fellow' and was probably conscious of the fact that should the Conservative candidate be defeated at this by-election then his own brother would face a strong challenge at the next general election.[110] When it was announced that Belmore's brother, Henry William Lowry-Corry, would be standing for the Conservatives, Abercorn, despite reservations about his candidacy, encouraged his own tenants and supporters to come out in favour of him and dispatched his agent to drum up support for him.[111]

Abercorn did, however, express his concerns about the ramifications of a defeat for Lowry-Corry. As one fellow Tyrone landlord, J. F. Lowry, put it: 'If Tyrone is lost at this time, every county in Ireland will have a Home Ruler next election.'[112] The Duke encouraged Belmore to think seriously about the possibility of withdrawing his brother from the contest, rather than see him defeated at the ballot box. He was confident that in the barony of Strabane 'very few will vote against a candidate I support', but he feared that indifference on the part of the electorate might cost Lowry-Corry votes. 'Macartney', he wrote, 'is a very unscrupulous man, and he has made good use of this infernal Ballot and of the present tenant right madness.' Furthermore, while Abercorn's supporters seemed lacking in any enthusiasm for the election, Macartney's were 'full of energy and animosity'.[113] As the Duke predicted, the day of the count was an anxious one; by a majority of only 36 votes Lowry-Corry was returned as the member for Tyrone.[114] For many in the landlord camp the result was too close for comfort.

Within a year of the by-election a general election was announced in which Ellison Macartney again took on the establishment, this time competing with both sitting MPs for one of the two Tyrone seats. It was suggested by various individuals, including Disraeli, that Lowry-Corry, being the junior partner to the more experienced Hamilton, should stand aside in order to avoid an embarrassing defeat.[115] Having just fought a costly election campaign – he estimated his expenses to have been about £100 per day for 23 days, not counting fees and car hire – Lowry-Corry refused to do this.[116] The relationship between Lowry-Corry and Lord Claud does not appear to have been the most cordial, and it is possible to detect from the surviving correspondence a degree of suspicion between them. All three candidates addressed the land issue, though it was Ellison Macartney who won over the tenant right movement. He was also able to draw upon Catholic support while at the same time retaining his Orange backing. The result of the poll was a resounding victory for Ellison Macartney, with Lowry-Corry elected in second place over 1,500 votes behind. Lord Claud trailed in a further 400 votes behind Lowry-Corry. He took his defeat very badly and reputedly declared that he would never set foot in Tyrone again, his main grievance being a lack of support from his fellow gentrymen.[117] Lord Claud's anger simmered away under the surface for over a year before boiling over in a 'very unpleasant fracas' on 13 July 1875 at a meeting of the Conservative

Society in Omagh.[118] He openly accused a Major Stewart of 'treachery [and] dishonourable conduct' in ensuring that Lowry-Corry stood at the previous year's election.

Second term as viceroy

When the Conservatives returned to power with a secure majority in February 1874, the Duke seemed the obvious choice for the Irish lord lieutenancy. Disraeli sought to encourage him to accept the appointment, arguing that the prospects were good for the Conservatives remaining in power for a number of years and that it was therefore necessary to have a viceroy who was prepared for a 'long and undisturbed reign'. The Queen herself was anxious that the Duke should accept an important office of state, if not in Ireland then in England.[119] Abercorn, however, at first refused the position, citing personal reasons, but when it was also declined by the Dukes of Marlborough and Northumberland, he consented to the appointment. Both the Queen and Disraeli were delighted, with the latter writing to the Duke on 24 February:

> I was at Windsor this morning, and can bear witness to the extreme satisfaction of the Queen on learning that you were again to be Her Representative. I know that this act involves, on your part, great personal sacrifices, and I am proud of a colleague as distinguished by his patriotism as he has long been, by his acknowledged abilities and his successful sway.[120]

In one of his earliest public addresses after taking up the lieutenancy in April he declared that it was his intention to 'administer the law with firmness and impartiality, and to work in the spirit of a generous and benignant policy'.[121] Abercorn's second term as viceroy was not as fulfilling as the first and at times he felt frustrated in his role. In April 1875 the Duchess reassured him:

> I think however irksome your duties may be, you must feel an inward compensation, that your life is not an entirely useless one. God has endowed you with intellect and ability above the average, which you have had little opportunity of exercising to advantage.[122]

Lord George Hamilton later wrote that his parents found the 'climate of Dublin too enervating for a continuance of office'.[123] The first viceroyalty had been enjoyed immensely by the younger members of the family, but this was not the case with the second. Lord George reflected that the 'gilt was off the gingerbread' and 'the artificiality of the semi-regal atmosphere in which we moved was much more apparent and much less endurable'.[124] In December 1875 it was reported that Abercorn wished to retire as viceroy.

Gossip that he was about to announce his resignation persisted into early 1876. 'I was told today that you had said that you should give up the lord lieutenancy in April', wrote the Duchess to her husband on 15 February, '[and] that you were not going to spend more of your private money in Ireland.'[125] Clearly the Duke was frustrated at his position, but, much to the government's relief for it saved it the trouble of finding a replacement, he continued in the role for the remainder of the year. The reference to the Duke's 'private money' suggests that he was becoming annoyed at the personal expense the role cost him. It was later calculated by his son Claud that in addition to the annual allowance of £20,000 the Duke had spent £60,000 of his own money during his time as lord lieutenant.[126] Cricket no doubt provided a welcome diversion from routine duties and Abercorn, though now in his mid-60s, continued to play regularly for the viceregal team. According to Lord Ernest, though he was probably exaggerating slightly, the Duke selected his entourage on the basis of their cricketing abilities, even going so far as to seek out clergymen with sporting talents as official chaplains. In the summer of 1875 Abercorn took a blow in the face from a cricket ball which injured his eyes. Following a social gathering, Disraeli described him as 'the beautiful viceroy in goggles', adding 'he excels in the game as in everything'.[127]

The Duke playing the part of Charles I at the 'Fancy Ball' he hosted in St Patrick's Hall, Dublin Castle, in March 1876.

In early December 1876 Abercorn resigned his lieutenancy, ostensibly because of his wife's ill-health. For a number of years she had been suffering from what was possibly depression, for many of her letters of this period reflect a certain melancholy. A contributory factor to Abercorn's resignation was the furore at Court arising from the conduct of his son-in-law, the Marquess of Blandford. Blandford, who was married to the Duke's daughter Albertha, had been involved in an adulterous relationship. The embarrassment that this had caused for his parents, the Duke and Duchess of Marlborough, made it expedient for Marlborough to be exiled to Ireland as lord lieutenant. It is unlikely that Abercorn felt any particular sadness on having to resign his position. Some commentators even felt that the Duke's return to England would be to the government's advantage in the Lords.[128] Though relinquishing the lord lieutenancy, Abercorn continued to discharge various responsibilities. In 1878, he travelled to Italy as Envoy Extraordinary for the investiture at Rome of King Humbert with the Order of the Garter.[129] In 1881, the Duke was appointed Chancellor of the Royal University of Ireland. In this capacity he conferred the honorary degrees of Doctor of Laws and Doctor of Music on, respectively, the Prince and Princess of Wales during another royal visit to Ireland in 1885.

Barons Court

Having disposed of his English properties by the mid-1850s, and notwithstanding the consideration he gave in 1856 to selling his Irish estate *en bloc*, Abercorn began to take much more of an interest in Barons Court. One indication of this was the construction of a new church there in 1855. A small building with structurally divided nave and chancel and a bellcote over the west gable, it was intended to be the family's place of worship when in residence in Tyrone. He also began to increase his plantations about Barons Court. In addition, two model farms were established in the vicinity of Barons Court, each one of over 1,000 aces and provided with suitable buildings. The management of these was intended to set a good example to farmers in the neighbourhood.[130] These model farms 'boasted a water-race, a mill-wheel and fascinating sluice-gates which could be raised or lowered with most exciting results', remembered Lord Ernest.[131] These activities involved the removal of a significant number of tenants occupying farms in the vicinity of Barons Court. An article on the evictions was published in *The Irishman*, a copy of which managed to find its way to Karl Marx. Marx was of course intrigued by the story and wrote to his friend Friedrich Engels in November 1867: 'The Irish Viceroy, Lord Abicorn (this is *roughly* the name), has "cleared" his estate of thousands within recent weeks by compulsory evictions. Among the evicted are well-to-do farmers whose improvements and capital investments are confiscated in this fashion.'[132] The claim that thousands had been forcibly evicted was an exaggeration. Nonetheless, for a time feeling was high.

Touring through Ireland in the early 1880s, Margaret Dixon McDougall, who wrote under the pseudonym 'Norah', noted that Abercorn was 'spoken of as a model landlord' whose 'published utterances were genial, such as a good landlord, father and protector of his people would utter'. However, the memory of the earlier clearances was still strong, and Mrs McDougall was critical of the Duke's actions in this regard:

Plans to build Barons Court Church were underway by the mid 1830s. On 22 February 1837, F. N. Clements wrote to his mother, Lady Leitrim, that 'Lord Abercorn is going to build a small church for about £300, [with] a parsonage house, and endow it with £120 or £150. That church will be between Barons Court and a new village, almshouse, etc, he is building' (A. P. W. Malcomson, *The Clements Archive* (Dublin, 2010), p. 461). There seems to have been a lengthy delay in proceeding with church's construction for nearly nineteen years later, on 4 November 1855, Major Humphreys wrote, 'His lordship has just built a remarkably nice church at the end of the demesne, and is very anxious to have it consecrated that service may be performed in it' (PRONI, D623/A/269/59). The church was consecrated on 24 March 1858.

The garden terrace alongside Lough
Fanny is clearly visible.
Further improvements to the gardens
were executed in 1876 by Ninian
Niven who designed a garden of three
terraces with balustrading on the
south front.

Someone who thought His Grace of Abercorn was sailing under false
colours, that his published utterances and private course of action
were far apart, published an article in a Dublin paper. The article
stated that the Duke had evicted over 123 families, numbering over
1,000 souls, not for non-payment of rent, but to create a lordly
loneliness about Barons Court. His Grace did not like tenantry so near
his residence. Those tenants who submitted quietly got five years' rent
– not as a right, but as a favour given out of the goodness of his
heart.[133]

In 1878, the Duke finally decided to make Barons Court his usual
residence. He was approaching 70 and was no doubt growing weary of
having to find a new country house every few years. The dream of a
permanent English residence was over. To begin with he was reluctant to
introduce to the house the works of art and other treasures that had once
beautified The Priory. Lord Ernest remembered the 'home-made furniture'
in the bedrooms at Barons Court, the 'drugget carpets' and 'dimity curtains',
and the 'huge baize-lined hampers' used to store turf for the fire.[134]
Eventually in the winter of 1879 his family persuaded him to decorate the
house with the paintings, statues, books and furniture that had been in
storage for over 30 years. The move to Barons Court coincided with, and

perhaps contributed to, the Duchess's return to health and the social scene. In June 1879 Disraeli commented to Lady Chesterfield that a dinner he had recently attended was 'remarkable for one thing – the return to society after six years of ill-health and solicitude of the Duchess of Abercorn'.[135] Lord Frederic described the happy times the couple enjoyed at their Tyrone home in their declining years.

> My father had one peculiarity; he never altered his manner of living, whether the house was full of visitors, or he were alone with my mother, after his children had married and left him. At Baron's Court, when quite by themselves, they used the large rooms, and had them all lighted up at night, exactly as though the house was full of guests. There was to my mind something very touching in seeing an aged couple, after more than fifty years of married life together, still preserving the affectionate relations of lovers with each other. They played their chess together nightly in a room ninety-eight feet long, and delighted in still singing together, in the quavering tones of old age, the simple little Italian duets that they had sung in the far-off days of their courtship.
>
> As his years increased, my father did not care to venture much beyond the circle of his own family, though as thirteen of his children had grown up, and he had seven married daughters, the two elder of

whom had each thirteen children of her own, the number of his immediate descendants afforded him a fairly wide field of selection. In his old age he liked to have his five sons round him all the winter, together with their wives and children. Accordingly, every October my three married brothers arrived at Baron's Court with their entire families, and remained there till January, so that the house persistently rang with children's laughter. What with governesses, children, nurses and servants, this meant thirty-three extra people all through the winter, so it was fortunate that Baron's Court was a large house, and that there was plenty of room left for other visitors. It entailed no great hardship on the sons, for the autumn salmon fishing in the turbulent Mourne is excellent, there was abundance of shooting, and M. Gouffe, the cook, was a noted artist.[136]

On 25 October 1882, the Duke and Duchess celebrated their golden wedding anniversary. At 8am on that frosty morning the rector of Ardstraw assembled a choir of schoolchildren under their bedroom window to sing an epithalamium specially composed by Mrs Cecil Frances Alexander, daughter of their former agent, Major Humphreys. The Barons Court Temperance Band then played 'Auld Lang Syne' and 'Haste to the Wedding'. Shortly before noon 120 estate employees, accompanied by a local brass band, paraded to Barons Court. In returning thanks to those gathered, the Duke said: 'Our married life has been a happy one. I believe rarely has half a century of married life been passed with more affection or with more mutual sympathy in feeling, and in the pursuits which lead to domestic happiness

A view of the gallery in the late nineteenth century.

and long-lived peace and satisfaction.' At 5pm 240 labourers and 'female friends' were entertained in the granary, while following a family dinner at Barons Court a ball was held in the granary that night. Among the many presents received was a large photograph from the Queen of the Royal Family.[137]

The land issue

Through his status, connections and political influence, Abercorn was one of the key figures in the defence of the landowners of Ireland in the late 1870s and early 1880s at a time when they were coming under attack from various quarters. The emergence of the Land League, which called for an end to landlordism, posed a serious threat for Irish landlords, while the general election of 1880 again demonstrated how the balance of political power was shifting away from the landed classes. The campaign of that year was fought against the background of serious land agitation brought on by poor harvests and falling prices in 1878–79. Lord Claud Hamilton believed that this election provided him with an opportunity to return to the Commons and so stood for the Conservatives, but was narrowly defeated. On this occasion the formerly troublesome Ellison Macartney, who stood with official Conservative backing, and a Liberal candidate, who campaigned strongly on issues that appealed to tenant farmers, were elected. Lord Claud would not have another opportunity to return to the Commons, and he died in 1884 aged 70.

Feeling that they were coming under ever greater pressure, at the beginning of January 1882 a protest rally was held in the Exhibition Palace in Dublin by the landowning classes, angry at the rent reductions being imposed on them by the Land Commission, a body established by the government in the previous year. It was a huge gathering with some 3,000 people present.[138] The Duke chaired the meeting, and in opening it he set out what he felt its purpose should be:

> In meeting here today our object is not to condemn or to criticise the Land Act itself, which, whatever may be our opinions of its injustice or its necessity, we still accept as a legislative enactment. Neither do we wish to enter into any political question. Our object is to condemn and criticise the mode in which the Land Act had been administered by the Sub-Commissioners.

These civil servants, whose qualifications, impartiality and experience he questioned, were the targets for Abercorn's anger. He accused them of carrying out their work in an 'offhand and haphazard manner' and said that reductions in rent based on their valuations were simply a means of buying off the Land League 'by the sacrifice of the landlords' income'. He launched a scathing attack on the Land League: 'We will not allow our fortunes and the birthright of our children to be sacrificed in a vain attempt to perpetuate and appease a seditious and homicidal Land League.' The gathering was afterwards described by the Duchess to the Queen as the 'most important meeting ever held in Ireland'.[139]

Abercorn also used his seat in the House of Lords to condemn the treatment of Irish landlords. During the debate on the Address at the opening of the 1883 session he severely criticised government policy in Ireland, declaring that 'history would record the name of Mr Gladstone as that of the statesman who, without evil intentions, had wrought greater ruin and desolation on Ireland, and greater degradation of its national character than any minister who for two centuries had governed that country'. Not surprisingly, Abercorn's outspokenness on this and other issues drew criticism. An article by 'Kosmos' published in the *World* in 1883 begins with what seems to be praise, but it is soon apparent that the writer uses mockery in describing the Duke with statements such as 'Abercorn is an eternal institution' before dismissing his 'twopenny omnipotence'.[140]

Death and burial

The monument to the 1st Duke at Barons Court Church.

In mid-October 1885, while at Barons Court, the Duke became ill. His condition fluctuated over the next two weeks and at various points he seemed to be making a recovery. Even from his sickbed he continued to take an interest in public affairs. However, in the last week of October his illness worsened and he passed away at 9.30pm on Saturday, 31 October. He was in his 75th year. With the exception of his daughter Harriet, who was on the Continent, all the members of his family had gathered at Barons Court during the final stages of his life. Early the following morning news of his passing reached the Queen at Balmoral. Several times the previous day she and the Prince of Wales had telegraphed asking to be kept informed. The Queen wrote in her journal that she was 'very much aggrieved' to hear of Abercorn's death – 'such a noble, handsome-looking man, and take him all in all, one will not see his like in Ireland again. He was a clever, good man, and very useful in Ireland. The poor Duchess nursed him throughout.'[141] She sent a telegram to the Marquess of Hamilton, now the 2nd Duke, expressing her 'deep concern at this sad news', adding, 'My children join in truest sympathy.' Over the coming weeks and through the Christmas period the Queen continued to be in regular communication with the Duchess as she sought to comfort her during her grief.

The Duke was mourned deeply, not just by his family, but by those with whom he had come into contact over a long and active life. His son George wrote that he was a 'most kind and considerate parent'. His obituary in the *Times* observed: 'The Duke of Abercorn was one of the few members of the nobility and lords of the soil who amid all the trouble and turmoil of the last few years, which have shattered many popular reputations, retained the good opinion and good will of all classes of people.'[142] Lord Ernest wrote that while his father usually treated those among whom he lived in his latter years *de haut en bas*, he 'inspired them with an unbounded admiration which very nearly approached worship'.[143] The monument erected to his memory at Barons Court Church was designed by Walter G. Doolin of Dublin and is in the form of a Celtic cross.

The Dowager Duchess of Abercorn

The Duchess survived the Duke by nearly 20 years, remaining remarkably active in spite of her advancing years. She moved to at Coates Castle, Fittleworth, Sussex, where she continued her well-established practice of visiting the needy in her neighbourhood and doing what she could to help them. Though living on her own, she was visited on a regular basis by her large family circle. With her 'inextinguishable love of a joke', she was hugely popular with her grandchildren and great-grandchildren. On one occasion,

The Dowager Duchess of Abercorn celebrating her 82nd birthday at Montagu House, Whitehall, in July 1894, with 101 of her descendants. A photograph of a similar gathering held in 1903 for the Dowager Duchess' 91st birthday, again at Montagu House, shows her with 146 of her 205 direct descendants.

when in her 86th year, her nurse found her in the garden demonstrating to her great-grandson the art of walking on stilts. When she had turned 87, she was described as appearing 'as young as a kitten and really only looks about 60, walks three miles a day and thoroughly enjoys life.' On another occasion, when aged 90, she was found with a stable-boy, both of them armed with sticks, at the back of a barn intently watching a rat-hole into which a ferret had been inserted.

In her 90th year she was present at the coronation of Edward VII. This was also the age at which she was persuaded to no longer try to be present at the weddings of her descendants. She continued to make an annual autumn visit to Scotland, which she enjoyed immensely. During the Boer War, in which many of the younger men in the family were engaged, she knitted stockings and tam-o'-shanters for the troops. She died on the morning of 31 March 1905 at Coates Castle after only a few days' illness. It was suspected that she had caught a chill while out driving which developed into pneumonia. At her death it was calculated that she had 245 descendants, of whom around 160 were still alive. She was, in the words of her son Ernest, 'the one golden link that held together some fifty families scattered here and there about the United Kingdom'.[144]

Many people marvelled at the energy shown by the Dowager Duchess of Abercorn. According to her son Lord Ernest, even in her old age she possessed an 'irrepressible *joie de vivre* that many a girl of twenty might have envied'.

This remarkable monument at Barons Court Church bears the legend: 'The Tables of the Ten Commandments were placed in this Church and the Chancel was paved with marble in loving memory of Louisa Jane Duchess of Abercorn by her Grand Children, Great Grandchildren, and Great-Great Grandchildren together with their Husbands and Wives, whose names stand inscribed above. 1906'.

The younger sons of the 1st Duke of Abercorn

Of the seven sons of the 1st Duke of Abercorn, one, Cosmo, died when he was only a month old, while another, Ronald, died at the age of 18. The remaining five sons, all educated at Harrow, reached adulthood and would go on to have successful careers in a number of different spheres of activity. In 1885, four of the brothers successfully stood for election to the House of Commons, while the eldest, the 2nd Duke, took his seat in the Lords.

The sons of the 1st Duke photographed in 1874. Standing is Lord Hamilton and sitting from left to right are Lords George, Frederic, Claud and Ernest.

Lord Claud (1843–1925)

Lord Claud John Hamilton represented more constituencies than any of his brothers and his parliamentary career stretched from 1865 to 1918, though with two short interruptions and one long one lasting from 1888 to 1910. He was a young officer in the Grenadier Guards when, in 1865, he was elected MP for the city of Londonderry. The choice of Lord Claud as the Conservative candidate had revealed deep divisions within the local Protestant community. The Hamiltons were viewed as anti-Presbyterian by the local populace and during the election campaign Lord Claud had gone out of his way to counter this. The 1868 election in Derry was a heated affair. Supporters of his challenger, the Liberal candidate Richard Dowse, afterwards Baron Dowse, had a chant along the lines of:

> Dowse for iver! Claud in the river!
> With a skivver through his liver.[145]

Lord Claud was defeated by just over 100 votes, with Dowse's victory attributed to the support he received from a significant number of Presbyterian electors. The following year Claud was returned as MP for King's Lynn in Norfolk in a by-election, holding this seat until 1880 when he was defeated in the general election of that year. He was absent from Parliament for only a few months for he was the victor in a by-election in Liverpool in August 1880. In November 1885, following the reorganisation of parliamentary constituencies, he was returned for the West Derby division in Liverpool.

175

In the aftermath of this election Lord Claud refuted a number of allegations made against his family in the *Liverpool Mercury*, specifically that the Hamiltons had held between them some 27 offices and had received £116,800 from the public purse.[146] In what was described as 'a crushing reply' Claud countered every argument made against his family. He pointed out that in the last half century, his late father had expended £70,000 on the 18 elections contested by members of the family. Few of the alleged offices received support from public funds and in most cases the Hamiltons were forced to use their own finances in order to discharge the attendant duties. Claud acknowledged that he had been Lord of the Treasury, but this was for only a few weeks prior to the 1868 election and that he had 'paid more away in stamp duties and uniforms that I received in official salary'. Lord Claud resigned as MP in 1888 to concentrate on his business interests, but returned to the Commons over two decades later in January 1910 as MP for South Kensington which he represented until retiring in advance of the 1918 general election. In 1917, he was made a privy counsellor.

He was probably best known for his lengthy chairmanship of the Great Eastern Railway which began in 1893 and lasted until 1922. When the company introduced a new class of express passenger trains in 1900 it named the first of these new locomotives after him and in fact the entire class became known as the Claud Hamiltons. He was popular with his staff and showed genuine concern for their welfare. Lord Claud was also chairman of the Railway Clearing House and the Railway Association. In addition, he presided over the board of the East London Railway Company and was a director of the Sheffield District Railway Company. Away from politics and business, he held a number of positions, including the presidency of the London branch of the Grenadiers Old Comrades Association and the chairmanship of the Carlton Club. He was an aide-de-camp to Queen Victoria from 1887 to 1897 and during the First World War was a commandant in the Special Constabulary.

In July 1878, he married Carolina Chandos-Pole. They had two children, Gilbert Claud, who served with distinction during the Boer War, and Ida. He remained active into old age. His obituarist remembered Lord Claud, by this time past the age of 70, shooting partridges from breakfast on a hot September day and then changing into flannels and playing tennis from late afternoon until dusk.[147] He was remembered as a 'well-meaning, warm-hearted man', slow to form an opinion, but fixed in it once he had. He died in 1925 aged 81.

Lord George (1845–1927)

Born in Brighton in 1845, Lord George Francis Hamilton was the most successful parliamentarian of the 1st Duke of Abercorn's sons. In 1864, he joined the Rifle Brigade and four years later transferred to the 1st Battalion of the Coldstream Guards. Unexpectedly, in 1868, he was invited to stand as

Lord George Hamilton photographed in 1875.

the Conservative candidate for Middlesex. He accepted, but only after Disraeli encouraged him with the words, 'all right, little David, go in and kill Goliath'. Few imagined that he would be successful, however, while the Duke himself was warned:

> Let nothing induce you to allow G. to come forward for Middx, if there is still any thought of it. The Election would cost you from 12 to 14 thousand – and I can assure you positively beyond all doubt that he wouldn't have a ghost of a chance; not a scintilla: I know this.[148]

However, after the sitting MP, Henry Labouchere, had made critical remarks about the Hamiltons the Duke indicated his willingness to bankroll George's election campaign. Labouchere dismissed Lord George as 'a young gentleman who had lately joined the army – an unfledged ensign who was getting on with the goose step and preparing himself for the onerous duties connected with the Horse Guards'. Others mocked his youthfulness with the cry, 'Milk for the baby!'[149] To the surprise of many political commentators, George was elected with a comfortable majority. He held the seat until 1885 when, following the redrawing of constituency boundaries, he was elected MP for Ealing. As an MP representing constituencies with large middle class populations, Lord George became well informed on the political aspirations of this sector of the electorate and was a valuable asset to the Conservative Party in this regard.

In 1874, having turned down a position in the Foreign Office on the basis that his French was limited, he was made Under-Secretary for India, representing the government on India in the Commons, the Secretary of State for India being a member of the Lords. His first ministerial statement earned Disraeli's high praise, with the Prime Minister telling the Queen, 'Both sides of the House were delighted with him; with his thorough knowledge of the subject; his fine voice; his calmness, dignity and grace.' Four years later he became Vice-President of the Council, which effectively made him the minister for education, a role he found frustrating. In 1885, he was appointed First Lord of the Admiralty and worked heard to modernise the Royal Navy. Among the reforms he implemented was the creation of a naval intelligence department and the introduction of a more strategic approach to future expansion.

Implacably opposed to Home Rule, he nonetheless supported land reform in Ireland. In December 1886, he advised his brother, the 2nd Duke, to accept the inevitability of having to begin the process of transferring the farms on the Abercorn estate to the tenants. At times his position on the land issue brought him into conflict with his own family. In September 1892, for instance, in the face of further legislation on the land question, the 2nd Duke wrote to Col. Edward Saunderson, 'I look upon him as a traitor and don't like him now'.[150] In 1895, George became Secretary of State for India, holding this position until 1903 when he resigned because of his opposition to tariff reform which he believed was inimical to India's economic interests. By this time, he had also become largely disinterested in domestic politics and retired from the Commons in advance of the 1906 general election.

Lord George Hamilton as depicted by Spy in *Vanity Fair* on 5 April 1879. In the accompanying description it was observed of him: 'He is a young man of engaging appearance and great readiness of speech.'

He continued to be active in public life and served as chairman of the Royal Commission on the Poor Law from 1905 to 1909. He later chaired the Mesopotamia Commission in 1917 which investigated defeats suffered by the India army. Outside of politics he was an enthusiastic cricketer – he was president of the MCC in 1881-2 – and cyclist. He died at his London home in 1927. In 1871, he had married Lady Maud Caroline, daughter of Henry Lascelles, 3rd Earl of Harewood. They had three sons, Ronald, Anthony and Robert, all of whom served in the First World War and survived.

Lord Frederic (1856–1928)

Though in general the Hamiltons were considered great company, few were as popular and universally liked as Lord Frederic Spencer Hamilton. His father having decided that his son should pursue a career in the diplomatic service, Frederic he left Harrow at the age of 17 to spend time on the Continent – at Nyons in the south of France and Brunswick in Germany – improving his language skills. Having passed his entrance examinations, he joined the Foreign Office at the age of 20. His first experience of foreign courts was in 1876 when he was part of a Special Mission to Rome that was led by his father. Ten months later he was sent to Berlin as an Attaché, also spending some time 'on loan' to Vienna. Later he would serve under Lord Dufferin, his godfather and the man after whom he was named, at St Petersburg where he enjoyed himself immensely and made a wide circle of friends.

Following the appointment of his brother-in-law, Lord Lansdowne, as Governor General of Canada, Lord Frederic was sent to Ottawa. Here he launched with great enthusiasm into winter sports and believed that he had been the first to introduce the art of skiing to Canada (for a time he thought that he had been the first to introduce skiing to the North American continent). According to his own account, '... in January 1887, I brought my Russian ski to Ottawa, as I fondly imagined, the very first pair that had ever been seen in the New World. I coasted down hills on them amidst universal jeers; every one declared that they were quite unsuited to Canadian conditions.' When Lord Lansdowne was appointed Viceroy of India in 1888, Lord Frederic moved with him to Calcutta. Other postings in his diplomatic career included Lisbon, Argentina and Brazil.

Away from the Foreign Office, Lord Frederic served two terms as a Conservative MP, though he seems neither to have been an effective nor an enthusiastic member. In 1885-6 he represented Manchester South-West. In 1892, he was selected as the Unionist candidate in North Tyrone, the seat that had previously been held by his brother Ernest and which was one of the most marginal seats in Ireland. While campaigning in North Tyrone, Lord Frederic made the rather surprising admission that he was a believer in the compulsory sale of estates as a means of resolving the land issue. Although brother to one of the largest landowners in Ireland, he pointed out that that he was not a landlord himself and so land reform would not affect him personally. He won

Lord Frederic Hamilton. Taken in 1876, the year in which Lord Frederic had his first experience of foreign courts, spending time in Rome and Berlin.

The monument to Lord Frederic
in Barons Court Church.

by a narrow majority, but served only one term,
retiring in 1895.

Lord Frederic is best known for three largely
autobiographical volumes, *The days before yesterday*,
Here, there and everywhere, and *The vanished pomps of
yesterday*. While full of humorous anecdotes and
amusing observations – 'The Austrian aristocracy were the
most charming people. … Though brainless, they had
delightful manners' – they also provide an insight into the
activities of foreign embassies and the jostling for power by the
great European empires of the latter part of the nineteenth century. He
was also editor of the *Pall Mall Gazette* for a time, and created the fictional
detective, Mr P. J. Davenant, a 'youthful Sherlock Holmes'. Many people
testified to his charm and good company. A fellow traveller on a voyage from
Quebec to Liverpool in 1909 – Lord Frederic was returning from the Far East
– remembered him as one of the most popular men on board and a 'bright and
entertaining conversationalist, a man who could talk well and had an
amazingly extensive repertoire of experiences and stories', ranging from his
schooldays, to diplomatic career and electioneering in England and Ireland.'[151]
Lord Frederic died unmarried in 1928.

Lord Ernest (1858–1939)

The fourteenth child and youngest son of the 1st Duke of Abercorn, Lord
Ernest William Hamilton was born in 1858 at Brocket Hall in Hertfordshire,
the family's then English home. Following schooling at Harrow, he entered
Sandhurst and in 1878 was commissioned into the 11th Hussars; he was
promoted to captain in 1884. The death of his father in October 1885 resulted
in him standing as MP for the constituency of North Tyrone, his brother
James, the original candidate, having succeeded to the dukedom. In the
ensuing contest in December of that year Lord Ernest defeated the prominent
Nationalist John Dillon by 3,345 votes to 2,922. During his election campaign
Lord Ernest adopted a conciliatory tone and in his victory speech thanked the
Presbyterians and Liberals who had voted for him.[152]

In the election of the following July, Lord Ernest was again returned, though
with a slightly reduced majority, after defeating a Gladstonian Liberal, J. O.
Wylie, a Presbyterian barrister and land commissioner. Wylie had Nationalist
backing while it was also hoped that he would win sufficient support from the
Presbyterian tenant farmers to oust Lord Ernest. However, as Ernest was later
to reflect, this group disliked the idea of Home Rule even more than voting for
a member of the landed aristocracy.[153] After entering the Commons Lord
Ernest quickly became deeply disillusioned with parliamentary life. By his own
admission he was an 'unwilling victim' and made few contributions to
parliamentary debate.[154] In order to relieve some of the boredom surrounding
life at Westminster he would race with his brother Frederic on bicycles
borrowed from dining room attendants.[155] On another occasion he went

Lord Frederic made his appearance
in *Vanity Fair* on 7 February 1895
and among the comments made of
him were: 'He is a traveller who
has visited the greater part of the
world, and a sportsman who has
had notable sport in South America
and India. He can jabber more or
less correctly in five tongues; he is
generally musical; and he is blessed
with a host of friends. He is
probably the worst billiard-player
in Europe. But he is a popular
fellow.'

fishing in Norway during a parliamentary session. Not surprisingly, he retired from politics after one full parliamentary sitting.

Following his withdrawal from representative politics, Lord Ernest pursued a number of different interests. His brother Frederic acknowledged that he was a man 'with a fatal facility for doing everything easily'. Because of his many talents, his ambitions in life kept changing. Frederic believed that Ernest could have been a great cricketer, while he also excelled at steeple-chasing, golf, music and photography. His frequent changes of direction were a source of frustration for his family, but in response 'he pleaded in extenuation that versatility had very marked charms of its own', and even wrote a poem, 'The Curse of Versatility'[156] He travelled to various locations, including the Klondyke and Peru, on behalf of mining syndicates, and accepted several directorships. He wrote prodigiously on a range of different subjects from history to religion. His consciousness of his Scottish ancestry comes through in his novels, such as *The outlaws of the marsh* (1897), which is set in the Borders during the sixteenth century, and in his historical writings, including *The soul of Ulster* (1917). He also wrote *The first seven divisions: a history of the fighting to Ypres* (1916), a work of 'instant history'. Two historical works published after the war, *Elizabethan Ulster* (1919) and *The Irish rebellion of 1641* (1920), are regarded as well researched and written books, even if they reveal too much of the author's bias.

In 1922, he published his autobiography, *Forty years on.* Following its appearance, Lord Ernest was by sued for libel by a local priest, Fr John McConnalogue, for suggesting that the cleric, a leading Nationalist, had joined in celebrating Lord Frederic's victory in the 1892 general election in North Tyrone, enjoying his fair share of Moët and Chandon in a Strabane hotel. The story was fictitious and the matter was settled out of court with Lord Ernest making a public apology and paying costs and damages to McConnalogue. Lord Ernest was the last of the fourteen children of the 1st Duke to die, passing away at his London home on 14 December 1939. He married Pamela Campbell in 1891 and they had two sons – Guy Ernest Frederic and John George Peter – and two daughters – Mary Brenda and Jean Barbara Bertha Elizabeth.

Lord Ernest

The seven daughters of the 1st Duke of Abercorn

It has frequently been commented on that each of the seven daughters of the 1st Duke and Duchess of Abercorn married a man of no lower rank than an earl. Disraeli remarked in 1863, 'His daughters are so singularly pretty that they always marry during their first season, and always make the most splendid matches'.[157] G. W. E. Russell wrote, 'Few sets of sisters have been so universally liked and admired, and none have better deserved the good fortune which awaited them, or were more perfectly fitted to the positions which they were called to fill.'[158]

Harriet, the eldest, married the 2nd Earl of Lichfield in 1855, having thrice turned down an offer of marriage from the Duke of Manchester. She bore eight sons and five daughters. She died in 1913. Beatrix married the 2nd Earl of Durham in 1854. She would bear thirteen children over the next seventeen years and died just a few days after the birth of her youngest child in January 1871 aged only 35. She was remembered by her brother Ernest as 'a very beautiful woman with the face of an angel'. Louisa married the future 6th Duke of Buccleuch in 1859 and was the mother of six sons and two daughters. Known as 'Tiny', it was said of her that she had the 'charm of perpetual youth' and 'abhorred all friskiness and riskiness, all the craving for notoriety, all the disregard for convention, which in later years had become fashionable.'[159] She served as a Mistress of the Robes to Victoria during two separate periods – 1885–92 and 1895–1901, and continued as a Mistress of the Robes under Queen Alexandra.

Katherine married the future 4th Earl of Mount Edgcumbe and was the mother of four children. The Mount Edgcumbes had a villa near the Croix des Gardes, Cannes, and every winter for a number of years Katherine went there with her mother to Cannes for the benefit of their health and were joined by other members of both families. Georgiana was the last of the sisters to marry. Considered by Disraeli to have been 'very pretty', she had been pursued by a succession of suitors, but as her mother was in indifferent health Georgiana felt it was her duty to remain at her side. In 1882, however, she married the 5th Earl Winterton. Their only child, Edward, was born in the following year. She died in 1913. In 1863, she had been one of the eight bridesmaids at the wedding of the Prince of Wales to Princess Alexandra.

Abercorn family group, 1858 (Royal Collection). From left to right, standing: Lord Claud Hamilton; Lord Ronald Hamilton; Lady Katherine Hamilton; James, Lord Hamilton; Lady Louise Hamilton; Louisa, Marchioness of Abercorn with Lord Frederic Hamilton; James Hamilton, Marquess of Abercon; Lord George Hamilton. Seated: Harriet, Countess of Lichfield with Thomas, Viscount Anson; Lady Maud Hamilton; Lady Georgiana Hamilton with John, Viscount Lambton; Hon. Frederick Lambton; Lady Albertha Hamilton; Beatrix, Countess of Durham with baby, probably Hon. Charles Lambton.

181

Lady Georgiana Hamilton as
Queen Elizabeth, wife of
Charles IX of France, at the
'Fancy Ball' in Dublin in 1876.

What was perhaps considered the greatest match was the marriage of
Albertha to the Marquess of Blandford, heir to the dukedom of Marlborough.
The wedding took place on 8 November 1869 in Westminster Abbey with a
huge gathering of royalty and nobility present. Four children would follow,
including the future 9th Duke of Marlborough. The marriage, however, was
deeply unhappy with the couple having very little in common. One historian
has written that she was 'as good as she was beautiful, as pious as she was
innocent, and really rather stupid'.[160] Blandford himself complained that his
only choice in marriage was which of the Abercorn daughters to take.
Nicknamed 'Goosie', some of the Churchill family thought Albertha a fool
and she became known for her practical jokes – such as putting soap she had
cut into wedges on to the cheeseboard and placing ink pots on the tops of
doors. Blandford, deeply flawed, but highly intelligent, quickly bored of her
and began an affair with the wife of Lord Aylesford. She had previously been a
mistress of the Prince of Wales and while her husband was prepared to turn a
blind eye to the royal liaison, he was less indulgent when it came to the affair
with Blandford.

In an attempt to stop her husband from issuing divorce proceedings, Lady
Aylesford gave Blandford compromising letters to her from the Prince of
Wales. These were then used to blackmail the Prince into using his influence
with Lord Aylesford to stop him from divorcing his wife. This he succeeded in
doing, but the fallout was huge with the Prince boycotting any house open to
Blandford.[161] It also had consequences for Albertha's father for he was forced,
not very reluctantly it must be admitted, to relinquish the Irish lord
lieutenancy so that it could be given to the Blandford's father, the Duke of
Marlborough, not as a reward, but so he could be 'exiled' across the Irish Sea.
After Blandford's affair with Lady Aylesford came to light Albertha sought a
judicial separation. He attempted a reconciliation with her, but it was not a

success and he continued his affair with Lady Aylesford, fathering a child with her in 1881. In 1883 Blandford and Albertha divorced.[162] Until her death in 1932 she preferred to be known as Albertha, Marchioness of Blandford, though she was entitled to be called the Duchess of Marlborough as her former husband had succeeded to the dukedom shortly before their divorce.

Her obituarist wrote that 'her most outstanding characteristic was the unshakeable benevolence of her outlook'.[163]

On the same day that Albertha married the Marquess of Blandford, her younger sister, the 'graceful and placid' Maud, married the 5th Marquess of Lansdowne and would go on to bear four children. Lansdowne was successively Governor General of Canada (1883–88) and Viceroy of India (1888–94). Among the appointments that Maud held was that of Lady of the Bedchamber to Queen Alexandra. At the outbreak of the Boer War in 1899, she was instrumental in founding the Officers' Families Fund, of which she was president, and during the First World War she and her husband provided their London home, Lansdowne House, as its headquarters. After the War she was made a Dame Grand Cross of the Order of the British Empire (GBE). She was the last of the sisters to die, passing away in October 1932.

The farewell demonstration at Barons Court on Lord and Lady Lansdowne's departure for Canada in October 1883. With hundreds of participants, this elaborate farewell for the Duke's daughter Lady Maud and her husband had been weeks in the planning and included performances by the Barons Court Brass Band and the Barons Court Church Choir.

The Duke as a young man.

8
James Hamilton,
2nd Duke of Abercorn
The survival of the estate

When the 2nd Duke of Abercorn succeeded to the title in the autumn of 1885 it was at the most critical point in the family's more recent history. The landed estate, which had experienced a period of stability for nearly three centuries, was on the eve of breaking up as the tenantry took advantage of a series of land acts to purchase their farms. Politically, Ireland was in a state of upheaval in 1885 as the country was gripped by the first Home Rule crisis and its ramifications. History has not been as kind to the 2nd Duke as it has to other members of the family in the past 150 years. He has been described as weak and ineffectual, a man who promised much but delivered little. A description of him from 1881 rather mockingly noted, 'He has not done much, but he has done nothing badly.' Such comments probably have more to do with expectation than with reality. Unlike his father and his son, the 2nd Duke of Abercorn never held an important office of state. Whereas his father was lord lieutenant of Ireland on two occasions, and his son governor of Northern Ireland for over 20 years, at no point was he entrusted with a position of political importance. Whatever his failings, he shepherded the family and estate through a period of great turbulence. That both still exist today is testament to the fact that he did so successfully.

Early life and marriage

James Hamilton, the future 2nd Duke of Abercorn, was born at Byam House, Brighton, on 24 August 1838, the fourth child and eldest son of the 2nd Marquess of Abercorn and his wife Louisa. He was baptised in the parish church of Brighthelmston, Sussex, on 1 September following. During his childhood the family had no settled home, but rather moved from country house to country house. There were regular visits to Barons Court, as well as to Scotland, but most of his early life was spent in England. Like his father, he was educated at Harrow and then Christ Church, Oxford, receiving his

BA in 1860 and MA in 1865. As a young man, one of his closest friendships was with the Prince of Wales. They regularly dined together, and the heir to the throne would look to him for advice on the direction his life should take. In March 1872, for example, we find that one of Hamilton's concerns was that the Prince of Wales should be found some meaningful occupation. The two men talked this over on several occasions before Hamilton approached Colonel Ponsonby, one of the Queen's equerries and later her private secretary, to discuss the matter with him. Hamilton was convinced that the Prince needed some 'congenial employment' and thought that he might like to be taught the business of the various departments of government. Whatever employment he was found, Hamilton was convinced that the Prince would do his best.[1]

Hamilton travelled widely in his younger days. By the mid-nineteenth century the European 'Grand Tour', enjoyed by earlier generations of Hamiltons, had given way to sporting expeditions to India, and towards the end of 1860 Hamilton set out on such a tour in the company of Col. Harvey Tower and Lord Listowel, returning the following year with a large cache of trophies. When he was planning a trip to Copenhagen in April 1865 the Prince of Wales arranged for him to deliver some photographs to the King and Queen of Denmark, the Prince's parents-in-law. The following year he was appointed a lord of the bedchamber and accompanied the Prince on an official visit to Russia to attend the wedding of the future Czar Alexander III. In January 1868 Hamilton travelled to Vienna where he attended the funeral of Maximilian, the former Emperor of Mexico, who had been executed the previous summer, and whose body had been brought back to Austria for burial. There he was shocked by the lack of sympathy shown by the aristocracy, writing to the Prince to express his dismay at this.[2] Later that year Hamilton was involved in the Prince and Princess of Wales' visit to Ireland as guests of his father, the viceroy. In fact, it was Lord Hamilton who suggested that the Prince go to the Punchestown races on the basis that so many people would be in attendance.[3]

In consequence of his father's elevation to a dukedom in August 1868, Hamilton was given the honorary title of Marquess of Hamilton. (Previously he had been styled Viscount Hamilton.) In the same month Hamilton had a fortunate escape when the train on which he and his mother and five of his siblings were travelling collided with a goods train loaded with petroleum at Abergele in north Wales. Thirty-four people died in the accident, but the number might have been many more but for Hamilton's quick-wittedness. His brother Frederic, who was with him on the train, recounted the story in his autobiography *The days before yesterday*:

> It occurred at once to my eldest brother, the late Duke, that as the
> train was standing on a sharp incline, the uninjured carriages would,

'Hamly', aged 30, and Mary, aged 20, in January 1869, the month in which they married.

if uncoupled, roll down the hill of their own accord. He and some other passengers accordingly managed to undo the couplings, and the uninjured coaches, detached from the burning ones, glided down the incline into safety. From the half-stunned guard my brother learned that the nearest signal-box was at Llandulas, a mile away. He ran there at the top of his speed, and arrived in time to get the up Irish mail and all the other traffic stopped. On his return my brother had a prolonged fainting fit, as the strain on his heart had been very great. It took the doctors over an hour to bring him round, and we all thought that he had died.[4]

On 7 January 1869 at St George's Church in Hanover Square, London, he married Lady Mary Anna Curzon-Howe, daughter of the 1st Earl Howe. Lord Richard Grosvenor MP was the Marquess' best man, while the bride was attended by eight bridesmaids, among them Hamilton's sisters Albertha and Maud. Afterwards 150 guests, including several members of the Royal Family, were invited to Curzon House for the wedding breakfast. Hamilton and Mary would have seven sons and two daughters, though four of their sons died in infancy. The eldest child was James Albert Edward, the future 3rd Duke of Abercorn, who was

The Duchess and her children, c. 1885. From left to right: Lord Hamilton, Gladys, the Duchess, Jack and Phyllis. Claud Nigel had not yet been born.

186

born at Hamilton Place, Piccadilly, on 30 November 1869. The other sons to reach adulthood were Lords Arthur John Hamilton and Claud Nigel Hamilton, the former of whom was killed in the opening months of the Great War. Of the Duke's two daughters, Lady Gladys Mary married the 7th Earl of Wicklow, while Lady Alexandra Phyllis was single at the time of her death in the sinking of the RMS *Leinster* in 1918.

Early political career

In June 1860 Hamilton announced that he wished to put himself forward as a Conservative candidate for the forthcoming by-election in County Donegal. A vacancy had arisen following the death of one of the constituency's two MPs, Sir E. S. Hayes, and for a time it looked like there would be a contest, as A. J. R. Stewart, a landlord in the north of Donegal, had also put himself forward as a Conservative candidate. However, Stewart withdrew and on 17 July Hamilton was returned unopposed.[5] He was still only 21 and totally untried as a public representative. However, it was a well-established tradition in his family to enter parliament relatively soon after coming of age. He joined his uncle, Lord Claud Hamilton, MP for Tyrone, in the Commons, and by the end of the decade two of his younger brothers, Claud and George, were also MPs. Throughout the 1860s Hamilton made little contribution to parliamentary life and was preoccupied with other matters, such as Court affairs and foreign travel. A story that survives from his early period as a Donegal MP concerns a visit to the west of the county in 1864. On this trip he met a young woman, the soon to be married Miss Coane, who 'evinced a great interest in the success of his election'. Hamilton responded to this by promising to send her a wedding gift on the occasion of her marriage. True to his word, on hearing of her marriage he sent off a number of 'costly articles of bijouterie for the work table' and wished her every happiness for the future.[6] In the 1865 general election Hamilton and the other sitting MP, Thomas Conolly, were returned unopposed.

By the time of the 1868 election land reform was a contentious issue, and the movement for tenant right was increasing in strength. The proposed disestablishment of the Church of Ireland was also a major issue. Conscious of the sizeable Catholic proportion of the Donegal electorate, Hamilton made clear that he opposed disestablishment, not because he wished to defend the Church of Ireland, but on the grounds that it threatened to undermine the constitution and destabilise society. He also promised to give consideration to the issue of land reform, but was prepared to do no more than that at this stage. Though the appearance of a Liberal candidate seemed a possibility at one stage, in the end both Hamilton and Conolly were again returned unopposed.[7] The land question had became even more of an issue by the time of the 1874 general election, so much so that whereas in 1868 Hamilton merely promised to give it his attention, he now had to announce a declaration of support for the Ulster Custom (the expectation that a departing tenant-farmer had the right to receive a payment from the incoming tenant). The two Conservative candidates faced a strong challenge from the Kennedy brothers, Evory and Tristram, who had the support of the tenant-right associations as well as a number of Catholic and Presbyterian clergy. The result was close, but both Hamilton and Conolly were re-elected.

Though the 1874 election had resulted in the return to power of the Conservatives, Hamilton was under no illusions about the seriousness of the threat to the Conservative position in Ireland from those agitating for land reform. In June 1874 he wrote to Disraeli's secretary, 'I am convinced in my own mind that if the present government do not do something in the way of amending the Land Acts themselves, that at the next election the few remaining Conservative seats in Ulster will go also.'[8] His warnings were ignored, however, and the government offered no support to initiatives designed to address the land question. In the by-election caused by the death of Thomas Conolly in 1876 the Conservative candidate, William Wilson, a Presbyterian solicitor from Raphoe who gave strong backing to tenant-right issues, won with a margin of less than a hundred votes against the Liberal candidate, Thomas Lea. A further by-election arising from Wilson's death in 1879 saw the Conservative candidate comfortably defeated by Lea, who again stood for the Liberals.

In the aftermath of this election result, Hamilton again argued that the government should take the land issue seriously and, in a further missive to Disraeli's secretary in January 1880, pointed out that:

> There is only one subject that these tenant farmers in the north of Ireland at the present time care about – and that is the land question. It is all-absorbing to them. They care little about general policies or foreign policies, but the whole of their thoughts absolutely and without exception is concentrated upon the land.[9]

Hamilton recognised the seismic shift in politics in Ireland, writing, 'It makes me very unhappy and uneasy as the whole political aspect of these northern parts is gradually altering.'[10] Disraeli was not impressed at his hectoring, and called Hamilton a 'whipper-snapper'. Nonetheless, the Donegal MP felt frustrated that the Tory administration had repeatedly ignored his calls for the land question to be addressed. In this regard, it can be said that he was prepared to put the Conservative ascendancy in Ulster above his family's economic self-interest – a very different position, it may be observed, to the one he was to adopt after he succeeded to the dukedom and estate.[11]

Aware that his chances of being returned to Westminster hung in the balance, Hamilton tried to reassure the Donegal electors on the land issue as well as play up his support for local issues during the 1880 election campaign. In the months leading up to the election, Hamilton championed a number of causes. At the beginning of the year, for example, he had led a deputation that met with the Chief Secretary seeking his support for a government loan to complete the Donegal and Fermanagh railway line.[12] In the vote, however, his fears were realised and he came third behind the two Liberal candidates. The result was close – he was a mere 61 votes behind the second of his two opponents – and in fact in early reports he had been proclaimed the victor.[13] Accusations were made that eviction notices had been served on Abercorn tenants in the St Johnstown area of County Donegal who had voted against Hamilton, though on being challenged about this Thomas Lea was forced to admit in the Commons that these stories were not true.[14]

Life in Belgrave Square

By this time Hamilton had moved with his family to Belgrave Square. He remained active in the political arena and was also involved in promoting a number of innovative exhibitions in South Kensington in the 1880s. In August 1881 he was elected a vice-president of an International Fisheries Exhibition in London, and he was apparently the one who came up with the idea for illuminated gardens and outdoor music at the event. This was followed by exhibitions promoting health and inventions – the 'Healtheries' and the 'Inventories', as they were known. Against the background of Hamilton's involvement in these exhibitions, in the summer of 1885 *The World* published an article which provides a rare insight into his home in London.

> It is in one of the more modest of these pleasant dwellings … that the heir to the Dukedom of Abercorn was to be found any morning during the past season busily engaged in devising some new and irresistible attraction for the "Inventories", in endeavouring to pour oil on the troubled waters of Herr Eduard Strauss's last grievance, in holding with judicial impartiality the balance between Mr Dan Godfrey and his many rivals, in calculating with pardonable anxiety the cost of modern illuminations on scientific principles, in answering some urgent application or appeal from his old friends the fishermen or Freemasons of Donegal, or in procuring by the powers of persuasion he has used so effectually, some notable addition to the marvellous musical collection he has brought together beneath the dome of the Albert Hall.
>
> The vestibule at the entrance of Lord Hamilton's house is filled with time-worn Chippendale furniture. Beneath the old-fashioned bureau with brass handles is the stuffed head of an Indian *arnee* – a relic of Lord Hamilton's memorable sporting tour of 1861; above it hangs

The 2nd Duke of Abercorn in *Vanity Fair*, 5 March 1881:
'He has enjoyed the friendship of illustrious persons, and, oddly enough, he has deserved it. … He is good-looking which is a matter of course with his family. … He is full of tact, agreeable, and endowed with the good manners which oblige even Radicals to admit that blue blood has its advantages.'

189

the dutiful address of his father's faithful tenantry, which was presented to him when he paid his first visit to Baronscourt after his marriage. On the walls are some of Hogarth's best prints in their original frames; and over the mantelpiece opposite is a unique German engraving, in which some sixteenth-century artist, working in those dark days when the De Rothschilds and the Bleichroders were yet unborn, graphically depicts "ye bloodie sentence of the Jews against Christ the Saviour of the World."

The first door to the left brings you at once to Lord Hamilton's study, a large oak-panelled room, from the lofty windows of which he can look across screens of pale painted glass, ornamented with tracery and flowers, on to the turf and foliage in the square beyond. A Turkey carpet covers the polished floor, a great mahogany writing-table nearly fills the lightest corner, and on the wainscot above it you will notice the portraits of Lord Beaconsfield and the late Admiral Glyn. A painting of Anne Plummer, Countess of Abercorn, occupies the carved panel over the fireplace. On the mantelshelf beneath it, between the bronze Pompeian candlesticks, which were a present from the Prince of Wales (Lord Paisley's godfather), and by the side of a likeness of the Princess of Wales (the godmother of his sister), are many things which remind you of the many phases of Lord Hamilton's career.

Here, for instance, is a photograph of the bonny Belgian fishwives who came to Kensington in 1883, and there is an invitation "to meet her Majesty's ministers," together with a dozen or more official notices of urgent meetings of the Executive Council of the Inventions Exhibition and the governing body of the Training School for Cookery, which must, in a measure, recall to their recipient the memories of the much-underlined whips of parliamentary life. Half a dozen quaint folding-tables with twisted legs are scattered about the room, around the sofa of Turkish saddle-bags and amidst the morocco-covered chairs: a row of Moorish pottery finds a congenial resting-place on the frieze between the panelling and the ceiling; and the top of a Dutch press near the door is in possession of a number of blue stoneware jars. The stuffed heads of several formidable bison and buffaloes, slain in India, adorn the walls and materially assist some Eastern guns, ancient brass warming-pans and pictures in Florentine frames, in relieving the sombre tints of the old oak, which also forms a background for Sir E. Landseer's sketches of the poor dead and gone "Toddy," a much-cherished memorial of the great painter's visit to Brocket Hall in the summer of 1858.

Behind a tall carved screen which shuts out any possible draught from the door, Richmond's crayon portrait of Lady Hamilton rests on an easel, and the round table before it is crowded with relics of no common interest. Close to the photographs of the Duke of Abercorn and Lady Lansdowne, in Italian frames of inlaid ebony and ivory, may be seen, amidst medals, miniatures and silver punch-ladles, a gold and diamond snuff-box, presented to Lord Hamilton by the King of Denmark, the crosses and ribbons of the orders of the Daneborg, the Iron Crown, and St Anne (mementoes of his presence "in attendance" at several foreign State ceremonials), and a much-prized silver cigarette case, given him by the Prince of Wales. A large case, placed against the wall opposite the picture in the panel, contains a goodly array of books of reference, and above these are suspended, in methodical order, a display of sporting guns, English fishing rods, Indian weapons, tigers' skulls, and the dried tails of Ceylon elephants. Between this capacious bookcase and the window a stuffed "capercailzie" (killed last autumn) seems to gaze compassionately on a straw-coloured Chippendale chest of drawers, which is well-nigh weighed down with the load of neatly-bound literature which the "Fisheries" and "Healtheries" have offered as a contribution to contemporary science.

Lord Hamilton sits with exemplary patience for some hours each day on a Dutch chair before his serviceable writing-table, with his despatch-boxes open beside him, and clad in a blue smoking jacket of dark-blue silk. He will probably not be sorry to snatch a moment's rest from his interminable correspondence, to talk to you with refreshing frankness of Irish political prospects or the future of South Kensington exhibitions. He may perhaps even be induced to show you the little dining-room behind his study, with its Queen Anne sideboards and cabinets filled with rare Derby and Worcester china, over which hang Pannini's beautiful pictures of the interiors of the two great Roman churches; the staircase, with its walls lined with prints and engravings; and the drawing-room above, which Lady Hamilton has furnished so charmingly, and where you will not fail to admire the light-blue draperies, the abundance of flowers, the Sèvres plates, the ormolu sconces, the Chinese screen, with its wonderful porcelain plaques, and Sir Thomas Lawrence's famous picture of Sir William Hamilton's beautiful wife.

Home Rule

Parliamentary reform in the period 1883–85 transformed electoral politics in Ireland. The Franchise Act dramatically increased the number of voters, giving many Catholics and labourers of all denominations the right to vote for the first time. The Redistribution of Seats Act saw the abolition of the old two-seat county divisions and the creation of single-member constituencies. These changes had major ramifications for opponents of Home Rule, whether Conservative or Liberal. Recognising the seriousness of the situation, Hamilton was active in seeking common ground between Conservatives and Liberals during the months prior to the general election of 1885. In August he chaired a meeting at Belvoir Park, Belfast, home of

Sir Thomas Bateson, the object of which was to establish a pro-Union body called the Loyal Irish Union. In addressing the gathering, Hamilton indicated that what had attracted him to it was the fact that the association was being established on broad lines and there was nothing in its prospectus that could not be supported by pro-Union Liberals. He emphasised that at this time it was essential for all those opposed to Home Rule to work together whatever other political opinions they may have had.[15]

These were more than just sentiments for the Marquess of Hamilton. He succeeded in persuading the Conservative candidate in East Donegal to stand down in order to give his former Liberal opponent, Thomas Lea, a clear run.[16] He also won the support of the leading Liberal in North Tyrone, the industrialist E. T. Herdman of Sion Mills. It was in North Tyrone that Hamilton himself intended to stand, hoping to revive his Commons career. That changed, however, with the death of his father on 31 October and Hamilton's succession to the dukedom, meaning that he now had to stand aside from the electoral contest. His youngest brother Lord Ernest Hamilton took his place. In the ensuing vote in North Tyrone, Lord Ernest defeated the prominent nationalist John Dillon by 3,345 votes to 2,922. During his election campaign Lord Ernest adopted a conciliatory tone and in his victory speech thanked the Presbyterians and Liberals who had voted for him.[17] Three of the Duke's other brothers – Lords Claud, George and Frederic – were also successful candidates in the 1885 general election, all returned for English constituencies. For possibly the only time in history, there were five brothers simultaneously at Westminster – one in the Lords and four in the Commons.

The results of the 1885 general election showed clearly the political direction in which Ireland was heading. In the election of that year 16 of the 33 Ulster seats were won by Conservatives, with the rest taken by Nationalists. None was won by a Liberal. At Westminster, Irish Nationalist MPs now held the balance of power. For the time being, there was still a minority Conservative government, led by the Marquess of Salisbury, and the Conservatives in Ireland were anxious that it should preserve their interests. In order to reassure them, Salisbury invited Abercorn to move the Address in the Lords on the opening of the new parliament, telling him that this would provide comfort to the Unionists as to the government's intentions towards them. Recognising the importance of the occasion, the Duke took this seriously, inviting the leading Irish Unionist Colonel Edward Saunderson, recently returned as MP for North Armagh, to lunch on 15 January to help him prepare his speech. Saunderson afterwards wrote to his wife that he found the Duchess to be a 'very nice friendly woman, not pretty but nice looking'.[18]

On 21 January, wearing his lord lieutenant of County Donegal uniform, the Duke rose to move the Address to the Queen. The Queen's Speech, which was read by the Lord Chancellor, had already set out the government's opposition to interfering with the legislative Union, and Abercorn used this opportunity to put forward the cause of the Irish Unionists, contrasting recent imperial successes abroad with the 'cloud of gloom hanging over a part of this Kingdom'. 'I regret to say,' the Duke observed, 'that capital is no longer being invested in that country, trade is at a standstill, property is without security, and in some parts of Ireland even life is insecure, and the country is gradually sinking into ruin.' He condemned the activities of the Irish National League and its use of boycotting as a means of intimidating its opponents, claiming that 'respectable merchants and tradesmen have been ruined by it; whole families have been nearly starved by it'. He rounded on proponents of Home Rule, argued that severing the Union threatened the integrity of the Empire, and placed the issue in a wider British context:

> Have the people of Scotland, who follow with affection their kith and kin to every distant quarter of the globe, realized the fact that within 20 or 30 miles of their own shore there is a loyal population— Irishmen, no doubt, but of Scottish descent—one with them in language, in customs, and in religion—a population which at the present moment is in serious peril, struggling for its very existence against those who regard them as enemies and aliens? Moreover, have the people of England realized that a large portion of the population of Ireland which is of their own race and creed has, through good and evil report, alike in weal and woe, for more than two centuries maintained their loyalty to England, has been a connecting link between England and Ireland, and has, no doubt, largely contributed to the well-being of both countries? There is again, in Ireland, a considerable Roman Catholic element, who have always clung to the Union as their only protection against the never ending experiments of schemers and dreamers who in many ways endeavoured to upset the existing state of things. To sacrifice them would be even more disgraceful.

Moves to unite the pro-Union forces in Ireland were given added urgency when, in February 1886 and with the support of Irish Nationalist MPs, Gladstone again became Prime Minister, with a promise to introduce a Home Rule bill. As the Loyal Irish Union had not been a success, it was dissolved and Abercorn and others instead focused on the Irish Loyal and Patriotic Union, with the Duke taking an executive position within the organisation.[19] At a more local level, Abercorn, with the support of fellow Tyrone landlord Hugh de Fellenberg Montgomery and Herdman, made another attempt to bring together Unionists of all persuasions in the north-west of Ireland. On 9 January 1886 a meeting was held in Omagh under the chairmanship of

Abercorn which established the Northwest Loyal Registration and Electoral Association (NLREA).[20] Conservative and Liberal representatives from 10 divisions in the north-west – the four constituencies in Tyrone, North and South Londonderry, North and South Fermanagh, Derry City and East Donegal – were invited to the meeting. The Duke was elected president and he was to be advised by a directorate chosen annually from the constituencies through co-operation between Conservatives and Liberals.[21]

The Duke worked tirelessly for the Unionist cause during the winter of 1885–86 and through the following summer. He was much more than simply a figurehead for those opposed to Home Rule, but was actively engaged in mobilising support for Unionism. He recognised the need to bring together all pro-Union elements in a common cause even if he had reservations about some of these groupings. For example, he was cautious about the effectiveness of the Orange Order, commenting to Salisbury on one occasion, 'These Orangemen are many of them good fellows, but their leaders are vain and foolish to any degree.'[22] He was especially conscious of the need to ensure that Presbyterians consistently voted for Unionist candidates in parliamentary elections, rather than Liberal candidates, standing with Nationalist support, who promised land reform. He therefore made a point of reaching out politically to Presbyterians. Speaking in Lifford at the beginning of March, the Duke expressed his pleasure that so many Liberals were in attendance and referred to 'Presbyterian Liberal loyalty', adding, 'The Liberals of the North of Ireland are just as true and just as loyal as the Conservatives.' He concluded with a warning that severing the Union would ruin the country and ultimately lead to civil war.[23] In June 1886 he presented a petition to parliament from the General Assembly of the Presbyterian Church in Ireland opposing Home Rule.[24]

Abercorn's ability to unite all shades of Unionist opinion was put to the test in his own constituency of North Tyrone in the general election of July 1886. A Gladstonian Liberal, and therefore Home Ruler, J. O. Wylie, a Presbyterian barrister and land commissioner, challenged Lord Ernest. Wylie had Nationalist backing while it was also hoped that he would win sufficient support from the Presbyterian tenant-farmers to oust the sitting MP. However, as the Duke's youngest brother was later to reflect, this group disliked the idea of Home Rule even more than voting for a member of the landed aristocracy and Lord Ernest was returned to parliament, though with a slightly reduced majority. Once again Herdman and the local Liberal association broke ranks with the Gladstonian Liberals and supported Hamilton.

In the years that followed, the Duke continued to make friendly overtures to Presbyterians. This can clearly be seen in a letter of early December 1888 that he wrote to W. E. Ball, secretary of the Nonconformist Unionist Association,

> Fancy if I in my humble position in the north of Ireland, instead of bringing all parties together, had taken a different course and had proclaimed the Presbyterian ministers to be a radical class of men not worth relying upon – why, it would have made every body hostile to each other and would have done no end of mischief.[25]

The Duke did remain somewhat suspicious of Presbyterian intentions, however, something that probably dated back to his time as MP for Donegal, writing to Salisbury in 1896 that 'during the last few years the Presbyterians have behaved very well to us. As a rule they are a nasty radical lot, but the Home Rule question has altered their former political opinions to a great degree.' One of the few Presbyterians with whom he did enjoy a good relationship was John Ross QC, a close friend of the family. In January 1896 he wrote to Cadogan on Ross's behalf, recommending him for a position on the bench and pointing out that Ross's promotion would 'gratify a very large amount of Presbyterians in the North of Ireland'.

Abercorn was also aware of the need to promote the cause of Unionism to as wide an audience as possible. In a letter to the journalist William Henry Hurlbert, which was subsequently published in the *New York Tribune*, Abercorn set out the Conservative position on Home Rule to an American audience in August 1886. He emphasised that the Conservatives were anxious that 'their fellow-countrymen in Ireland of every creed and class should enjoy equal political rights and equal consideration, and have equal social liberty granted to them by law and secured to them by its observance'. He was critical of Gladstone, writing, '[He] has, in my opinion, sadly missed the opportunity which his position and his previous services gave him for conciliating the growing elements which sever English and Irish feeling.' The Protestant Ascendancy was a 'thing of the past', insisted the Duke, and no-one wished to see its political character revived. He continued:

> To give the greatest possible scope to the natural aspirations of the people for self-government without impairing the Parliamentary union, and to hasten the time when Irishmen, like Scotchmen, shall fill all the administrative posts in their own country, to insist meanwhile that the poorest as well as the richest shall have the protection of the law for person and property – this I apprehend is the genuine Conservative policy.[26]

The Ulster Convention of 1892

The defeat of the first Home Rule bill and the fall of Gladstone in July 1886 ushered in a new Conservative-led, and pro-Union, government. However, long before the 1892 general election was held, it was expected that Gladstone's Liberals would secure victory and that a new Home Rule bill would be brought before parliament. In response to this the Unionists in Ulster began to make plans for a convention that would clearly demonstrate their continued opposition to self-government for Ireland. On 17 June 1892 12,000 delegates from all over the province assembled in Belfast in a specially constructed hall in Botanic Gardens. Giving one of the keynote addresses was the Duke, who had been chosen as the chairman of the rally – the Great Convention as it has become known. In his address Abercorn emphasised the broad sweep of support for Unionism and denied accusations that the gathering was simply an Orange demonstration. He also drew on the history of the province to show that Ulster was different from the rest of Ireland, arguing that it had been industrialised through the hard work of the settlers who arrived during the Ulster Plantation. He expressed his hope that the Unionists in Ulster could rely on their Scottish neighbours with whom they shared many characteristics, and on Englishmen since Ulstermen had done so much to further the British Empire. The Duke was not a first-rate public speaker and to begin with some of those present found his speech somewhat laboured, though all listened respectfully. However, towards the end of his address Abercorn began to speak with greater vigour and his speech reached a climax with the memorable words, 'Men of the North, once more I say, we will not have Home Rule!' He then roused the delegates to their feet, and called on them to repeat after him, 'We will not have Home Rule!'

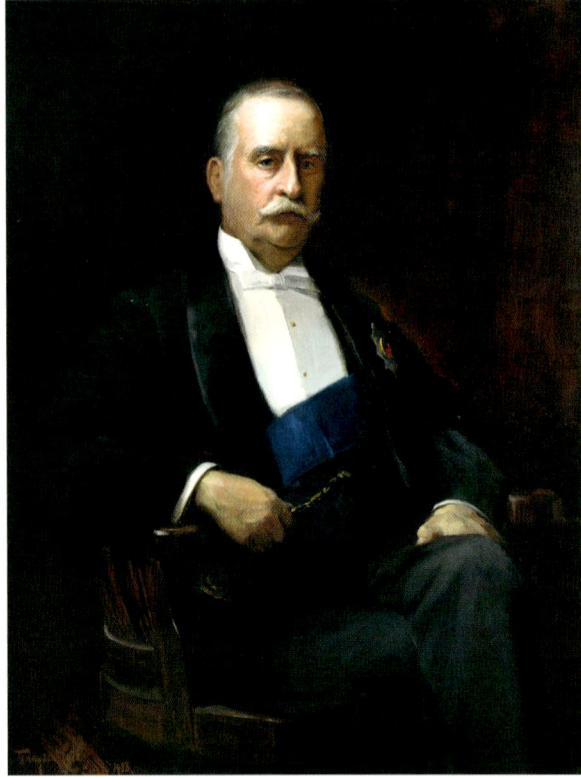

The Duke of Abercorn wearing the Garter Riband and Star. The Duke was made a Knight of the Garter in 1892.

Though this was not the first time he had used these words – he had done so some time before this at a farmers' meeting in Enniskillen – it was at the Great Convention that he used them with greatest effect and it is with this maxim that he has forever been associated. Letters of congratulation poured in. His mother, the Dowager Duchess, called him the 'joy and pride of my heart' and told Abercorn that his father would have been very proud of him. The Marquess of Dufferin and Ava wrote from Paris to congratulate Abercorn on the success of the Ulster Convention: 'Your speech read excellently and I am told nothing could be more effective – moderate, eloquent, dignified – it had every good quality, and I am sure we ought all to be very much obliged to you for the trouble you have taken in the matter.' A month later Salisbury wrote to the Duke to tell him that he had forwarded his name to the Queen for the Garter, adding, 'But immediately after the

Ulster Convention I think it is a matter of congratulations on public grounds that at this juncture the Queen has the opportunity of bestowing this mark of her grace.' The following April the Duke presided over a massive gathering of Unionists at the Albert Hall in London where he again enunciated the words, 'We will not have Home Rule' to loud cheers. During 1893 he took part in numerous public demonstrations against Home Rule throughout the United Kingdom. It was not, however, the force of popular opposition to Home Rule that resulted in the defeat of the bill in September 1893, but rather opposition in the House of Lords. Though he did not take part in the parliamentary debates, Abercorn played an important role in mobilising opposition to Home Rule in the Lords, where the bill was overwhelmingly rejected. For the next decade and a half, Home Rule ceased to be a major political issue.

Tyrone politics in the 1890s

Fighting elections was a costly exercise and there were also expenses associated with the registration courts, where solicitors fought to ensure that everyone qualified to vote was actually on the electoral register. Raising the necessary funds was always a struggle. In September 1886 the Duke lamented, 'The people up here are not like those in England and it is with the greatest difficulty that we can get them to subscribe to anything.' The general assumption was that a wealthy landowner would underwrite all electioneering costs. Thus the North Tyrone Unionist Association depended heavily on financial support from the Duke of Abercorn. In 1890, for instance, of the total registration expenses of £750, the Duke contributed £400.[27] Even for a man of his means this was a considerable strain on resources. In March 1888, E. T. Herdman commented to Hugh de Fellenberg Montgomery, 'none of the Hamiltons wish to contest the seat as the Duke thinks the amusement too costly'.[28] Lord Ernest Hamilton was himself deeply disillusioned with parliamentary life following his initial election victory in December 1885. By his own admission he was an 'unwilling victim', only standing because his eldest brother was forced to withdraw on the eve of the poll.[29] He made few contributions to parliamentary debate, though on one occasion he joined with the Liberals in dismissing talk of civil war in Ireland as 'absurd and childish nonsense'.[30] In order to relieve some of the boredom surrounding life at Westminster he would race with one of his brothers on bicycles borrowed from dining room attendants.[31] Not surprisingly, he retired from politics after one full parliamentary sitting.

Despite Abercorn's reservations about the cost of electioneering, the Unionist successor to Lord Ernest was actually his brother, Lord Frederic Spencer Hamilton, who had previously been MP for one of the Manchester constituencies. While campaigning at Castlederg, Lord Frederic made the rather surprising admission that he was a believer in the compulsory sale of estates as a means of resolving the land issue. Although brother to the largest landowner in Tyrone, Lord Frederic pointed out that that he was not a landlord himself and so land reform would not affect him personally. His advocacy of compulsory purchase at this stage was remarkable given his class background coupled with the fact that this issue was so controversial in a number of other constituencies. In the heaviest poll yet witnessed in North Tyrone, Lord Frederic was elected ahead of the Presbyterian Liberal, Rev. Prof. James Brown Dougherty, though with a greatly reduced unionist majority. He retired after just one parliament and his failure to publish a farewell address provoked one correspondent to the *Tyrone Constitution* to accuse him of not having as much devotion to the constituency as other family members.[32] To begin with it was anticipated that Dr Edward Thompson of Omagh would come forward as the Unionist candidate for North Tyrone in 1895. However, his candidature did not materialise, perhaps because Abercorn did not approve. Months later the Duke was to write to the Earl of Belmore concerning Thompson, stating that he was 'mad' about getting into parliament and 'very nearly played "hanky panky" in North Tyrone'.[34]

The Unionist selected to contest North Tyrone in 1895, William Wilson, pledged to support any measure to secure the interests of the tenant but which would not damage those of the landlord.[35] From the wording of Wilson's address it is clear that he was mindful of the Duke's patronage. However, in the ensuing election Wilson was defeated by the Gladstonian Liberal, Charles Hemphill. The seat was never regained by the Unionists despite some extremely close results, mainly because the Nationalists chose to run Liberals such as Hemphill, who were quite often Protestants, rather than Catholic members of the Irish Parliamentary Party. However, it would also seem to be the case that once the personal involvement of the Abercorns in electoral politics ceased in the mid-1890s, the Unionist cause in North Tyrone suffered a setback. At the same time, the Duke's influence in politics in North Tyrone remained immense. Following the passing of the Irish Local Government Act of 1898, the Duke became a member of Tyrone County Council, serving as its first chairman.

Barons Court

The 2nd Duke of Abercorn inherited from his father a vast landed estate in Counties Tyrone and Donegal, as well as properties in Scotland. Early in 1888 the American journalist with whom he had previously corresponded, William Henry Hurlbert, visited Barons Court and left an interesting account of his time there.[36] He noted a number of initiatives that were providing employment for locals and relief for the poor. Some time before Hurlbert's visit a storm had resulted in the destruction of over 100,000 trees in the demesne. An 'enterprising Scot' named Kirkpatrick came to an arrangement with the Duke to turn the fallen trees into timber. He built a 'neat wooden cabin and stables' and constructed a small steam-powered sawmill. He brought a couple of men over with him from Scotland, but for the most part employed local people. Another local enterprise reported by Hurlbert was the responsibility of Mrs Dixon, the English wife of the house steward at Barons Court. This was the cottage woollen industry which had been established following a talk on thrift that had been given by the then Marquess of Abercorn at a temperance meeting in the area. The old Duke and Duchess had provided the funds needed to buy yarn from Edinburgh and knitting needles. The then Marchioness acted as the corresponding clerk and business agent of the initiative. Since it started 300 families had been involved in the industry, between them producing 20,000 pairs of socks which were supplied to the British Army. Nearly all of those involved were from mountain farms around Barons Court, but not actually on the Abercorn estate.

In the summer of 1888 *The Times* published an account of the Abercorn estate that painted a very positive picture of the property at that time. This report is printed in full below.

> The British public hears of little but fighting between landlord and tenant in Ireland, and it may be of interest to them to have some account of a great estate, which is well managed, and on which, though this is by no means the exception in this country, the most friendly relations subsist between the owner and tiller of the soil. Such an estate is that of the Duke of Abercorn, situated in North Tyrone and the adjoining part of Donegal, and comprising 63,000 acres in a ring fence. The property was granted by James I at the time of the plantation of Ulster to Lord James Hamilton, whom he created Earl of Abercorn, on condition that he kept up three castles and 300 men all armed.[37]
>
> At the siege of Derry two of the family fought on opposite sides, Claude, the fourth earl, being with the forces of James II, while Captain Hamilton, who afterwards succeeded as sixth earl, took part with the defenders inside the walls; and close to the house at Baron's Court is to be seen a huge anchor, said to have belonged to the French war vessel *Lausun* on which James II embarked in Waterford Harbour after the battle of the Boyne, accompanied by his aide-de-camp and kinsman, Claude, fourth Earl of Abercorn. They departed in such a hurry that the cable was cut, and the anchor was dredged up and presented to the late Duke, when Lord Lieutenant, by the Harbour Commissioners as a mark of their respect for his Grace, and as a memento of the period in which his ancestor bore a gallant and devoted part.

The demesne, or park, as it would be called in England, includes 5,000 acres of undulating ground, the greater part of which is beautifully wooded, while some 1,500 acres are devoted to the maintenance of two home farms. The house is a very fine one, and stands on a broad plateau, with terraces and Italian gardens leading down to the lake. From the top of a hill known as Bessy Bell, which rises from the demesne to a height of over 1,300 ft, a splendid panorama of the estate and surrounding country is obtained. The distant view is fringed with mountains on every side, and no fewer than 300 bonfires were counted from this point on the night of the Jubilee celebration.

To the east lies the Monteloney range, the Clara Mountains and Lough Erne to the west, and to the north the Donegal Mountains, with the peaks of Muckish and Errigal. At the foot of the hill on the eastern side is situated the village of Newtownstewart, where James II slept the night after the raising of the siege of Derry, and which he burnt next morning. The house which he occupied has never been rebuilt, and its ruined walls form a conspicuous feature in the town. Further north on the banks of the Mourne are the Sion flax spinning mills, where Mr. Herdman, a tenant of the Duke's, employs 14,000 hands, for whose accommodation he has built a village of houses.

A few miles further on is the town of Strabane, which forms the centre of the property, and almost within a stone's throw of it, on the other side of the river Foyle, is Lifford, in Donegal probably the smallest county town in the United Kingdom, the population numbering only about 500. Ardstraw, in another part of the property, is the site of one of the oldest ecclesiastical establishments in Ireland, having been the seat of the Bishopric of Derry, which was moved in the sixth century to Maghera, and thence to Derry; and St. Eugene, a disciple of St. Patrick, is said to have died there. The Derg valley in which it is situated is famous for its large race of men, and was one of the great battle grounds between the O'Neills and O'Donnells.

The estate lies in a fine undulating country, with good-sized farms and comfortable homesteads, the haggards filled with neat and well-thatched stacks of oats and hay, and showing unmistakable signs of industry. The farmers are the descendants of the Scotch planters, being mostly Presbyterians, and are a sturdy, hard-headed, independent race of men. The crops they chiefly depend on are flax, oats, turnips, and grass, and if they could get a good price for flax and cattle they would be well enough off. The price of the former was a little better last year than in 1886, being from 50s. to 55s. per cwt. In the time of the American war, when it was as high as £6, they made money freely, but they also lived up to it, and built houses in many cases altogether out of proportion to the size of their holdings.

They are generally low about the prospects of farming and see no hope of a change for the better without Protection, which they seem to be in favour of to a man. Some of them, on the other hand, say they have been doing well enough; that though they have to sell their cattle low they can also buy them low; and that the price of feeding stuffs and cost of living are both much less than they were; though they complain that labour has not fallen, and, indeed, that it is difficult to get labourers at all, as most of the able-bodied men from the district are emigrating to America, Australia, and New Zealand. 'If we had the land they have in the South,' said one man, 'I think we'd do, rent and all. They have splendid land, and don't work it.' 'I've been down there,' he added, 'and I don't like them. They're a different people, and I wouldn't live there for anything.' They also complain that the long-continued agitation has affected the circulation of money, and thereby added largely to the general depression.

The uncertainty of the future makes them shy of land purchase, and they do not like the prospect of the hard and fast rules which they anticipate would have to be adhered to under the State; whereas the Duke's office is open for rent-receiving every Tuesday in the year, and they can suit their convenience as to the time of payment. One townland on the property was, however, sold to the tenants last June for 20 years' purchase of the reset, or judicial, rents, and some further sales have since been arranged. It was suggested to me that they would prefer to pay a smaller yearly instalment than that provided for under Lord Ashbourne's Act, and let it be a continual charge, as they think that posterity should bear some share in the burden, and that it would be an advantage to have some control kept over the land, with the view of preventing subdivision.

Of one thing I was assured on all sides, that there is no danger of the Protestant farmers of the North going over to Home Rule. They do not believe the country could prosper under a Parnellite Parliament in Dublin; they fear increased taxation, and above all they have the dread of being ruled by Rome. Tyrone is not a great Orange county, but I am told the Orangemen have increased considerably in numbers since Mr Gladstone's Home Rule proposals. 'They have increased,' said a big, broad-shouldered man of 6ft 4in., with a twinkle in his clear blue eye, 'for I have a way of knowing.' 'And they'll never submit to be ruled by Parnell,' he declared, adding, with another twinkle, 'for I have a way of knowing.' Ninety per cent, I was told, of the property in the district belongs to loyalists, but they are in danger of being swamped by the lower orders, who are nearly all Roman Catholics, but few of whom hold any land. The proclivities of the farmers are Liberal, but in the face of a common foe they sank all differences to return a Unionist, and are at present represented by Lord Ernest Hamilton.

There are 1,815 tenants on the Duke's property, about half of whom have had judicial rents fixed, chiefly by agreement, only 141 having gone into court. There were a number of leases made in 1834 [1835], no doubt with the object of creating votes, and of these a considerable proportion are still subsisting. About 100 expired in 1882, and there has been as yet no change in these rents, though the tenants are now seeking an abatement. There are also some leases made since 1870, but the Duke voluntarily reduced the rents in these cases two or three years ago, thereby anticipating the new Land Act. The tenant-right on the estate has always commanded high sums, rising to as much as 60 years' purchase, a farm of 28 statute acres rented at £15 4s. 5d. having sold in 1878 for £915. Thirty, 40, and 50 years' purchase have been frequently given, anything under 20 years being the exception, and the average sale of tenant-right in 1886 came to 22 years' purchase.

The best feeling appears to subsist between the Duke and his tenants, though with so large a number it would probably be too much to say that there is no disaffection whatever. There are 80 labourers' cottages at Baron's Court, all well-built slated houses with two rooms and offices. They most of them have gardens in front, and ivy or creepers on the walls, presenting a pleasing contrast to the bare white-washed wall of the ordinary Irish cabin. A hundred and eighty hands are employed all the year round, the annual labour bill coming to £6,000, or, if estate management be added, over £7,000 expended in wages. There, is a clothing club for the labourers, who have any money they put in doubled by the Duke. An old man is still living on the estate who remembers when 'the peace was proclaimed after '98.' The whole country was illuminated, and whisky was 3d. a pint, and there were 'no gaugers.' He also remembers 'the old Marquis,' who used to gallop for miles through the rides and drives of Baron's Court but never go outside, and 'always wore his sash,' or riband of the Garter.

For the benefit of the poorer classes outside the estate, who are not so well off, a knitting industry, known as the Baron's Court Cottage Industry, was established three or four years ago, and has now, thanks to the unremitting energy of the Duchess of Abercorn, attained extensive dimensions. Several regiments, both of Regulars and Militia, are supplied with socks, and there are different patterns for the Guards, Rifle Brigade, Hussars, &c. Any orders, large or small, are gladly received. Mrs. Dickson, the steward's wife, weighs the yarn and gives it out, and the goods are brought back the following week, weighed again, and paid for. It is an immense boon to the people during the winter months and they come in from a radius of ten miles to get the work, which makes an addition to the earnings of a family varying from 6s. to 12s. a week. They also knit gloves, shawls, knicker-bocker stockings, &c., and are very clever at embroidery. Oddly enough, they cannot work from patterns, but if they are told to do a shamrock, rose, or so forth they bring back the devices beautifully done.

The Baron's Court Cottage Industry obtained a diploma and medals at the Edinburgh Exhibition, and the Duchess organized the collection of Irish women's work of all kinds for the Glasgow Industrial Exhibition. If such a place as Baron's Court were broken up, or the means of expenditure seriously reduced, it is obvious that it would be an immense loss to the whole district. The Duke resides on the estate during a great part of the year, and takes an active interest in all that concerns its management and the welfare of the people.[38]

The report provides a fascinating insight into the estate at this juncture, but it must be acknowledged that it downplays the fact that significant portions of the estate were in fact in the process of being sold off to the tenants and that there was an increasing degree of agitation among the tenantry. The break-up of the estate as a result of the land acts is discussed below, but it cannot be overstated that this was a period of immense change for the estate. By the late nineteenth century there was an increased emphasis on direct farming and maximising the resources of Barons Court itself. An individual who was to play a very important role in this was Robert Bell who, in the spring of 1889, was appointed steward of Barons Court, beginning an association with the estate that would last until his death in 1931, On the eve of his arrival the Duke wrote to him with various instructions, though giving him the freedom to 'form your own ideas for improvement in the system of working.' Among the tasks that Bell would soon have to oversee was the construction of a new stable block. The Duke also gave his opinion on the key members of estate staff at this time. David McNally, the foreman gardener, was 'a thoroughly respectable honest man upon whom you can rely', while Newton, the gamekeeper, was 'a good man'.

The stable block at Barons Court in the process of construction, 1889–90. Designed by the Belfast architect, Joseph Bell, the foundation stone for the new stable block – 'partaking in general features in what is known as the Baronial' – was laid on 18 September 1889. The contractor was J. Ballantine of Derry.

203

The Abercorn coat of arms on the stable block.

Also praised by the Duke were Cowie, the forester, 'an active intelligent young man', and Bradley, the mason, 'a most intelligent workman'.[39]

The break-up of the estate

Though not as strong as in other areas, the movement for tenant right gained some support among the tenants on the Abercorn estate from the 1870s onwards and by the early 1880s its tenants were openly calling for land reform. Dealing with this trend, which was inseparably bound up with contemporary political developments, was to prove a major challenge for the Duke of Abercorn. As previously noted, in the 1885 and 1886 general elections the Presbyterian farmers on the Abercorn estate, who constituted a majority of the tenants, had almost to a man supported the candidature of the Duke's youngest brother, Lord Ernest, in the North Tyrone parliamentary constituency. However, as soon became apparent, opposition to Home Rule did not necessarily equate to satisfaction at the existing tenancy arrangements and demands for reform on the Abercorn estate became ever more forceful. At Christmas 1886 Lord George Hamilton wrote to his brother on the matter of land reform, advising him to, as he saw it, bow to the inevitable and begin to sell his estate to the occupying tenants:

> I strongly advise you to take at wherever you can. Rents won't rise, but are certain to fall. ... I daresay even twenty years' purchase would curtail your existing income, but in a few years hence you will get less and the longer you delay making up your mind, the more what you have to sell recedes in value. ... Nothing in my mind can save Irish landlords ultimately. ... Sell out now before made to.[40]

Some limited action was taken in this regard. At the beginning of 1887 the Duke's agent sent out a circular to the tenants in a number of townlands in the Donegal portion of the estate offering them the opportunity to purchase their holdings at 21 years' purchase. This was dependent on a sufficient number of tenants availing themselves of this offer.

The tenants do not seem to have been enthused by this and instead over 100 of them gathered in the school-house in St Johnstown in February 1887 to demand a 25% reduction in their rents, claiming that the current state of agriculture left them with no alternative. The challenge to the family by the tenantry was exploited by Nationalist MPs in the House of Commons, especially as it was emanating from predominantly Protestant tenants who could not be accused of aiding and abetting the mainly Catholic National League. In the House of Commons John Dillon, the MP for East Mayo (and the defeated candidate in North Tyrone in the 1885 general election), claimed that the influence of the Hamiltons was viewed in Ireland as 'most sinister and anti-Irish' and that they were in favour of a Coercion Bill which would force tenants to pay rents. In response, Lord George Hamilton denied this and defended the family's relationship with the tenants on the estate.

Persisting in their demands, some months later the tenants on the estate asked for a 30% reduction in their rents; otherwise they would go to the land courts and have their rents judicially fixed. They also asked for an early reply so that, should their request be rejected, they would have time to have their cases entered with the land courts by 31 October. The Duke responded by stating that an immediate reply could not be given and that he would have to consult with other members of the family. He did promise to treat all cases filed before 1 January as if they had been entered before 1 November. Early in November 1887 a large number of the tenants, most of whom seem to have been from the Tyrone manor of Dunnalong, gathered at the estate office in Strabane where they were informed by the agent, James McFarlane, that the Duke was unwilling to grant any reduction whatsoever in the rents. Furthermore, they were at liberty to take whatever course of action seemed best to them, but Abercorn would only go so far as to sell out on whatever terms could be agreed. The Duke's response took the tenants by surprise and caused considerable annoyance, if not anger.[41]

However, while rejecting the request for a reduction in rents, the Duke had held out the prospect of 'selling out' to the tenants under the terms of the Ashbourne Act of 1885: in other words, of enabling the tenants to purchase the farms they were then in possession of and so become outright owners of these farms. This offer was limited to those tenants in the Donegal portion of the estate and the manor of Dunnalong. The tenants responded positively and by mid-December the process was underway. *Freeman's Journal* explained the practicalities and significance of the move as it affected the estate:

> Speaking generally, the terms are twenty years' purchase of a rent fixed by a mutual arrangement. The annual payments by the purchasing tenants will be considerably under the judicial rents, and, of course, at the end of forty-nine years the farms become the absolute property of the occupiers.[42]

The Duke's agent at this time was a man who had served the family in various capacities for over 40 years. James McFarlane had been appointed agent by the 1st Duke in 1883 during a particularly contentious episode in the history of the estate. He succeeded T. W. D. Humphreys, Major Humphreys' son, who, in McFarlane's opinion, had mishandled the response to the creation of the Irish Land Commission resulting in numerous instances of legal proceedings between the estate and its tenants. McFarlane later claimed that once he had been appointed agent all such litigation ended. At the time of the autumn 1887 agitation, McFarlane believed he had held his nerve in the face of considerable unrest among the tenantry and a degree of anxiety on the part of the Duke. As a result of his firmness, 'I obtained the highest price for any estate in Ireland with the lowest outlay and [a] very trifling loss as regards arrears.' He further claimed that through his conduct he had been able to preserve the 'good feeling … between you and your tenants past and present'.[43]

The Abercorn estate was one of the first in Ireland to undergo the selling off of a substantial portion of its acreage, and in all just under 28,000 acres was transferred from landlord to tenant at this time. In permitting the sale of part of the estate to the tenants, the Duke seems to have adopted a pragmatic approach, even if it was done with a degree of reluctance. He was later accused of selling merely the outlying and least valuable parts of his estate. It is true that the lands sold at this time were those furthest from Barons Court, but in fact these were among the most valuable portions of the estate and the sale of these holdings raised £267,000. It must not be thought that the Duke had simply resigned himself to meekly watching his estate disintegrate before him. Abercorn had spent much of 1887 working with other landlords to create a body which would represent their interests. The concerns he had for his own class can be seen in a letter drafted by him which was read at a gathering of Tyrone landlords in Omagh in August of that year: 'The Irish landlords are to be sacrificed on the base excuse of maintaining the Union, and the whole of Ireland is to suffer for a few disturbed counties.' Before the end of the year the Irish Landowners Convention had been established and he became its first president.

Because of his wealth and status, as well as his many connections, Abercorn continued to be the dominant figure in Irish landlordism through the 1890s and into the twentieth century. It was a largely frustrating aspect of his career. Parliamentary legislation continued to weaken the position of the landlord and Abercorn, along with other landowners, felt that they were victims of political expediency designed to satisfy the demands of those calling for land reform. It even led to a family rift when the Duke and his brother Lord George Hamilton fell out over the land issue, with Abercorn writing to Saunderson in September 1896, 'I look upon him [i.e. George] as a traitor and don't like him now.'[44] The operations of the land courts were a particular cause of concern and the Duke frequently made representations to Lord Cadogan, the Irish viceroy, on appointments to the bench and other positions. In proposing one particular candidate for a judicial position, Abercorn pointed out that:

> a man should be chosen who has fought and sacrificed for his [the word 'country' is deleted] party, who has shown his own personal worth by his political actions, in preference to others who have been the happy possessors of safe seats and whose abilities and eloquence have been extolled by an admonitory and greedy lot of Dublin lawyers and officials.[45]

It was felt that those involved in the land courts were often biased against the landlords. In one fit of exasperation Abercorn wrote to Cadogan enclosing a letter from his own agent to show the 'wickedness of the farce that is now going on in the Courts'.[46] It was also true that overall he saw his influence ebbing away when it came to patronage. Though he bombarded Cadogan with recommendations for even the most inconsequential of positions, his choices were frequently rejected. For example, in 1898 his candidate for the Congested Districts Board, who happened to be the secretary to the Landowners' Convention, was rejected.

What he found particularly galling was the apparent apathy of English 'friends' of Irish landowners. In January 1897, he wrote to Cadogan, 'I have not much faith in our Unionist friends', referring to the Liberal Unionists, adding,

> there is too much of the old Whig about some of them and this I detest. Of all the political sections I think the Whig section of days gone by is the worst and the meanest, but much of the blood of those old time servers ... remains in some members of the present government.[47]

At times Cadogan showed little patience with Abercorn's continual badgering. In March 1898, for example, he wrote to the Duke:

> It is unfortunate that, at a time when proposals for affecting great constitutional changes in Ireland are under consideration, we are

confronted as usual with a personal difficulty which appears to absorb
the attention of those to whose guidance and advice in more
important matters it would be natural to look.[48]

The following year later the Irish landowners threatened a resolution
against the government in the Lords. 'You can have no conception of the
feeling of disgust, mingled with despair and hopelessness', Abercorn wrote
to Cadogan, 'which the Landowners in Ireland feel towards the
Government.' The Duke demanded and won a private audience with
Salisbury on the afternoon of 21 January. Naturally this infuriated Cadogan,
who felt that his position was being undermined. However, in calming the
lord lieutenant's fears, Salisbury expressed his surprise that Abercorn had
gone to so much trouble to say so little.[49]

One of the landowners' most persistent critics was the Scotsman T. W.
Russell, a former temperance reformer and latterly MP for South Tyrone.
Abercorn accused him of having caused a number of electoral contests
through his insistence on compulsory purchase, and also of fomenting
discord between Anglicans and Presbyterians. Writing to Salisbury, Abercorn
described Russell as a 'vicious, little, teetotal, radical Scotchman'. Salisbury
in reply wrote, 'I think he would keep his head better if he returned to
alcohol.' Though the Duke did have the satisfaction of seeing Russell
dismissed from the Local Government Board in 1900, the enmity between
the two lasted until the Duke's death in 1913.

The Irish land act of 1903 (popularly known as the Wyndham Act, after
George Wyndham, the Chief Secretary of Ireland) is generally regarded as
the most important. It originated in a conference held in December 1902,
chaired by Lord Dunraven, which brought together landlord and tenant to
discuss further land reform. Though he had rejected an invitation to attend,
Abercorn was somewhat surprised by the generosity of the report of the
conference, as far as the landlord interest was concerned, and at an Irish
Landowners Convention meeting the following January he recommended
that the government give it serious consideration. In the following months
he used his influence to win over the broad mass of Irish landowners to
Wyndham's land bill. However, despite his support for the legislation, he did
experience the sadness of knowing that it would continue the break-up of
his estate. In the Lords, the Duke spoke during the Irish Land Bill debate on
3 August 1903. After pointing out that he spoke in support of the bill, he
continued:

> I rise with feelings of grief mixed with pride – grief in thinking of the
> extinction that is about to take place under this Bill of what is called
> the landlord class in Ireland, and the consequent separation that has
> for so many generations existed between the landowners and their
> tenantry, and of pride in being connected with that class that has

suffered so much and so patiently under the land laws of Ireland. I think it only right that I should publicly recognise the great liberality of the financial provisions of this Bill. ... The Bill now before your Lordships is one of the most important and far-reaching that has ever been introduced into Parliament for dealing with the land question in Ireland, and for effecting a final settlement, equitable as far as possible, and satisfactory between landlord and tenant. In fact, it tends to perform a social revolution. To part with an estate that has been in your family for generations, to sever your connection with your tenants with whom you have lived on the best of terms, is an unpleasant wrench. Money, even in these days, is not a compensation for everything. Money cannot obliterate the old associations connected with family ties, and, I might almost say, with historic connections. To part with the familiar acres, and to receive in lieu thereof money, the investment of which is always attended with anxiety and is never free from risk, is not a very agreeable exchange. No class has been so shamefully treated by legislation as the Irish landlords, and I believe that in no other civilised country but England would such treatment have been tolerated, and this treatment meted out to the most loyal men, and, taking them as a class, the very backbone of their country.

Abercorn was one of the first landlords to initiate the sale of much of what remained of his estate under the terms of the Wyndham Act. Within a short time of its passing, the a circular was issued to the tenants encouraging them to take advantage of this legislation to purchase their farms. The tenants responded positively, and by 1912 almost all of the remaining portion of the estate in County Donegal had been sold off, while in County Tyrone only around 15,000 acres remained.[50]

British South Africa Company

Away from politics and estate management, in the late 1880s Abercorn became involved in matters of imperial importance when, in July 1889, he accepted the invitation to serve as chairman of the British South Africa Company, having been persuaded to do so, it is believed, by none other than Cecil Rhodes himself. It does not appear that Abercorn had had any previous interest in African affairs and it would seem that the choices of him as chairman and the Duke of Fife as vice-chairman were to enhance the standing of the company and especially its board. Ostensibly they were also there to represent the public interest. Abercorn himself gladly consented to the position, believing it to be for the good of the Empire. He also benefited financially from his involvement in the company. As chairman he received a salary of £1,200 and was able to acquire large numbers of shares at par, which he was subsequently able to sell for an excellent return when prices

rose. He was delighted when Rhodes named a town at the southern end of Lake Tanganyika after him. The Duke was fairly easy-going when it came to company business. He apparently enjoyed his role at the head of the company, though he does not appear to have had 'any taste for the drudgery of reading reports and overseeing the company administration'.[51] This also suited Rhodes, as it allowed him a free hand to pursue his own agenda in South Africa.

One example of Abercorn's somewhat nonchalant approach comes in an incident recalled by Rhodes's private secretary. The two men had arrived late in London in January 1891 to be met by Abercorn and taken to the Westminster Palace Hotel for a meal. The Duke showed himself to be not terribly interested in what Rhodes had to say about company matters, 'because when His Grace should have been paying closest attention to Mr Rhodes he turned to me and said, "We have had a capital black-cock season this year …" and Mr Rhodes' face was a study.' Admittedly the incident occurred in the early hours of morning, when the Duke may have been wishing he was in his bed.[52] However, other comments point to Abercorn being a man whose mind could wander. For example, Lord Balcarres described him as 'quite a typical Duke: with so little power of concentration that he can scarcely concentrate his mind long enough to read a little article in the *Daily Mail*'.[53] Evidence to the contrary, showing that the Duke did have the ability to act decisively, is found in the following amusing anecdote. In the spring of 1912 the committee of the Carlton Club was mulling whether or not to get rid of its 'lymphatic secretary'. Lord Londonderry had been tasked with terminating the secretary's employment, but was unable to stomach this. Some of the other committee members had a word with Abercorn, who told Londonderry that if he did not sack the secretary before the meeting, he (Londonderry) would have the unpleasant task of sacking him publicly at the meeting. This intervention had the desired effect. Afterwards the David Crawford, Lord Balcarres mused, 'How valuable at times is a Duke in second childhood. Whenever in doubt we whispered something to Abercorn who promptly distributed it *coram populo*.'[54]

What can be said about Abercorn and the British South Africa Company is that the Duke placed a great deal of confidence in Rhodes, believing him to be its mainstay, and was reluctant to take action against him when he seemed to be overstepping the mark. For example, when Rhodes became prime minister of Cape Colony in July 1890 Abercorn protested that this was incompatible with his role in the company, but did not force him to choose between the two. A few months later, when Salisbury had reportedly had enough of him, the Duke defended Rhodes, saying that though he was 'a little bit of an autocrat' he was a man of 'great influence, power and knowledge'. On a subsequent occasion, in response to the brutality being shown to the natives by those acting on behalf of the company, Abercorn remonstrated only half-heartedly with Rhodes.[55] The one occasion when it seems that Rhodes really did annoy the Duke was when his alternate on the Board, Rochfort Maguire, was returned as a Nationalist MP in an uncontested by-election in County Donegal in 1890. Abercorn took personal offence at this and was 'greatly shaken' in his opinion of Rhodes, though the latter's response was to offer the opinion that '[Charles Stewart] Parnell is acting wisely in putting a better class of man into the House of Commons'.[56]

The main controversy of his chairmanship was the Jameson Raid of 1896, a failed attempt to start an uprising among British settlers in the Transvaal. With Abercorn's relaxed attitude to company affairs, there is no reason to believe that he was aware of the preparations for the raid. The Duke was at Barons Court when news of the Jameson Raid broke. A representative of Central News rushed there to ascertain his views on the actions of Dr Jameson. Abercorn admitted that the reports from South Africa were a major shock, but declined making any official statement. He did say that the Board had had no hint of what Jameson was planning, but hoped that a satisfactory explanation would be received in due course. The controversy surrounding the Jameson Raid rocked the company. Abercorn, along with most of the Board, recognised that Rhodes's resignation had to be accepted, but failed to act decisively, retreating to his position that without Rhodes the company was doomed. Eventually, under considerable political pressure, the Board accepted Rhodes's resignation. Despite the furore surrounding the raid,

Abercorn continued as chairman, a position he held until his death. One artefact from this period, no longer at Barons Court for it was later donated to Salisbury Museum, was a finely crafted pistol which the Duke intended to present to Lobengula, the chief of the Matabele. Before the presentation could be made the Matabele revolted, and so the pistol remained with the Duke. It may be noted that Mbala in Zambia was formerly named Abercorn in honour of the Duke, while there is also a village called Abercorn in Swaziland.

Visit to the northern courts of Europe

Abercorn's close connections with the Royal Family continued throughout his life. In 1886, he was appointed a Groom of the Stole, and, as previously noted, in 1892 he was awarded the Order of the Garter. The most important role performed by the Duke on behalf of the Royal Family was acting as 'His Britannic Majesty's Special Ambassador' to announce the death of Victoria and accession of his close friend Edward VII to the throne to the northern courts of Europe. At the time of his appointment, March 1901, he was recovering from a bout of flu, and his brother Frederic anxiously wrote to him prior to his departure with advice on the most appropriate footwear for the Russian spring, warning 'Melting snow is a most deadly thing, and many people have lost their lives getting their feet wet in it.' Abercorn packed accordingly and on 22 March left Charing Cross on a journey that would cover 3,600 miles. Travelling with him were his son, the Marquess of

The Duke and Duchess of York (the future George V and Queen Mary) at Barons Court in early September 1897 while on a tour of Ireland. While staying with the Hamiltons, a garden party was held in their honour. Over 1,500 invitations were issued and the Duke of Abercorn arranged for 150 carriages to ferry guests from the railway station in Newtownstewart to Barons Court.

Hamilton, and the Earl of Kintore, Major General Sir Archibald Hunter, and George Clerk of the Foreign Office. A detailed journal has survived which provides an absorbing account of the expedition.[57]

The visits to Copenhagen and Stockholm were enjoyable, if relatively uneventful. In the latter the party was taken on a tour of the Zoological Gardens, while the Duke and his son received an enthusiastic welcome from a large contingent of the Hamilton family in Sweden: 'a very fine looking and pleasant lot of men they were'. During the tour there were occasional expressions of disapproval for the Boer War, then being fought, and in Sweden the King was 'clear and to the point in the military criticisms of events in South Africa'. After Stockholm the next stop was St Petersburg, which the party reached on 1 April. They stayed at the Winter Palace, where the Duke was accommodated in rooms last occupied by the Emperor of Austria. The Russian court was in residence at Tsarkoe Selo, some 16 miles south of St Petersburg. The party travelled there by train, with the Duke then being transferred to a carriage drawn by six white horses accompanied by the Grand Marshall of the Court. A warm welcome awaited them from the Tsar and Tsarina, and the Tsar had even donned the uniform of a Scots Grey to greet them. In St Petersburg the Duke visited Faberge, 'that delightful robber', and spent £125 on various articles.

Journeying on from St Petersburg by train, the party arrived at Berlin late on the evening of 7 April. It had been arranged that on the 9th the Kaiser would meet the Duke at the Royal Schoss. Escorting the group was a detachment of Queen Victoria's Regiment of Dragoons, a unit of the German army, the first time a party other than royalty had been escorted in this way. The Duke and his fellow travellers were ushered into an anteroom where a large number of senior figures in the German army and navy had assembled. The room contained a series of glass cases containing models of the latest battleships in the German navy. The Kaiser was 'in excellent spirits and looked remarkably well'. He drew the Duke's attention to a Union flag which hung as a curtain to the Kaiser's own quarters, proudly telling him that it had been draped on the coffin of the late Queen. After dinner the Kaiser presented Abercorn with a large marble bust of himself. The conviviality lasted late into the night as the Kaiser waxed lyrical on a broad range of subjects – war, finance, art and colonisation.

The following day the party dined with Queen Victoria's Regiment of Dragoons. The Duke in his speech emphasised 'the necessity of cementing bonds of friendship and ties of comradeship between the two nations, and armies and navies.' After dinner the party was treated to a quite extraordinary spectacle. The tables were cleared and the officers formed up to parade past the Duke.

> The Colonel was armed with a broom, the officers placed silver mugs, wine coolers, or anything metal procurable on their heads as helmets; they were variously armed with tongs, pokers, shovels, broomsticks, and wrapt up in table cloths and napkins, they marched past the Duke as steadily as they could.

This apparently was an honour usually only paid to heads of state and crown princes. After this horses were brought into the room for a demonstration of equestrian skills. The night was still young, for the party still had a supper to attend. As they returned to their hotel to change, the Duke made sure that none of them were 'hiccoughy' before allowing them to attend this late evening meal.

The Kaiser thoroughly enjoyed entertaining his guests. Writing to Edward VII afterwards, he commented:

> They made an excellent impression here and were most respectfully treated by the public. We are doing out best to make them feel comfortable and at home in Berlin. ... I have already had the great satisfaction of hearing from Captain Hamilton's own mouth that, notwithstanding his having a height of nearly two yards, yet his bed was really long enough!

The final royal visit was to the King of Saxony on 13 April. Four days later the party arrived back in London. George Clerk calculated that the mission had spent in all £1,534, which he did not consider excessive.

A few months after the visit of Abercorn's delegation the Kaiser's mother died. She had been the eldest child of Queen Victoria, and the Duke's late sister Katherine, wife of the Earl of Mount Edgcumbe, had been one of her bridesmaids. Abercorn wrote to the German emperor to express his sympathies and received the following telegram in reply:

> The amount of work and woe I had to go through during and after the horrible time have kept me from immediately answering your very kind letter as I ought to. I am most touched by your kind words of sympathy; thank God, dear mother at least could peacefully pass away after such fearful suffering as she went through. She often talked about your sister her bridesmaid, and I will remember the visit at Mt Edgecumb[e] when I accompanied mama as a boy.[58]

The success of the Duke's mission did not lead to his being drawn into the world of European politics. When the German statesman Friedrich von Holstein, the dominant figure in the Kaiser's Foreign Office, wondered whether the Duke would be a suitable person to involve in discussions on Anglo-German relations, the response from Baron Eckardstein, the First Secretary of the German Embassy in London, was that while Abercorn was agreeable enough, he was a 'confused and politically ignorant person'.[59]

Hampden House

Following the death of his father, the 2nd Duke moved his London residence to Hampden House in Green Street, which became his home in the capital for the remainder of his life. Hampden House was well known for its social gatherings, which were regularly reported in the press. In June 1889, for example, the Duchess hosted a reception at Hampden House which was attended by the Turkish Ambassador, the Italian Chargé d'Affaires, and numerous members of the British aristocracy and members of parliament. 'The house was beautifully decorated with flowers and the gardens illuminated with coloured lamps', while a military band played in the balcony throughout the evening. Two days later a ball was held here with the Prince and Princess of Wales as guests of honour. Further examples of such gatherings include a ball in May 1894 with the Russian ambassador, the Austro-Hungarian ambassador, the Italian ambassador, the Portuguese minister and the Brazilian minister present, while a reception in November 1897 was in honour of Indian and colonial visitors to London.[60]

Such occasions were more than simply social gatherings. In May 1890 the King of the Belgians dined at Hampden House. With other representatives of the British South Africa Company in attendance, and with Belgian colonial ambitions in Africa of great interest to the company at this time, the occasion provided an opportunity to discuss issues of interest in a convivial atmosphere. The house was also opened for other events. In February 1893, for instance, the Duchess hosted an exhibition of English and Irish hand-made lace at Hampden House in advance of the lace being sent to the Chicago World Fair. When Lady Knightly of Fawsley visited the house in June 1889 she remarked that she was 'delighted with it, such a nice old fashioned stately abode with some good pictures … and the finest silver chandelier I ever saw'.[61]

Even after he became King, Edward VII was a regular luncheon or dinner guest here, providing him with an opportunity to discuss politics and other matters, while Queen Alexandra was also a frequent visitor to the Duchess. One interesting insight into life in Hampden House is provided by Consuelo Vanderbilt, the American wife of the 9th Duke of Marlborough, who described meeting the Duke on a visit to his London home:

The Duke of Abercorn seated and holding a cigar.
As he told a young Somerset Maugham, 'when I come to dinner with a widow lady I always bring my own'.

> The Duke, a small fragile man, was seated near the fire; he had embroidered slippers on his feet, and a velvet smoking jacket, for he was convalescing from some minor ailment. … The Duke was restless and fussy and ran around the room pointing out family portraits by Lawrence, of which there was a lovely collection.

He admired Consuelo's fur coat and compared it to his own, which he believed was not as good.[62] Another amusing account of the Duke's behaviour is provided by the writer Somerset Maugham, who years afterwards recalled an evening when he was seated beside Abercorn at a dinner. At one point the Duke produced a large cigar case and asked Maugham if he liked cigars, opening the case to reveal several handsome Havanas. The young writer replied that he did (though he did not admit that he could not afford them and only smoked one when it was offered to him). 'So do I', said the Duke, 'and when I come to dinner with a widow lady I always bring my own. I advise you to do the same.' And with that Abercorn chose one of the cigars for himself, snapped the case shut and put it back in his pocket.

Another anecdote from this time concerns the Duchess and the reaction among her friends to Thomas Hardy's controversial novel of 1891, *Tess of the d'Urbervilles*. Hardy himself left this account of the impact it was having on dining arrangements at Hampden House:

> The Duchess of Abercorn tells me that the novel has saved her all future trouble in the assortment of her friends. They have been almost fighting across her dining table over Tess's character. What she now says to them is, "Do you support her or not?" If they say "No indeed. She deserved hanging. A little harlot!" she puts them in one group. If they say "Poor wronged innocent!" and pity her, she puts them in the other group, where she is herself.[63]

The third Home Rule crisis

Though by the early twentieth century it was clear that the leadership of Ulster Unionism had shifted decisively towards the business and professional classes of Belfast and away from rural patricians, the Duke continued to be an important figure within the wider Unionist family. In 1905, for instance, he was chosen as the first president of the Ulster Unionist Council. By 1910 Home Rule was once again a major political issue. Due to illness, Abercorn was unable to be present at the annual meeting of the Ulster Unionist Council and Ulster Union of Constitutional Associations in January 1910, but sent the following letter which set out his views on the impending crisis:

> We have to contend against an absolute fact, namely, that the Government have actually gone in for Home Rule. It is all nonsense

for Mr Asquith to talk about Home Rule without separation. That is a mere blind, for every one who knows anything about Ireland is quite aware that if Home Rule were given to Ireland separation must eventually follow. The demonstration will, I hope, have one good effect, namely, that it will enlighten the eyes of the English public against the effects of Home Rule, in the same way as the great meeting over which I had the honour to preside in Belfast in 1892 was the means of pointing out to the electorate of those days in England how fatal the policy of Mr Gladstone would have been if carried into operation.[64]

The re-emergence of the Home Rule threat refocused attention on constituency contests. By 1910 the Duke's own division of North Tyrone had become the most marginal constituency in Ireland; in the general election of 1906 and the by-election of 1907 the Unionist candidate had been defeated by, respectively, nine and seven votes. Because of the expenses incurred as a result of the revision courts, the North Tyrone Unionist Association (NTUA) was heavily in debt and once again Abercorn found himself having to use his own resources to help finance the Unionist campaign in advance of the January 1910 election. He took a personal interest in this election and intervened directly to dismiss the proposed candidature of W. W. Barnhill, a local Unionist he believed was weak and unpopular, arguing that E. C. Herdman, chairman of the NTUA, should stand instead. What particularly angered Abercorn was the fact that he believed that should his own son have been standing he would have been expected to pay all the election expenses himself, which he was not in a position to do.[65] Barnhill succumbed to the pressure and withdrew. In the ensuing election Herdman lost by over 100 votes.

In advance of the general election of December 1910, the North Tyrone Unionist Association met to select a suitable candidate.[66] Their choice – Lord Arthur John (Jack) Hamilton, the Duke's son and a captain in the Irish Guards – was received with much enthusiasm.[67] E. C. Herdman, addressing the meeting at which his candidature was announced, said that he was glad the candidate was 'a member of a family which had always worked for the good, not only of North Tyrone, but the country generally'. However, not even the popularity of the son of the Duke of Abercorn could prevent another victory for the Liberal candidate. After the result was announced, Hamilton admitted that he was only a beginner in politics and was proud of his first efforts.[68] The editorial of the *Tyrone Constitution* had already commented, 'having youth on his side, he will be a leader in the van of Unionism in the days to come'.[69] However, this was not to be, for on 6 November 1914 Jack was killed in action in France. The Duchess of Abercorn also became involved in the political opposition to Home Rule, serving as the first president of the Ulster Women's Unionist Council formed in 1911.

Final years and death

The final years of the 2nd Duke were marred by illness. He never fully recovered from an operation to remove an abscess from his liver in 1910, and his public engagements steadily decreased. He did, however, become involved in an organisation founded in 1911 that was originally known as the Volunteer Police Force and subsequently the Civilian Force. The Duke was its president and wrote several letters to the press appealing for support. In these, he set out the aims of the movement: 'mainly the preservation of public order and the protection of life and property in times of strike, riot and disturbance' – essentially to support public services during periods of industrial action and unrest.[70] The emergence of this organisation was viewed with concern by some who regarded it as a semi-military, strike-breaking movement acting outside of normal policing. In early December 1911 the Secretary of State for the Home Department criticised the Civilian Force in the Commons, though he declined to raise the matter with its president directly, adding, 'I should think the Duke will be aware of what takes place in this House.' The following February, Abercorn insisted the 'Force is purely non-political and takes no side in any trade dispute, but confines itself to assisting in the preservation of the peace, the protection of law-abiding citizens, and the maintenance of the public services'.[71] The government became even more concerned when the Duke published a letter proposing to enlist a company to be known as the Indian Service Force which would be made up of, among others, officers of the Indian Army. This proposal seems to have come to nothing and the deterioration of his health lessened his involvement in such schemes.

The Duke of Abercorn, *c.* 1910.

A fascinating insight into the Barons Court household in the Duke's final years is provided by the 1911 census. The only members of the family at Barons Court on the night of the census – 2 April – were the 2nd Duke and Duchess and their daughter Lady Alexandra Phyllis. The census records that the Duke and Duchess had been married for 42 years and had had nine children, of whom five were still alive. There were thirteen servants in the household: Ina Sutherland, the housekeeper; Sarah Jane Aiken, the Duchess' maid; Margaret Robson, Lady Phyllis's maid; housemaids Ellen Florence Dare, Rebecca Hamilton and Mary Ellen Allsopp; kitchen maids Sarah Annie Marshall and Rebecca Rodgers; James Attride, the Duke's valet; footmen

Thomas Thompson and Sidney Childerley; Ethel Smith, a professional nurse ('hospital' is written in brackets after her occupation); and, finally, Edmund Douglas Bennett, the Duke's secretary. Seven of the servants had been born in England, two in Scotland and the remaining four in County Tyrone. Their ages ranged from 41 (the housekeeper) to 18 (one of the kitchen maids). The census reveals that there was a remarkable preponderance of Scots among the estate staff at this time. The estate manager, Robert Bell, was a native of Scotland, as was his son David who assisted him. So too were Robert Taylor, the gamekeeper, John Robson, the forester, John J. Wallace, the farm manager at Letterbin, and two of the gardeners, William Allan and John McIntyre. George Yea, the head gardener, had been born in England, though his wife Isabella was a Scot.

Due to ill-health the Duke was unable to play a prominent role during the Unionist campaign against the third Home Rule Bill in 1912. In one of his few public appearances, he presided at the rally addressed by Sir Edward Carson on 20 September in Londonderry, one of the events in the campaign leading up to 'Ulster Day' when the Ulster Covenant would be signed. He himself was too weak to travel to Belfast to sign the Covenant with the other leaders of Unionism on 28 September. Instead, he signed it at Barons Court Church under an oak tree, watched by the drilled ranks of men from the local Unionist Clubs. This was the last occasion

Footmen at Barons Court, late 1800s.

The Barons Court staff, late 1800s.

on which he took part in any public gathering. Though he planned to spend Christmas at Barons Court, he left there hurriedly at the beginning of December 1912, travelling to London.

The Duke signing the Ulster Covenant at Barons Court Church on 28 September 1912. The Duchess headed the local list of signatories of the Women's Declaration.

NATIONAL MUSEUMS NORTHERN IRELAND

It was later reported that the last thing he did while on his way to England was to bring to the Tyrone County Hospital in his own car a poor man whose hand had been crushed in an accident.[72]

On Christmas Eve he visited the West London Hospital, of which he was president, to distribute gifts to the patients. Just after Christmas he was back at the hospital to receive Queen Amelia of Portugal who was paying a visit to the institution. However, a chill quickly developed into pneumonia and he passed away at Hampden House at 5.30pm on 3 January 1913. On the evening of his passing a lone piper played outside Hampden House: his identity remained a mystery and it was thought that he was a personal acquaintance of the Duke's or someone who had received assistance from him in some way.[73] The funeral service was held at St Mark's Church, North Audley St, London, on the following Monday. Because of the interest he had shown in the London Fire Brigade, many uniformed firemen lined the streets from Hampden House to the church.[74] Following the service his body was brought back to Tyrone and interred at Barons Court, in the grounds of the small Church of Ireland church built by his father.

Opinions on the Duke and his legacy varied. His obituarist in *The Times* believed that 'he occupied, on the whole, a less conspicuous position in the world than several of his brothers and sisters'. A political opponent, the Protestant Home Ruler, Rev. J. B. Armour of Ballymoney, commented:

> The Duke of Abercorn, the author of the snatch 'we will never have Home Rule', is gone and the Unionists are in mourning. Personally he was very kindly and the sorrow for him about Newtownstewart is real but the race of which he was the big man was never very reliable as the members of the family always liked to play with both ends of the stick.[75]

Others were more complimentary in their tributes. Upon hearing of the death of the Duke, David Crawford, Lord Balcarres, wrote in his journal:

The Duke of Abercorn, who died yesterday, was a droll little man, void of intellect, but endowed with an address and dignity which more then compensated for other shortcomings. He was a power in Ireland and this was owing to a friendliness of gesture which won hearts.[76]

The *Irish Times* noted that he was not a 'platform speaker of the first rank'.[77] Few would have disagreed, though Thomas MacKnight would remember him as 'One of the most kindly and least demonstrative of noblemen in Ulster, his language was very simple'.[78] The Duchess survived him by over 16 years, dying on 11 May 1929 at her London home, 115 Park Street West, at the age of 81. Friend of the family John Ross described her as 'one of those noble, selfless women of whom the world is not worthy'.

Lord Arthur John Hamilton (1883–1914)

Known within the family as Jack, Lord Arthur John Hamilton, son of the 2nd Duke of Abercorn, was born in Devon in 1883 and educated at Wellington College. In 1901, he enlisted in the Militia, serving for a number of months before joining the Irish Guards. He was promoted to captain in 1909. In December 1910 he stood as the Unionist candidate for North Tyrone in the general election, but was defeated. Having retired from active service, he joined the Special Reserve with the rank of captain in March 1913 and in the same year was appointed Deputy Master of the Household. At the outbreak of the First World War he rejoined the Irish Guards and landed in France in August 1914. On 19 September *The Times* incorrectly reported that he had been killed in action. He regularly wrote to his mother from the front and the Duchess kept this correspondence, labelling it 'Letters and cards from my precious Jack. Last letter 16th October – last postcard 2nd November 1914'. A few days after his last postcard he was killed in action near Klein Zillebeke in Flanders.[79]

Lord Arthur John Hamilton.

His body was never recovered and for some time there was uncertainty as to what had happened to him and whether he had been killed or captured. It was not until 24 November that the War Office sent the Duchess a telegram reporting that Jack had been missing since 6 November, but pointing out that this did not mean that he was dead. For some months he was listed as missing, but it came to be accepted that he had been killed on 6 November. In 1916, his uncle Lord Ernest Hamilton described the encounter in which he perished:

November 6th saw a certain renewal of the enemy's activity. The day opened very foggy, but by eleven o'clock there was a bright sun. ... The German bombardment, with which they as usual opened the day, was more than usually severe, and lasted the whole morning, and about 2 p.m.

it was followed by an infantry attack before which the left of the French and the right of the Irish Guards was driven in. As a result of this cave in the line, the left of the Irish Guards, which remained in the trenches, suffered considerably, Lord John Hamilton, Captain King-Harman and Lieut. Woodroffe being killed.[80]

For years afterwards his mother tried to find out what had happened to him. She was able to track down Lewis Gage-Brown, an officer in the Life Guards, who wrote to her on 17 March 1918 from the Hotel v. d. Abeelen in Scheveningen – in Holland where many Allied POWs had recently been transferred – to tell the Duchess 'I can give you but scant news', but going on to relate what he knew about her son's death:

> On November 6 1914 we came into action at Klein Zillebeke close to Ypres in support of the remnants of the Irish Guards and Grenadiers. Shortly after I was myself captured and taken to Lille, where I met some men of the Irish Guards, Dunne amongst them. He related that the regiment had had a very heavy bombardment and that there were very few survivors, some having been bayonetted as they lay helpless in the trenches. Your son was very seriously wounded and apparently half delirious. Dunne stayed with him, though he said he could have got away if he had left him. When he was captured the Germans sent stretcher bearers to your son. I cannot, I regret, remember exactly what happened then, but I am nearly sure that your son died very soon after and that Dunne was with him to the end. In any case I believe his sufferings were not very prolonged. I do not think that German treatment had anything to do with your son's death. … It will be some consolation doubtless to know that your son's end was very gallant and honourable.

Gage-Brown further related that Dunne had passed on to him Lord John's watch, but had not yet returned it to the family as he felt he could not guarantee its safe arrival. (On 26 November 1914, the *Belfast Newsletter* reported that the Duke had received a letter from an officer in the Life Guards who was a prisoner in Germany – presumably Gage-Brown – who informed him that he had come into possession of Jack's watch.)

In October 1920 the Duchess received from the War Office, via the Directorate of Graves Registration and Enquiries, Central Europe, Berlin, the translation of a letter from Major Rieder v. Riedenau, a former officer in the German army resident in Limburg an der Lahn. Returning Jack's diary, small pocket book, army whistle and orders, he provided an explanation of how he had come into possession of them. Quoting directly from his diary of 5 [sic] November 1914, he related that he and his men had carried out a successful attack on the English trench.

> There were still 8 men around me with whom I jumped into the trench. We only found dead and wounded there. The trench was entirely shelled. I took half a dozen prisoners and drafted them back. I then

intended to advance, but my attention was drawn by one of my men calling out: 'Herr Hauptmann here lies a severely wounded English officer!' I stepped to the side and saw a badly wounded Engl. Captain leaning against a shattered tree who had been the Commander of that Battalion. He had been shot through head and chest and his eyes were closed. Beside him was kneeling his Orderly sobbing. As the battle was still going on I had little time to spare; however, I went to him, asked him if I could help him and if he had any special wishes. He opened his eyes and recognised me and pointed to his chest. We unbuttoned his waistcoat (leather) which was soaked with blood and I removed his pocket book. According to his papers, it was Lord John Hamilton who seemed to hold a high position at the Royal Court in the Buckingham Palace. In the pocket book were photos, some dried flowers and also a signed photo Miss Kitty Light, London. From Miss Kitty Light were also various letters addressed to him which have got lost. ... I rested him as best I could ... and asked what more I could do for him. He spoke with great difficulty and very indistinctly. I could not remain with him, but had to leave him as the fighting was going on. I offered him my hand which he took whilst lying on his back and pressed saying: Adieu mon Camarade. His Orderly was taken prisoner. He himself probably died on the spot. ... It was a pitiful picture that remained in my memory for a long time afterwards. This British Officer made upon me a most distinguished and Chevalrsec impression.

Three days later Riedenau was himself wounded on the same spot. Though he did not know what had happened to Lord John's body, he remembered clearly the place where he had found him: 'about 600 m. N. W. Kleinsillebeke on the Border of the Herethage Woods.' The Duchess replied to Riedenau to thank him for the letter and effects which had brought her some comfort and to ask if he had any further information on Jack's death and in particular if he had suffered greatly. His responded to say that he regretted he knew nothing more than he had originally told her, but assured her that the wounds he observed on Jack's body were such that 'he could not have suffered much pain', adding, 'When I left him he was already almost unconscious, quite comatose, and passed away shortly afterwards.'

Lord Arthur John Hamilton is commemorated on the Ypres (Menin Gate) Memorial in Belgium. His name also appears on the Duddingston Kirk War Memorial, at Barons Court Church, and on the First World War Memorial Window in St Bartholomew's Church in Ottawa, Canada, that was commissioned by the Duke of Connaught.

IN THIS CHURCH FOR MOST YEARS OF
HIS LIFE WORSHIPPED AND PRAYED
ARTHUR JOHN HAMILTON
CAPTAIN IRISH GUARDS 5TH SON OF
JAMES 2ND DUKE OF ABERCORN K G
HE WAS BORN AUGUST 20TH 1883 AND
WAS KILLED IN THE TRENCHES NEAR
YPRES BELGIUM NOVEMBER 6TH 1914
THIS TABLET IS DEDICATED TO HIS DEAR
MEMORY BY HIS SORROWING MOTHER
"I WILL GO DOWN INTO THE GRAVE
UNTO MY SON MOURNING" GENESIS XXXVII 35
HIS LAST WORDS WERE
"I AM GOING — TELL MY MOTHER
HOW I DIED AND PRAY FOR ME"
AND HE DIED WITH A SMILE ON HIS LIPS

The memorial to Lord Arthur John Hamilton in Barons Court Church.

Lady Alexandra Phyllis Hamilton
(1876-1918)

The older of the two daughters of the 2nd Duke of Abercorn, Lady Alexandra Phyllis Hamilton was born on 23 January 1876. As a young woman, Lady Phyllis, as she was generally known, developed a keen interest in archaeology. In the course of 1907 she began to make firm plans for carrying out a number of excavations, contacting several individuals who were only too happy to help or offer advice. The rector of Strabane provided information on how to acquire Ordnance Survey maps, while both the steward at Barons Court, Robert Bell, and the agent, Colonel John Baillie, were fully supportive in assisting with the necessary arrangements. A prehistoric megalithic monument (an unusual pairing of portal tombs within a long cairn) in Ballyrenan, on the west facing slopes of Bessy Bell overlooking Barons Court, was investigated first. (The site had been visited in 1890 by the Royal Society of Antiquaries of Ireland at the invitation of Phyllis's father, who was a Fellow and Patron of the Society.) In late October 1907, under Phyllis' direction, workmen cleared the monument of stones and rubbish so that excavations could begin. Among the artefacts discovered were some stone beads, fragments of pottery and bone, and some flints including 'a lovely little arrow-head in perfect preservation'. The care with which she undertook the excavation is reflected in her own account of the discovery of the beads: 'Carefully sifting every spadeful, we got altogether seven large beads, four of them round and flat, and two long-shaped, of a greenish stone, and another very light and black – all perforated.'[81]

Lady Alexandra Phyllis Hamilton.

Excited by her finds, Phyllis wrote to Robert Cochrane of the Royal Society of Antiquaries of Ireland who thanked her for her report and asked if a notice of the excavation could be published in the next issue of the Society's *Journal* which Phyllis happily approved.[82] She also corresponded with George Coffey, the Keeper of Antiquities at the Dublin Museum of Science and Art (now the National Museum of Ireland – Archaeology) who was very positive about her investigations, writing, 'If I may say so, you have displayed much care as well as zeal in what you have done already.' Members of her family were enthusiastic about what she had achieved, with her father writing, 'What an excellent "antiquarian" you have become & you deserve the greatest credit for all your energy which has been rewarded.' Her uncle Frederic was similarly positive, writing to her that the account of the excavations had interested him 'immensely'. The site would be excavated again in 1936 by the archaeologist Oliver Davies with the support of the 3rd Duke.

At the same time that she was excavating in Ballyrenan, Phyllis was looking into the possibility of carrying out investigations at a number of other locations. One of these was in the townland of Beragh to the south-east of Barons Court at a particular spot marked on maps as 'Grave Yard' – probably a long disused burial place. As Beragh lay outside the family's estate, permission from the landowner had to be secured. This was readily granted, though the agent for this estate had the following cautionary note for Phyllis: 'It occurs to me to remind you that although there is no country where graveyards are so neglected or ill kept as in Ireland there is no place where people are so easily excited at any interference with them.' Whether or not this was enough to put Phyllis off – Robert Bell had similarly warned her against interfering with this site – there is no evidence that she proceeded further with excavations in Beragh.

Ballyrenan megalithic tombs

Where she did investigate was the small island in Lough Catherine known as Island MacHugh which included the remains of a medieval castle. Excavations were carried out here in the summer of 1908 and coincided (probably deliberately) with the temporary lowering of the lakes at Barons Court. This lowering of the water level revealed that stakes had been driven into the 'beach' all the way round the island showing that it was in fact a crannog, something that had not been apparent before. No evidence for a causeway to the island was discovered, but among the finds were large quantities of flint as well as bones. No report of her work on Island MacHugh seems to have been published in any scholarly journal and it seems that Phyllis did not carry out any further archaeological investigations, though why this should have been so is not clear.

In 1915, Phyllis went to France, working as a YMCA volunteer in support of British troops. In a letter to her brother, the 3rd Duke, on 2 June 1915 she wrote, 'I think most of them think we are paid bar-maids, but the few who have grasped that we are not & that we pay our own expenses here to be with them are really surprised & pleased & grateful.' While in France, she kept up a regular correspondence with her brother Claud who was serving with the Grenadier Guards. His letters to her survive and are generally positive in tone, though the stresses and strains of war still come through strongly: 'there has been very hard fighting and our losses have been very heavy … The papers have exaggerated our gains'; 'sentimentality soon vanishes in war'; 'I wish I was back in England, I have had enough of war and rumours of war'.

A contemplative Lady Phyllis.

In October 1918 she and her mother were staying at Shelton Abbey, near Arklow, the home of her brother-in-law, Ralph Howard, Earl of Wicklow (whose wife Gladys, Phyllis's younger sister, had died in March 1917). When her mother left for London, Phyllis stayed on an extra week so that she could spend time with a local man, home on leave from the army.[83] Remaining with her were Martha Bridge, the family's cook, and her lady's maid, Ellenor Strachan. All three boarded a mail steamer, the RMS *Leinster*, at Kingstown on 10 October. However, shortly after setting sail for Holyhead the vessel was torpedoed by a German submarine. Over 500 people lost their lives in the sinking, including Phyllis, whose body was never recovered, and the two servants. Shortly after the sinking, Frances, Lady Ashbourne wrote to the Duchess with a report she had heard via her brother that she thought might bring her some comfort. One of the officers on board the *Leinster*,

said he was astounded at the calmness and courage of Lady Alexandra. He saw her with another lady (her maid) on board, putting on life belts, and went to them to try to give them any help he could, but she said "oh you must leave us at once – we are strong women, and are not afraid. Go to those who want you more." He said she was perfectly composed.

The family was later told by a survivor that as the ship was going down Phyllis gave up her life jacket to her cook, saying 'I'm a strong swimmer'.[84]

A memorial service was held in St Mark's Church in London on 14 October and at Barons Court Church five days later. The Dowager Duchess never quite recovered from the shock of the loss of her daughter. Responding to a letter of sympathy from Robert Bell, the estate manager at Barons Court, the Duchess wrote that she wished Phyllis could have seen the hundreds of letters of condolence – 'she who always tells me "she was so dull, so stupid, no-one ever really liked her".' The Duchess had now lost three children during the course of the First World War, two of them as a direct result of the conflict – Jack and Phyllis – and Gladys. 'The agony of going on living without my 3 darlings is quite indescribable', she told Bell, 'and this last blow worse than all.' Today the family still holds great affection for Lady Phyllis.

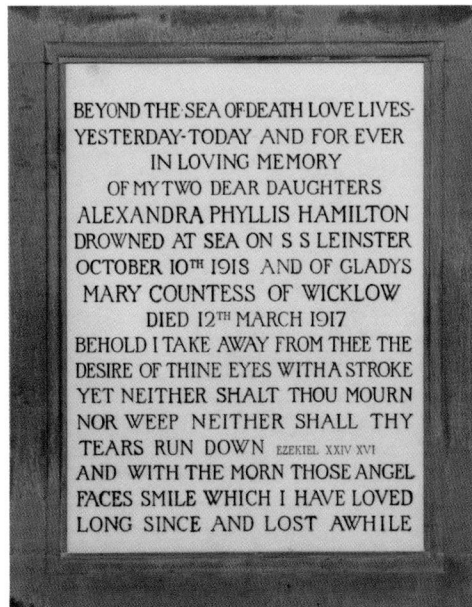

The memorial to Lady Phyllis and Lady Gladys in Barons Court Church.

227

Drawn by Lord Paisley
April 1879

The nine-year-old future
3rd Duke displays his talents as
an artist.

RIGHT: The Duchess of Abercorn

9
James Hamilton, 3rd Duke of Abercorn
A Northern Irish duke

If his father had assumed the headship of a family at a time of crisis, then the same could be said for the 3rd Duke. On both occasions the crisis was the threat of Home Rule. In 1913 that threat was even more serious, though the issue of land reform, which had been of critical importance in 1885, had more or less been resolved. Following the partition of Ireland, the 3rd Duke accepted the invitation to become Northern Ireland's first Governor, a position he held for over two decades. His conduct as Governor won widespread praise even from his political opponents.

James Albert Hamilton was born at Hamilton Place, Piccadilly, on 30 November 1869, the oldest child of the Marquess of Hamilton and his wife Lady Mary Anna Curzon-Howe. The Prince of Wales was his godfather. He was educated at Eton from 1883 to 1886 and then joined the army, serving initially in the Royal Inniskilling Fusiliers before transferring to the 1st Life Guards. It was a matter of some frustration to him that, unlike many of his cousins, he did not serve in the Boer War. Only 150 men of the 1st Life Guards were required and as the officers were selected on the basis of seniority, Lord Hamilton, being at this time a relatively junior officer, was overlooked. He would later serve as a major in the North Irish Horse. In 1894, he married Lady Rosalind Bingham, daughter of the 4th Earl of Lucan. They had two sons, James Edward, the future 4th Duke, and Claud David, and three daughters, Mary Cecelia Rhodesia, Cynthia Elinor Beatrix, and Katherine.

One of the Marquess' passions was natural history, and it was said of him in jest that he was envious of the superintendent of the Zoological Gardens. He was also a keen sportsman and in 1894 made an expedition into the heart of Africa to hunt big game, travelling long distances on foot accompanied by a lone servant. This resulted in many dangerous and exciting experiences, and the trophies of his adventure were at one time on display in the smoking room at

The 3rd Duke in the uniform of
the 1st Life Guards

The Hamilton siblings. From left to right: Claud, James, Katie, Cynthia and Mary

Hodge

Barons Court. Hamilton retained an interest in Africa all his life and, like his father, held the presidency of the British South Africa Company. At one point he seriously considered emigrating to South Africa and buying an estate there.

MP for Londonderry

Like many members of his family, the Marquess entered politics. The Unionists of North Tyrone sought his candidature in advance of the 1895 general election, but he declined their offer, telling them that his army duties prevented him from standing. In 1900, the Unionists of Derry City chose him as their candidate for the general election of that year. In the 1860s this seat had been held briefly by his uncle Lord Claud Hamilton. The 2nd Duke was initially reluctant to allow his son to contest the election, fearing that a defeat in Derry would be hugely damaging to the family's reputation. He had in fact telegraphed the Unionist association in Derry refusing to allow them to put his son up for election, but had been persuaded to change his mind by his close friend, John Ross, who believed the Marquess had a strong chance of success.[1] In 1900, the Nationalist candidate was the outgoing MP, Arthur Moore, a Tipperary landlord and papal count. A close contest was anticipated and the result was victory for Lord Hamilton by a mere 67 votes. In 1906 Hamilton was returned unopposed, while in the January and December elections of 1910 the Marquess was returned by margins of 57 and 105 votes, respectively, his opponent on both occasions being Shane Leslie of Castle Leslie, County Monaghan. The story is told that once while out campaigning for her husband in Derry, Lady Hamilton, after introducing

On 16 February 1899 the future 3rd Duke of Abercorn was the subject of the 'Men of the day' column in *Vanity Fair*, and, though written with a degree of gentle mockery, the sketch does provide an insight into how others saw him at this time: 'Nature has given him brains; and, like all clever men, he is a little diffident. He is not so energetic as some busy people are, but he is nevertheless a keen soldier, who will only leave the service at the call of duty. For he has ambition and it is expected that he will some day make a name for himself. ... [He] is a good unaffected fellow, with a bright and sunny disposition; and altogether he is a genial giant, upon whose bulk sits a courtly and very prepossessing manner.'

herself, was met with an angry response from a householder who exclaimed 'Get you away you wanton woman – I've heard of your carrying on with Lord Nelson!'

It is not insignificant that Hamilton represented an Irish constituency, and specifically a constituency in north-west Ulster, that part of the island with which his family had been so closely associated for nearly 300 years. As Lord Cadogan observed to the Marquess of Salisbury in April 1900, 'the Abercorns think more of Derry than Cork'. Despite their rural base, one historian has written that the Abercorns 'unified all the different elements of urban unionism into a monolithic whole'.[2] While an MP, Hamilton served for a number of years as Treasurer of the King's Household, and later as an opposition whip. It does not appear that he particularly enjoyed his parliamentary career, making few contributions to the debates at Westminster. Even before he had to stand down on succeeding his father as Duke in January 1913, Hamilton had intimated his desire of retiring from the Commons. Writing of the succession, the David Crawford, Lord Balcarres commented that the new head of the family would make a 'good outdoor duke', and added, 'now that the fatigues of parliament are removed from his shoulders, [he] will be a much happier man'.[3] On his father's death the now 3rd Duke of Abercorn inherited what remained of the estate in Ireland – around 15,000 acres, including the demesne and house at Barons Court – as well as property in Scotland.

Home Rule and the Great War

When the 3rd Duke succeeded to the title, Ireland was in the throes of the third Home Rule crisis. His family had been prominent supporters of the Union, with his father an important figurehead for the opponents of Home Rule, and the Duke continued to demonstrate his commitment to this political cause. One of the responses to the crisis was the formation of an armed force to oppose any attempt to introduce Home Rule to Ulster. This organisation, the Ulster Volunteer Force (UVF), owed much to the leadership

The Ulster Volunteer Force training camp at Barons Court, October 1914.

A parade of the officers of the Tyrone Regiment in front of the stable block.

of the landed classes. The commanding officer of the Tyrone Regiment was the Duke. An important priority for the UVF leadership was the training of suitable men to act as officers in the organisation. In early October 1913 a training camp was established at Barons Court, the first of its kind in Ulster. Of the 300 men present, just over half were farmers, seven were members of the clergy, three were from the legal profession, 10 were linen and woollen manufacturers, while most of the rest were shopkeepers and tradesmen. When Sir Edward Carson visited Barons Court on 4 October, at the invitation of the Duke, he found the men at musketry training.[4] The Duke

The training camp staff outside the 'Agent's House' with the Duke seated in the centre. Standing behind the Duke's right shoulder is Robert Bell, the estate manager at Barons Court. Sitting to the Duke's right is Captain Ambrose St Quintin Ricardo, the driving force in the Tyrone Regiment. Seated on the far right of the photograph is Philip Cruikshank, the editor of the *Tyrone Constitution*.

231

himself, in an act of camaraderie, performed the duties of a waiter in serving refreshments to the men. At the same time, Abercorn was somewhat apprehensive about the political direction in which Ireland was heading. One visitor to Ireland at this time commented, 'The Duke is sincere enough, but I should say he is d___d uncomfortable at heart in the position in which he finds himself. ... Nevertheless he can't move back now.'[5] Abercorn was not alone in his uneasiness. Like others of his class he felt compelled to fulfil his responsibility as a leader of society, and yet at the same time feared that events were overtaking them. A further training camp at Barons Court began on 30 May 1914 with over 1,000 officers and men present.

A few months later the British Empire was at war with Germany. In the early months of the conflict Abercorn was actively involved in trying to recruit volunteers for the army, though not always with success. In January 1915, W. C. Trimble, the editor of the Enniskillen-published *Impartial Reporter*, wrote to Carson: 'His Grace of Abercorn (whom we all admire) had been here twice or three times to obtain recruits for the North Irish Horse, and had not got one recruit.'[6] Two of the Duke's siblings died as a direct result of the conflict. Lord Arthur John Hamilton, a captain in the Irish Guards, was killed in action near Klein Zillebeke in Flanders on 6 November 1914. The Duke's youngest brother, Lord Claud Nigel Hamilton, also fought in the war, serving as a captain in the Grenadier Guards. On the day after his brother was killed, he wrote from the trenches to his brother-in-law, the Earl of Wicklow, reporting that

Lord Claud Nigel Hamilton and Lady Violet Ruby Hamilton at the Coronation in 1953 A man of small stature like his father, Lord Claud Nigel Hamilton was twenty years younger than his brother, the 3rd Duke. He is remembered as a dextrous, energetic man who was interested in everything. After the First World War he was an Equerry to the Prince of Wales and in 1921 was appointed a Deputy Master of the Household. He was an Extra Equerry to the Queen at the time of his death in 1975.

> Out of 30 officers and 1,100 men who landed about a month ago, there are now 4 officers and 180 men. I don't know what will happen to us, we cannot go on like this: the last officer was hit about ten minutes ago it will be my turn any minute, but as long as it does not hurt too much it does not matter except for poor Mamma.[7]

At the beginning of December 1914 Lord Claud was made a Companion of the Distinguished Service Order, his citation reading: 'Commanded machine gun for five days and nights in forward trenches without relief, with great effort and under severe fire.'[8] During the War, he was one of the closest companions of the Prince of Wales, himself an officer in the Grenadier

Guards. In 1918, he was made an Officer of the Order of the Crown of Italy and awarded the Croix de Guerre. The Duke's sister, Lady Phyllis, also went to France in 1915, working as a YMCA volunteer in support of British troops. At one point it looked like the Duke himself would have an opportunity to go to France as a 'town major' (an official who would liaise between military and civil authorities), something he was desperately keen on doing, but political commitments prevented him from leaving Ireland.[9] A few weeks before the war ended the family suffered a further blow with the death of Lady Phyllis who drowned on 10 October 1918 following the torpedoing of the RMS *Leinster*. The Dowager Duchess never quite recovered from the the loss of her son and daughter, and indeed the entire family mourned their deaths deeply.

Throughout the war years the Duke remained politically active in the discussions over the future of the island. In 1915 he was elected president of the Ulster Unionist Council in succession to Lord Londonderry.[10] Though by this time Ulster Unionism had become increasingly dominated by a Belfast-centred business and professional elite, there was still tremendous symbolic value in having a leading aristocrat as the head of the movement. The Duke was one of around 100 delegates at the Irish Convention convened by Lloyd George in 1917 in an attempt to formulate a political settlement for the island. The Convention met between July 1917 and April 1918 under the chairmanship of Sir Horace Plunkett. At one point during its deliberations the Duke claimed that he 'spoke for the small farmers and farm labourers of his part of Ulster', no doubt to the derision of Nationalists, while he also acknowledged the beneficial results of the Local Government Act of 1898. He moved that the 'Royal Irish Constabulary and the Dublin Metropolitan Police should both remain as reserved services under the control of the Imperial Government for at least six years', though this amendment was defeated. Ultimately, the Convention was a failure and Abercorn lamented the 'weary months' that he had spent attending its meetings in Dublin. After it had ended he wrote to fellow Unionist, Hugh de Fellenberg Montgomery of Fivemiletown, in a tone of exasperation: 'To talk of any "settlement" now is fatuous, with the country ... in its present condition ... it is bound to be a measure that will please nobody, of course the Ulster Unionists will object, and it cannot go far enough to please or placate the Nationalists, so I am at a loss to fortell its fate.'[11]

Raid on Barons Court

On the same night that the Duke wrote the above letter to Montgomery, 17–18 May 1918, Barons Court was raided by a gang of masked men. None of the family was present at the time, but Abercorn himself wrote to *The Times* to give the version of events that had been provided to him.[12] Around midnight a 'party of Sinn Feiners' arrived at the estate in eight motor cars. They overpowered the gate-keepers, broke into the house, and cut its telegraph wires. The men then spent two hours searching the house from top to bottom for 'non-existent arms', in the process frightening witless three maidservants, the sole occupants of the house. Failing to find the arms they had supposed were hidden in the house, the men made off, taking with them six antique swords of decorative value, but no practical use. What perplexed the Duke was how a convoy of eight cars full of men had travelled such a distance without being stopped by the police. Where they had found the petrol for the journey also puzzled Abercorn. Clearly frustrated at the disregard of the rules and regulations imposed on other parts of the UK for the furtherance of the war, he posed the question, 'how much longer is Ireland going to be treated as a neutral country?' What Abercorn did not reveal was that in one of the passages, the raiders wrote 'Good Old King William'.

The Duchess was unable to contain herself with the excitement created by the raid. Lilian Spender wrote to her husband Wilfrid, who was on active service, on 21 May with news that the Duchess was 'very full of the Baronscourt raid', adding:

The 3rd Duke, *c.* 1915.

It was a really big affair, nearly 100 men and 20 cars [*sic*], all the house and grounds picketed, telephone wires cut, and they ransacked the house for two hours, but found not one cartridge, much less a rifle! They didn't even find a revolver and some ammunition in a cupboard in the Duke's bedroom, for tho' they broke it open, they broke the wrong half![13]

The raid even made it into a debate in the Lords on 11 June on the stringency with which the Defence of the Realm Regulations were being applied in Ireland. Lord Willoughby De Broke, in reference to the availability of motor fuel, remarked:

Now we also know that petrol must have been used for the highly patriotic purpose of rifling the Duke of Abercorn's house to see if there were any arms that would be available at some future time. I do not suppose the noble Earl[14] knows any more than I do where the petrol came from which these bandits used when they went to the Duke of Abercorn's to take down the swords of his ancestors from the gallery with a view to cutting somebody's head off when they got an opportunity of doing so.

Partition and appointment as Governor of Northern Ireland

In the immediate aftermath of the war, the political situation in Ireland became even more fraught. Unionists in Ulster were concerned that support from their one-time allies in Britain was waning. At a large meeting of Unionists in Omagh on 1 October 1919 the Duke condemned those who had been elected on a pro-Union platform, but who were now 'very much milk and water Unionists'. The Duke also warned the meeting that 'the great and powerful organization, the Northcliffe Press, was no longer on their side' and was continually trying to undermine their position. However, nothing that had happened in the previous five years had made them any less determined not to accept the authority of a parliament in Dublin.[14] In August 1920 the Duke accepted an invitation to become honorary colonel of the Tyrone Regiment of a reorganised Ulster Volunteer Force. That autumn he took part in the debates in the Lords over the Government of Ireland Bill. Speaking on 23 November in support of the bill, he explained why the Unionists of Ulster were in favour of it:

> They are tired, after thirty years of political intrigue, gerrymandering, and wire pulling. They are a solid race, a race of great courage who believe in themselves and believe that under a Northern Parliament they can work out their own salvation, continue their business and their agriculture, and be more or less independent of outside interference.

Quoting from John Stuart Mill, he commented on what created a sense of nationality. However, the common sympathies that Mill thought essential were not present throughout Ireland where 'ever since the plantation of Ulster the Ulster people have been more or less at variance with their fellow-countrymen'. Though acknowledging that this was deplorable, he admitted that there was no denying the facts of history. He also hoped, somewhat optimistically, that if separate legislatures in the north and south of Ireland were successful 'at some future date the two may coalesce and form a united Parliament'. However, this would be on only one condition – 'joint loyalty to the Crown and to the Empire'.

Due to the considerable unrest at this time, Barons Court itself was not considered safe for the family to visit. In December 1921 Bell, the estate manager, warned the Duchess that if the Duke and his son, Lord Hamilton, came to Barons Court there was the very real threat of them being kidnapped.[15] This was a particularly tense time for the family. A month before, on 19 November, the Duchess had been present for the dedication of the Memorial Tower at Thiepval, erected in memory of the men of the 36th (Ulster) Division. She unfurled the Union flag and French tricolour from the tower.[17] As part of the ceremony, trees were planted, including one by the Duchess for the 'women of Ulster'. The event left a deep impression on all those gathered. 'It was a day not to be forgotten', the Duchess wrote to Colonel Fred Crawford on 27 December, 'charged with such glorious memories on that hallowed ground.' The reality of the political situation in Ireland was also weighing heavily on the Duchess, as she confided to Crawford her anguish at the course of events:

> Like you, my feelings are too deep and bitter for words, but if we hold tight, and keep that unalterable confidence in our right cause which has sustained us hitherto in all crises, we shall once more triumph. I am sure of it, but it is hard to keep quiet and calm others when one rages within! Let us pray that 1922 will see our attitude justified. Best wishes to you for it and the succeeding years, and may Ulster be only true to herself.[18]

With no satisfactory settlement possible for the island as a whole, the partition of Ireland took place in 1921 and Northern Ireland was created. Under the new arrangement a Governor would be the representative of the King in each part of Ireland. It was officially announced on 11 December 1922 that the new Governor of Northern Ireland would be the Duke of Abercorn. His swearing in took place the next day in a simple ceremony in the Record Chamber of the County Courthouse in Belfast, with an absence of formality save for a police guard of honour.[19] In many ways the Duke was the obvious choice as Governor. As Ulster's leading aristocrat, a firm supporter of the Union, and coming from a family long established in the province, he had impeccable credentials. Adopting a conciliatory position, he said in his first speech:

> I desire to express the earnest hope that the time may not be too far distant when the Executive of the Irish Free State and the Executive of Northern Ireland may meet to settle in an amicable conference those outstanding questions which affect the welfare of both areas.[20]

A few days later the King invested the Duke with the insignia of the Order of St Patrick. A state entry to Belfast was planned for early the following year and was eventually arranged for 26 February. The events of that day began at Stormont Castle with the presentation of a gold key from the Lord Mayor of Belfast to the Governor. It had originally been planned that the key would be presented on a specially constructed platform on the Newtownards Road near the city boundary, but this had been abandoned in the face of heavy rain and strong winds. The day finished with a reception at the City Hall. In his speech the Duke said: 'We live in times of difficulty, not merely in Ireland, but in Europe and far beyond. In such times there is one clear signal which every man may confidently obey – the signal to devote himself to his duty and to the task that is ready to his hand.' He finished his speech with a saying used by merchantmen of old, 'And so God send the good ship to her desired port in safety.' On that evening the Duke sent a telegram to the King, 'With humble duty I beg to inform your Majesty that

I have today received a most enthusiastic and loyal welcome as your representative in Northern Ireland upon my official entry into Belfast.'[21]

In 1928, the Duke agreed to serve as Governor for a further term. In the same year, he was made a Knight of the Garter. In February 1931, on the recommendation of R. B. Bennett, the prime minister of Canada, Abercorn was offered the position of Governor-General of the dominion. The Duke turned this down, giving as his reason his desire to remain in Northern Ireland. In conveying George V's regret at Abercorn's declining this position, Lord Stamfordham, the King's private secretary, wrote, 'Indeed as I told you His Majesty was afraid that you could not relinquish the very important and responsible office which you occupy as Governor of Northern Ireland.' Later that year the Duke surrendered 20% of his salary as Governor at a time of economic difficulties for the country at large. In July 1934 Royal approval was issued for the Duke to be reappointed Governor for a third term.

The governorship

As the governorship was a new position in a new state, the Duke was left to formulate his own precedents and procedures as the constitutional head and King's deputy in Northern Ireland.

The Duke of Abercorn wearing the Garter Riband and Star.

He was spared much of the criticism that was directed at government ministers on account of his straightforwardness and sincerity, and even his political enemies recognised that he had the best interests of Northern Ireland at heart. He was described as a man of 'splendid physique and commanding presence' who 'possessed courage and resolution, as well as dignity, tact and an attractive geniality'.[22] In late 1924 it was agreed that Hillsborough Castle, the former seat of the Marquess of Downshire, would become the official residence of the Governor. In October of the following year the Duke and Duchess moved in, and for most of the next 20 years this was their primary residence. In responding to a welcome from the people of Hillsborough the Duke admitted that they were, comparatively speaking, strangers to the townsfolk, but he hoped that over the next number of years 'we may all get to know each other very much better'.[23]

The Duke was a firm believer in the positive good of the British Empire and of Northern Ireland's position in it, and in a speech in Londonderry on 7 October 1926, when he was presented with the freedom of the city, declared: 'Surely it is a great thing to belong to a brotherhood of Empire in

the formation of which so many of our relatives have taken part, and who, especially in the case of Irishmen, find themselves scattered over the globe.' During Empire Week in May 1930 he issued a statement that read: 'I would like all to translate the special activities of this week into a firm conviction and habit of purchasing Empire goods.' Again he drew attention to the closeness of the people of the province and those in the colonies and dominions.

The Duke recognised the symbolic value of visits to Northern Ireland by the Royal Family, accompanied by appropriate demonstrations of loyalty. In March 1924, 'on behalf of the people of Northern Ireland', he invited the Duke and Duchess of York (the future George VI and Queen Elizabeth) to the province. This would be the first royal visit to Northern Ireland since the opening of parliament by the King in June 1921, and as its success was considered vital much careful planning went into preparing for it. The young couple, accompanied by the Governor, arrived from Stranraer at Bangor on Saturday, 19 July to find thousands gathered to welcome them. The Duke had taken over Clandeboye for the weekend and as the Duchess was ill, their daughter Lady Katherine, a close friend of the Duchess of York, acted as hostess. The royal couple thoroughly enjoyed their stay there, so much so that on one of the evenings the Governor was forced to press the Duke of York to go up to bed as the official guests were yearning to go home. The following week was to be a busy one, with a visit to Belfast where the Yorks were given honorary degrees by Queen's University, a stopover at Barons Court, followed by a visit to Derry. From there the party returned to Belfast by train, stopping at Coleraine, Ballymoney and Ballymena. The last day of their visit was spent at Mount Stewart as guests of the Londonderrys before the Yorks departed on the 26th.[24]

When it came to the official opening of Parliament Buildings at Stormont in 1932, the Duke, who had laid the foundation stone in May 1928, sought a visit from a senior member of the Royal Family and issued an invitation to the Prince of Wales, which was accepted. The Prince, however, was anxious that the ceremony be handled sensitively, given the current economic situation, and that costs should be kept to a minimum, writing to the Governor that the opening would 'remind those thousands who are unfortunately unemployed and almost starving, that, since the War, an enormous amount of money had been expended on bricks and mortar'.[25] While in Northern Ireland, the Prince stayed as a guest of the Duke and Duchess at Government House, Hillsborough. On one evening, after dinner, he decided to go for a walk through the village. He was quickly recognised and surrounded by a large crowd. A drumming party was at that time in the midst of performing and the Prince, to the delight of those gathered, accepted the invitation to beat a Lambeg drum.[26]

The celebration of the Royal Jubilee in 1935 provided another opportunity for a demonstration of loyalty. The Governor invited Prince George to Northern Ireland, but was advised that the King and Queen wished to have all their family with them at a special thanksgiving service in St Paul's Cathedral on 6 May. Instead the Duke of Gloucester acted as the royal representative to Northern Ireland, where a special service was held in St Anne's Cathedral on 12 May.[27] On 28 January 1936 the Abercorns were present at Windsor Castle for the King's funeral. The Duchess provided Fred Crawford with an account of the proceedings:

> We were in the Choir at St George's Chapel at the Funeral and nothing has ever impressed me more. It was so beautiful, yet so simple, and when the coffin sinks below the floor it is heartrending. The Queen is a marvel, and the King has been wonderful to her. I hear Loyal Ulster has shown its sorrow in no uncertain way.[28]

In May 1937 the Duke was one of four Knights of the Garter who carried the canopy over George VI at the coronation. Back at Barons Court 2,000 people were entertained at a special picnic and nearly 600 children were presented with coronation souvenirs.

Though viewed as part of the Unionist establishment in Northern Ireland, the Duke was anxious to be seen to be politically neutral in his role as Governor. When E. W. Ross, his estate manager at Barons Court, was invited to join a local Unionist association in 1933, Abercorn cautioned against it, arguing, 'I have always tried to avoid being connected with politics in any way & to appear as impartial as possible, and if you were to join, the Nationalists might try to make out that you were acting on my behalf.' He used his speeches to express his hope that mutual support would bring the different factions in Northern Ireland together. For instance, in the aforementioned speech in Londonderry in 1926, the Duke stated that he could not enter the field of politics, but hoped that everyone would endeavour to work in a 'peaceful, law abiding, and constitutional manner'. Interestingly, in preparing this speech he had wished to quote from a recent speech made by Cardinal O'Donnell in the city in which the cleric had expressed his hope that change would come 'as the fruits of goodwill on all sides'. However, as the main thrust of O'Donnell's speech had been condemnation of the partition of Ireland, the Duke was advised not to refer to him and so the line was removed.

On the opening of Royal Courts of Justice on 31 May 1933 he asked his audience to be mindful of the generosity of the British Government 'in providing for every sphere of activity'. He also implored his listeners to live in harmony with each other:

> May I make an earnest plea that there be peace in our midst. It is well for us to remember that we are living in a very difficult age, in which

it is essential that each man should help his neighbour. Let you, one and all, therefore decide that from now onwards you will live in peace and concord, conducting yourselves with pride and dignity in whatever state of life it has pleased the Almighty to place you.[29]

The Church of Ireland bishop of Down and Connor and Dromore, the Methodist president and the Presbyterian moderator took part in this ceremony. It was felt important to include all three major Protestant denominations in such events, though achieving the right balance between them was not always easy. In March 1936, during discussions on religious services on 'National' occasions, the Duke wrote to Lord Craigavon indicating his frustration at the situation:

> I fully understand the difficulties owing to there being no Established Church in Ulster, and clerics are often very narrow and tiresome in these matters, but, after all, the reigning king, whoever he may be, is, as such, the head of the Church of England, and equally of the Established Church of Scotland, which is Presbyterian, so there should be no cavilling in the matter.[30]

A sense of humour comes through in the Duke's speeches on public occasions. For instance, at the opening of the harbour airport in 1935 the Duke is supposed to have said that anyone who wanted to fly was mad and that the only flight he wanted to take was when he flew to heaven. The complexity of the Northern Irish situation for outsiders was also a concern to him. When an Englishman was appointed the county commandant of the Tyrone 'B' Specials the Duke raised concerns that he might 'not thoroughly understand the idiosyncrasies of character of our people here'.[31]

In July 1939 the Duke attended a luncheon party in London to which Joseph Kennedy, the American ambassador, was also invited. As they conversed, Kennedy expressed his desire to visit Northern Ireland and the Governor indicated that he would be more than happy to host him at Hillsborough. The ambassador also told the Duke that he quite liked the idea of being awarded an honorary degree by Queen's University, Belfast. As the Duke subsequently explained to Craigavon, it was 'not that [Kennedy] valued these degrees in the slightest', but the ambassador thought that it would be well received in the US if he, a Roman Catholic, were to be awarded a degree by the 'university of "Protestant" Ulster'. The Duke liked the idea, as did Neville Chamberlain, with whom he had discussed the matter. Craigavon's response is not known, but in any case the outbreak of war put an end to it. Abercorn found Kennedy an intriguing character, writing to the Northern Ireland Prime Minister, 'I like what I have seen of Kennedy, a bit of a "crook" perhaps, but a pleasant and amusing one.'[32]

Fire at Hillsborough Castle

On the morning of 7 August 1934, there was a fire at Hillsborough Castle. It was spotted by an official who had gone up on the roof to lower the flag to half mast as a mark of respect following the death of the German president, Field Marshall Von Hindenburg. The staff hurriedly began to remove furniture and furnishings from the upper floor (including a Van Dyck that the Duke was particularly fond of) and were soon joined by the police and local people. The Belfast Fire Brigade arrived in record time and soon brought the conflagration under control. However, the scale of the destruction was apparent, with fire damage to the upstairs and water damage to the ground floor. Subsequent investigations revealed that the fire had originated in the quarters used by Commander Oscar Henderson, the Governor's Private Secretary, who was on holiday in the south of England. The Duke and Duchess were not in residence at the time. A press release issued later that day stated that the house and contents were fully insured and taxpayers would not be footing the bill for the repairs. Soon afterwards, the Duke visited the house and, in response to an expression of sympathy from the King, telegraphed: 'The house is almost totally gutted, but owing to the excellent work of all concerned the majority of the furniture and other contents have been removed to safety.'[33]

The restoration of the Castle took place over the next year and a half. The completion of the work was held up by the slowness of the firm responsible for the interior decoration. This firm had been chosen by the Duke himself against the advice of officials. In the meantime, Wilmont House at Dunmurry provided gubernatorial accommodation. Opinions have varied on the end result of the restoration work – 'weak, modernised Georgian', according to one architectural historian. Another has observed that 'the opportunity was taken of inserting much formal, not to say regal, plasterwork in a style which might fittingly be described as Late (British) Empire'.[34] One source of controversy at the time was the proposed removal of the gates from Richhill Castle to Hillsborough. In November 1936 the inhabitants of Richhill issued a resolution deploring the appropriation of the castle gates which they claimed had been there for over 200 years. However, the removal went ahead and the gates are still in place at Hillsborough Castle.

Conduct as Governor

Abercorn was personally liked and respected by members of the Northern Ireland Government and probably exercised considerable indirect influence on ministers.[35] He and his wife enjoyed a strong friendship with Lord and Lady Craigavon, and with other senior figures in Ulster Unionism. In 1940 and 1943, the Duke oversaw the smooth transfer of the premiership from Craigavon to Andrews and then to Brooke. Despite his Unionist and establishment credentials, Abercorn had the respect of many Nationalists for the manner in which he conducted himself as Governor. During a debate in the Commons in 1955 on whether the Governor's salary should be increased, Cahir Healy, Nationalist MP for Fermanagh and South Tyrone, reflected on that fact that during his time as holder of this office the Duke had 'discharged his duties with efficiency and to the satisfaction of everybody concerned'. Healy was generous in his praise:

> He also got the credit for bringing a number of industries to Northern Ireland. I am sure that he did his best. The name of the Duke of Abercorn was such that it might appeal to many industrialists across here. There was nothing Socialist or Nationalist about him. ... He entertained, he dined, he wined, he did everything pertaining to his office, and I never heard anything but praise of his social qualities.

In the course of this debate it was pointed out that the Duke of Abercorn had used his own money to finance some of his activities as Governor. Sir Douglas Savory claimed that 'especially during the latter part of his Governorship, the Duke of Abercorn was out of pocket by thousands of pounds', while H. Montgomery Hyde added: 'I certainly knew of my own personal knowledge, because I had the friendship of the late Duke of Abercorn, that he was substantially out of pocket. He put his hand into his own pocket to pay the expenses, and he was too decent a man to make a protest at that time.'

A detailed picture of the Governor's expenditure is provided by Oscar Henderson in a document entitled 'Position of the Governor of Northern Ireland', dated 23 May 1945.[36] At this time the Governor's total annual salary was £8,000, £6,000 of which was tax free. The Governor was responsible for paying his staff and all expenses in connection with the office. The Governor's staff comprised a Private Secretary and Comptroller, Personal ADC, Assistant Private Secretary, and Confidential Clerk. A government messenger was also paid for by the Governor. In addition the Governor was responsible for all lighting and heating in Hillsborough Castle, including the public rooms and office. He supplied all pictures, ornaments, linen, china and cutlery used there and provided his own servants, brought from Barons Court, and official car and driver. Henderson reckoned the Duke donated £500 to various charities every year and the Duchess another £200–300 when she attended charity functions. Prior to the Second World War, the Duke hosted an annual garden party at Hillsborough attended by over 2,000 people. This, together with the St Patrick's Day celebrations, cost as much as £1,000 to put on. It is little wonder that the Duke was forced to dip into his own pocket to cover the full costs of the governorship. A former senior civil servant in the Irish Free State fondly remembered the evening receptions hosted by the Duke and Duchess on St Patrick's Day, which he described as 'an informal delight for both possessed the knack of making people feel happy'. Lady Moyra notes that her grandfather was proud of both his Irish and British heritage.

The 3rd Duke and Barons Court

By the time that the 3rd Duke inherited the title and estate, the issue of land reform that had confronted his father and grandfather had been largely resolved. As a result of the various land acts of the late nineteenth and early twentieth centuries the greater part of the estate had been sold to the tenants prior to 1913. What remained was still substantial – around 15,000 acres – though obviously the income from it was considerably lower than that collected by the 1st Duke prior to 1885. The 3rd Duke's responsibilities as Governor meant that he had little time for the management of Barons Court. The estate manager until his death in 1931 was Robert Bell, and the Duke seems to have been content to let him operate as he thought best. The 1920s was a difficult time for farming in general and this comes through in Bell's letters to the Duke. In May 1922, for instance, the manager wrote, 'Farming remains a disappointing business, much worse than before the war, but surely things will regain a working balance soon.' From the 1930s, however, the Duke's heir, Lord Hamilton, became much more involved in running the estate, which was certainly to its benefit. Of considerable importance in the history of the estate in the twentieth century was the lease from the Duke to the Forestry Commission of just under 3,000 acres of land at Barons Court in 1920. The duration of the lease was nominally 150 years, but a clause was included which allowed the lease to be ended in certain circumstances. In 1927, the lease was assigned to Forest Service of Northern Ireland.

The Duke standing in front of the main portico of Hillsborough Castle.

The present Duke recalls that his grandfather, whom he remembers as a tall (he was 6 feet 4 inches), kindly and distinguished figure, was always ready to welcome his grandchildren to Barons Court. It was during one such visit to Barons Court that disaster nearly struck the family. Early on the morning of 13 January 1940, a fire was discovered in the north wing of the house. Sleeping in this part of Barons Court were the Duke's three young grandchildren: Moyra, James, and Anthony. They were quickly woken and moved to safety. The Duke and Duchess had been asleep in another part of the house. The fire was initially fought by the Duke's guard led by Captain

The entrance hall at
Barons Court which was
used as a sitting room by
the 3rd Duke.

Martelli, and by the estate fire brigade under Captain Ross. Valuable tapestries, ornaments, furniture and paintings were removed to the lawn by estate workers. The Londonderry City Fire Brigade arrived on the scene within three-quarters of an hour and laid a hose to the lake.[37] Through their endeavours the fire was brought under control and extinguished, though not before considerable damage had been done to the wing. There were no suspicions that the fire was malicious and it seems simply to have been an unfortunate accident. The fire at Barons Court was a devastating blow for the Duke, and one from which he never really recovered. Nonetheless he and the Duchess continued to visit Barons Court on a regular basis, spending much of each summer there, as well as Christmas.

The war years

The outbreak of war in September 1939 brought fresh challenges. Shortly after hostilities began the Duke issued the following statement:

> At this time of gravest anxiety, I, in my capacity as your Governor and as an Ulsterman, feel sure that all the people of Northern Ireland will remain calm and stand resolute. Please try to do everything you can to assist the government in the prosecution of the war and cheerfully carry out such orders as are issued for the defence and safety of our people, especially the children.[38]

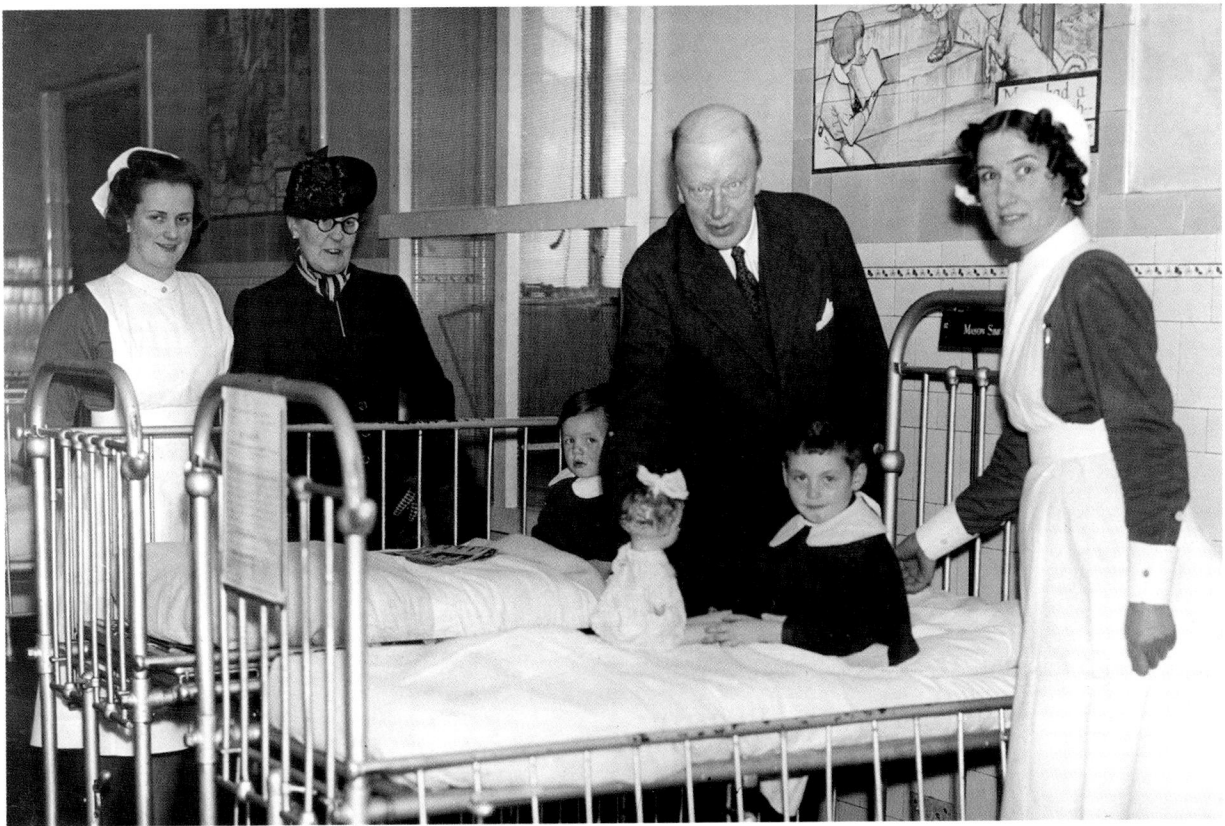

A few weeks later the Duke announced that he was setting up the 'Governor's Fund' to raise money for the Red Cross and St John War Organisation. By the end of November over £5,000 had been raised, the donations also going to support the Ulster Gift Fund. The latter organisation had been established in September 1939, with the Duchess as its president, to support the war effort through, for example, providing clothing and bandages to military hospitals, and later assistance to prisoners-of-war from Northern Ireland. Its headquarters was in Bedford Street, Belfast, while there were some 300 depots across the province. Throughout the war the Duke and Duchess were indefatigable in their support of various causes, visiting, for example, camps, hospitals and training schools. During this time, the Duke made Northern Ireland his absolute priority, forgoing meetings in London and elsewhere. He also agreed, in 1940, to stay on as Governor for a fourth term. In 1941, shortly after the Belfast Blitz, Abercorn privately recommended that conscription be introduced to Northern Ireland, believing that it was right to 'strike when people's feelings are hot', though in the end nothing came of this.

Many of Ulster's big houses were requisitioned during the war and their grounds used for military camps. In October 1940 a party of officers inspected Barons Court with a view to establishing an artillery camp there. However, they decided against it because of a scarcity of water and the softness of the roads leading to it. The estate manager, Captain Ross, was opposed to having the main house taken over by evacuees for a school or

The Duke and Duchess visiting injured children in the Children's Hospital, Belfast, April 1941.
BELFAST TELEGRAPH

being used as a 'Convalescent Depot' because of the insufficiency of the water supply during the summer. At the beginning of March 1941 the Sub-Area Quartering Commandant visited Barons Court looking for a site for 100 huts. Because of the undulating nature of its terrain, it was not considered suitable for a permanent camp. However, soon afterwards a suitable site for a camp at Barons Court was identified and in early May Ross informed the Duke that two infantry battalions and the Field Ambulance were comfortably settled there and were enjoying their new environment. A hospital had been established as well as a dental surgery. Ross made sure that the 2,000 troops knew which areas were out of bounds, and that shrubs, trees and nests were not to be tampered with. 'They are so far as I can see', he wrote to the Governor, 'a very quiet and well behaved crowd, and I do not think we will have any trouble at all.'

The Duke and Duchess were well known for their hospitality, and during the War extended warm welcomes to a number of distinguished visitors to Northern Ireland. In the spring of 1941 Robert Menzies, the Prime Minister of Australia who had travelled to Britain to discuss wartime strategy, was a guest of the Abercorns at Hillsborough Castle. In his autobiography Menzies described the Duke and Duchess as 'marvellous and full-hearted people'. The purpose of his visit to Ireland was to explore the possibility of opening up a channel of communication between Churchill and de Valera. This was a cause of concern to those in Northern Ireland who feared that the price of ending Irish neutrality would be the political reunification of the island. At Hillsborough, the Duchess asked him, 'Is Churchill going to sell us out to the South?' She was reassured when Menzies explained to her that he had come to Ireland without Churchill's blessing.

On 26 January 1942, the Duke was at the dockside to welcome to Northern Ireland the first American troops sent to Europe. Thereafter he took a great interest in their well-being. He was particularly interested in baseball, and attended several of the exhibition matches that were staged. One, on 4 July 1942 at Windsor Park, attracted a crowd of 10,000 and the Duke was there to 'throw the first ball'. In November 1942 the Duke welcomed Eleanor Roosevelt to Northern Ireland during a tour by her of American military and welfare establishments. Another visitor during the war years was the future American presidential candidate Adlai Stevenson who later remarked that spending time in the library at Barons Court had been for him one of the most peaceful and intellectually stimulating interludes during the war. The Duke also established a good relationship with David Gray, the American ambassador to Ireland, who was known for his hostility to Irish neutrality. Ensuring that the right image of Northern Ireland during the war was presented in America was of great concern to the Duke. In 1943, he took great exception to a hostile article by the Irish minister in

Washington which was printed in the *New York Times* and subsequently reprinted in the *London Evening Standard*, and insisted that this be challenged. In May 1945 he was greatly perturbed at reports that de Valera had offered his condolences to the German minister in Dublin following the death of Hitler.

Retirement

By the beginning of 1945 the Duke had decided in his own mind that he would retire once Nazi Germany had been defeated. In late January he wrote to his son, Lord Hamilton, outlining his reasons:

> As you may know, I have decided to resign the Governorship when the European war is over. I do not feel up to carrying on after that, as there are sure to be any amount of political, etc. difficulties then arising, & this country may then be in the same state as Greece or Poland! And I think I should, after all these years, leave when the going is good.

He had reached the age of 75 and with the war undoubtedly going the way of the Allies, felt that he had done his duty and it was time to make way for someone else. He was now near the end of his fourth term and had served for a much longer period than he could have imagined when he accepted the position in 1922. He kept his thoughts to his closest confidants, and it was not until mid-June that it was announced that the Duke would be standing down as Governor. He had recently sprained his knee as the result of a fall, and was probably more conscious than ever of his age.

In the address delivered to him by the Northern Ireland House of Commons on the occasion of his retirement, it was stated: 'Your own personality has done much to strengthen the ties which bind us to our traditional policy, while elsewhere principalities and powers less firmly founded have crumbled into ruin.' In reply the Duke paid tribute to Northern Ireland's war effort:

> I am confident that the spirit which has brought us to victory will endure into the days of peace. I am sure that with courage, foresight and goodwill the tasks will be worthily performed and that Northern Ireland will enjoy a prosperous and happy future.[39]

On 8 September 1945 a civic garden party with 1,000 guests in attendance was held in Brooke Park, Derry, in honour of the Duke and Duchess and to bid farewell to them. Shortly after this the couple moved to London. Though both of them had declared quite strongly their opposition to making 68 Mount Street their retirement home, it was here that they were to spend the rest of their lives together. On 31 October the Duke was sworn in as a member of the Privy Council and in early December he had an audience with the King to acknowledge his retirement as Governor. Of course, the Duke did not sever all connections with Northern Ireland. He presided at a meeting on 29 March 1946 to revive the Ulster Association in London. The following September he was back at Barons Court, where he was presented with gifts by Lord Londonderry on behalf of the people of Northern Ireland for his time as Governor.[40] A year later he again visited Barons Court to view the changes being implemented under the direction of the architect Sir Albert Richardson. In London, he enjoyed visiting museums and read extensively. The Duke celebrated his eightieth birthday at Mount Street in 1949. The Duchess provided their granddaughter Moyra with an account of the celebration:

> Grandfather thoroughly enjoyed his birthday, the wires poured in all day. Cynthia transferred her family tea party here as I had been indulging in a horrible cold. She arrived with a lovely cake, & all sorts of good food. Mary, Jock, Sandy, both sets of Clauds & wives, & of course the Spencers. We drank Grandfather's health, & were all very happy.

The 3rd Duke of Abercorn died on 12 September 1953, in his 84th year. He had not enjoyed the best of health in his final years and had missed the Coronation due to illness. In tribute, the Prime Minister of Northern Ireland, Lord Brookeborough, said of him:

> For a long time to come the Duke of Abercorn will be remembered as a man of great personal charm, a devoted servant of the state and one

of Ulster's most distinguished sons. In earlier life his experience as a
soldier and parliamentarian helped to prepare him for higher office
and greater responsibilities. As first Governor of Northern Ireland he
created a splendid tradition and has set a noble example of public
duty. He knew and loved the Northern Ireland people, entered into
their joy and shared their sorrows. Endowed with many natural gifts
and graces, the Duke was the soul of honour and, in the finest sense
of the word, a gentleman.

Tributes were also paid to him in the House of Lords. The Marquess of
Salisbury described him as having 'courage, a shrewd common sense and a
simple kindliness which endeared him in a rare degree to the people of Ulster:
he loved them and they loved him'. Earl Jowitt, the former Lord Chancellor,
in referring to the Duke's low profile in the Lords, observed:

> The Duke of Abercorn reminds us of this fact: that those who are
> shallow enough to think that because we do not see noble Lords at
> Westminster taking part in our activities here, therefore they are not
> doing useful service, are taking a completely short-sighted view. Here
> is an illustration of a man who was, quite naturally, able to devote
> only a small time to the service of this House, but who, in another
> capacity, was rendering most useful service to his State and to the
> country. The fact that for some twenty-three years he held in Northern
> Ireland the great position which he did hold, and the fact, which I
> think is common knowledge, that he was offered the opportunity of
> serving His Majesty as Governor-General in Canada, but declined to
> accept the position because he felt that he ought not to leave Ulster, is
> a tribute to his simple sense of duty.

The Duke's body was cremated in London and his ashes were brought back
to Barons Court for burial. There was never any doubt that this was his true
home. Following the Duke's death, the Duchess moved to 44 Mount Street,
London, where she lived until her death on 18 January 1958.

Lord Claud David Hamilton

Lord Claud David Hamilton
(1907–68)

The second son of 3rd Duke of Abercorn and his wife Rosalind, Lord Claud David Hamilton was born on 13 February 1907. He was educated at Eton and then Christ Church, Oxford, from where he graduated with a BA in 1929. He then pursued a legal career and was admitted to the Inner Temple in 1930. The present Duke remembers him as a 'quiet, elegant, intelligent and kind man'. While working in London, Lord Claud lived for a number of years with his brother's family in Cambridge Square. During the Second World War he served in the Irish Guards, reaching the rank of captain. His niece Lady Moyra believes that he blossomed during the war years and overall enjoyed his time in the Irish Guards, despite the horrors he encountered during the campaign in north-western Europe in 1944–5.

Letters, invariably written on '2nd Armd Bn Irish Guards' headed paper, that he sent to his sister-in-law, the Marchioness of Hamilton, provide an insight into some of his wartime experiences. Claud's battalion was not part of the first wave of troops that landed at Normandy on D-Day, but followed just under a month later. On 3 July 1944, he wrote to 'Kath' that he and his comrades had arrived in France the day before:

> I had a rather rough crossing in a small tank-landing-craft in which I was frequently refreshed by mugs of tea from one of the sailors who had a beard & came from Dungannon! The shipping off the beach-head was the most impressive sight I have ever seen – really breath-taking – and what remains of Hitler's Western Wall looks like some of London did in 1940. ... Some of the villages are very knocked about & others seem quite untouched, according to how quickly the Germans withdrew.

His frustration at the failure of Operation Market Garden in the early autumn of 1944 comes through in a letter he wrote on 12 October:

> It was too tragic for words that we couldn't get to the airborne men in time. ... On the way up here we met US airborne troops at all the canal and river bridges. One of them said: "Gee, we're glad to see you – we've been here sandwiched between two lots of Germans & the bacon is getting mighty thin"!! ... The town [Nijmegan?] was a most impressive sight one night when I crossed the river – flares falling from enemy 'planes, several houses ablaze and thousands of our coloured tracer A/A shells bursting in the sky. But in the daylight, these battlefield scenes always fill me with the deepest gloom – ruined homes, smashed vehicles, in an air of utter desolation, & if there are dead men it is worse still. Please heaven, the whole foul business ends before the real winter begins, but I very much fear that the "over by Xmas" school of thought are too optimistic.

A letter of 19 December shows that there were occasional diversions from army duties and that he had the opportunity to build friendships with some of those being liberated:

> The town I am living in has got a small railway running down the main street – like the old Clogher Valley Railway! ... I have "palled up" with a doctor who lives a few miles away & went duck-shooting with him today. Unfortunately, there were no ducks! The doctor was up to his eyes in the resistance movement & looked after numbers of wounded partisans & RAF men who had been shot down in these parts. He was imprisoned by the Germans & remained thus until 3rd Sept when his warders decamped before the Allied troops arrived. ... I have recently been driving a small German 'Volkswagen' which makes a noise like a squadron of tanks & has a disconcerting habit of swinging broadsides across the road when the breaks are applied.

He was even able to have a quiet Christmas as a letter of 27 December reveals:

> The very charming owners of a nearby country house gave me a most hospitable Christmas. Three of us lunched there and stayed until midnight. We provided a plum pudding and some captured champagne which was greeted with ironic cheers as it was marked "*Reservé à la Wehrmacht*". ... My present abode is a large farm built (in a square round a monumental manure heap) in 1645 – white walls and red tiled roofs. Very comfortable and attractive to look at, but the sanitary arrangements are a bit whimsical. As usual the inhabitants can't do enough to make life easy for us.

Accompanying a letter of 10 April 1945 were some German collar badges for the young Hamilton children that had been found in a barrack store. In the same letter, he was critical of the manner of the media's reporting of their campaign:

> The BBC and the Press have been so outspoken about our movements that I suppose I can tell you that I crossed the Rhine on Good Friday, over a very long 'Bailey' pontoon bridge. It was such a slow process that a Grenadier sergeant found time to be seasick.

Two days after that a close friend was killed, prompting Claud to write, 'it makes one sick to read in the Press that "all organised resistance has ceased!"'.

A letter penned on 13 May, less than a week after the war had ended, was written about half-way between Hamburg and Bremen:

> As a matter of fact we weren't "careering so fast & furiously" as you think – every bridge had been blown up & the roads cratered by exploded sea-mines. Some of these places were also defended by small parties of extremely gallant German marines. But, towards the end, the prisoners came in faster & faster & it became obvious that it was all

> over … And now one can hardly realise that all the horror & suffering
> is over & it is too strange for words to be saluted by German soldiers.
> … The present situation is very unreal – it really is impossible to realise
> peace has come & at the same time some of the worst aspects of war
> are beginning to fade from one's memory.

Quite naturally his thoughts turned to civilian life: 'I simply can't imagine what I am going to do when I leave the army – it should be early autumn. Any suggestions?'

One of the first things he did after leaving the army was to marry Genesta Mary Heath, a friend of his sister Mary, on 21 February 1946.[41] They had met for the first time on D-Day, when Claud's regiment was in the midst of preparations for its crossing to France. Genesta's memories of the encounter were that he was 'a tall officer with a kind face and inquiring eyes'. They regularly wrote to each other during the campaign and he told her of the horrors of encountering concentration camps. Following their marriage, the couple moved to Genesta's large ranch in Kenya. Claud also fulfilled the role of a part-time magistrate in Nakuru. While in Kenya, he took a deep interest in the Masai tribe. Among his papers which were deposited in the Bodleian Library of Commonwealth & African Studies at Rhodes House, Oxford, are letters on the Masai tribe with collections of tribal folk-tales and songs, articles on life in Kenya and a manuscript history of the Masai. In 1953, Claud and Genesta returned for the Coronation where Claud was a gold staff officer, wearing the full dress uniform of the Irish Guards. They returned permanently to London in the mid 1960s which he found a thoroughly miserable experience. He died on 15 February 1968 aged only 61 and was buried in Christ Church churchyard, Coldharbour, Surrey, where a small Celtic cross marks his grave. Genesta died in 1990; the couple had no children.

10
James Hamilton,
4th Duke of Abercorn
A gentleman and a scholar

The twentieth century brought many challenges for landowning families. The land acts of the late nineteenth and early twentieth centuries had resulted in a significant reduction in the quantity of land they directly owned. Adjusting to these changes was difficult enough, but additional taxes, death duties, the rising cost of labour, among other things, all increased the financial strain on landed estates. Some landowners adapted better than others. In the case of the Abercorn estate, enormous credit is due to the 4th Duke, who worked tirelessly to ensure its future viability. The fact that he had a lower profile than his antecedents, not holding important political office, does not diminish his significance in the family's story over the past four centuries.[1]

The 4th Duke of Abercorn as a boy.

The future 4th Duke of Abercorn was born on 29 February 1904 and baptised on 30 March in the Chapel Royal, St James' Palace, the King being one of his sponsors. His earliest years were partly spent at Coates Castle in Sussex, the house that his great-grandmother, the widow of the 1st Duke of Abercorn, had retired to in her final years. Initially he was styled Lord Paisley and, from the death of his grandfather in 1913, Marquess of Hamilton. Among the earliest surviving letters of the young Marquess are several written to his father from Ludgrove School in 1915. It is clear that he enjoyed sports, for in one letter he proudly told his father about a game of football in which he scored a goal, and in another he wrote that he had taken eight wickets in a cricket match, but scored only four runs. The war was never far from his mind, however, and in his letters he included sketches of aeroplanes, which he saw occasionally, and drawings of German soldiers. The reality of the horrors of war was brought home to him through the deaths of his uncle Jack (Lord Arthur John) and his aunt Phyllis, whom he adored. He continued his education at Eton and then went to Sandhurst, after which he was commissioned into the Grenadier Guards as a Second Lieutenant.

The 4th Duke around the time of his marriage.

253

ABOVE: Lady Kathleen Crichton, the future Duchess of Abercorn, in 1908.

LEFT: The wedding of the 4th Duke, 9 February 1928.
BELOW: The scene outside the St Martin's in the Fields Church, London.

The Hamiltons return to Barons Court after their honeymoon.

Lord Hamilton married Lady Kathleen Crichton, daughter of the late Lt-Col. Henry William Crichton, Viscount Crichton, and Lady Mary Cavendish Grosvenor, on 9 February 1928 at St Martin-in-the-Fields Church, London. Giving the bride away was her brother John, the 5th Earl of Erne, while the Marquess' younger brother, Lord Claud, was his best man. Officiating at the ceremony was the Archbishop of Armagh. News of the wedding had generated huge public interest, and a large crowd gathered outside the church to await the arrival of the King and other guests; a cold prevented the Queen from being at the service, though she was able to attend the reception at the London house of the Duke and Duchess of Devonshire in Carlton Gardens. The following day the Marquess' mother wrote to him of her joy at their marriage: 'The simple dignity of the service impressed everybody. ... you both radiated happiness and the atmosphere of the church was one of peace and complete accord.' The couple honeymooned at Shillinglee Park in Surrey, which had been lent to them by Lord Hamilton's cousin, Lord Winterton, before travelling to Malaga in Spain. It was to be the beginning of over half a century of devoted companionship.

Though Lord Hamilton loved the army, he recognised that if he was to provide for a family, he needed to find a more remunerative position. He

The christening photograph of James, 1934. The newest addition to the family is cradled by his mother, with his father, Lord Hamilton, standing behind. To the left of the 3rd Duke is Lord Craigavon, the Prime Minister of Northern Ireland, and standing to his left is Lord Claud Hamilton, in front of whom is the 5th Earl of Erne. Standing on the far left of the photograph is Captain Martelli, who was in charge of the Governor's guard, while seated in front of him is Robert Bingham, the US ambassador.

therefore, resigned his commission to become a stockbroker, working in the City for the firm Williams de Bröe. Three children followed over the next 11 years: Moyra Kathleen in 1930; James, the future 5th Duke, in 1934; and Claud Anthony in 1939. Though the Hamiltons lived in London – their home was 22 Cambridge Square – the Marquess remained in close contact with Barons Court through regular correspondence with the estate manager. He was also anxious to be kept up to date with what was happening in the locality. For example, in 1936 he gave instructions that he wished to be sent the *Tyrone Constitution*, the principal local newspaper.

Moyra, Anthony and James

Lord and Lady Hamilton's position in society meant that they moved in Court circles. In 1935, for instance, they were guests of the King and Queen during Ascot week. In January 1936, following the death of the King, Lord Hamilton wrote 'London is such a sad place just now', adding 'Lady Hamilton and I mourn him as one who has been very kind to us personally.' He recommended to the estate manager that the employees of Barons Court be given the morning off on the day of the funeral as a mark of respect. The following year he was an usher at the Coronation of George VI; the Marchioness and Lady Moyra watched the event from the stands.

The estate in the 1930s

The last major piece of legislation that affected landed estates in Northern Ireland was the Land Act of 1925. Due to earlier land transfers, this affected the Abercorn estate to a lesser degree than other landed estates in the province. Several in the east of the province had remained virtually intact after the earlier land acts and were only now transferred to the tenants. At this time the Barons Court estate was reduced in extent to 5,500 acres, though it remained one of the largest estates in Northern Ireland in private ownership. In February 1928 the remaining lands were settled on the Marquess on the occasion of his marriage.[2] From this time onwards Lord Hamilton became much more closely involved in the management of the estate. There were numerous challenges facing estates at this time, mostly financial in the form of income tax and surtax, death duties and the increased costs of labour. The Abercorn estate may have been better positioned than most to come through these difficulties, but even here there were trials.

In September 1931, Robert Bell, the long-serving estate manager, died. His replacement was Captain E. W. Ross, a Scotsman and veteran of the First World War; he had been gassed and the consequences of this remained with him for the rest of his life. Ross arrived at Barons Court at the beginning of November 1931 and his initial impression of the estate was that it would be difficult to increase income significantly, but he hoped that it would be possible to cut expenditure considerably. As a landlord, Lord Hamilton showed himself to be sympathetic to the difficulties faced by his tenants. In one instance from November 1932 he made the following offer to Ross in relation to a tenant in financial difficulties, 'if he is *really* in need, I would be quite prepared to make a voluntary payment of two shillings or half a crown per week'. On another occasion, in February 1933, the Marquess was reluctant to prosecute the owner of a dog that had destroyed many of the ewes, 'but that is only because I do not like taking money from a man who has only a modest living'. At the same time he realised that he needed to take a firm stand on this incident, writing to Ross, 'I don't want to be hard on anyone, but people must learn that we are not going to be trifled with, and we were very lenient to those two poachers.' The sheep-mauling incident continued to irk him, however, and he soon afterwards wrote to Ross, 'I still feel furious about that blasted dog!'

His career in finance, however much he disliked it, had given him a grasp of economics that, it would not be unfair to say, was not shared by his father, who was content to allow the Marquess a relatively free hand in the running of the estate. Lord Hamilton was acutely aware of the need to improve efficiencies and make savings where possible. He was also alive to the impact that external factors could have on the fortunes of the estate. For example, in April 1932 he wrote to Ross:

> No-one expects very much relief from the Budget, but there seem to be definite signs of slight revivals in trade, and the unemployment figures are slowly shrinking. If the Free State abolish the oath & become a Republic, it will surely help us in the North, both in industry and farming.

One approach adopted in the interwar years by a number of landowners in Northern Ireland, among them the Earl of Antrim and Lord O'Neill, to lessen the impact of taxation and death duties was to create an estates company. Early in 1933 Lord Hamilton and his father talked over the possibility of reorganising the estate along these lines. The Marquess explained to Ross that this would enable them to change the way Barons Court was run and to centralise everything. Ross's task was to assemble the necessary financial paperwork on the estate over the previous six years, a task he found difficult due to the rather disorganised manner in which the previous estate manager had left things. Lord Hamilton fully appreciated his efforts, writing to him in March: 'It is you, entirely, that we thank; as it is you who have borne all the drudgery and worked so efficiently.' Moves to create the estates company were delayed until a Scottish company had been established so that shares from it could be transferred to the Barons Court one. However, by January 1934, the new Barons Court Estates Company had been established with Lord Hamilton as its chairman.

The creation of this company did not immediately result in a transformation of the estate's economic position. The year 1936/7 was a particularly bad one for the Barons Court estate. While it was not expected at this time that the estate would cover all of its costs, neither could it sustain heavy losses. Its total income in 1937, from farming, rent receipts, etc., came to £3,427. The cost of running Barons Court came to £9,125. With the remittance from Coutts coming in at £4,800, that left an overdraft of £898. The excess of payments over receipts was as follows: woods £1,297; gardens £634; game £919; dairy £101; management £1,517; and mansion house £893. In his analysis of the accounts, Ross admitted that things were not good, but refused to blame the performance of the farm for the difficulties.

Lord Hamilton was not impressed by either the accounts or Ross's explanation of them. He carefully dissected the figures, seeking clarification on certain points and drawing attention to inconsistencies in others. He also recognised that there was an urgent need for action, issuing the following instructions to Ross:

> I would like you to summon all heads of department and impress on them the very serious need for every economy. I know that a lot has been done in this line, yet I am sure that amongst the men, a certain amount of wastage of material, etc, still goes on and I should like them to point out to their men that unless things go better we shall have to reduce the number of employees. I should be very loath to do this as I have always felt that one of the justifications for the continued existence of Barons Court is the amount of men it employs, but we cannot go on indefinitely increasing the overdraft.

There is no doubt that the Barons Court estate was a major employer. A list of employees drawn up around this time showed that there were three byers (i.e. men who worked in the byers), two ploughmen, three horsemen, one pigman, one shepherd, five oddmen (including two drainers), one foreman, and one poultry maid on the farm alone. In addition, the staff in the dairy comprised a manager, a dairymaid and an engineman. The stock on the home farm at this time included seven horses, 170 head of cattle (of which 45 were dairy cows), 203 sheep, 93 pigs, and 614 poultry. In May 1940 the staff comprised 20 persons employed on the farm, 13 in the woods, seven with responsibility for game, 10 in the gardens, six tradesmen and five workers in the demesne. The total wages bill each week came to £81 17s. 2d.

Despite Lord Hamilton's concerns, a radical overhaul of the management of the estate was not introduced at this time. The absence from Barons Court for much of the year of both Lord Hamilton and his father made implementing change difficult. Ross battled on manfully and a number of cost-cutting measures were introduced. For example, the area under cultivation was substantially increased to help alleviate the cost of purchasing animal foodstuffs. At the same time, it was still obvious that a significant reordering of the management of the estate was needed if Barons Court was to have a secure future. That, however, would have wait until another world war had been fought and won.

The war years

The outbreak of hostilities in September 1939 was to cause considerable disruption to Lord Hamilton and his family. At the beginning of the war, the

John Erne fishing in the River Mourne.

Marquess rejoined his old regiment, the Grenadier Guards, while Lady Hamilton volunteered as an auxiliary nurse at St Thomas' Hospital in London. The young Hamiltons were already in Ireland for their summer holidays and instead of returning to London spent the final months of 1939 with their cousins, the Crichton children, at Crom before going to Barons Court for Christmas with their grandparents. Less than three weeks after Christmas they had a narrow escape when a fire broke out in the west wing where they were sleeping.

The Marquess was never sent overseas and spent most of the war in London at Wellington Barracks, the headquarters of the Grenadiers in Birdcage Walk. His brother-in-law John Erne, who had been an officer in the Royal Horse Guards, was active in reconstituting the North Irish Horse. While on attachment to the 12th Royal Lancers, he died from wounds received in action near Dunkirk on 23 May 1940, leaving an heir still short of his third birthday. Not only was this a devastating blow for the family, it would have repercussions for Lord Hamilton, who was one of the trustees of the estate. The Marquess' younger brother Lord Claud, known in the family as Claudie, was an officer in the Irish Guards and was part of the Allied advance across Europe following the Normandy landings in June 1944.

From the summer of 1940 the Marchioness and her children lived at Greenlands, near Henley on Thames, the country house of Viscount Hambleden, a descendant of W. H. Smith of bookselling fame. The family took up residence in The Bothy, the house where the unmarried male gardeners, most of whom had joined up at the start of the war, had lived. Even in this rural idyll they could not entirely escape the war. At the beginning of October 1940 Lady Hamilton wrote of having witnessed a 'dogfight of 50 aeroplanes between us and the hill where we collect acorns on the way to church. They looked lovely, gleaming silver against the blue sky, diving at one another.' During her absences at St Thomas', the children were looked after by their nanny, Catherine Blackwood. She was from Edinburgh and is remembered by Lady Moyra as the 'most heavenly woman in the world'.

Now separated for long periods, Lord and Lady Hamilton kept up a regular correspondence throughout the war years. The Marquess' letters were generally upbeat in tone and he never, of course, discussed operational matters. Occasionally he commented on news not directly related to his own duties, such as the effects of air raids on London. Any incident involving St Thomas's was conveyed to his wife. On 11 September 1940 he reported that the hospital had been hit and that there had been some fatalities. He visited the hospital himself to see the damage and observed, 'everyone is so wonderfully calm and more determined than ever, though it is, of course, tiring'. On a subsequent visit a few days later, he gave an account of what he had witnessed:

> They have rigged up some cellars and basements as emergency casualty wards, as they refuse to close down for a minute, and they particularly wanted you to know that they were performing an acute abdominal within a quarter of an hour of the explosion. ... They are without telephone, gas, light and water, but it was a wonderful to see their courage.

Lord Hamilton also made sure that representatives of the American press had the opportunity to see the damage for themselves and so report the story across the Atlantic.

There were occasions when he could see the lighter sides of things in the midst of the gloom. For example, on 18 September 1940 he wrote to the Marchioness: 'I adored your story of the Italians bombing their own cruisers, it is one of the nicest things which I have heard for a long time.' He was quick to dismiss as German propaganda a warning that had come, via a crashed Luftwaffe pilot, that he should always have with him his gas mask. There is no doubt that the effects of the war weighed heavily on the family, though both the Marquess and Marchioness remained hopeful for the future. At the beginning of December 1940 Lady Hamilton wrote to her husband, 'As you say, good times will assuredly come again which we shall enjoy and appreciate with deeper significance for the stern days we are passing through.'

In the spring of 1943 Lord Hamilton was appointed adjutant at Windsor in succession to Captain R. G. Briscoe MP, who had resigned to take up the position of lord lieutenant of Cambridgeshire. In commenting on the implications of these changes, the regimental news-sheet reported:

> The Training Battalion's gain is the Regimental Orderly Room's loss and it is one from which the survivors are reeling. His experience after 3 years and 4 months was unequalled and his patience inexhaustible. All the compassionate side of the Regimental Orderly Room's activities fell to him, and many of the messages of appreciation which parents and wives are sometimes kind enough to send to Headquarters are attributable to his care and forethought.

The Marquess had been a popular figure at regimental headquarters and left behind many friends when he moved to Windsor; a letter has been preserved from his long-time friend, Major Arthur Penn, the regimental adjutant who was also a member of the Royal Household, who wrote to him to express his sadness at his departure and to thank Lord Hamilton for his many kindnesses to him.

With army duties preventing him from making frequent trips to Barons Court, Lord Hamilton relied on others to keep him informed on happenings there. In December 1943 Lord Claud visited Barons Court and provided his brother with an update on the state of affairs. One concern was poaching, and he observed with a degree of humour that pheasants were becoming commonplace on the Christmas dinner tables around Newtownstewart. In another incident a Barons Court deer provided an enjoyable Christmas feast for local families during the war: on one of their patrols the local Home Guard opened fire on what they thought was a German paratrooper, but instead shot a deer. One of the men was a butcher and so they brought it home, had it prepared, and venison was served for Christmas.

As the war progressed, Lord Hamilton felt able to be more open about it in his letters to his wife. On 7 June 1944, the day after D-Day, he wrote to Lady Hamilton:

> Well, whatever may yet have to be faced, that appalling tension has ended, and it looks as though things are going quite well; though the next few days are going to be critical. … If only events continue to move favourably in the West, in Italy, and in Russia, who knows what may happen.

The move to Barons Court

Though he was able to make only occasional visits to Northern Ireland during the war, Barons Court was never very far from Lord Hamilton's mind and neither were the many issues relating to its future. In August 1944 his wife and children holidayed there with the Duke and Duchess. A number of problems were apparent to the Marchioness, who nevertheless remained optimistic: 'never before, even in the present dilapidated condition, have I seen it so enchanting.' In the following month Lord Hamilton himself visited Barons Court and was dismayed by some aspects of the estate's management. In particular, he was 'shocked' at the condition of the gardens, which were 'fast deteriorating'. He turned for advice to Dr George Scott-Robertson, the Permanent Secretary at the Ministry of Agriculture for Northern Ireland. Pointing out to Scott-Robertson that the gardens were 'becoming more & more of a market concern and needing expert and modern management', he expressed anxiety at the fact that the head gardener at Barons Court was getting old and 'losing all sense of method with the inevitable result that what should be a valuable source of food in the shape of fruit and vegetables, is now producing only a fraction of what under careful management it undoubtedly could'. He added:

> I am convinced that estates like B.C. are very valuable assets to the country, but to justify their future existence (& incidentally to pay their way!) they must serve as examples to the countryside in the excellence of their products & the efficiency of their management. This I hope to achieve in farming, forestry & gardening so that the estate may show to everyone what may be achieved by new ideas applied to careful husbandry.

Scott-Robertson sent an encouraging response, offering advice and telling Lord Hamilton that he fully agreed that a large garden such as that at Barons Court could become a profitable concern quite easily. Thanking him for his reply, the Marquess commented, 'One hopes that the people of Ulster may become more "vegetable-minded", the soil and climate being ideal for that'.

Lord Hamilton was well aware that at some point he would make Barons Court his permanent home. At the same time, he was anxious not to offend his parents by any presumption of what they might do following the retirement of the Duke as Governor of Northern Ireland. However, he was curious to find out what the intentions of his parents were after his father relinquished this position. In mid-January 1945 Lord Hamilton wrote to his mother, outlining his views on the future of the estate. There is no doubt that he had deliberated long and hard before committing his thoughts to paper. He fully recognised the scale of the task awaiting him in Tyrone, expressing his opinion that: 'Of one thing I am certain: it will require every effort in the way of supervision in the running of the estate to make living there possible & even then much modification will have to be faced when it becomes possible to face the rebuilding.'

In weighing up the options his parents could choose from, he ruled out dividing their time equally between Barons Court and London on the basis that it was not economically viable. Furthermore, it would not provide the constant supervision that the estate needed at this critical time. In this he meant no criticism of Ross, who had 'carried on manfully & with great success through these v. difficult years'. With the future of the estate still at risk, Lord Hamilton was firm in his belief that 'it is only right that I should assume the responsibility of running B.C. especially as I am convinced that estates where the family are content to take a back seat & leave the management to their agent are doomed'.

His mother had previously mooted the idea of dividing Barons Court between them, but Lord Hamilton did not think this would be feasible: 'Your idea of a combined ménage at B.C. was charming of you to suggest, but I can't see it working in practice, especially as with the drastic modifications in rebuilding which I envisage, there just wouldn't be room for 2 separate households to live.' He also reassured his mother that he was not trying to force them to leave Barons Court before they were ready to do so:

> Please don't imagine for one moment that I am trying to supplant you and Daddy, but wouldn't you feel very lonely & rather lost living in the depths of Tyrone after the very full life of these last 22 years and your many activities which would cease when Daddy retires? ... I am afraid that the alterations to the house, which I regard as absolutely inevitable if the family is even to continue to live there would hardly be acceptable to Daddy who had put so much into the interior decoration of rooms which I fear will never again be occupied.

He was also concerned for the needs of his own family, writing: 'Without complaint, Kath has lived in something approaching squalor for the last 5 years and I do so want her to live henceforth in comparative comfort. Moreover, I feel it is high time that the children had a definite home of their own in which to develop their roots.'

If he was worried what his parents would think of his suggestions, his fears were soon allayed, for his mother wrote to him on 21 January:

> Your letter received last night was a real comfort & help – your Father & I thoroughly agree about BC; it requires a young and strong man out of doors & a practical, sensible woman within. We agreed a little time back that we were no longer up to it, & so when we leave here, which I most earnestly hope may be this next Decr, we would like to go into a flat in London, large enough, if possible, to take in any stray members of the family who want a lodging; we don't want ever to go back to Mount St – out of the question for expense & servant point of view. There is enough furniture in store in England and at BC to set up a flat well. This is only a rough sketch, of course, but we do thoroughly agree that you should take over BC, & make whatever alterations you & a good architect devise.

Soon afterwards Lord Hamilton's father wrote to him along similar lines, confirming once and for all that they were more than happy for him to make Barons Court his permanent home:

> We do not wish to continue living at B.Ct. It is really, fond as I am of it, not a place for old people. One would be quite cut off from everything there, and with the short time probably left to one, it would not be worthwhile doing anything which would really be of interest. Also, a small detail, journeys back & forward, are very trying to the aged, and those I would have to make. Again, after so long in my present position, I would be sure to be approached by many people to use my influence with my successor, whoever he may be, so I am sure it is wisest to clear out of Ulster, when the time comes. I think

also we had better get rid of Mount St & live in a good flat, if possible; it would probably cost less, & be easier with servants, etc.

On 31 January Lord Hamilton wrote to his wife, enclosing this letter from his father. Though the Marquess recognised the Duke's concerns regarding the 'future difficulties which are certain to arise with his succession were he to remain in Ulster', he had concluded that 'his chief reason is his complete loss of interest in anything at B.C. which I thought very apparent last summer and which probably dates from the fire'. A few days later he again wrote the Marchioness on their future in Northern Ireland:

> It is tragic to think of his relief at leaving Barons Court; it is so essentially a place to have love and care bestowed on it. I think subconsciously we realised that it lacked this, but in the past it was not possible to remedy. However, the fervent love which we all bear it will restore everything. ... I can still hardly realise what a wonderful promise of the future holds out to us, darling, and hope it is not tempting the fates to dream as I do and plan all sorts of delicious things and improvements.

Lady Hamilton replied with similar enthusiasm:

> Yes, darling, isn't it wonderful to dream about Barons Court and what we shall be able to give it, all of us, so easily and joyfully. I cannot feel that it will take long to respond and become the home that it was always meant to be; especially after the alterations the homeliness will be even easier.

In early February Lord Hamilton wrote to the Marchioness on the eve of their wedding anniversary with 'fervent hopes' that their next anniversary would be spent together at Barons Court: 'How heavenly that would be after these long, long years of semi-separation which at the same time have been wonderfully fortunate in that we have been so close to each other and yet terribly tantalising.' The end of the war in Europe brought huge relief, though it was also tinged with sadness at the thoughts of those who had died in the conflict. Shortly after VE Day, Lord Hamilton wrote to his wife:

> I fully realise though I have been unable to put it into words what poignant memories the end of the war must have inevitably brought ... it is so hard not to pine and long for those whom one loves not to be here to enjoy their victory with us.

He again looked to their future together at Barons Court: 'Thank God, it really won't be long before we can resume our life together, and in a home that we both love so much. What joy that will be, and also to see the children growing up where they ought to.' In July Lady Hamilton and the children moved to Barons Court, to be followed a couple of weeks later by the

Marquess. Life at Barons Court was to prove a very happy experience for the young Hamiltons. Lord Anthony, who, as the youngest, spent the most time there in the immediate post-war period, remembers that it was 'paradise' in comparison with the rather restricted life they had in England.

The reconstruction of Barons Court

One of the first challenges facing Lord and Lady Hamilton when they took over the estate in 1945 was the house itself. Because of his duties as Governor of Northern Ireland, the 3rd Duke had spent most of the previous 20 years at Hillsborough Castle and Barons Court had not been his main priority. There had also been the fire of January 1940, which had gutted the west wing on the north front of the house. Times had changed considerably from the days when his great-grandfather, the 1st Duke, had a house full of children and grandchildren, and an army of servants to look after them. Lord Hamilton had three children and a greatly reduced household staff.

Shortly after moving in Lord Hamilton set himself the task of trying to reorganise the house in preparation for the building work. The bibliophile Marquess found himself easily distracted when it came to sorting through the books in the house. He wrote to his wife on 11 November 1945: 'I am having an absolute field-day with the books in the Billiard Room – I thought I knew most of the books there, but never realised the amount of rubbish among them!' A few days later he updated her on how things were progressing:

The reconstruction of Barons Court in the late 1940s.

> You will need all your nerve when you view the pile of furniture – and junk, which today's shift has brought to the front! The men worked like Trojans, but even so I have had to take two for tomorrow as we

haven't yet begun on the polygon or Hamilton rooms. All the servants' rooms are cleared and the contents fill up the portico under tarpaulins. Outside the portico, to rid them of dust, lie a whole forest of antlers and heads!

At the end of the following January an auction of surplus furnishings from the house was held.

Early in 1946 Lord Hamilton wrote to his friend, the architect Hal Goodhart, for advice on how best to go about the reconstruction of Barons Court. Explaining that there had been a serious fire in 1940, the Marquess set out his views on the house and the architect they needed:

> Calamitous as this then seemed, it gives us the opportunity of a serious reduction in the house's size when it may become possible to rebuild. What we are now eagerly seeking is an architect, a specialist in the late Georgian style, who would advise us how best to accomplish the above, with modernisation, & yet enable us to retain the essential character of the house. My wife and I have a fairly concrete idea of how to start & what we want, but we have now reached a stage where we must consult an expert. I have written rather fully hoping to show thereby that we have already planned as far as we are able, & that our architect would have to be prepared to follow our ideas as far as may be feasible … This is a much loved house, and I am prepared to take the v. greatest pains in order to get the right man for the job – a job of overwhelming importance to us & as may be, I hope, to many future generations of my family.[3]

In response, Goodhart recommended several architects. Interestingly, the man who was to be commissioned was not among them, though Goodhart did admit that he had deliberately omitted other well-known architects.

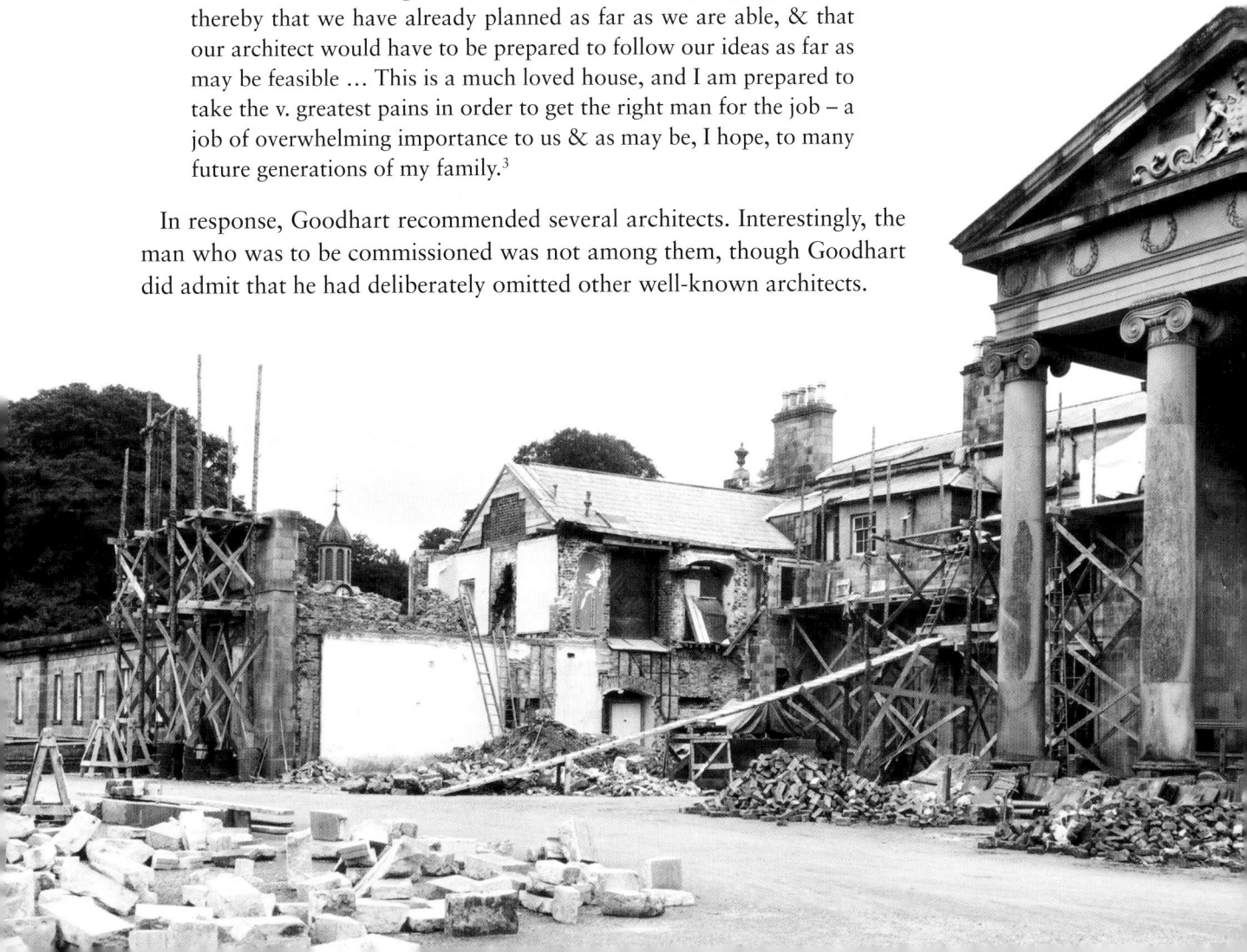

Lord Hamilton also looked to others for advice, and it was his brother-in-law, Lord Spencer, who suggested Sir Albert Richardson. Richardson was one of the most distinguished architects of his day. In 1947 he was awarded the Royal Gold Medal for Architecture and in 1954 he was elected President of the Royal Academy. As an admirer of the work of Sir John Soane, Richardson certainly had the right credentials to undertake the work at Barons Court. On 4 September 1946 Richardson wrote to Lord Hamilton telling him that the prospect of being involved in work at Barons Court 'appeals to me very much'. A visit duly followed, the two men discussed the house and what could be done with it, and Richardson left to give further thought to the matter. Lord Spencer was again consulted, but Richardson did not agree with his suggestion that the great staircase should be 'eliminated'. 'I told him', the architect wrote to Lord Hamilton on 24 October, 'this would leave another great volume of space … the objective should be as little interference as possible with the existing structure.' Richardson was still giving thought to Barons Court in mid-November, but was not yet able to give details on the proposed work. However, he did promise that he would 'give the closest study to reducing wherever possible'. In the meantime, Matthew McDermott of the Department of Architecture, National University, Dublin, had been commissioned to produce an accurate survey of the house from which Richardson could work. McDermott made two visits to Barons Court and got on well with Lord Hamilton. The two men discussed the *Táin Bó Cúailnge* and McDermott was impressed with the Marquess' reading material on this.

By early February 1947 Richardson had prepared outline plans and presented these to Lord Hamilton on one of the latter's visits to London. The Marchioness was not able to be present, but her husband arranged for her to see Richardson in person and told her to think of 'some stiff conundrums to put to him'. Working with Richardson seems to have been a happy collaboration for the Hamiltons, and Lady Hamilton was very much an equal partner throughout the process. In May outline specifications for the alterations to Barons Court were drawn up. In summary, the main works to the exterior of the house were: to pull down the gutted west wing on the north front; reduce in length the corresponding east wing to give balance to this side of the house; face up the walls where the wings had been removed with stone obtained from what had been demolished; and construct screens on either side of the main block with square granite columns, the cornices to be from the existing masonry. On being sent drawings of the elevations, Lord Hamilton commented that they were 'most attractive'. Work began soon afterwards, the first task being to demolish the burnt-out wing. By the end of the second week of June this was 'fast disappearing'. By late September work to the interior of the house had begun, the Londonderry firm, Robert Colhoun Ltd, having been engaged to carry out much of the joinery etc. Shortly before this the 3rd Duke had visited Barons Court and gave his approval to the remodelling.

At times there were frustrations, due to delays caused by the weather or illness among the workmen. Finding men skilled in certain activities also proved difficult. Early in the reconstruction, for instance, Lord Hamilton lamented to Richardson that it was proving difficult to find skilled masons. 'Too old and senile' was how he described those who had thus far been identified. Later, in November 1948, he wrote to his wife that they had found someone who could supply men adept in building with stone, but not in cutting it. Post-war shortages of building materials, especially cement, also caused delays. Nonetheless the work proceeded at a steady pace, and by January 1949 the Marquess informed Richardson that the exterior of the house was in sight of completion. By the end of March that year, £10,675 had been expended on the works, with another £6,000 expected to be spent. In relation to Richardson's fee, in April 1949 the architect pointed out that the RIBA scale was 12% of the total cost of the works, plus travelling expenses. However, 'in view of your cooperation and the special nature of the reconstruction', he told Lord Hamilton that he was willing to accept 10% and that to include travelling.

Work continued on the house into the early 1950s. In May 1952 Lord Hamilton admitted to Richardson that he did not think the screens to the portico would be completed that year as it would take three-four months' work. The delay in the completion of the work was, explained the Marquess, due to the urgency in carrying out repairs that had been put on hold while

The Duke and Duchess with Sir Albert Richardson at Barons Court

the reconstruction of the house was proceeding. During the previous summer farm buildings had been rebuilt and this summer the garage roof and lead gutters to the old servants' quarters needed attention. In actual fact it seems that the screens were finished before the end of the year. On receipt of his final payment in December 1952, Richardson wrote to Lord Hamilton, 'I am so pleased that the work has been completed and that the house is no worse for the very drastic alterations.' The family was certainly pleased with

269

the end result. In the summer of 1950 a radio documentary series on Ulster houses included an episode on Barons Court. The script was read by the Marquess' younger brother, Lord Claud, who in discussing the ongoing alterations to the house commented that 'for all the changes, it keeps that warm, friendly atmosphere which has made so many and such different kinds of people feel that it is, first and foremost, a home'.

Externally, the works carried out at this time can be principally seen on the north front. The most commented on effect of these alterations is that as a result of the dismantling of the west wing and shortening of the east wing, as well as the removal of the parapet, the *porte-cochère* now stands out even more prominently – a 'stranded giant' in the words of one architectural historian. The ends of the former wings retain their recessed, though now blank, arches and are linked to the *porte-cochère* by a screen of square piers of Mourne granite. Internally, one of the principal changes by Richardson was the division of the gallery into three rooms – just as it had been in Steuart's original house. He did so by having thin partitions, glazed at the top to still allow a full-length view of the ceiling, fill out the screens of columns. The room at the east end of the gallery was used as a dining room, while the adjoining library (with its bookcases simply boarded over) was used as a pantry. These alterations were easily reversible – vitally important when David Hicks carried out his redecorations in the 1970s.

In 1963, the artist Derek Hill, who produced portraits of several members of the family, wrote an article on Barons Court for the art magazine *Apollo*. Written with the Duke's assistance and providing a tour through the house, it described the living quarters then pertaining, along with the paintings and artefacts, before concluding:

> The charm of the house lies … in the fact that nothing is studied in its presentation and no object is shown off, whatever its merits may be, more than another. They all take their place quite naturally and quietly with the family around them and appear to be used and loved rather than locked away and merely hoarded up against the bad day. If ever the term 'gracious living' could be used correctly it would be the one to describe more aptly this great, yet friendly, Irish house.[4]

Though remaining their private home, the Duke and Duchess frequently opened Barons Court to visitors, hosting numerous events for various causes. In afterwards thanking the Abercorns for their hospitality, one visitor commented: 'other stately homes are opened to the public, but yours is shared. There is a vast difference!' Another commented: 'you obviously have the knack of making your guests feel happy and wonderfully at home'.

The revitalisation of the estate

Following his permanent settlement at Barons Court, Lord Hamilton worked indefatigably to ensure the continued viability of the estate at a time when many landowners were finding the stark economic conditions very difficult to adjust to. He was very much 'hands-on' in his approach to the management of the estate – as willing to work with scythe or spade as review the accounts – and his immense knowledge of dendrology would contribute to its changed fortunes. It was due to his vision, astuteness and hard work that Barons Court came through this difficult period and was set on a sound footing that ensured its future. Many other 'big house' owners across Ireland could not adapt to radically different economic conditions to those enjoyed by their fathers and grandfathers, and were forced to part with their homes and what remained of their estates.

This would certainly have happened to Crom had it not been for the determination of Lord Hamilton. The Marquess was one of the trustees of his late brother-in-law John Erne's estate. When others were suggesting that Crom be sold, Lord Hamilton was quite insistent that this should not happen. He had his way, and today Crom Castle remains the private home of the present Duke's cousin, the 6th Earl of Erne. Others among Lord Hamilton's wider family circle were not so fortunate. The Marquess was dismayed to hear in the summer of 1948 that his cousin Billy Wicklow (the 8th Earl of Wicklow) was planning on selling what remained of his estate, as he simply could not make it pay its way. Later that year Lord Charlemont wrote to him that he was quitting his home at Drumcairne, near Stewartstown, County Tyrone: 'I am too decrepit to run a place now as I can't walk round it and see what was doing ... Then there was the insoluble problem of SERVANTS; to live at Drumcairne in these days the householder must be able to cook, make beds, be self-sufficient, that is, and independent.' The difficulties facing owners of country seats were reinforced following a visit that the Marquess and Moyra paid to an aristocratic home, which had left them 'subdued at the unhappiness of the house ... as black as night'. At the same time, Lord Hamilton was aware that there was no point in holding on to property simply for the sake of it. For instance, in the early 1950s Duddingston House, near Edinburgh, was sold. It had been designed by Sir William Chambers for the 8th Earl and was one of Scotland's finest eighteenth-century houses. However, it had not been occupied by members of the family for over 30 years and there was little prospect of their doing so again.

During the war there had been the usual boost to agriculture and forestry, which had benefited the estate. In May 1942 Ross wrote to Lord Hamilton that even though wages had increased by 85%, every department, with the exception of gardens and game, had shown a substantial profit. Two years later in June 1944 Ross felt confident enough to write to Lord Hamilton, 'I do feel we are now on an even keel and the prospects for the future are fairly good.' For several years the Barons Court Estates Company operated at a profit, mainly due to heavy timber sales. For example, in August 1944 an order had been received from the County Down Railway Company for 500 sleepers. This provided an opportunity to sell hardwood that could not be marketed in normal circumstances. However, an immediate consequence of the end of the war was that the sale of timber practically ceased.

Soon after moving to Barons Court, Lord Hamilton again turned to Scott-Robertson for advice. He wrote to him in the spring of 1946, acknowledging that he felt he could not progress his ideas on farming without the advice of the Ministry of Agriculture. He admitted that he was 'as yet no practical farmer, yet I know enough to value when things are wrong'. What concerned him in particular was the lack of policy on the Barons Court farm. This was especially true of pastoral farming, for 600 acres was running only 200 head of cattle. What the Marquess wanted was for one of the Ministry of Agriculture's experts to visit Barons Court and advise on the grasslands and on the farm buildings, for the byres were in a 'most parlous condition'.

Barons Court continued to be a major source of local employment. Lord Anthony remembers that in his childhood just after the war there were 15 foresters, 12 employees working on the farm, five in the gardens, three gamekeepers, and three maintenance men. It was undoubtedly overmanned, but the present Duke has observed that the family felt a moral duty to provide employment to the local community. The harvest was a major feature of the agricultural calendar. The crops grown on the estate included oats, barley, potatoes and turnips. The ties between the family and the estate workers continued to be very strong. When Lord Claud and his wife Genesta visited Barons Court shortly after their marriage in February 1946, the latter commented that the people 'adore the family'. Lady Moyra remembers that estate workers were well looked after. They had free milk from the estate and a plot of land for potatoes and vegetables. At Christmas food and clothing was distributed to the families of the estate workers. There was also a Christmas party at Barons Court for local children where presents were given out. One of the great characters on the estate at this time was Joe Duncan, the head gamekeeper, with whom Lord Anthony spent a great deal of his time during holidays and who taught him to love Barons Court. The Marquess also looked to the material needs of the people around Barons Court. At a meeting of the local Women's Institute in February 1947, 'when asked what they most wanted in their houses, they gave a unanimous request for electricity, water and sewerage'. Only the first of these was in the power of the Marquess to grant, but he hoped to be able to provide that to them.

The difficulties facing the estate at this time were compounded by the fact that Captain Ross had been ill since early 1945 and his health gradually deteriorated to the point where he could no longer play an active part in the running of the estate. He died in November 1947. The Marchioness was not at Barons Court at the time and Lord Hamilton wrote to her, 'So the poor fellow has gone to his rest and has been spared much suffering.' The farm steward was also in a poor state of health and unable to discharge his duties effectively. The direct management of the estate thus fell on Lord Hamilton's shoulders. In early March 1948 he wrote, 'I am less and less satisfied by the lack of method with the [farm], and this will make it easier, when the time comes, to make the great change.'

Finding the right people to fulfil important roles was vital. A new farm steward, William Houston, arrived in the autumn of 1948 and immediately impressed Lord Hamilton. On 4 November he wrote to the Marchioness: 'We are now really on the upgrade … the farm is, I am pretty certain, under capable management.' Both Lord Hamilton and Houston realised that a 'considerable smartening up is necessary', but agreed that this needed to be done gradually. Nonetheless, Lord Hamilton wished to give the farm workers a 'pep talk', as he put it, which seems to have been a rather forthright statement of intent. A few days later it was reported back to him that 'the farm men were considerably shaken by my little harangue to them'. However, it seems to have had the desired effect, with Lord Hamilton writing: 'There is certainly a new feel about the farm, though this may only be to impress Houston. But he has sized them up pretty well for himself, and I have little doubt that he will handle them properly.' Notwithstanding the genuine sense of responsibility to provide local employment, gradually the number of staff working at Barons Court was reduced in the following years.

In the post-war period the estate witnessed the introduction of greater mechanisation as well as the modernisation of farming techniques. In July 1948 a new tractor was delivered to Barons Court. Lord Hamilton wrote that it 'looks so immense it almost frightens me'. Later that year he ordered a Landrover, which he believed would 'prove its weight in gold'. Around the same time, Lord Hamilton was pleased to report an increase in milk yields which he ascribed to 'judicious feeding'. By the following July a 'vast silo pit' was nearly ready. Depending on the asking price, when farms adjoining the estate were put up for sale the Marquess purchased them and let them to tenants. Not everything attempted was a success. For instance, the market garden was a financial failure, being too far away from any potential market. Nonetheless, gradually the estate began to pay its way, and forestry was to play no small part in this.

In the midst of a busy and sometimes punishing workload, the Marquess was able on occasion to visit his friends and enjoy himself. In late January 1947, for instance, he travelled to Ballywalter Park to stay with the

Dunleaths. Rising just after at 4 o'clock on the morning of the 26th, he and his hosts set off for a day's shooting at Downpatrick. After parking the cars there was:

> Then an eerie walk in the dark along the railway line to the marshes … where we waited for the light. It wasn't really cold & the dawn shining up the cathedral and the Mournes was beautiful indeed, but the real thrill was hearing the chatter of hundreds of geese and thousands of duck, just ahead of us. I have never seen anything like it and it is a never to be forgotten experience. It was all so wild and beautiful …

Amid the excitement, the Marquess had a pang of sadness as he thought about his brother-in-law John Erne who had died in 1940: '[it] made me somehow think very much of John & of how much he would have adored it & an intense longing for him for him to be there.' 'Finally', he continued, 'the geese rose with a deafening roar and the shooting was fast and furious till 9.30. At first I was so excited that I hit nothing, but later retrieved myself & really shot rather well.' There were some breaks for refreshments, but the shooting went on until late afternoon. The others in the party included Johnny Blakiston-Houston ('of course, he ran out of cartridges about an hour after shooting started') and Lady Mairi Bury. In summing up the experience, the Marquess considered it 'a wonderful day'. Opportunities like this to relax with friends were not common in the immediate post-war years, and Lord Hamilton made the most of them.

Though now based at Barons Court, the Marquess regularly visited London, which provided him with an opportunity to catch up with his parents and wider family, not to mention his many friends, as well as to deal with business matters. However, it is clear from his letters that his distaste for city life was in no way lessened by merely being a visitor to the capital. In the second week of February 1947 he visited London and was horrified by what he found. At this time coal shortages, exacerbated by the exceptionally wintry conditions, were affecting electricity supplies as well as the transport system, not to mention the heating of homes. 'London is a city of dreadful nights', he wrote to Lady Hamilton, who was visiting their daughter in Switzerland, 'and it really makes one's blood boil to think that such gross incompetence has brought things to such a pitch. It must surely do the Socialists a great deal of harm, especially the inevitable growth of unemployment & one can only hope that people will learn from this tragic example.' He added that his parents had somehow managed to acquire some anthracite which he reckoned would keep them going for around 10 days.

It was a relief for the Marquess to escape back to Barons Court. Soon after arriving he wrote to his wife, 'It is heavenly to be back home, and although cold, it is *nothing* like London. The last two days there were a nightmare, and one's heart just bled for those pitiable shopgirls, shivering in overcoats, in premises with a few candles. At the moment they are just apathetic, but later they will surely get very angry.' The following evening he was due to address a social gathering of the British Legion in Castlederg. 'They may not like it', he wrote to Lady Hamilton, 'But I am just going to weigh in on how fortunate they are to live here & how people in England are suffering & that we will all have to work like never before to make up precious lost time.'

In May 1948 the Hamiltons received an invitation to stay at Windsor Castle for Ascot week. Perhaps because he had not been at such a gathering for some time, Lord Hamilton wrote to his wife asking whether 'knee breeches are still worn at Windsor in the evenings' and if there were any other changes in dress. A couple of months later the Marquess dined with friends in Derry. Prince Philip, whose ship had docked in the city's harbour, was also present and regaled the party with the story of how he and some fellow officers had gone to a small hotel in Buncrana, where a 'mini incident' had occurred. The Prince had been recognised and a large number of the townspeople had 'flocked outside the hotel [and] gave him a terrific ovation as he left!' There followed an 'apologetic complaint' from the Irish police to the RUC for not being informed of the Prince's visit, which prevented them from ensuring that he was able to enjoy his meal in peace. On hearing this story, Lady Hamilton wrote, 'I don't think anyone realises the Buncrana escapade over here and your father says, "what a splendid thing for Donegal" ... Perhaps the Edinburghs may yet reign in Dublin!'

'A terrific partnership' is how Lady Moyra characterises her parents' relationship, and without doubt the support that Lord Hamilton received from his wife in the difficult days of the post-war period was critical to what he was able to achieve. This was in spite of the fact that during the late 1940s and through the 1950s the Hamiltons were frequently separated due to the regular visits that the Marchioness made to England to care for her mother, who had suffered a terrible riding accident around 1909 and had never walked again. After losing her husband during the First World War, she married the Hon. Algernon Stanley, son of the Earl of Derby, and bore two more children – a son, Anthony, who was killed in action during the Second World War, and a daughter, Constance. The Stanleys made their home at Sopworth, near Badminton. In her later years she endured periods of ill-health requiring her daughter Kathleen's regular care and attention until her death in January 1959. During these periods of separation the Hamiltons wrote to each other almost on a daily basis – the careful preserving of these letters by Lady Moyra is one of the main sources of information on the family and estate during this period.

Forestry

There were few things that the 4th Duke of Abercorn was more passionate about than forestry, and through practice and intense study he became a highly respected authority on dendrology. He worked energetically to ensure that the woodlands at Barons Court were placed on a commercial footing and made sure that there was good proportion of hardwood planting. When he moved to Barons Court in 1945 there were 800 acres of woodland in the direct control of the estate, 400 acres of which were of rhododendron. He considerably extended the woodland acreage, introducing new species of trees, among them faster-growing varieties from the southern hemisphere. The Duke's appointment as president of the International Dendrological Society was a clear indication of his world standing on forestry matters. At a local level, in 1960 he was appointed chairman of a committee established by the Ministry of Home Affairs on nature conservation in Northern Ireland. Its report from 1962 recommended the creation of an independent nature conservancy funded by government and with strong links to Queen's University, Belfast. The Duke was also president of the Royal Forestry Society from 1964 to 1966. His obituarist in the *Quarterly Journal of Forestry*, in noting that this was one of the society's 'most profitable and tranquil periods', commented:

> This was no accident, for he was the most conscientious, kindly and approachable of men; the sort of leader to whom a Society such as ours, with its wide spectrum of membership, most readily responds. No journey was too tedious, no ceremony too trivial, no meeting too small for him to travel and be there to lend his charm and expertise to the proceedings. And expertise as well as charm he had in plenty.

In penning his own tribute to the Duke, Langshaw Rowland, a former president of the Royal Forestry Society, recalled a visit to Barons Court in the 1950s. At the time he had been director of forestry of the Westminster Estates and interested in finding out more about forestry practices at Barons Court. An invitation was duly issued and Rowland spent an enlightening couple of days at the estate. He was very impressed with a plantation of *Nothofagus obliqua*, a South American species of beech native to Argentina and Chile, which he considered 'outstanding', though unfortunately it was subsequently flattened by gale-force winds. Rowland's attention was also drawn to very fine group of Scots pines by the lakeside in the park. He suggested that a rabbit fence should be erected around the group and the ground scarified a little to encourage regeneration. The Duke wholeheartedly agreed, and a fence was up before nightfall. That was not the end of the story as Rowland recollected:

Two or three years after my prescription for perpetuating this fine stand on the lakeside, the Duke was staying at Eaton and I took him to look at my woods at Pendugwm in Montgomeryshire. It was soon after I had bought 80 acres of derelict woodland which adjoined. We had just started replanting and, as we came to a hill crest, the Duke said "What a site for hemlock". He gave me a quizzical look and then said "you remember the Scots pine at Barons Court and your prescription for regeneration?" I replied that I did and hoped that it had been a success. Whereupon he laughed and said "There is only one Scots seedling among the finest regeneration of hemlock I have ever seen – from an excellent tree just outside the fence". He then asked me if I would accept about a thousand of the hemlock seedlings and plant them on this site. Needless to say I was very happy to do so and the result is a hemlock plantation which, at the age of 22 years, is far and away the best conifer plantation I have at Pendugwm. We always refer to it as the Abercorn Plantation and, as it adjoins the summer house, I often amuse visitors by recalling its history.

During Rowland's initial visit to Barons Court the Duke sought his advice on establishing a forestry society in Northern Ireland. Rowland did not think that this was feasible, and instead suggested that a Northern Ireland division of the Royal Forestry Society should be formed. This was indeed what happened. Following a visit to Northern Ireland of the Royal Forestry Society in the summer of 1955, during which they were entertained at Barons Court by the Duke, it was decided that there should be a division of that society in Northern Ireland. This was created the following February at Barons Court with the Duke as its first chairman, and a programme of activities and meetings organised.

In the autumn of 1959 the Duke attended the Commonwealth Parliamentary Conference in Canberra. Lady Moyra (who had visited Australia just a short time before with Princess Alexandra) remembers her father dreading the thought of another long journey – earlier that year he had been to British Columbia with the Duke and Duchess of Westminster – but once he reached Australia he thoroughly enjoyed his time there. For the Duke the trip presented an opportunity to explore the flora of Australia, and his frequent letters home convey his enthusiasm for this. In Perth he found 'every form of flowering trees from palm trees downwards'. After an outing to the Forestry Department's plantations he wrote that he had experienced 'a fascinating day, both from the forestry point of view and from the real beauty of the country'. Similar experiences are recounted on trips to other parts of the continent, and overall he was very impressed with the Australian approach to forestry management. The following June he visited Russia, which he enjoyed immensely, for this provided a further opportunity to learn about forestry in a very different setting. When Pomeroy House was opened as a forestry school by the Duke in 1961, he used the opportunity to call for the creation of a chair of forestry at Queen's University. He was distraught when, in September of that year, Hurricane Debbie caused enormous damage to the trees at Barons Court, destroying several hundred acres of deciduous woodland. In all, around a quarter of the plantations (some 300,000 trees) at Barons Court were destroyed (and this on the back of devastating storms in 1957 and 1959). Though it took years to repair the devastation, the Duke applied himself to the task with the same steady determination that had characterised his previous endeavours.

Public life

Almost as soon as he was permanently settled in Northern Ireland, Lord Hamilton began to be involved in public life and local affairs to a much greater extent than before. Prior to the war he had entertained thoughts of embarking on a career in politics, but his father's position as Governor and desire to be seen as politically neutral prevented him from pursuing this. In 1946, Lord Hamilton was appointed High Sheriff of County Tyrone and in the same year was elected to Tyrone County Council, going on to serve as its chairman. He became a member of the Northern Ireland Senate in 1949 (serving until 1962), and two years later was appointed Lord Lieutenant of County Tyrone. The present Duke believes his father enjoyed membership of the Senate more than that of the County Council, which he often found tedious – 'very boring' was how he described one council meeting to his wife in 1948. It was said that his speeches in the Senate were devoid of sectarian comment and that he never distinguished between Catholics and Protestants.[5] The causes he supported were those that affected people of all backgrounds. In the summer of 1958, for instance, he actively campaigned against the closure of the GNR line between Portadown and Derry. At a rally in Omagh town hall he told those gathered that protesting against the closure was not enough – what they should also do was to give the railway their fullest support and encourage their friends to do likewise. In November 1968, 15 unemployed residents of Derry, in a demonstration designed to show that they were anxious for work, planted 100 Japanese larch saplings donated by the Duke.[6]

He was a firm believer in the Union and believed that greater efforts should have been made to attract Catholic support for it. However, he was not a high-profile Unionist, but rather exercised a calming influence behind the scenes during times of tension. Such a situation arose in 1956 following the

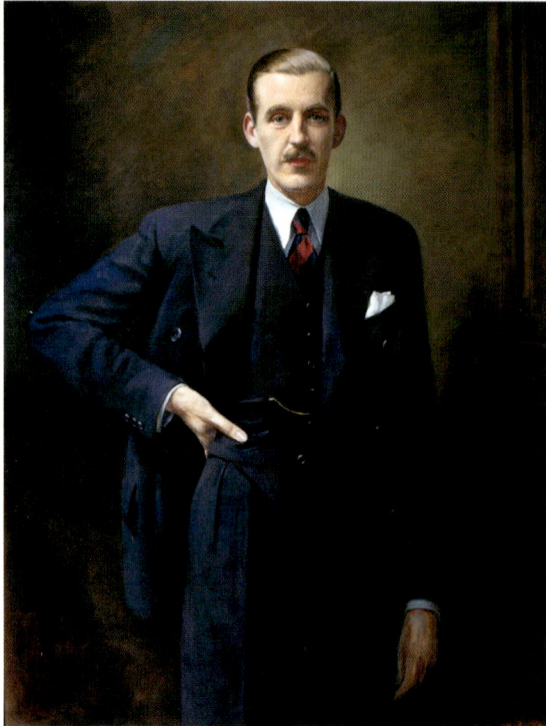

Portrait of the 4th Duke by John A. A. Berrie

by-election victory of George Forrest as an Independent Unionist in Mid Ulster. This was against a background of difficulties for a number of Unionist politicians which Brookeborough, as Prime Minister, was anxious to resolve. Bringing Forrest into the 'official' party fold was felt to be one solution. The Duke, as chairman of the Mid Ulster constituency association, was willing to do this sooner rather than later, telling Brookeborough, 'I first thought we should delay this as I thought tempers might soothe, but the opposite seems to be the case, and in view of the general "sticky wicket", I feel pretty sure that we will be doing the right thing.' At the same time, he was worried that this would be seen as a concession by the Unionist extremists and expressed his concerns if 'the "wild boys" got the reins'. In the late 1960s the Duke supported the policies of the Prime Minister of Northern Ireland, Terence O'Neill, and in early 1969 he publicly declared his opposition to the defection from O'Neill of the local MP in North Tyrone. At the Stormont election in that year he supported his son-in-law, Commander Peter Campbell, during his campaign in Derry. A long-time vice-president of the Ulster Unionist Council, the Duke resigned in January 1974 out of sympathy for Brian Faulkner's support for power-sharing.

The Duke loved art and heritage and had a keen interest in Irish history and civilisation. He was the first president of the Ulster-Scot Historical Society, founded in December 1956 and now known as the Ulster Historical Foundation. At a widely welcomed speech in Strabane in September 1956, at the opening of a new grammar school, he emphasised the importance of educating the young to appreciate the arts. He also invited young people to Barons Court to view its art treasures. He had a strong sense of his own family's history and the way this was told through the house and its contents. For instance, in October 1952, in response to an expression of interest in the portrait of Mrs Hawkins from the Trustees of National Galleries, he wrote to his father: 'I would very strongly deprecate any sale of the picture. It is such a beautiful one, and although not one of the family, it has very strong family interest, especially for B.C.' Given his own interest in the natural environment, it is not surprising that he was fascinated by Charles Hamilton of Painshill and spent some time translating the correspondence between Hamilton and the leading French horticulturalist, the Abbé Nolin.

In May 1960 the Duke was invited to act as chairman of an organising committee advising on the preparation of an exhibition of paintings from country houses in Ulster. He brought his enthusiasm for and knowledge of the subject to the committee, and allowed a dozen of his own paintings from Barons Court to go on display. There was a feeling that this could be the last opportunity to do something like this, and in the preface to the exhibition catalogue the Duke wrote:

Many of the larger country residences, both north and south, have already disappeared from the Irish economy; others will inevitably follow and in years to come it may be impossible to organise an exhibition on this scale from private sources, since the larger canvases will not be available.

On 5 April 1962 the Belfast Museum and Art Gallery became a Northern Ireland national institution – the Ulster Museum – when it was formerly handed over to the Duke, as chairman of the museum's trustees. He continued to serve as chairman of the trustees until 1972. Among his other positions, the 4th Duke was appointed Honorary Colonel in the service of the 5th Battalion, Royal Inniskilling Fusiliers (Territorial Army) in 1963. The following year he was one of the patrons of the Irish Himalayan expedition. He was also an active and conscientious president of the Royal United Kingdom Beneficent Association.

Of his many public roles, probably the position he enjoyed most was that of Chancellor of the New University of Ulster. He had been nominated for the chancellorship of Queen's University, but in a vote was defeated by the theatrical director Sir Tyrone Guthrie. The Duke was actively involved in the establishment of the New University of Ulster at Coleraine, leading its appeal for funds from September 1967; by the following summer it was halfway towards its target of £1,500,000.[7] He also provided trees from Barons Court for the campus grounds. On 15 September 1970 the Duke was installed as Chancellor 'in a brief, but colourful ceremony' in front of an invited gathering of 500 persons. The first graduates were presented with their scrolls and six honorary degrees were awarded. Unfortunately, the student body boycotted the ceremony, claiming that a charter had been imposed without consulting staff or students.[8]

The Duke and Duchess at the opening of the Guy L. Wilson Daffodil Garden at the New University of Ulster in 1974.

The Duke began his speech on this occasion with a consciousness of the honour that had been bestowed on him and the hard work that had made the creation of the institution possible: 'I meet this with all humility, but with determination to serve the interests of the New University of Ulster in whatever way I can … I like to think that all here today will experience a thrill when we realise that only a few years ago this site was mere bare fields.' 'Ireland has been styled the land of "Saints and Scholars"', the Duke continued, 'and although it would appear that the former are nowadays sadly lacking in our troubled

community, yet there has always been an undoubted respect for learning quite apart from the material benefits that achievement of knowledge can bestow.' He went on to stress the importance of the natural sciences and conservation, praising the Forestry Division of the Ministry of Agriculture for the creation of forest parks. In addition he encouraged the study of Russian and Eastern European languages, arguing that 'if the greatly to be desired lessening of tension between East and West materialises, this will certainly assist the interchange of scientific, industrial and cultural thought.'

In August 1977 the Duke welcomed the Queen and the Duke of Edinburgh to the University. In his address on this occasion he looked back to 1613 when the town of Coleraine was granted a charter, and drew parallels with the founding of the university. In 1613, the townsmen of Coleraine had been granted permission to 'practise their arts, mysteries and manual occupations within the liberties of the town' – now the same activities 'peculiar to a university' were practised here. The Duke remained as Chancellor of the University until his death. In tribute to the Duke the coat of arms granted to the University of Ulster (created following the amalgamation of the New University of Ulster and the Ulster Polytechnic) in 1985 incorporated an antelope supporter on the left side, a device used in the Abercorn arms.

The Duchess of Abercorn

With regard to her own contribution to the public sphere, the Duchess was deeply concerned with medical provision and care for most of her adult life. Mention has already been made of her role as a VAD (Voluntary Aid Detachment) in St Thomas' Hospital, London, in 1939–40. For many years she was involved with the Red Cross. She joined the Berkshire Branch in 1940, working in the Maidenhead Division for the remainder of the war. On her permanent move to Barons Court in 1945 she joined the Northern Ireland Central Council Branch and later became president of the County Tyrone Branch. In 1959, she succeeded the Dowager Marchioness of Londonderry as president of the NI Central Council Branch, also chairing its Executive Committee. Under her direction the Red Cross was re-established in the city of Derry in 1961. In 1974, the Duchess became president of the newly created Western Branch, which covered most of the three former branches of Londonderry City, County Tyrone and County Fermanagh. The ease with which this amalgamation was achieved was largely due to her ability to produce a consensus among the different parties concerned.

In her role with the Red Cross, the Duchess was never simply a figurehead, but someone who worked hard in the best interests of the organisation, at both local and provincial levels. During her time as president, the Duchess encouraged the NI Branch to keep abreast of reforms and changes taking

The Duchess speaking at a Red Cross event at Englefield House, Berkshire, during the war.

place in the rest of the United Kingdom, frequently visiting London to represent Northern Ireland. The onset of the Troubles brought fresh challenges. The Duchess firmly believed that the neutrality of the Red Cross should be upheld through these years of difficulty. At the height of the civil disturbances in Derry she personally accompanied the meals-on-wheels service as it ventured into the 'no-go' areas of the city. She also volunteered for the Omagh district's emergency call-out register which required attending scenes of bombings, visits to the wounded in hospital, and providing assistance to the homeless and those in distress. In 1979, the Duchess received the Queen's Badge of Honour, the highest award in the Red Cross, in recognition of her many years of service and outstanding contribution to the organisation.

The Duchess' understanding of health provision was further utilised during her chairmanship of the Tyrone County Hospital. She was widely respected as someone who understood the pressures that medical staff faced, with one senior figure in the Ministry of Health and Social Services writing to her in 1968, 'May I say that as a nurse one always feels very safe to have you present because every nurse knows that in you we have an informed and understanding friend. Thank you for all you do for us as a profession and for the health services.' The Duchess was active in many other areas of public life in Northern Ireland. She was a patron of the NI Benevolent Fund for Nurses and the president of the British Commonwealth Nurses War Memorial Fund. She was also president of the Federation of Women's Institutes of Northern Ireland from 1946 to 1985; after her retirement she was made an honorary life member of the Federation.[9] The Duchess was also an active and knowledgeable gardener, generous in giving out advice and in sharing plants with her friends. Terence O'Neill's wife Jean wrote to the Duchess after one visit to thank her 'for all those lovely plants', adding, 'It is shocking to have raided Barons Court & walked off with so much … It is also wonderful to see Barons Court & all the lovely things with endless space and endless scope & the thought that it will go on getting better.'

The Duchess with nurses in Derry, 1960s.

In 1964, the Duchess was appointed a Mistress of the Robes to Queen Elizabeth, The Queen Mother, succeeding the Dowager Duchess of Northumberland. Among her duties was arranging the roster of the Ladies-in-Waiting, one of whom was always in attendance with the Queen Mother. The role required her attendance at major state occasions, while the Duchess also accompanied the Queen Mother on a number of overseas visits, including a tour of Canada in 1967, as well as trips to various parts of the United Kingdom. In this role, the Duchess was known for her modesty and friendliness, but also as someone with an 'independent spirit'. It was also commented on that she 'travelled with an almost impossibly light suitcase'.[10] She was made a Dame Commander of the Royal Victorian Order (DCVO) in 1969 and a Dame Grand Cross (GVCO) of that order in 1982.

Towards the end of his life the Duke did not enjoy especially good health, but bore it all without complaint and continued to fulfil his many duties. He and his wife celebrated their golden wedding anniversary in February 1978, and in the July of that year a party to mark this was held at the Westminsters' flat in London. On the evening of Sunday, 3 June 1979 the Duke took ill and was admitted to Tyrone County Hospital in Omagh, but died the following morning. His death came as a shock for his family and friends. The Duchess was on a cruise of the Western Isles with the Queen Mother at the time. She returned to Barons Court immediately, arriving that afternoon. Lady Moyra and her family had only recently arrived back from a holiday in Australia. Letters of sympathy from all over the world and across the religious and political divide in Northern Ireland poured in. One correspondent wrote that the Duke had been 'both friendly and courteous. These qualities, together with his high rank and unusual modesty, leave him a man of

The Duke and Duchess around the time of their 50th wedding anniversary.

whom Ulster can be justly proud.' Others drew attention to his 'delicious sense of humour', 'his gentle understanding of people', 'his legacy of kindness and courtesy', and the fact that he 'represented all that was good in his generation'.

As he had donated his body for medical research, a service of thanksgiving was held at Barons Court Church on Thursday, 7 June. The church was packed to overflowing, with many of those in attendance having to be seated in the open air. They heard his friend, Robin Eames, the Bishop of Derry and Raphoe, speak warmly of the Duke:

> The public life and service of the late Duke was immense and significant. His interests and influence were widespread in the Province and beyond. But it was as a man affectionately referred to in these parts as 'the Duke' that so many of us will remember him with pride and thanksgiving. He was a man of peace who loved the simple things of life. From such simplicity he found great strength and vision. And in the Tyrone countryside his love for the people of all shades of opinion and background, his family life and his deep personal faith in God gave him a stature we will not forget. He was a man of deep concern for all of the people of this Province. Yet his hope, his faith in the inherent decency of ordinary people and a strong conviction that peace was attainable for all people gave him a refreshing optimism which he could not conceal. Those who were privileged to know him will recall this gentle and compassionate man of peace with love and thankfulness.[11]

An employee expressed his views on the Duke in a very simple, but no less profound, way: 'Sir, I worked for a gentleman.' The Duchess survived her husband by over 10 years. She continued in her role as Mistress of the Robes to the Queen Mother, and fulfilled many other public duties, until her death at Barons Court on 2 February 1990.

Lady Moyra Campbell

The eldest child of the 4th Duke and Duchess of Abercorn, Lady Moyra was born at the family home in London, 22 Cambridge Square, in 1930 and christened in Barons Court Church, possibly the first member of the family to be baptised there. She was educated at a day school in London, then St Mary's, Wantage, before attending a finishing school in Switzerland in 1946–7. On 2 June 1953, she was one of the six Maids of Honour at the Coronation of Queen Elizabeth II in Westminster Abbey; 60 years later all six attended the anniversary ceremony in the Abbey. In April 1954, Lady Moyra was appointed a Lady-in-Waiting to Princess Alexandra, accompanying her on

LEFT: The Duke in his study at Barons Court.

Commander Peter and Lady Moyra Campbell.

many official visits overseas. In 1959, they travelled to Australia to take part in the celebrations to mark the centenary of Queensland, also visiting Canada, Fiji, Thailand and Cambodia. In 1960, they travelled to Nigeria for the freedom ceremonies. The following year they visited Hong Kong, Japan, Thailand and Burma. In 1963, Lady Moyra was appointed a Commander, Royal Victorian Order (CVO). She resigned as a Lady-in-Waiting when her husband stood as a pro-O'Neill Unionist in Derry in the Stormont election of February 1969.

For over 60 years she had been involved with the National Society for the Prevention of Cruelty to Children, joining its Central Executive Committee in 1954. She is currently a vice-president of the society. In the aftermath of the Coronation she put her Maid of Honour dress on display around Fermanagh and Tyrone, raising £600 for the NSPCC. In 2012, with the Queen's blessing, Lady Moyra again put her dress on display in order to raise money for the cross-border activities of the three charities with which she is most closely associated – the NSPCC, Early Years (originally the Northern Ireland Pre-School Playgroup Association), and the Northern Ireland Cancer Fund for Children. She has been involved with both of the latter organisations for over 30 years and remains deeply passionate about all three charitable bodies.

On 12 November 1966, at St Columb's Cathedral in Derry, she married Commander Peter Campbell, son of Major-General Sir Alexander Douglas Campbell and his wife Patience Loveday Carlyon. An experienced officer in the Royal Navy with a distinguished career record, Commander Campbell was a former Equerry to the Queen. He resigned from the Navy the day after he married and became a director of a Belfast shipping company. From 1974 to 1996 he was the Representative in Ireland for the Honourable the Irish Society, doing much to modernise the way its interests in County Londonderry were managed. Lady Moyra and Commander Campbell have two sons, Rory, a solicitor, and Michael, an entrepreneur. In the summer of 1969, they moved to Hollybrook, near Randalstown, County Antrim, where they continue to live.

Lord Anthony Hamilton

The younger brother of the present Duke of Abercorn, Lord Claud Anthony Hamilton, known as Anthony, was born in London in July 1939. He was in Northern Ireland at the outbreak of World War II and remained in the province for the rest of that year and into the early part of the next, surviving the fire at Barons Court of January 1940. He spent most of the war at Greenlands, near Henley on Thames, before moving with his family to Barons Court in the summer of 1945. He began attending prep school in England in 1948 and then went to Eton. In 1957, he was commissioned into the Irish Guards, serving in England and Cyprus. He left the army in 1961 and for the next thirteen years worked in merchant banking for firms including Kleinwort Benson and Colegrave & Co. Apart from a three-year period in Vancouver from 1968 to 1971, he was based in the City of London. Though he initially loved London, by 1974 he was ready for a change and returned to Northern Ireland to become the administrator of the National Trust properties of Castle Coole and Florence Court in County Fermanagh, a position he held for five years. He also joined the Ulster Defence Regiment, serving until 1979 and reaching the rank of captain.

In 1982, in Killinchy Presbyterian Church, he married Catherine Janet Faulkner, daughter of Sir Dennis Faulkner of Ringhaddy, County Down. Their first home was an old farmhouse near Enniskillen which Anthony had bought in 1979, and it was while living here that their two children, Anna, a teacher, and Alexander, a captain in the Irish Guards, were born. In 1988, they moved to Killyreagh, a Georgian-period house, where they continue to live. From 2005 to 2007 Anthony was president of the Royal Forestry Society, a position his own father had earlier held, and has also been chairman of the Northern Ireland division. For over 20 years he was chairman of the County Fermanagh Farming Society. He has also been active in the Fermanagh branch of the charity Riding for the Disabled Association. He is currently the Vice Lord Lieutenant for County Fermanagh.

Lord Anthony, Lady Catherine, Anna and Alexander.

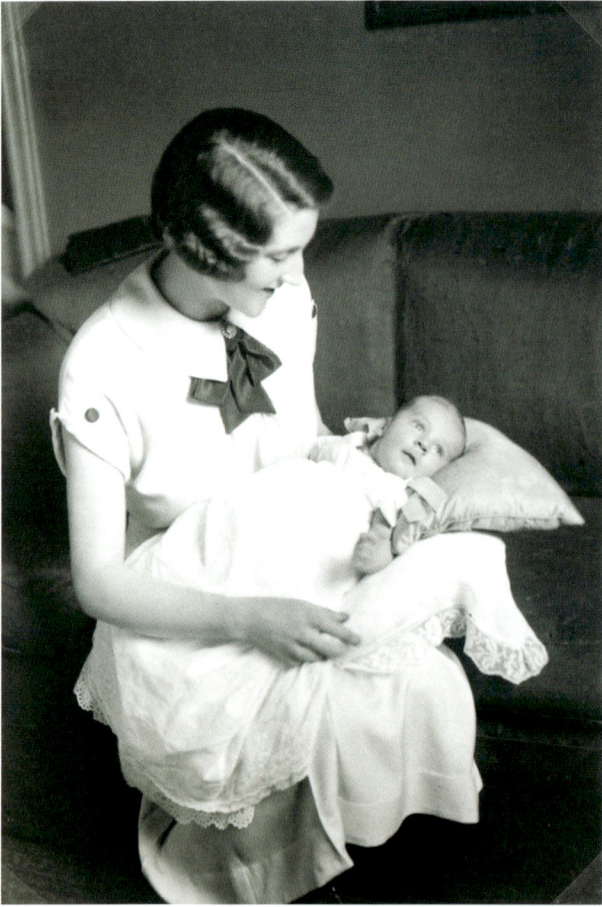

The infant Duke with his mother.

11
James Hamilton,
5th Duke of Abercorn
A modern duke

The present Duke of Abercorn is a thoroughly modern duke. One of only two dozen or so holders of a dukedom in the British Isles, leaving aside royal dukes, he is fully aware of the challenges facing his family and estate in an era of rapid change. In an age where the nobility no longer wields political power, and where traditional concepts of rank and deference have been largely eroded, the Duke of Abercorn still commands enormous respect. Under his guidance the estate has successfully adapted to the twenty-first century and is considered an exemplar of sound management in practice. The Duke considers himself a custodian of his inheritance, and that his responsibility is to pass it on to his successors in an even better condition than it came to him. A shrewd businessman and innovator, he is far from conforming to the conventional caricature of an aristocrat. A strong sense of duty, passed down to him from successive generations of Hamiltons, shapes most of what he does and is obvious in the fact that he has dedicated most of his life to the service of the people of Northern Ireland.

The future 5th Duke of Abercorn was born in London on 4 July 1934 and spent the early part of his life in the then family home at 22 Cambridge Square. When war was declared in September 1939 he was with his parents in Northern Ireland, spending the latter part of the year with his cousins at Crom and then Christmas at Barons Court with his grandparents. In January 1940 he had a narrow escape when a fire broke out in the wing of Barons Court in which he and his brother and sister were sleeping. Fortunately, no-one was injured. He spent much of the war with his mother and siblings at Greenlands, near Henley on Thames, while his father was based initially in London and afterwards at Windsor. In the summer of 1945 the family moved to Barons Court permanently. Though it was a very happy period for the family, the Duke remembers that times were hard, with much work needed to both the house and the estate. He was educated at Ludgrove School and then Eton, where he was able to indulge his passion for sport, enjoying cricket, football and swimming. He would later become the first man to water-ski between Ireland and Scotland. For four months he worked on a farm in France prior to receiving a commission as a Second Lieutenant in the Grenadier Guards in 1952; among his duties was standing guard over Nazi war criminals in Spandau prison in Berlin.

He left the army in 1956 and for the next few years began to prepare for when he would assume responsibility for running the estate. He gained experience in estate management while working for the Buccleuch estate in Scotland. Like a number of other sons of landed families in Northern Ireland, he studied at the Royal Agricultural College in Cirencester, graduating in 1962, after which he worked alongside his father in overseeing the management of the estate. Though his father would retain an interest in forestry management, the present Duke took an increasingly leading role in the running of other aspects of the estate. This was particularly true of the Scottish properties, which comprised arable farms in the Borders and Fife and forestry in the Borders and Argyllshire, which the Duke visited two or three times a year.

Member of Parliament

In October 1964 the Duke was elected MP for Fermanagh and South Tyrone in the Westminster election, winning over 55% of the vote. The seat had previously been held by his cousin, Lord Robert Grosvenor, later 5th Duke of Westminster. He retained the seat in the 1966 general election, again winning over 50% of the vote. The Duke acknowledges that it would be fair to describe him as a 'reluctant politician'. 'My sole involvement', he now admits, 'centred on a desire to encourage economic development in the west of the province, and to encourage good community relations. I freely admit that due to youth and inexperience I was in no way fully alerted to the complexities of Northern Ireland – from which I have been learning ever since!'

His maiden speech, made during a debate on the Finance Bill, was delivered on 24 November 1964 and he began with a note of appreciation for his predecessor, continuing: 'I have the honour of representing the most westwardly and one of the most beautiful constituencies. It is predominantly an agricultural constituency comprising small farms.' He went on to raise concerns about certain provisions in the Bill 'which could well extenuate our existing problems in Northern Ireland', while praising recent progress in the economy:

> Unhappily, one label which has become attached to Ulster is that it
> suffers from consistently high unemployment and has done so for far

too long. Yet the high percentage of Ulster's unemployment gives a false picture of both the economy and the industrial progress of the province. Few realise that through redundancy in our traditional industries 100,000 have been forced into the labour market since 1945. To counteract the decline in employment in our basic industries, the Northern Ireland Government have succeeded in sponsoring 178 new firms, providing 52,000 new jobs, since 1945. In fact, 25 per cent of those employed in industry are now working in factories built in Ulster since 1945.

However, the most satisfactory development is that the majority of those firms have expanded, and several have doubled their original production. This proves beyond doubt the adaptability of the Ulster worker and also the feasibility of profitable production in Ulster. We have for the first time a diversification of industry. In fact, Ulster today is one of the most widely diversified industrial communities in Western Europe, including a high concentration of man-made fibre groups, such as British Enkalon, I.C.I., Courtaulds, Chemstrand and du Pont.

Although we are not a wealthy part of the United Kingdom, we in no way want, or expect, to be treated as a poor relation – far from it. We want to be given the opportunity of playing a vital role in the economic expansion of the United Kingdom. Northern Ireland is a growth area and to prove my point industrial production rose by 38 per cent between 1954 and 1963 compared with 24 per cent for the United Kingdom as a whole. It is now an accepted fact that if we are to have real prosperity in the United Kingdom then every area and section of the community must have a fair share in it.[1]

The Duke represented an overwhelmingly rural constituency and was well aware of the importance of farming to the local economy. He concluded his maiden speech with a warning that the 'small farmer in Northern Ireland is definitely not getting his fair share of increased prosperity', adding: 'I am convinced that the small farmer has still a vital role to play in the future of this industry, providing he receives a fair deal from the Government.'

Issues relating to the farming sector in Northern Ireland continued to be raised by the Duke during Commons debates and he fully understood the differences in the industry in the province and other parts of the United Kingdom. In May 1966, in the course of the debate on the Agriculture Bill, the Duke observed:

Northern Ireland can be described as a country of small farms, and as the average holding is 30.5 acres compared with 79.2 acres in England the definition of a small-holding has a considerable difference in meaning in the two countries. Therefore, different circumstances exist in Northern Ireland. Amongst small farmers there is a general feeling that the Government is more concerned in implementing the

National Plan than in aiding agriculture ... This policy of integration is lacking in social content, for farmers have a social dignity as owner-occupiers which they can never regain in the countryside as employees, should they be fortunate enough to obtain alternative employment or, as unemployed should they fail to do so. In England, the redundant farmer has a far greater opportunity of obtaining alternative employment, thereby generally increasing his standard of living. Unhappily, this is not the case in Northern Ireland, especially in the constituency I represent. ...

I am convinced that the future prosperity of the industry depends on obtaining a larger share of the home market. The Government should recognise that this industry—it is still a great industry—has the manpower, mechanisation, will-power and ability to provide and produce food for the under-developed countries where the great majority are desperately under-nourished owing to the terrible shortage of food. The International Federation of Agricultural Producers is meeting in London at the moment. Delegate after delegate has been speaking on behalf of the under-developed countries which are crying out for more food. Here is an opportunity which the Government must seize.[2]

Throughout his parliamentary career the Duke was a strong promoter of manufacturing industry in Northern Ireland. In a letter to *The Times* in the spring of 1969 he pointed out that Northern Ireland possessed the three most essential elements for successful industrial development: '1. An available and willing labour force, with industrial training facilities ahead of any country in Europe; 2. An abundant supply of water; 3. Modern transportation facilities.' He argued that 'the majority of our new industries are located in the countryside or new towns, blending very successfully, as in Switzerland, with the local environment'.[3] During his time as MP, he visited the United States on several occasions to promote trading links with Northern Ireland and tourism to the province. On one occasion in Shreveport, Louisiana, he told reporters, 'We are literally buying jobs because our available labour market is the most valuable commodity anyone can offer', and highlighted the incentives being offered to American companies by the Government of Northern Ireland. The Duke was keenly aware of the wider benefits of tourism, arguing that there must be a new attitude towards tourists. They were not a 'necessary nuisance', but rather 'invaluable additional consumers, benefiting not only hotels, but many different trade and service industries'.[4] He believed that a better relationship between the two parts of Ireland would be to the benefit of the whole island in terms of tourism and told the Commons in February 1965 that tourism 'could prove to be one of our biggest growth industries, which would be of particular benefit to my constituency.' Today, the tourism industry remains one of the Duke's special areas of interest.

The politics of O'Neillism

In the mid to late 1960s the Duke was a firm supporter of the policies of the Prime Minister of Northern Ireland, Terence O'Neill, during a period of considerable unrest, the beginnings of the Troubles. Interviewed for a local newspaper in 1968, he lamented the fact that Northern Ireland's forwardness in technology was not matched by its politics. At this time, he was holding monthly advice centres in Dungannon and Enniskillen which provided him with an opportunity to meet the electorate face to face and learn of the real issues that mattered to his constituents. In November 1968, in response to claims that those in the pro-O'Neill camp were not being particularly vocal in their support for the premier, the Duke wrote a letter to a local newspaper in which he stated: 'I believe that at the present time it is essential that politicians should state in plain words what they believe in ... I am convinced that [O'Neill] is doing an excellent job for Northern Ireland under very difficult circumstances.' Looking back on this period today, the Duke reflects:

> In 1968 one knew immediately of the total necessity of bringing in reforms to ensure that Northern Ireland would be on a par with Great Britain with regard to equal rights legislation. I had great respect for Terence O'Neill, James Chichester-Clark, and Brian Faulkner for their determination in implementing these reforms and for converting the inevitable into reality.

In the 1969 Stormont election the Duke's brother-in-law, Commander Peter Campbell, stood as a pro-O'Neill Unionist in Derry. During his election campaign, he called for an end to segregation in schools, in housing and in the workplace. When the election result was announced Commander Campbell had come third with around 25% of the vote. It was afterwards reckoned that several hundred Catholics had voted for him prompting one historian to comment that this was 'probably the first time a Unionist in Derry had ever achieved this.'[5] Following O'Neill's resignation as Prime Minister in April 1969, the Duke observed, 'His resignation must not be regarded as a victory for extremes, since it should be remembered that in the struggle for moderation, which alone can save our British citizenship, there are bound to be casualties.'[6]

The Duke's support for the policies of O'Neill had placed him at odds with many within his own constituency party, and in advance of the 1970 Westminster election there was talk of a challenge to his candidature, though in the end this did not materialise. His subsequent election campaign was devoid of any party-political comment – though he did describe the attempts to select a single non-Unionist candidate as having all the ingredients 'of a James Bond thriller' – and instead he concentrated on economic issues. At a rally in Dungannon, he told his audience:

> I believe in complete fairness in every sphere of social need – housing, jobs and farm prices. In fact I believe that fairness and firmness are essential ingredients for the foundation of modern society. My sole reason for remaining in politics is because I am not prepared to see a lifetime's work given to this community by the older generation ruined through senseless violence. Nor am I prepared to see the young and able forced to emigrate through instability and hooliganism.[7]

Overall, his parliamentary career is not one that the Duke looks back on with particular enjoyment. 'Happily I was defeated in the May 1970 election', he reminiscences, 'and decided from that day onwards to remain apolitical and unattached to any political party.' The victor in the 1970 election, by a narrow margin, was Frank McManus; today he and the Duke work together on the Fermanagh Trust.

Marriage, family and move to Barons Court

On 20 January 1966, the Duke met Alexandra Anastasia Phillips at the wedding of the future Lord Pembroke in London. Better known as Sacha, she was the daughter of Lt-Col. Harold (Bunny) Phillips and his wife, Georgina (née Wernher). In May, during gloriously sunny weather, Sacha travelled across to Ireland for the first time. It happened that Lord Claud Nigel Hamilton, the 4th Duke's uncle, was also visiting Barons Court at this time and he is supposed to have remarked that he had met the woman whom he believed would become the next Duchess of Abercorn. During this visit, and while returning from Henry McElhenny's home at Glenveagh Castle in

The wedding photograph of the Duke and Duchess of Abercorn, 20 October 1966, taken at St James' Palace.

The christening of Jamie at Barons Court Church in 1969. The ceremony was performed by Alan Buchanan, the archbishop of Dublin. Prince Charles was Jamie's godfather.

Jamie, Lord Hamilton (right) carrying the train of the Queen at the Garter ceremony in 1983.

Donegal, the couple became engaged. They married on 20 October 1966, the wedding ceremony taking place in Westminster Abbey with the Queen, the Duke of Edinburgh, Prince Charles, Princess Anne, Prince Andrew (who was a page boy), the Queen Mother and Lord Mountbatten among the 1,200 guests. A party of tenants and estate workers from Barons Court was also present, and the reception afterwards was held at St James's Palace. The Hamiltons spent the first 10 years of their marriage living principally in London, though with regular visits to Ireland, especially during the time that the Duke was an MP. Their eldest son, James Harold Charles, the Marquess of Hamilton, was born in August 1969 and baptised the following November by the Archbishop of Dublin in Barons Court Church; the Prince of Wales was one of the godparents. The Duke and Duchess have two other children – Sophia Alexandra and Nicholas Edward Claud.

In the mid-1970s the Hamiltons and their two older children moved full-time to Barons Court, with the Duke's parents moving into a self-contained unit incorporating the White Library and the West Wing. The Duke and Duchess were determined to create a comfortable, modern family home and not long after settling there permanently they invited the renowned interior designer David Hicks – who was married to a daughter of Lord Mountbatten, the Duchess's godfather – to visit them and advise on the redecoration of the ground floor rooms. The Duke recalls that Hicks arrived one summer morning at 11am, having driven up from Classiebawn in

Portraits of Jamie, Sophie and Nicholas by Zsuzsi Roboz.

A graduate of Middlebury College, Vermont, James Harold Charles (Jamie) worked in television and film production for a number of years. He is now actively involved in the running of the estate. In 2004, he married Tanya Nation and they have two sons, Alfred and Claud.

Sophia Alexandra (Sophie) worked for the famous French fashion designer Givenchy in Paris and later co-founded her own fashion label, Hamilton Paris. In 2013, she became engaged to Hashem Arouzi and they are the parents of twins Caspian and Soraya.

After studying at Trinity College, Dublin, Nicholas Edward Claud moved to New York where he graduated from the Pratt Institute in 2008. He still lives in New York where he and his Russian-born wife Tatiana are professional photographers. They are the parents of Valentina.

The main staircase

County Sligo where he was holidaying with his family, and by 1pm he had finalised his scheme. It left the Hamiltons astounded, but also convinced that they had to employ him and his remarkable talents. The redecoration began in March 1977 and was completed by Christmas of that year.

Nearly all of the main rooms on the ground floor bear Hicks's touch. Under his direction the domed rotunda was turned into a formal dining room. He had the walls painted buttercup yellow and the dome various shades of grey. The carpet was woven in the Philippines to his own design. His use of dramatic colours is nowhere better seen than in the staircase hall. Top-lit, this space was often dull under grey skies. Hicks painted the walls a deep scarlet and the columns and plasterwork ceiling a brilliant white. Initially the Duke was hesitant when the designer proposed this treatment of the staircase hall. However, when he saw the end result he was taken aback with its effect. Hicks also convinced the Hamiltons that the long gallery should be restored to its original layout, removing the partition walls that had divided it into three rooms. Once again Barons Court boasted the longest room in a private house in Ireland.

Hicks also restored the library. Under Richardson this had been turned into a pantry and the bookshelves boarded over. An east-facing room, it was naturally darker than the other main rooms with their southern aspect. Hicks removed the boards, had the books replaced and used the purple velvet

curtains from the old dining room as the wall covering. His use of strong colours has had the effect of making the room a place of warmth and comfort. The carpet in this room was one of Hicks's own designs. His creativity was also expressed through his arrangement of the rooms. Thus, in the staircase hall he positioned two busts on scagliola pedestals, but otherwise left this as a largely empty space. The niches in the rotunda were used to display porcelain on glass shelves. In the Gallery the many items of furniture were carefully arranged so that the room does not appear cluttered.

Most ingeniously – and for some, most controversially – he had the idea of turning the old dining room into a family room. At the time, this was the largest room in the house with some of the most extravagant plasterwork from the Morrisons' makeover. Under Hicks the dining room was transformed into a space that fitted the needs of the family perfectly. He created three separate spaces – a kitchen unit at one end, a unit for storage, drinks and flower-arranging at the other, and in between a family dining area. His son Ashley summed up his father's achievement: 'He had taken the biggest, grandest, and most unusable room in the house, and treated it like a theatre stage, placing kitchen units like stage furniture, around which the action of their lives could be played out.'[8] These 'modern island skyscrapers', as Hicks himself called the tall green-painted cupboards he created for the units in the family room, are easily removable should any future member of the family desire a change.

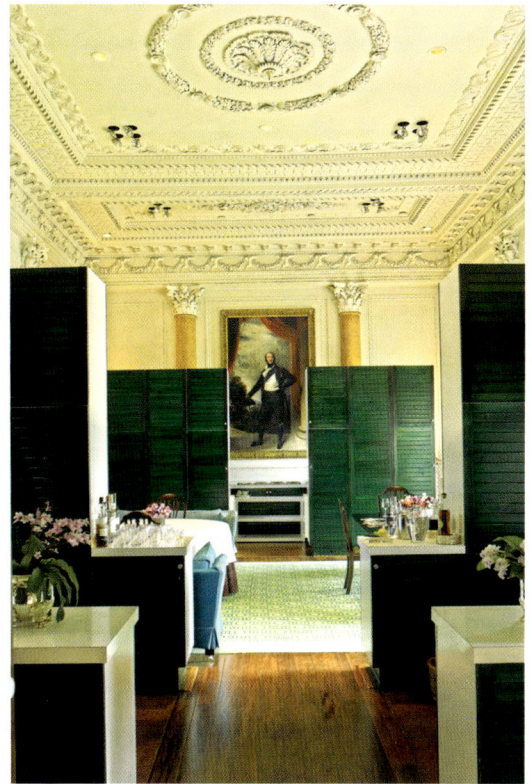

The family room

OPPOSITE TOP: The gallery
OPPOSITE BOTTOM: The library

The garage block at Barons Court designed by Raymond Erith. Built in 1970, this stands on the site of the former service wing.

299

Hicks achieved exactly what the Duke and Duchess wished him to. 'Although Barons Court might be described by some as a grand Georgian house', observes the Duke, 'many others have commented that Barons Court is a home in the truest sense of the word and not a private museum.' Hicks loved Barons Court, staying there every summer and using the opportunity to search out from the attics and cellars yet more treasures to be cleaned and positioned in the rooms. The Duke and Duchess have also employed the talents of Paul Kelaart, whom the Duke describes as a 'remarkable furniture restorer', and credit is due to him for the excellent condition of the furniture in the house. He visited Barons Court two or three times a year and, like Hicks, became a great friend of the family.

Business interests

It has been said of the Duke that he is much more of an entrepreneur than an academic. He is an astute businessman and highly respected by members of the Northern Ireland business community. The departure of the Duke from the Commons in 1970 meant that he had greater freedom not only to pursue business interests of his own, but to give of his time to promote the Northern Ireland economy in general. In the early 1970s he was responsible for the development at Newtownards of Northern Ireland's first out-of-town shopping centre. He has been involved with numerous bodies concerned with the economy and business development. Among other positions held, he has been a Member of Council of Europe (1968–70), a Director of the Northern Bank (1970–97), a Director of the Local Enterprise Development Unit (1971–77), a Member of the Economic and Social Committee, EEC (1973–78), a Director of the Northern Ireland Industrial Development Board (1982–87), President of the Building Societies Association (1986–92), Chairman of Laganside Limited (1987–89), Chairman of the Laganside Development Corporation (1989–96), and a Director of InterTradeIreland (1999–2003). He has also been President of NI Business in the Community, an organisation that promotes social responsibility, integration into the community and best practice.

Of the many such positions he has held, the Duke regards his period as Chairman of the Laganside Development Corporation as the most enjoyable and satisfying. When the 'Laganside Development (Northern Ireland) Order 1988' was discussed in the Lords in February 1989 the Duke spoke out strongly in favour of it, declaring:

> From the outset we in Laganside have adopted a policy of quality and, wherever possible, originality. My colleagues in Laganside believe that the people of Belfast deserve nothing but a development of the highest possible quality. Again there will be specific and important flagship developments which we hope will not only raise morale within the

community but also attract considerable positive interest from outside Northern Ireland. At the same time – and I wish to make this very clear – we are sensitive to the genuine concern of those who feel that a quality redevelopment will bar lower income groups from the undoubted benefits of the scheme. I wish to reassure not only this House but also those who genuinely harbour concern that good design need in no way involve high cost, as has been clearly demonstrated in recent years by the very successful Northern Ireland Housing Executive.

Inner city renewal is primarily an environmental challenge in order to create a change in image which in turn creates the right climate for commercial investment. Therefore I hope that this House will be interested to hear that earlier today in Belfast the Minister, Mr. Richard Needham, announced a comprehensive redevelopment of £20 million within the Laganside area but without a request by the successful developer for an urban development grant. I trust that the House will agree that that bodes well for the future. In fact through improving the all-important infrastructure with the implementation of the new weir by 1991 and continuing feasibility studies, progress is being achieved on all fronts with minimum delay. Since it is essential for a corporation to co-ordinate all the start-up work and to ensure the successful conclusion of redevelopment on either side of the River Lagan, I support the order.[9]

Looking back on the regeneration of 140 acres on both sides of the River Lagan, he considers his role as Chairman to have been 'energising and challenging, particularly as the political situation was so uncertain in those days.' From the outset, the Duke was determined that the infrastructure created was to be of the highest standard and of top-quality architecture. In an interview with Alf McCreary for his book *Titanic Port* (2010), the Duke said:

It's perhaps best for others to judge, but I believe that the Laganside Corporation achieved significant results during its term of office from 1989 onwards. It helped to raise morale tremendously, because over a long time the city and its people had turned their backs on the River Lagan. Now the area is a thriving location.

In 1997 he was awarded an honorary LLB by Queen's University, Belfast in recognition of his contribution towards revitalising the economy of Belfast's waterfront. The Duke has continued his association with the area through his involvement with the Titanic Quarter Company Ltd, of which he is a Director.

Interviewed for the *Belfast Telegraph* in the late 1960s, he said, 'I feel that anyone who has been given a fortunate start in life, like me, has a duty to

The Duke of Abercorn wearing the Garter robes.

pay back something to society.' His list of public appointments is long and impressive. The Duke was High Sheriff of County Tyrone in 1970, and in 1986 he was appointed Her Majesty's Lord Lieutenant of County Tyrone. In 2009 he relinquished this position on reaching the age of 75. On St George's Day 1999 he was appointed a Knight Companion of the Most Noble Order of the Garter (KG) and was granted the office of Chancellor of the Order of the Garter on 17 October 2012, in succession to Lord Carrington. Between 2001 and 2009 he was the Lord Steward of Her Majesty's Household. Since 1979, in succession to his father, he has been the President of the Royal United Kingdom Beneficent Association (now known as Independent Age). He is also President of the Ulster Historical Foundation, a Patron of the Fermanagh Trust and the Patron of the Ulster Cancer Foundation.

He has been a Patron of the Royal Ulster Agricultural Society (1990–95), a Trustee of the Winston Churchill Memorial Trust (1991–2002), and a Trustee of the Omagh Fund (1998–2003). The latter was established by Omagh District Council in the aftermath of the terrorist atrocity in the town in August 1998. In the Fund's final report in 2008 tribute was paid to the Duke for his contribution: 'His interest, involvement, advice and support were invaluable in those early years and the Trust is indebted to him.' In June 2003 the Duke was appointed to the Board of the Governors and Guardians of the National Gallery of Ireland, filling a position vacated by the Earl of Belmore, who had completed his term. The Duke immensely enjoyed his period as Colonel of the Irish Guards from 2000 to 2008. Though a regiment in the British Army, the Irish Guards draws its members from across the island of Ireland. In looking back on his association with the Irish Guards, the Duke reflects, 'Every regiment is a family; however, I found within the Irish Guards a very special and binding family relationship.'

The House of Lords

Following his succession to the dukedom, the Duke was entitled to sit in the House of Lords and duly took his seat on 25 October 1979. Over the next two decades, he

The Duke in the frock coat of the Irish Guards.

made numerous contributions to the debates and his areas of special interest lay primarily with improving the Northern Ireland economy, a subject that he was highly qualified to comment on. In his first contribution to a debate in the Lords, on 12 December 1979, on social and economic problems in the province, he began by telling the chamber:

> I should like to counteract a most unfortunate misconception that Northern Ireland has a constant begging bowl mentality and lacks the essential ingredients of self-help. Nothing could be further from the truth. Despite 10 years of violence and six years of slow economic growth, industry and commerce have shown a remarkable degree of resilience and determination not only to remain in business but also to expand whenever possible.[10]

Pointing out that 'Northern Ireland has a remarkably low level of industrial unrest, absenteeism and strikes' so that its 'industrial productivity during the past 15 years compares very favourably with Germany and outstrips both America and Great Britain', he acknowledged that 'unemployment remains

at a totally unacceptable level, despite a significant improvement in our infrastructure and an extremely attractive package of incentives to attract mobile industry'. He urged the Government to consider 'a tax-free concession on all manufacturing exports generated by new investment for a period of, say, 10 years'.

Whatever political problems existed in Northern Ireland, the Duke was convinced that progress in the economy was crucial and should not be overlooked. On 7 May 1981 in the Lords the Duke asked the Government whether it would consider introducing special and innovatory measures to assist the Northern Ireland economy. On this occasion he was highly critical of the Government, telling the Lords that as he read the Hansard report of a recent economic debate on the Northern Ireland economic situation, 'I became more and more depressed since the Government's response to a grave economic situation was indeed unimaginative, almost lethargic.' He urged a 'more inspiring and less mundane' approach to Northern Ireland's economic problems, warning that 'any society which insists on sticking to traditional economic methods and systems, instead of exploring new ideas, new technologies and new structures, will remain a static society and be left behind.' Among his concerns was the loss to the province through emigration of a significant portion of its skilled workforce, and so he argued for 'systematic detective work to find out where this expatriate management talent has emigrated to, then make contact and encourage a reverse brain-drain movement'. This could be achieved through financial incentives that would encourage 'expatriate managers to become entrepreneur owners of manufacturing firms in Northern Ireland'. Recognising the need to embrace the development of advanced technology, the Duke argued that this was possible through what was 'probably our greatest national asset ... the excellent and reliable labour force, of keen trained and educated men and women'.

In July 1982 the Duke urged caution with regard to proposals for a degree of devolved government in Northern Ireland, warning that 'the community are not only war-weary but also politics-weary' and dreaded a 'return of local politicians shouting at each other night after night in sterile argument on television'. 'The Government really must accept', he told the Lords, 'that, once outside the sterile arena of politics, ordinary people in Northern Ireland get on extremely well, and, through the common meeting ground of sport, voluntary schemes and organisations, people are slowly but actively assisting in the reconstruction of our society.' He used the opportunity to pay tribute to those engaged in such endeavours:

> The remarkable people who run these voluntary organisations have
> shown tremendous courage, tenacity and faith during the last 10 years
> and have proved beyond doubt that they are no longer prisoners of

the past. Again, countless thousands of other people representing every facet in Northern Ireland have proved that the heart of Northern Ireland is sound. I am now convinced that this heart needs strengthening—not political surgery—and this can only be achieved by a long recuperation from politics.[11]

Just as he had in the Commons, the Duke also used his seat in the Lords to champion the cause of agriculture in Northern Ireland, stating in 1981 that farming was 'and will always remain our biggest and most important industry, providing the only source of economic stability in rural areas.' He was also firmly of the opinion that forestry was critical to the health of the rural economy. In February 1988, during a debate on the state of afforestation in Northern Ireland, he expressed concern that the Department of Agriculture was slowing down its forestry programme and reducing the number of staff employed. He was critical of the fact that the 'Forest Service has been inadequately directed and led by the Department of Agriculture, since in the context of agriculture it has always been regarded as a poor relation.' Given that only 5.2% of Northern Ireland was afforested – compared with 12% in Scotland and a European Community average of 22% – he proposed that the Government should set a target of doubling this percentage by 2010.

He also recognised that it was crucial to the economic development of the region that its infrastructure was improved. Thus, in October 1998, he called on the Government to secure the necessary funds from Brussels to upgrade the A5 road connecting Ballygawley to Londonderry, which he called the 'commercial, industrial and social lifeline of the west of the Province and Donegal'. 'An improved A5 route', he believed, 'would play a critical role in enhancing the economic development of the region.'[12] This was his last contribution to debate in the Lords, for with the passing of the House of Lords Act in 1999 the Duke's career in that chamber ended.

The estate today

Throughout its history the family's adaptability to changed circumstances has been the key to its survival. This is as true today – and as necessary – as it was three centuries ago. The continued successful management of the various properties in Northern Ireland and Scotland is critical to Barons Court's survival. The estate is entirely rural-based and therefore it is vital to maximise all of its resources. Forestry remains a central part of the estate. Following Hurricane Debbie in the early 1960s, and again in the 1990s, the terms of the lease with the Forestry Service were renegotiated so that as and when the existing tree crop is clear-felled the land reverts to the estate. At present around 16 hectares a year is coming back to the estate from the Forestry Service, and by 2024 it will all have returned. In late 2001 the estate adopted the practice of continuous cover forestry. Though a more complex approach to forestry management, it has significant advantages over clear-felling for Barons Court, in terms of its impact on the landscape and the natural habitat of the sika deer for which the estate is famous. The topography of Barons Court, surrounded by steeply sloped hills, is also better suited to continuous cover forestry, which reduces the risk of flooding. It was felt important to work with nature and create the right conditions for the self-regeneration of the forest. This approach to forestry management has been widely praised, and in 2003 the estate was awarded the prestigious Royal Forestry Society's Duke of Cornwall's Award for its efforts toward forestry and conservation management.

In recent years the Hamiltons have been focusing on the potential to generate renewable energy from the resources of the estate. In 1995, 10 wind turbines were erected on Bessy Bell, which produce enough electricity to supply 5,000–6,000 homes. One of the biggest changes in the management of the estate is in the number of people directly employed by it. The estate used to have a much bigger staff, and much routine maintenance was carried out in-house. Now external contractors carry out such tasks. Farming is no longer carried out in-hand and the land is let in conacre. The horticultural enterprise in the walled garden that was established and managed by the estate is now leased to a tenant who runs a wholesale nursery business. The staff may be smaller, but it is a highly committed team.

There are two personalities who have given invaluable advice, dedication and expertise to Barons Court during the past 40 years and are greatly appreciated by the Hamilton family. Firstly, Robert Scott, the Agent since 1977, has managed and directed both Barons Court and the Scottish estates with remarkable skill and success. A man with real vision, leadership and in particular expertise in forestry, combined with the firm commitment that the estate must continuously evolve in order to secure its future, he has proved invaluable over the years to Barons Court. 'Barons Court', in Robert Scott's view, 'is a living memorial to all who have lived and worked here over the centuries.' Secondly, the Castlederg contractor Jack Lynch has supervised all the substantial building work at Barons Court and in particular the detailed work on the house during the past 40 years. With a remarkable knowledge and love of old buildings, he has been a great friend and neighbour of the Hamilton family. On his eightieth birthday in June 2011 the Duke and Duchess gave a reception at Barons Court for his family and friends to mark their gratitude and affection for him.

Robert Scott has been Agent since 1977. In 2009, he was appointed Lord Lieutenant of County Tyrone.

In more recent times the Duke has branched out into other areas of business. In 1991, he bought Belle Isle from Miss Lavinia Baird. An island in Upper Lough Erne with a fascinating history and a castle dating back to the seventeenth century, Belle Isle was purchased as a future home for his younger son Nicholas. Until he was ready to move into it, this stunning location offered the opportunity to develop a high-quality tourism product. The refurbishment of Belle Isle provided the Duke and Duchess with an opportunity to decorate a fine country house with fixtures and furnishings of their choosing – something they never had to do at Barons Court. Once again, the Hamiltons turned to their friend David Hicks for advice and direction on how to transform a decaying castle into a luxury retreat. The designer's touch can be seen in his use of bold colours, providing a dramatic backdrop for paintings by Sir Edwin Landseer, Paul Henry, Percy French and Derek Hill, porcelain by Mildred Mottahedeh, rattan sofas from the Philippines, and furniture by the renowned Victorian cabinetmaker James Lamb. Belle Isle is also host to a cookery school. The idea for this enterprise grew out of a conversation between the Duke and Michel Roux Senior and the desire to create something that would attract visitors to the area outside the normal tourism season. Today it is one of the best known cookery schools in Ireland.

The Duchess of Abercorn

As she readily admits, prior to her visit to Barons Court in May 1966, the Duchess of Abercorn had never been to Ireland, knew little about it, and was totally unprepared for the changes to her life that a move there would bring. However, in the period since she and the Duke made Barons Court their permanent home in the mid 1970s, the Duchess has made a widely admired and respected contribution to education and in doing so has brought together tens of thousands of schoolchildren from across political and religious divides in Ireland.

Though born in Tucson, Arizona, where her father had moved briefly for health reasons just after the War, Alexandra Anastasia Phillips grew up in Leicestershire with her parents, Lt.-Col. Harold (Bunny) Phillips and his wife Georgina (née Wernher), and four siblings, Nicholas, Fiona, Marita and Natalia. Better known as Sacha, she remembers her father as a great storyteller who loved regaling his children with tales that fed their

Portrait of the Duchess of Abercorn by Derek Hill.

307

Portrait of the Duchess of Abercorn by Evgeny Grouzdev.

imagination. Her formal education began in a school run from a farmhouse by a Mrs Thomas. For the future Duchess, exposed to the routine of farm life, this was an idyllic and formative experience. She then went on to St Mary's, Wantage, before completing three A-levels in a year at a school in Westminster. Following a long trip around South America with her parents, visiting Brazil, Argentina, Chile and Peru, she returned to England and enrolled on a secretarial course at St James' College, London. Later the Duchess would train as a professional counsellor in transpersonal and depth psychology; she has long been an admirer of the psychologist Carl Jung.

The move to Barons Court in the mid 1970s took place at the height of the Northern Irish Troubles when murders and bombings occurred on an almost daily basis. At the age of seven, her daughter Sophie began to have nightmares related to the Troubles. Not only was the Duchess anxious for the well-being of her own daughter, she was also concerned for the many other children in similar circumstances. Though feeling a 'horrifying sense of powerlessness as to what could be done', there was a deep desire to find a means by which children could express their thoughts and feelings creatively. This led to the creation of a project that would encourage creative writing in schoolchildren, the inspiration for it coming from the Duchess' own great-great-great-grandfather, Alexander Pushkin.

From an early age, the Duchess was conscious of her Russian ancestry. A major influence on her life was her maternal grandmother, Lady Zia Wernher, whose parents were Grand Duke Michael Mikhailovich of Russia, grandson of Tsar Nicholas I of Russia, and Countess Sophie Merenberg. Theirs was a morganatic marriage and for this they were banished from Russia, eventually moving to England via Germany. It is through Countess Sophie that the Duchess descends from Pushkin, widely regarded as the greatest of Russia's poets and a man whom she believes 'spoke for the very soul of Russia' and who gave its people a sense of their own literary identity. In February 1987, to mark the 150th anniversary of his death, a major celebration of Pushkin's achievements took place at Luton Hoo, her grandparents' home on the Bedfordshire-Hertfordshire border. She remembers vividly the impact that this event had on her: 'I instantly realised that I must carry its message safely back with me to my home in Northern Ireland to see how it might help the children of our troubled land to find a voice and tell us their story in writing.' Thus, the Pushkin Trust was born.

   With the support of Michael Murphy, the Chief Executive of the Western Education and Library Board, a pilot initiative was developed along the lines of a creative writing competition for poems and short stories. Named the Pushkin Prizes Project, it would have both cross-border and cross-community dimensions to it. In its first year, 1987, eight primary schools participated – four Protestant and four Catholic; four in County Tyrone and four in County Donegal. Shiela McCall, a Field Officer with the Western Board, and Harry Cheevers, a school inspector in Donegal, played an instrumental part in making the initial project a success. In the 27 years since, the work of the Pushkin Trust has witnessed many changes. By the mid 1990s the number of schools taking part had grown to 50, exchange visits involving teachers and pupils in Ireland and Russia had been organised, and a Summer School in Creative Writing for Teachers established. Later a Summer Camp of the Imagination would be held at Barons Court and a Partners in Education Programme founded. In 2002, the Creative Writing Programme was brought to a conclusion; in the 15 years of its existence, over 20,000 children had taken part from nearly every county on the island. In the following year the Pushkin Awards was established with 20 schools taking part in the pilot scheme. Today the focus of the Pushkin Trust is on inspiring educators to find   The Pushkin House

the spirit of Pushkin for themselves so that they can then pass that on to children. The Duchess continues to be deeply involved in the work of the Trust that was created by her vision and nurtured and sustained by her enthusiasm and commitment to its core aims.

The need for a suitable venue for the activities of the Pushkin Trust led to the construction of the most interesting of the recent buildings erected at Barons Court, Pushkin House. In the words of its architect, Richard Pierce, it was to be the 'architectural manifestation of the Pushkin Prizes', a place that would have 'something of a magic of the Pushkin's stories, a stimulation to the imagination.' In 2001, Pierce and the Duchess travelled to Russia looking for inspiration and found it at the Vitoslavlitsy Museum of Wooden Architecture. The reconstructed building that especially resonated with them was an eighteenth-century timber church, St Nicholas, which possessed the internal loftiness of space they wished to recreate in the Pushkin House. On returning from Russia, Pierce designed a dacha-style house that was 'symmetrical on both axes with the central space rising to a square lantern.' The house was built by Jack Lynch and was constructed entirely of wood.

The Duchess has been active in many other cultural and literary initiatives. Reflecting her passion for Russian arts, she is a patron of the Mariinsky Theatre Trust. She is also on the Council of St George's House, Windsor Castle, an organisation formed in 1966 by the Duke of Edinburgh as a forum for the discussion of contemporary issues. She was a governor of Harrow for 10 years. In the aftermath of the Omagh bombing of 1998 she became a trustee of the Northern Ireland Centre for Trauma and Transformation. In 2003, she published *Feather from the Firebird*, a volume of prose poems. In the same year she was awarded an honorary doctorate by the University of Ulster for her services to education through her work with the Pushkin Trust. Further recognition of her unique contribution to education include the Princess Grace Humanitarian Award that was presented to her by the Ireland Fund of Monaco in 2006, and her appointment as an Officer of the Order of the British Empire (OBE) in 2008.

The Marquess and Marchioness of Hamilton, Jamie and Tanya, with their sons, Alfred, Viscount Strabane, and Lord Claud.

Epilogue

In looking back over four centuries, the Duke of Abercorn has a very strong sense of the past, present and future of Barons Court:

> My family has always regarded both living at Barons Court and in Ireland as a real privilege which results in successive generations dedicated to Barons Court and in maintaining the family link with it. Each Duke of Abercorn has considered his tenure as a tenancy for life with the overriding responsibility of passing on the tenancy to the next generation in an improved order, both environmentally and financially.

The story of the Hamiltons of Barons Court has many more years left to run.

Abbreviations

Complete Peerage	G. E. Cokayne (ed.), *The Complete Peerage of England, Scotland, Ireland, Great Britain and the United Kingdom* (13 vols, London, 1910–59)
DIB	*Dictionary of Irish Biography* (9 vols, Cambridge, 2009)
Hamilton, *The days before yesterday*	Lord Frederic Hamilton, *The days before yesterday*: edition published in *The vanished world of yesterday* (London, 1950)
Hamilton, *Here, there and everywhere*	Lord Frederic Hamilton, *Here, there and everywhere*: edition published in *The vanished world of yesterday* (London, 1950)
Hamilton, *Forty years on*	Lord Ernest Hamilton, *Forty years on* (London, 1922)
HMC	Historical Manuscripts Commission
ODNB	*Oxford Dictionary of National Biography* (60 vols, Oxford, 2004)
PRONI	Public Record Office of Northern Ireland
Scots Peerage	J. B. Paul (ed.), *The Scots peerage: founded on Wood's edition of Sir Robert Douglas's Peerage of Scotland; containing an historical and genealogical account of the nobility of that kingdom* (9 vols, Edinburgh, 1904–14)
TCD	Trinity College, Dublin
TNA	The National Archives (London)

Notes

CHAPTER 1: THE SCOTTISH BACKGROUND

1 *Scots Peerage*, i, p. 37.
2 *Complete Peerage*, x, pp. 289–90.
3 Ibid., p. 290.
4 Harry Potter, *Edinburgh under siege, 1571–1573* (Stroud, 2003), p. 24.
5 W. M. Metcalfe, *A history of Paisley, 600–1908* (Paisley, 1909), p. 148.
6 George Hamilton, *A History of the House of Hamilton* (Edinburgh, 1933), p. 32.
7 Metcalfe, *History of Paisley*, p. 148.
8 Ibid., p. 149.
9 *ODNB*.
10 Ibid.
11 Quoted in *ODNB*.
12 Metcalfe, *History of Paisley*, p. 152.
13 *Complete Peerage*, x, p. 291.
14 Another version of this incident is that he was imprisoned in Edinburgh at this time, but was released when concerns were raised that he and his Catholic associates were going to seize the prison.
15 *Scots Peerage*, i, p. 39.
16 *Complete Peerage*, x, p. 291.
17 Metcalfe, *History of Paisley*, p. 194.
18 *Complete Peerage*, x, p. 292.
19 *The Peerage of Scotland* (Edinburgh, 1813), i, p. 1.
20 *ODNB*.

CHAPTER 2: THE SEVENTEENTH CENTURY

1 Michael Perceval Maxwell, *The Scottish migration to Ulster in the reign of James I* (London, 1973), p. 99.
2 Ibid., p. 123.
3 Ibid., p. 282.
4 Ibid., p. 302.
5 Raymond Gillespie, *Colonial Ulster: the settlement of east Ulster, 1600–1641* (Cork, 1985), p. 72.
6 Perceval Maxwell, *Scottish migration*, Ibid., pp. 161–2.
7 Ibid., p. 326.
8 George Hill, *An historical account of the plantation in Ulster at the commencement of the seventeenth century* (Belfast, 1877), p. 527.
9 Perceval Maxwell, *Scottish migration*, pp. 235–7.
10 Dawson Turner, *Descriptive Index of the Contents of Five Manuscript Volumes: Illustrative of the History of Great Britain, in the Library of Dawson Turner* (Sloman, 1851), p. 150.
11 An abstract of Mayerne's medical report was contained in a letter from Norman Moore MD to the Duchess of Abercorn, dated 21 Sept. 1906 (PRONI, D623/A/337A).
12 George Hill, *The Montgomery Manuscripts* (Belfast, 1869), p. 72, n. 11; George Hill, *The MacDonnells of Antrim* (Belfast, 1873), p. 233, n. 73.
13 'Extracts from the obituary of Robert Boyd of Trochrig' in *The Bannatyne Miscellany* (Edinburgh, 1827), i, p. 289; Abercorn's date of death was given in this account as 2 April.
14 Perceval Maxwell, *Scottish migration*, p. 107.
15 Sir William Fraser, *Memoirs of the Maxwells of Pollok* (2 vols, Edinburgh, 1863), i, p. 48, ii, p. 247.
16 Henrietta Haynes, *Henrietta Maria* (London, 1912), p. 121.
17 Ibid., pp. 163–4.
18 *Notes & Queries*, no. 14 (2 February 1850), p. 216; 'There is in the possession of an old lady living at Durham, in 1836, an original note in the handwriting of King Charles the Second, of which the following is a copy.'

19 Ibid.
20 Jane H. Ohlmeyer, *Civil War and Restoration in the Three Stuart Kingdoms. The political career of Randal MacDonnell, Marquis of Antrim* (Cambridge, 1993), pp. 26, 28.
21 National Records of Scotland, GD406/1/3184.
22 Ibid., GD406/1/7151.
23 Ibid., GD406/1/6840.
24 Fraser, *Maxwells of Pollok*, ii, pp. 217–18.
25 Ibid., ii, p. 254.
26 Ibid., ii, p. 268.
27 Bodleian Library, Oxford, Carte Ms 30, fol. 625.
28 Ibid., fol. 609.
29 Ibid., fol. 621.
30 *Calendar of the state papers relating to Ireland [CSPI], 1625–32*, pp. 510–13.
31 John Spalding, *The History of the Troubles and Memorable Transactions in Scotland from the year 1624 to 1645* (2 vols, Aberdeen, 1792), i, p. 19.
32 National Records of Scotland, GD75/667.
33 J. Lodge, *The peerage of Ireland*, revised, enlarged and continued to the present time by Mervyn Archdall (7 vols, London, 1789), v, 114. J. Graham, *Derriana* (Londonderry, 1823), p. 35.
34 *Extracts from the Presbytery book of Strathbogie* (Aberdeen, 1843), pp. xviii–xix.
35 David Stevenson, *Scottish Covenanters and Irish Confederates* (Belfast, 1981), p. 276.
36 *CSPI*, 1647–60, p. 628.
37 Bodleian Library, Oxford, Carte Ms 41, fol. 648.
38 HMC *Ormonde manuscripts*, new series, vi, p. 486.
39 National Records of Scotland, GD406/1/6185, /6242, / 7806, /10375.
40 *An account of a late engagement at sea* (London, 1691).
41 PRONI D623/B/4/38, 39; *The Case of the Earl and Countess of Abercorn* (no date [c. 1692]).
42 TCD, Ms 750/1/77, King to John Hough, bishop of Oxford, 8 June 1697.
43 Ibid.
44 *The Post Boy*, 10–13 April 1697.
45 PRONI, D623/B/4/44; *Complete Peerage*, i, p. 5; Nottingham University Library, Department of Manuscripts and Special Collections, Me C 4/2/5, Peter Mews to Edward Mellish, 22 July 1697; TCD Ms 750/1/77, William King to John Hough, bishop of Oxford, 8 June 1697.
46 National Records of Scotland, GD406/1/4510.
47 TCD, Ms 750/2/3/14-5, King to Robert Huntington, bishop of Raphoe, 24 June 1701; TNA (London), PROB/11/477.
48 Bodleian Library, Oxford, Carte Ms 42, fol. 210.
49 Ibid., Carte Ms 214, fol. 192r–v.
50 Ibid., Carte Ms 232, fol. 11–12.

CHAPTER 3: THE 6TH EARL

1 To quote Anthony Malcomson in his 'Introduction' to the Abercorn papers in PRONI.
2 PRONI, D623/A/5/10.
3 HMC, *Egmont manuscripts*, i, p. 458.
4 Malcomson, 'Introduction'.
5 The marriage licence was dated 24 January, though according to the bride's father the marriage took place on 21 January. Elizabeth was only in her mid-teens when she married Hamilton.
6 Lady Mary Baillie Hamilton, 'The later Earls of Abercorn and Captain the Hon. John Hamilton, R.N.' (unpublished typescript in the possession of the Duke of Abercorn; no date, but early twentieth century), p. 2.
7 Or Lord Hamilton of Bellamont.
8 *Scots Peerage*, i, p. 58.

9 Patrick Macrory, *The Siege of Derry* (London, 1980), p. 162.
10 W. R. Young, *Fighters of Derry, Their Deeds and Descendents, Being a Chronicle of Events in Ireland during the Revolutionary Period, 1688–91* (London, 1932), p. 230.
11 Edith Mary Johnston-Liik, *History of the Irish Parliament* (6 vols, Belfast, 2002), iv, pp. 340–1.
12 Patrick Walsh, *The Making of the Irish Protestant Ascendancy: the life of William Conolly, 1662–1729* (Woodbridge, 2010), pp. 30–1.
13 Shropshire Record Office, Ms 112/1/1661, Lord Rochester to the Hon. Richard Hill, 23 Sept. 1701.
14 PRONI, D1854/2/29a.
15 Toby Barnard, *A New anatomy of Ireland: the Irish Protestants, 1649–1770* (New Haven, 2004), p. 239.
16 PRONI, MIC/1/35.
17 PRONI, D623/A/5/10, Abercorn to Mr Nisbitt, 15 Jan. 1732–3.
18 PRONI, D623/A/5/1.
19 TCD, Ms 883/2.
20 PRONI, D623/A/5/1.
21 *Precedents and abstracts from the journals of the Trustees of the linen and hempen manufactures of Ireland* (Dublin, 1784), p. 2; HMC, *Egmont manuscripts*, ii, pp. 115–16.
22 TCD, Ms 1995–2008/1120, Abercorn to King, 20 Oct. 1704.
23 A. P. W. Malcomson, 'The politics of "natural right": the Abercorn family and Strabane borough' in G. A. Hayes-McCoy (ed.), *Historical Studies*, x (Galway, 1976), Malcomson, 'Politics of "Natural Right"', pp. 46–7.
24 David Hayton (ed) *The Letters of Marmaduke Coghill, 1722–1738* (Dublin, 2005), p. 162.
25 W. Graham (ed.), *The letters of Joseph Addison* (Oxford, 1941), pp. 137–8.
26 Graham, *Letters of Joseph Addison*, Addison, pp. 137–8.
27 C. I. McGrath, *The making of the eighteenth-century Irish constitution*, (Dublin, 2000), pp. 229–30.
28 *Journal to Stella*, Letter 10.
29 Ibid., Letter 22.
30 Malcomson, 'Politics of "natural right"', p. 46.
31 PRONI, D/623/A/3/2.
32 Johnston-Liik, *History of the Irish Parliament*, iv, p. 341.
33 PRONI, D623/A/3/2.
34 HMC, *Egmont manuscripts*, ii, pp. 115–16.
35 PRONI, D623/A/3/12.
36 PRONI, D623/A/3/17.
37 Sean Connolly, *Religion, law and power: the making of Protestant Ireland, 1660–1760* (Oxford, 1992), pp. 253–4.
38 HMC, *Ormonde manuscripts*, new series, viii, p. 242.
39 *ODNB*.
40 Clyve Jones, '"This Waye of Proceeding would Remoove the Umbrage, and Uneasynesse, of Courte, and Country Heere": The Earl of Abercorn's 1708 Scheme for Reforming the Election of the Scottish Representative Peers', *The Scottish Historical Review*, vol. 86 (April 2007), pp. 27–49.
41 National Records of Scotland, GD406/1/5857.
42 Ibid., GD406/1/7464.
43 *Journal to Stella*, Letter 43.
44 *Scots Peerage*, i, p. 59.
45 National Records of Scotland, GD406/1/8135.
46 Ibid., GD406/1/11818.
47 *Journal to Stella*, Letter 58.
48 PRONI, D623/A/3/16.
49 PRONI, D623/A/3/16.
50 R. E. Burns, *Irish parliamentary politics in the eighteenth century* (2 vols, Washington DC, 1989), pp. 120–23.
51 *ODNB*.
52 HMC, *Egmont manuscripts*, i, p. 372, ii, p. 135.
53 TCD, Ms 2537/151–2, 21 Aug. 1724.
54 HMC, *Egmont manuscripts*, i, pp. 103, 412.
55 Ibid., ii, p. 135.

CHAPTER 4: THE 7TH EARL

1 HMC, *Portland manuscripts*, iv, p. 118.
2 Daniel Defoe, *A Tour Thro' the Whole Island of Great Britain* (London, 1724), p. 16.
3 H. E. Samuel, 'John Sigismond Cousser in London and Dublin' in *Music & Letters*, 61, no. 2 (Apr. 1980), p. 161.
4 C. W. Hughes, 'John Christopher Pepusch' in *The Musical Quarterly*, 31, no. 1 (Jan. 1945), pp. 62–3.
5 HMC, *Egmont manuscripts*, ii, p. 155. The piece was in fact banned until after 1771.
6 L. E. Miller, 'Rameau and the Royal Society of London: new letters and documents' in *Music & Letters*, 66, no. 1 (Jan. 1985), p. 21.
7 In 1751, his nephew, the 8th Earl, explained that Charles was always with his, i.e. the 8th Earl's, grandmother, who was so old he could not leave her (PRONI, D623/A/14/49).
8 *ODNB*.
9 Count Frederick Kielmansegge, *Diary of a journey to England in the years 1761–1762* (London, 1902), p. 55–7.
10 Peter Cunningham (ed.), *The Letters of Horace Walpole, Earl of Orford* (London, 1859), ix, p. 68.
11 PRONI, D623/A/7/1, /9/1.
12 PRONI, D623/A/8/23.

CHAPTER 5: THE 8TH EARL

1 Lady Mary Baillie Hamilton, 'The later Earls of Abercorn and Captain the Hon. John Hamilton, R.N.' (unpublished typescript in the possession of the Duke of Abercorn; no date, but early twentieth century), p. 24.
2 Published in London in 1813.
3 Baillie Hamilton, 'The later Earls of Abercorn', p. 24.
4 A. P. W. Malcomson, *Pursuit of the heiress: aristocratic marriage in Ireland, 1740–1840* (Belfast, 2006), p. 234.
5 Baillie Hamilton, 'The later Earls of Abercorn', p. 23.
6 PRONI, D623/A/12/19, Abercorn to John McClintock, 21 Aug. 1745.
7 PRONI, D623/A/12/15, Abercorn to William Edie, 1 June 1745.
8 PRONI, D623/A/23/47, Abercorn to James Hamilton, 26 May 1778.
9 PRONI, D623/A/17/12, Abercorn to John Sinclair, 24 Feb. 1761.
10 PRONI, D623/A/24/92, Abercorn to James Hamilton, 13 March 1781.
11 PRONI, D623/A/23/7, Abercorn to James Hamilton, 10 Jan. 1778.
12 PRONI, D623/A/26/137, Abercorn to James Hamilton, [?] Feb. 1787.
13 PRONI, D623/A/12/65, Abercorn to John Colhoun, 17 Nov. 1747.
14 PRONI, D623/A/20/69, Abercorn to James Hamilton, 6 June 1771; /23/22, same to same, 7 March 1778.
15 PRONI, D623/A/21/54, Abercorn to James Blair, 18 Sept. 1773.
16 PRONI, D623/A/14/84, Abercorn to Rev. Dr Pelisser, 1 Aug. 1753.
17 W. H. Crawford, *The management of a major Ulster estate in the late eighteenth century: the eighth earl of Abercorn and his Irish agents* (Dublin, 2001), p. 7.
18 Malcomson, 'Politics of "Natural Right"', pp. 43–81.
19 PRONI, D623/A/12/46, Abercorn to Nathaniel Nisbitt, 3 March 1747.
20 PRONI, D623/A/36/165, Inhabitants of Strabane to Abercorn, n.d. [*c.* Oct. 1764].

21 Malcomson, 'Politics of "natural right"', p. 58.
22 PRONI, D623/A/24/26, Abercorn to James Hamilton, 7 Nov. 1779.
23 PRONI, D623/A/13/89, Abercorn to Mr Hamilton of 'Donemanagh', no date.
24 PRONI, D623/A/14/15, Abercorn to John Colhoun, 7 May 1751.
25 PRONI, Abercorn to John Hamilton, 13 July 1768.
26 Baillie Hamilton, 'The later Earls of Abercorn', pp. 61–4.
27 Ibid., p. 55.
28 Ibid., pp. 55–9.
29 Ibid., p. 59.
30 PRONI, D623/A/23/23, Abercorn to Mrs Cameron, 10 March 1778.
31 Baillie Hamilton, 'The later Earls of Abercorn', p. 28.
32 Ibid., p. 31, quoting from *The Argus*.
33 Ibid., p. 37; in 1874 the Duke of Abercorn sold this estate and a large part of Easter Duddingston to the Benhar Cal Company for *c*. £150,000.
34 John Connachan-Holmes, *Country Houses of Scotland* (Colonsay, 1995), pp. 58–60.
35 PRONI, D623/A/17/125, Abercorn to Walter Scott, 8 Oct. 1764.
36 Baillie Hamilton, 'The later Earls of Abercorn', p. 50.
37 Metcalfe, *History of Paisley*, p. 367.
38 Baillie Hamilton, 'The later Earls of Abercorn', p. 52.
39 Alistair Rowan, *The Buildings of Ireland: North West Ulster* (Harmondsworth, 1979) p. 133.
40 PRONI, D623/A/12/8, Abercorn to Colhoun, 26 Feb. 1745.
41 PRONI, D623/A/12/9, Abercorn to Colhoun, 7 March 1745.
42 PRONI, D623/A/13/28, Abercorn to Colhoun, 28 Jan. 1747.
43 PRONI, D623/A/12/63, to James Broomfield, 22 Oct. 1747.
44 In October 1750 Abercorn discovered that Broomfield had disposed of whatever property he had in Scotland and returned to Strabane.
45 PRONI, D623/A/18/90, Abercorn to James Hamilton, 12 April 1767.
46 PRONI, D623/A/23/117, Abercorn to Arthur Pomeroy, 16 March 1779.
47 Rowan, *North West Ulster*, p. 131.
48 Ibid.
49 Baillie Hamilton, 'The later Earls of Abercorn', p. 69.
50 Ibid., p. 70. Mary Baillie Hamilton suggests that, from the length of time between his death and burial, his body may have been embalmed.
51 Baillie Hamilton, 'The later Earls of Abercorn', p. 73.
52 Malcomson, 'Politics of "Natural Right"', p. 67.
53 *Statistical account of Scotland*, xviii (Edinburgh, 1796), p. 379.
54 *The Peerage of Ireland* (Dublin, 1789), v, p. 125.
55 *The Scots Magazine*, xvii (1755), p. 611.
56 Sir James Prior, *Life of Edmond Malone, Editor of Shakspeare* (London, 1860), ii, p. 405.

CHAPTER 6: THE 1ST MARQUESS

1 A. P. W. Malcomson, 'A lost natural leader: John James Hamilton, First Marquess of Abercorn (1756–1818)', *Proceedings of the Royal Irish Academy*, 88C, no. 4 (1988), p. 66.
2 A. P. W. Malcomson, 'The Gentle Leviathan: Arthur Hill, second marquess of Downshire, 1753–1801', Peter Roebuck (ed.), *Plantation to Partition: Essays in Ulster History in Honour of J.L. McCracken* (Belfast, 1981), p. 108.
3 Lord Ernest Hamilton, *Old Days and New* (London, n.d. [*c*. 1922]), p. 23.
4 As the Marquess of Abercorn was in the habit of describing the Stuarts.
5 Malcomson, 'A lost natural leader', p. 67.
6 Hamilton, *Old Days and New*, p. 25.
7 PRONI, D2433/D/5/2.
8 Lady Mary Baillie Hamilton, 'John James, 1st Marquess of Abercorn, K.G.' (unpublished typescript in the possession of the Duke of Abercorn; no date, but early twentieth century), p. 20.
9 East Looe was possessed at this time by the Buller family who were related to the Copleys.
10 Baillie Hamilton, 'John James, 1st Marquess', p. 23.
11 Ibid., p. 24.
12 Sir N. W. Wraxall, *Posthumous Memoirs of His Own Time* (London, 1836), i, pp. 61–2.
13 PRONI, Pitt to Abercorn, D623/A/226/13.
14 Wraxall, *Posthumous memoirs*, pp. 6–56.
15 *The Quarterly Review*, vol. lvii, no. cxiv (Sept. & Dec. 1836), pp. 453–5.
16 Baillie Hamilton, 'John James, 1st Marquess', p. 39.
17 Malcomson, 'A lost natural leader', p. 69.
18 Baillie Hamilton, 'John James, 1st Marquess', pp. 46–7.
19 Malcomson, 'A lost natural leader', p. 65.
20 PRONI, T2541/IK/11, p. 12, Abercorn to Henry Pomeroy, 19 Feb. 1790.
21 PRONI, D623/A/75/9, Abercorn, to the Rt Hon. Robert Hobart [Dec. 1789–Jan. 1790].
22 A lease for lives was one that would not expire until the last of the individuals named in the lease as lives had died.
23 PRONI, D623/A/76/2, Abercorn to Thomas Knox, 5 Jan. 1792.
24 Thomas Bartlett (ed.), *Life of Theobald Wolfe Tone* (Dublin, 1998), p. 171.
25 Marianne Elliott, *Wolfe Tone: Prophet of Irish Independence* (New Haven, 1989), pp. 201–02.
26 Malcomson, 'A lost natural leader', p. 78.
27 *The Morning Post or Dublin Courant*, 14 Sept. 1793.
28 Quoted in Malcomson, 'A lost natural leader', p. 79.
29 PRONI, D3030/T/3.
30 Quoted in Malcomson, 'A lost natural leader', p. 66.
31 *The Journal of Elizabeth Lady Holland (1791–1811), edited by the Earl of Ilchester* (London, 1908), ii, p. 67.
32 Peter Marson, *Belmore: the Lowry Corrys of Castle Coole, 1646–1913* (Belfast, 2007), p. 82.
33 Malcomson, 'A lost natural leader', p. 81.
34 D623/A/76/14, Abercorn to Thomas Knox, 5 Feb. 1792.
35 *Complete Peerage*, i, p. 7.
36 Wraxall, *Posthumous memoirs*, p. 64.
37 Baillie Hamilton, 'John James, 1st Marquess', p. 40.
38 Ibid., p. 48.
39 Quoted in Malcomson, 'A lost natural leader', p. 70.
40 Ibid., p. 70 (Lord to Lady Minto).
41 Baillie Hamilton, 'John James, 1st Marquess', p. 65.
42 Cecil died in 1819. She bore Copley two daughters, Elizabeth Mary and Maria, the latter of whom married the 3rd Earl Grey.
43 W. A. Maguire, *Captain Cohonny: Constantine Maguire of Tempo, 1777–1834* (Belfast, 2002), p. 12.
44 Lawrence was paid £50 for the painting.
45 Cassandra Albinson, Peter Funnell, Lucy Peltz (eds), *Thomas Lawrence: Regency Power and Brilliance* (New Haven, 2010), p. 12.
46 Maguire, *Captain Cohonny*, p. 17.
47 PRONI, D623/A/337A.
48 Quoted in Desmond Murphy, *Derry, Donegal, and Modern Ulster: 1790-1921* (Derry, 1981), pp. 35–6.
49 Quoted in Marson, *Belmore*, p. 97.
50 Marson, *Belmore*, p. 109.
51 PRONI, T3030/7/26, Redesdale to Perceval, 4 Nov. 1804.
52 Johnston-Liik, *History of the Irish Parliament*, iv, pp. 234–6, vi, p. 342.

53 A. P. W. Malcomson, *John Foster: The Politics of the Anglo-Irish Ascendancy* (Belfast, 1978), pp. 314–15.
54 Quoted in Malcomson, 'A lost natural leader', p. 84.
55 PRONI, T3456/6, Abercorn to William Pitt, 15 Jan. 1805.
56 Quoted in Hamilton, *Old Days and New*, p. 35.
57 Joan Haslip, *Lady Hester Stanhope* (London, 1934), p. 34.
58 Malcomson, 'A lost natural leader', p. 81.
59 PRONI, T2627/3/2/295.
60 PRONI, D623/A/75/96, Abercorn to George Steuart, 14 Jan. 1791.
61 PRONI, D623/A/87/20, Hamilton jun. to Abercorn, 14 May 1791.
62 PRONI, D623/A/87/22, Hamilton jun. to Abercorn, 29 May 1791.
63 PRONI, D623/A/108/9 Galbraith to Abercorn, 15 Dec. 1796.
64 PRONI, D623/A/89/15, Hamilton jun. to Abercorn, 15 December 1796.
65 PRONI, D623/A/80/30, Abercorn to Stewart, 23 Dec. 1796.
66 PRONI, D623/A/84/3, Abercorn to Burgoyne, 6 Dec. 1808.
67 PRONI, D623/A/124/32, Burgoyne to Abercorn, 12 August 1810.
68 PRONI, D623/A/125/16, Burgoyne to Abercorn, 11 April 1811.
69 PRONI, T3472/3/9, Abercorn to Aberdeen, 24 Dec. 1813.
70 *The Beauties of England and Wales*, x, pt iv (London, 1816), p. 678.
71 Hamilton, *Old days and new*, p. 38.
72 *Beauties of England and Wales*, p. 679.
73 PRONI, T3472/3/7, Abercorn to Aberdeen, 14 Oct. 1813.
74 PRONI, D623/A/226/2, O'Byrne to Abercorn, 8 Dec. 1789.
75 Albinson, Funnell, Peltz (eds), *Thomas Lawrence*, pp. 2, 10, 196.
76 PRONI, D623/A/227/35, James Durno to Sir William Hamilton, 16 Dec. 1791.
77 PRONI, D623/A/75/198, Abercorn to Thomas Knox, 16 Dec. 1791.
78 Sholto and Reuben Percy, *The Percy Anecdotes* (London, 1826), xiii, p. 38.
79 Baillie Hamilton, 'John James, 1st Marquess', p. 47.
80 Hamilton, *Old days and new*, p. 38.
81 Malcomson, *Pursuit of the heiress*, p. 33.
82 *The Miscellaneous Prose Works of Sir Walter Scott* (Edinburgh, 1835), xx, pp. 182–3.

CHAPTER 7: THE 1ST DUKE

1 PRONI, D623/A/85/52, Abercorn to Eliot, 28 Sept. 1812.
2 PRONI, D623/A/247/16; the letter is undated, but postmarked 15 Dec. 1817.
3 Hamilton, *Forty years on*, pp. 34–5.
4 G. W. E. Russell, *Portraits of the seventies* (Dublin, 1916), p. 254.
5 PRONI, D623/A/252/8, Aberdeen to Abercorn, no date [*c.* 1829].
6 *The Times*, 23 Feb. 1832.
7 Ibid., 18 March 1833.
8 PRONI, D3007/H/6/13, Belmore to Wellington, 16 Nov. 1829.
9 T2772/2/6/23.
10 *Belfast Newsletter*, 10 Jan. 1837.
11 PRONI, D623/A/254/4, Aberdeen to Abercorn, 14 Jan. 1837.
12 Hansard: House of Commons Debates, vol. 26, col. 276.
13 PRONI, D3007/H/14/31.
14 PRONI, D3007/H/7/25.
15 PRONI, DIO/4/11/12/1.
16 PRONI, D623/A/251/6, Abercorn to Duchess of Bedford, n.d.
17 W. V. Monypenny and G. E. Buckle, *The life of Benjamin Disraeli* (London, 1929), ii, p. 498.

18 Hamilton, *Days before yesterday*, pp. 307–08.
19 Hamilton, *Forty Years On*, p. 35.
20 *Morning Post*, 6 July 1853.
21 Hamilton, *Forty Years On*, p. 37.
22 PRONI, D623/A/283/1.
23 *The Times*, 1 April 1905.
24 Ibid.
25 *Days before yesterday*, p. 42.
26 PRONI, D623/A/310/14, Lady Abercorn to Abercorn, 8 May 1875.
27 Hamilton, *Days before yesterday*, pp. 43–4.
28 *Ordnance Survey Memoirs, County Tyrone*, vol. 5, p. 10.
29 PRONI, D623/A/267/1-25.
30 See his three articles on 'Baronscourt, Co. Tyrone' in *Country Life*, 12, 19 and 26 July 1979.
31 Henry Heaney (ed.), *A Scottish Whig in Ireland, 1835–38: the Irish journals of Robert Graham of Redgorton* (Dublin, 1999), p. 306.
32 PRONI, D623/A/266/1-25.
33 PRONI, T1282/1.
34 *DIB*.
35 Malcomson, 'Introduction' to the Abercorn Papers in PRONI.
36 *Belfast Newsletter*, 13 Feb. 1846.
37 Hamilton, *Days before yesterday*, p. 31.
38 *Leaves from the journal of our life in the Highlands, from 1848–1861: To which are prefixed and added extracts from the same journal giving an account of earlier visits to Scotland, and tours in England and Ireland, and yachting excursions*, edited by Sir Arthur Helps (London, 1868), p. 88.
39 Hamilton, *Days before yesterday*, pp. 37–8.
40 PRONI, D623/A/257/12.
41 Hamilton, *Days before yesterday*, p. 37.
42 Lord George Hamilton, *Parliamentary reminiscences and reflections, 1886–1906* (London, 1922), p. 5.
43 PRONI, D623/A/269/1, Humphreys to Abercorn, 19 Jan. 1841.
44 Norfolk Record Office, MC 97/150, 541X7; this purchase comprised the properties of Dale Park, Tortington and Eastergate, though collectively they were frequently referred to simply as Dale Park.
45 PRONI, D623/A/278/9, Froggatt to Humphreys, 18 July 1849.
46 PRONI, D623/A/279/9.
47 PRONI, D623/A/271/1, /4, /5.
48 PRONI, D623/A/269/7.
49 PRONI, D623/A/278/1.
50 PRONI, D623/A/276/7.
51 PRONI, D623/A/276/24.
52 PRONI, D623/A/278/15.
53 London Metropolitan Archives, ACC/0502/027.
54 *The Times*, 13 April and 30 April 1853.
55 PRONI, D623/A/269/33.
56 PRONI, D623/A/269/34.
57 PRONI, D623/A/281/37.
58 PRONI, D623/A/269/59.
59 James Hamilton, *Consultation pour James Hamilton, marquis d'Abercorn ... contre le duc d'Hamilton. Maintien et confirmation du titre héréditaire de duc de Châtellerault* (Paris, 1865).
60 PRONI, D1551/19.
61 PRONI, D623/E/5, pp. 16–17.
62 S. M. Hussey, *Reminiscences of an Irish land agent* (London, 1904), p. 165.
63 PRONI, D623/A/299/1–3.
64 G. E. Buckle (ed.), *The letters of Queen Victoria*, 2nd series (3 vols, London, 1926–28 i, p. 352.
65 Hamilton, *Parliamentary reminiscences and reflections*, p. 5.
66 Hamilton, *Days before yesterday*, pp. 94–6.

67 *Freeman's Journal*, 28 May 1867.
68 PRONI, D623/A/309/16, Cullen to Abercorn.
69 PRONI, D623/A/311/32, Disraeli to Abercorn, 28 Feb. 1868.
70 Quoted in James H. Murphy, *Abject loyalty: Nationalism and Monarchy in Ireland During the Reign of Queen Victoria* (Washington, 2001), p. 163.
71 PRONI, D623/A/306/7, copy letter to Abercorn from Lord Mayo, 4 March 1868.
72 PRONI, D623/A/306/10.
73 PRONI, D623/A/327/42.
74 Peter Galloway, *The Most Illustrious Order of St Patrick* (Phillimore, 1983), pp. 29–33.
75 Hamilton, *Days before yesterday*, pp. 99–100.
76 Quoted in Desmond Bowen, *Paul, Cardinal Cullen and the shaping of modern Irish Catholicism* (Dublin, 1983), p. 143.
77 James H. Murphy, 'Fashioning the famine Queen' in Peter Gray (ed.), *Victoria's Ireland? Irishness and Britishness, 1837–1901* (Dublin, 2004), p. 19.
78 Murphy, *Abject loyalty*, p. 166.
79 PRONI, D623/A/306/21.
80 PRONI, D623/A/257/15.
81 *Belfast Newsletter*, 6 April 1868.
82 PRONI, D623/A/311/48, Disraeli to Abercorn, 26 July 1868.
83 It was actually the Duke of Edinburgh who held the earldom of Ulster, not the Prince of Wales.
84 W. V. Monypenny and G. E. Buckle, *The life of Benjamin Disraeli* (London, 1929), p. 414.
85 Hamilton, *Parliamentary Reminiscences and Reflections*, p. 6.
86 Joseph Robins, *Champagne and silver buckles: the viceregal court at Dublin Castle, 1700–1922* (Dublin, 2001), pp. 134–5.
87 Mrs George Cornwallis-West, *The reminiscences of Lady Randolph Churchill* (London, 1908), p. 72.
88 Quoted in Robins, *Champagne and silver buckles*, pp. 134–5.
89 Monypenny and Buckle, *Life of Benjamin Disraeli*, ii, p. 576.
90 *The Times*, 16 Oct. 1829.
91 Eleanor Alexander (ed.), *Primate Alexander, Archbishop of Armagh: a memoir* (London, 1913), pp. 146–7.
92 Buckle (ed.), *Letters of Queen Victoria*, i, p. 611.
93 PRONI, D2777/8/55.
94 PRONI, D2777/8/56.
95 R. B. McDowell, *The Church of Ireland, 1869–1969* (London, 1975), p. 56.
96 PRONI, D623/A/322/1.
97 PRONI, D4160/K/22.
98 Christopher Tyerman, *A history of Harrow School, 1324–1991* (Oxford, 2000), pp. 426–7.
99 *The Times*, 16 June 1871.
100 Hamilton, *Forty years on*, p. 35.
101 PRONI, D623/B/8/47.
102 Hamilton, *Forty years on*, p. 108.
103 Ibid. p. 109.
104 R. W. Kirkpatrick, 'Origins and development of the land war in mid-Ulster' in F. S. L. Lyons and R. A. J. Hawkins (ed.), *Ireland under the union: varieties of tension* (Oxford, 1980), pp. 208–9.
105 *Belfast Newsletter*, 4 Dec. 1855.
106 Lowry-Corry was First Lord of the Admiralty, while Hamilton had been Treasurer of the Household.
107 Hamilton, *Days before yesterday*, p. 36.
108 B. M. Walker, *Ulster Politics: the formative years, 1868–86* (Belfast, 1989), p. 85.
109 PRONI, D3007/P/17
110 PRONI, D3007/P/28, Abercorn to Belmore, 15 March 1873.
111 PRONI, D3007/P/101, Abercorn to Belmore, 4 April 1873.
112 PRONI, D3007/P/66, J. F. Lowry to Belmore, 23 March 1873.
113 PRONI, D3007/P/101, Abercorn to Belmore, 4 April 1873.

114 All election results are taken from B. M. Walker, *Parliamentary election results in Ireland, 1801–1922* (Dublin, 1978).
115 PRONI, D3007/P/137, Disraeli to Belmore, 28 Jan. 1874.
116 PRONI, D3007/P/139, H. W. Lowry-Corry to Belmore, 29 Jan. 1874.
117 PRONI, D3007/P/158, Lowry-Corry to Belmore, 16 Feb. 1874.
118 PRONI, D3007/P/162, R. Lowry to Belmore, 15 July 1875.
119 PRONI, D623/A/319/3.
120 PRONI, D623/A/319/4, Disraeli to Abercorn, 24 Feb. 1874.
121 *Irish Times*, 21 April 1874.
122 PRONI, D623/A/310/4, Lady Abercorn to Abercorn, 11 April 1875.
123 Hamilton, *Parliamentary reminiscences and reflections*, p. 112.
124 Ibid., p. 113.
125 PRONI, D623/A/310/38, Duchess of Abercorn to Abercorn, 15 Feb. 1876.
126 *Essex Standard*, 26 Dec. 1885.
127 Monypenny and Buckle, *Life of Benjamin Disraeli*, ii, 730.
128 *Jackson's Oxford Journal*, 28 Oct. 1876.
129 PRONI, D623/A/322/7.
130 PRONI, D623/E/5, p. 25.
131 Hamilton, *Forty years on*, p. 49.
132 K. Marx and F. Engels, *Selected correspondence, 1846–1895* (New York, 1942), p. 228.
133 Margaret Dixon McDougall, *The Letters of 'Norah' on her tour through Ireland* (Montreal, 1882; reprinted 2004), p. 78.
134 Hamilton, *Forty years on*, p. 42.
135 Monypenny and Buckle, *Life of Benjamin Disraeli*, ii, 1310.
136 Hamilton, *Days before yesterday*, p. 303.
137 *Belfast Newsletter*, 26 Oct. 1882.
138 *The Times*, 4 January 1882.
139 George Earle Buckle (ed.), *The letters of Queen Victoria* (2nd series, London, 1928), iii, p. 257.
140 *Freeman's Journal*, 7 Nov. 1883.
141 Buckle (ed.), *Letters of Queen Victoria*, iii, p. 706.
142 *The Times*, 2 Nov. 1885.
143 Hamilton, *Forty years on*, p. 43.
144 Ibid pp. 300–2.
145 Hamilton, *Here, there and everywhere*, p. 736.
146 *Liverpool Mercury*, 26 Nov. 1885.
147 *The Times*, 27 Jan. 1925.
148 PRONI, D623/A/313/14.
149 *ODNB*.
150 PRONI, T2996/3/1.
151 John Waters Kirwan, *My Life's Adventure* (1936), p. 143.
152 *Tyrone Constitution*, 4 Dec. 1885.
153 Hamilton, *Forty Years On*, pp 211-2.
154 Ibid, p. 203.
155 David Cannadine, *The Decline and Fall of the British Aristocracy* (New Haven, 1990), p. 193.
156 Hamilton, *The Days Before Yesterday*, p. 123.
157 W. V. Monypenny and G. E. Buckle, *The life of Benjamin Disraeli* (London, 1929), ii, p. 498.
158 G. W. E. Russell, *Half lengths* (London, 1913) p. 96.
159 *The Times*, 18 March 1912.
160 A. L. Rowse, *The later Churchills* (London, 1958), p. 253.
161 Anne Jordan, *Love well the hour: the life of Lady Colin Campbell* (Leicester, 2010), pp 43–4.
162 Allen Horstman, *Victorian Divorce* (London, 1985), pp 135–6.
163 *The Times*, 9 January 1932.

CHAPTER 8: THE 2ND DUKE

1 Buckle (ed.), *Letters of Queen Victoria*, 2nd series, ii, pp. 201–2.
2 PRONI, D623/A/327/39.
3 Murphy, *Abject loyalty*, p. 164.

4 Hamilton, *Days before yesterday*, pp. 82–3.
5 *Belfast Newsletter*, 18 July 1860.
6 *Caledonian Mercury*, 11 Nov. 1864. Miss Coane was Ellen Coane who married Patrick Donnelly from Omagh in Killybegs on 11 Oct. 1864.
7 Walker, *Ulster Politics*, p. 55.
8 Ibid., p. 120.
9 Ibid., p. 129.
10 Ibid., p. 132.
11 A. B. Cooke, 'Sir Stafford Northcote's diary of a visit to the province in October 1883' in *Proceedings of the Royal Irish Academy*, lxxv, sec. C, no. 4 (1975), p. 66.
12 *Belfast Newsletter*, 3 Jan. 1880.
13 Ibid., 8 April 1880.
14 *Irish Times*, 29 May 1880.
15 *Belfast Newsletter*, 10 Aug. 1885.
16 PRONI, D623/A/331/20.
17 *Tyrone Constitution*, 4 Dec. 1885.
18 PRONI, T2996/1/64.
19 D.C. Savage, 'The Origins of the Ulster Unionist Party, 1885–6' in *Irish Historical Studies*, xii no. 47, (March 1961), p. 194.
20 *Tyrone Constitution*, 15 Jan. 1886.
21 Savage, 'Origins of the Ulster Unionist Party', p. 199.
22 Ibid., p. 187.
23 *Belfast Newsletter*, 3 March 1886.
24 *The Times*, 23 June 1886.
25 PRONI, D2396/3/11.
26 *Freeman's Journal*, 14 Aug. 1886.
27 Alvin Jackson, *The Ulster Party: Irish Unionists in the House of Commons, 1884–1911* (Oxford, 1989), p. 205.
28 PRONI, Montgomery Papers, D627/428/40, E. T. Herdman to Hugh de Fellenberg Montgomery, 20 March 1888.
29 Hamilton, *Forty years on*, p. 203.
30 Quoted in Jackson, *Ulster Party*, pp. 127–8.
31 Cannadine, *The decline and fall of the British aristocracy*, p. 193.
32 *Tyrone Constitution*, 19 July 1895.
33 Ibid., 28 June 1895.
34 PRONI, D3007/P/187, Abercorn to Belmore, 3 Nov. 1895.
35 *Tyrone Constitution*, 12 July 1895.
36 W. H. Hurlbert, *Ireland under coercion* (2008, originally published Edinburgh, 1888), i, pp. 132–7.
37 The writer is incorrect on these details: see Chapter 2 on the 1st Earl of Abercorn.
38 *The Times*, 15 Aug. 1888.
39 PRONI, D623/A/335/4, Abercorn to Robert Bell, 30 April 1889.
40 Quoted in Olwen Purdue, *The Big House in the north of Ireland* (Dublin, 2009), p. 72.
41 *Freeman's Journal*, 5 Nov. 1887.
42 Ibid., 14 Dec. 1887.
43 PRONI, D623/A/335/5, James McFarlane to Abercorn, 19 May 1890. The background to this letter and the assertions made in it was McFarlane's annoyance at not being paid as much as agent as he felt he should have been.
44 PRONI, T2996/3/1, Abercorn to Saunderson, Sept. 1896.
45 House of Lords Record Office, CAD/829.
46 Ibid., CAD/1010.
47 Andrew Gailey, *Ireland and the death of kindness* (Cork, 1987), p. 146.
48 House of Lords Record Office, CAD/1329.
49 Gailey, *Ireland and the death of kindness*, p. 118.
50 Purdue, *The Big House in the north of Ireland*, p. 83.
51 John S. Galbraith, *Crown and Charter: the early years of the British South Africa Company* (Berkeley, 1974), p. 114.
52 R. I. Rotberg and M. F. Shore, *The Founder: Cecil Rhodes and the pursuit of power* (Oxford, 1988), p. 315.

53 John Vincent (ed.), *The Crawford Papers: The Journals of David Lindsay, Twenty-seventh Earl of Crawford and Tenth Earl of Balcarres (1871–1940), during the years 1892 to 1940* (Manchester, 1984), p. 97.
54 Ibid., p. 273.
55 Rotberg, Shore, *The Founder: Cecil Rhodes*, p. 431.
56 PRONI, D623/A/334, Rhodes to Abercorn, no date [1890].
57 PRONI, D623/A/341/1.
58 PRONI, D623/A/336/38.
59 Norman Rich, *Friedrich von Holstein: politics and diplomacy in the era of Bismarck and Wilhelm II* (Cambridge, 1965), ii, p. 645.
60 *The Morning Post*, 1 July 1889, 24 May 1894, 29 Nov. 1897.
61 Peter Gordon (ed.), *Politics and society: the journals of Lady Knightly of Fawsley, 1885–1913* (Routledge, 2005), p. 174.
62 Consuelo Vanderbilt Balsan, *The Glitter and the Gold* (New York, 1953), p. 57.
63 Florence Emily Hardy, *The later years of Thomas Hardy 1892–1928* (New York, 1930), p. 6.
64 *The Times*, 5 Jan. 1910.
65 Ibid.
66 *Tyrone Constitution*, 25 Nov. 1910.
67 Ibid., 2 Dec.1910.
68 Ibid., 23 Dec. 1910.
69 Ibid., 9 Dec. 1910.
70 *The Times*, 23 Nov. 1911.
71 Ibid., 27 Feb. 1912.
72 *Irish Times*, 7 Jan. 1913.
73 *The Times*, 6 Jan. 1913.
74 *Irish Times*, 7 Jan. 1913.
75 PRONI, D1792/A/3/4/3.
76 Vincent (ed.), *The Crawford Papers*, pp. 296–7.
77 *Irish Times*, 4 Jan. 1913.
78 Thomas MacKnight, *Ulster as it is* (2 vols, London, 1896), ii, p. 299.
79 Documents relating to Lord Arthur John Hamilton's service in France are in the Abercorn collection in PRONI (D623/A/344).
80 Ernest Hamilton, *The first seven divisions: being a detailed account of the fighting from Mons to Ypres* (London 1916), pp 294–5.
81 Some of the papers of Lady Phyllis Hamilton are found in PRONI (D623/A/343).
82 Robert Cochrane, 'Cromlechs at Barons Court, County Tyrone, *Journal of the Royal Society of Antiquaries of Ireland*, xxxvii (1907), pp. 399–403.
83 Ninety-five years later, the Duke of Abercorn received a letter from Mr Edward R. Bayly of Ballyarthur House, County Wicklow, informing him that the young man in question was his father, Major Edward A. Bayly.
84 Mark Bence Jones, *Twilight of the Ascendancy* (London, 1987), p. 186. Philip Lecane, *Torpedoed! The RMS Leinster Disaster* (Cornwall, 2005), pp 172–3.

CHAPTER 9: THE 3RD DUKE

1 John Ross, *Years of my pilgrimage: random reminiscences* (London, 1924), p. 173.
2 Desmond Murphy, *Derry, Donegal and Modern Ulster: 1790–1921* (Derry, 1981), pp. 169–70.
3 Vincent (ed.), *The Crawford Papers*, pp. 296–7.
4 Ian Colvin, *Carson the Statesman* (New York, 1935), p. 217.
5 Paul Bew, *Ideology and the Irish Question: Ulster Unionism and Irish Nationalism, 1912–1916* (Oxford, 1998), p. 97.
6 PRONI, D1507/A/11/5.
7 National Library of Ireland, Wicklow Papers, MS 38,626/2.

8 *The Times*, 2 Dec. 1914.
9 Margaret Baguley (ed), *World War I & the Question of Ulster: The correspondence of Lilian and Wilfrid Spender* (Dublin, 2009), p. 239.
10 PRONI, D1507/A/11/28.
11 PRONI, D627/434/17, Abercorn to Montgomery, 17 May 1918.
12 *The Times*, 23 May 1918.
13 Baguley (ed), *World War I & the Question of Ulster*, p. 399.
14 Lord Curzon, the Leader of the Lords.
15 *The Times*, 2 Oct. 1919.
16 PRONI, D623/A/364/193.
17 *Belfast Newsletter*, 21 Nov. 1921.
18 PRONI, D640/17/5, Duchess of Abercorn to Fred Crawford, 27 Dec. 1921.
19 *Irish Times*, 13 Dec. 1922.
20 Ibid., 16 Dec. 1922.
21 Ibid., 27 Feb. 1923.
22 *The Times*, 14 Sept. 1953.
23 Ibid., 12 Oct. 1925.
24 William Shawcross, *Queen Elizabeth: the Queen Mother: the official biography* (London, 2009), pp. 211–13; Hugo Vickers, *Elizabeth, the Queen Mother* (London, 2006), pp. 84–5.
25 Quoted in Gillian McIntosh, *Force of culture: Unionist identities in twentieth-century Ireland* (Cork, 1999), p. 38.
26 *The Times*, 18 Nov. 1932.
27 McIntosh, *The Force of Culture*, p. 48.
28 PRONI, D1700/5/6/47, Lady Abercorn to Fred Crawford, 31 Jan. 1936.
29 *The Times*, 1 June 1933.
30 PRONI, CAB/9/T/5/1.
31 *Irish Times*, 2 Jan. 1989.
32 PRONI, CAB/9/T/5/1.
33 *The Times*, 10 Aug. 1934.
34 C. E. B. Brett, *Buildings of North County Down* (Belfast, 2002), p. 91.
35 Cannadine, *Decline and Fall of the British Aristocracy*, p. 175.
36 PRONI, CAB/9/T/5/1.
37 *Belfast Newsletter*, 15 Jan. 1940.
38 *The Times*, 9 Sept. 1939.
39 *Irish Times*, 14 Sept. 1953.
40 *The Times*, 23 September 1946.
41 Genesta Hamilton, *A Stone's Throw: Travels from Africa in Six Decades* (London, 1986).

CHAPTER 10: THE 4TH DUKE

1 This chapter is primarily based on the personal correspondence between the 4th Duke and Duchess, which remains with the family, and other family correspondence.
2 PRONI, D623/B/2/143.
3 PRONI, D623/D/4/32.
4 *Apollo* (July 1963), pp 12–17.
5 *Irish Times*, 14 Oct. 1966.
6 Ibid., 25 Nov. 1968.
7 Ibid., 21 June 1968.
8 Ibid., 16 Sept. 1970.
9 She was succeeded as president by her daughter-in-law, Lady Anthony Hamilton.
10 *The Times*, 6 Feb. 1990.
11 *Tyrone Constitution*, 15 June 1979.

CHAPTER 11: THE 5TH DUKE

1 Hansard: House of Commons Debates, 24 Nov. 1964, vol. 702 cc1087–234.
2 Ibid., 6 May 1966, vol. 727 cc2020–114.
3 *The Times*, 1 April 1969.
4 Letter to *The Times*, 14 May 1968.
5 Niall O Dochartaigh, *From civil rights to armalites: Derry and the birth of the Irish Troubles* (Basingstoke, 2005), p. 85.
6 *Irish Times*, 29 April 1969.
7 Ibid., 12 June 1970.
8 Ashley Hicks, *David Hicks: a life of design* (New York, 2009).
9 Hansard: House of Lords Debates, 21 Feb. 1989, vol. 504 cc591–600.
10 Ibid., 12 Dec. 1979, vol. 403 cc1212–63.
11 Ibid., 8 July 1982, vol. 432 cc899–954.
12 Ibid., 29 Oct. 1998, vol. 593 cc2145–54.

Bibliography

MANUSCRIPT AND UNPUBLISHED SOURCES

The main source of information for this book was the Abercorn Papers in the Public Record Office of Northern Ireland (D623). This vast collection of documents from the early thirteenth century through to the present day includes, according to it PRONI's own catalogue, '*c.* 29,300 individually numbered documents, 759 volumes, 88 bundles and 40 PRONI boxes'. Anthony Malcomson has provided a comprehensive 'Introduction' to the collection which I have referenced in the text. I am grateful to the Deputy Keeper of the Records for permission to cite from these papers. In addition, I was able to access material still at Barons Court and in the private possession of members of the family. Other manuscript sources are cited in the references to each chapter. In addition, two unpublished typescript volumes were made available by the Duke of Abercorn. Both written Lady Mary Baillie Hamilton, one is entitled 'The later Earls of Abercorn and Captain the Hon. John Hamilton, R.N.', and the other 'John James, 1st Marquess of Abercorn, K.G.' Though undated, they were probably written in the early twentieth century. There are also copies of these volumes in PRONI (D2152/1-2).

PUBLISHED SOURCES

Albinson, Cassandra, Peter Funnell, Lucy Peltz (eds), *Thomas Lawrence: Regency power and brilliance* (New Haven, 2010)

Alexander, Eleanor (ed.), *Primate Alexander,. archbishop of Armagh: a memoir* (London, 1913)

Baguley, Margaret (ed), *World War I & the question of Ulster: the correspondence of Lilian and Wilfrid Spender* (Dublin, 2009)

Barnard, Toby, *A new anatomy of Ireland: the Irish Protestants, 1649–1770* (New Haven, 2004)

Bartlett, Thomas (ed.), *Life of Theobald Wolfe Tone* (Dublin, 1998)

Bence Jones, Mark, *Twilight of the Ascendancy* (London, 1987)

Bew, Paul, *Ideology and the Irish question: Ulster unionism and Irish nationalism, 1912–1916* (Oxford, 1998)

Bowen, Desmond, *Cardinal Paul, Cardinal Cullen and the shaping of modern Irish Catholicism* (Dublin, 1983)

Brett, C. E. B., *Buildings of north County Down* (Belfast, 2002)

Buckle, G. E. (ed.), *The Letters of Queen Victoria*, 2nd series (3 vols, London, 1926–28,)

Burns, R. E., *Irish parliamentary politics in the eighteenth century* (2 vols, Washington DC, 1989)

Cannadine, David, *The decline and fall of the British Aristocracy* (New Haven, 1990)

Cochrane, Robert, 'Cromlechs at Barons Court, County Tyrone', *Journal of the Royal Society of Antiquaries of Ireland*, xxxvii (1907)

Colvin, Ian, *Carson the Statesman* (New York, 1935)

Connachan Holmes, John, *Country houses of Scotland* (Colonsay, 1995)

Connolly, Sean, *Religion, law and power: the making of Protestant Ireland, 1660–1760* (Oxford, 1992)

Cooke, A. B., 'Sir Stafford Northcote's diary of a visit to the province in October 1883' in *Proceedings of the Royal Irish Academy*, 75C, no. 4 (1975)

Cornwallis-West, Mrs George, *The reminiscences of Lady Randolph Churchill* (London, 1908)

Crawford, W. H., *The management of a major Ulster estate in the late eighteenth century: the eighth earl of Abercorn and his Irish agents* (Dublin, 2001)

Cunningham, Peter (ed.), *The letters of Horace Walpole, Earl of Orford* (London, 1859)

Defoe, Daniel, *A tour thro' the whole island of Great Britain* (London, 1724)

Elliott, Marianne, *Wolfe Tone: prophet of Irish independence* (New Haven, 1989)

Fraser, Sir William, *Memoirs of the Maxwells of Pollok* (2 vols, Edinburgh, 1863)

Gailey, Andrew, *Ireland and the death of kindness* (Cork, 1987)

Galbraith, John S., *Crown and Charter: the early years of the British South Africa Company* (Berkeley, 1974)

Galloway, Peter, *The Most Illustrious Order of St Patrick* (Phillimore, 1983)

Gillespie, Raymond, *Colonial Ulster: the settlement of east Ulster, 1600–1641* (Cork, 1985)

Gordon, Peter (ed.), *Politics and society: the journals of Lady Knightly of Fawsley, 1885–1913* (Routledge, 2005)

Graham, J., *Derriana* (Londonderry, 1823)

Graham, W. (ed.), *The letters of Joseph Addison* (Oxford, 1941)

Hamilton, Genesta, *A stone's throw: travels from Africa in six decades* (London, 1986).

Hamilton, Lord Ernest *The first seven divisions: being a detailed account of the fighting from Mons to Ypres* (London, 1916)

Hamilton, Lord Ernest *Old days and new* (London, n.d. [*c.* 1922])

Hamilton, Lord Ernest, *Forty years on* (London, 1922)

Hamilton, Lord Frederic, *The days before yesterday*, *The vanished pomps of yesterday* and *Here, there and everywhere*: all three books published in one volume as *The vanished world of yesterday* (London, 1950)

Hamilton, James, *Consultation pour James Hamilton, marquis d'Abercorn ... contre le duc d'Hamilton. Maintien et confirmation du titre héréditaire de duc de Châtellerault* (Paris, 1865).

Hamilton, George, *A history of the house of Hamilton* (Edinburgh, 1933)

Hamilton, Lord George *Parliamentary reminiscences and reflections, 1886–1906* (London, 1922)

Hardy, Florence Emily, *The later years of Thomas Hardy 1892–1928* (New York, 1930)

Haslip, Joan, *Lady Hester Stanhope* (London, 1934)

Haynes, Henrietta, *Henrietta Maria* (London, 1912)

Hayton, David (ed), *The letters of Marmaduke Coghill, 1722–1738* (Dublin, 2005)

Heaney, Henry (ed.), *A Scottish Whig in Ireland, 1835–38: the Irish journals of Robert Graham of Redgorton* (Dublin, 1999)

Hicks, Ashley, *David Hicks. A life of design* (New York, 2009)

Hill, Derek, 'Barons Court' in *Apollo* (July 1963)

Hill, George, *An historical account of the plantation in Ulster at the commencement of the seventeenth century* (Belfast, 1877)

Hill, George, *The Montgomery manuscripts* (Belfast, 1869)

Hill, George, *The MacDonnells of Antrim* (Belfast, 1873)

HMC, *Ormonde manuscripts*, new series

HMC, *Egmont manuscripts*

HMC, *Portland manuscripts*

Horstman, Allen, *Victorian Divorce* (London, 1985)

Hughes , C. W., 'John Christopher Pepusch', *The Musical Quarterly*, xxxi, no. 1 (Jan. 1945)

Hurlbert, W. H., *Ireland under coercion* (2008, originally published Edinburgh, 1888)

Hussey, S. M., *Reminiscences of an Irish land agent* (London, 1904)

Jackson-Stops, Gervase, 'Baronscourt, Co. Tyrone' in *Country Life*, 12, 19 and 26 July 1979

Jackson, Alvin, *The Ulster Party: Irish Unionists in the House of Commons, 1884-1911* (Oxford, 1989)

Johnston-Liik, Edith Mary, *History of the Irish parliament, 1692–1800* (6 vols, Belfast, 2002)

Jones, Clyve, '"This Waye of Proceeding would Remoove the Umbrage, and Uneasynesse, of Courte, and Country Heere": The Earl of Abercorn's 1708 scheme for reforming the election of the Scottish Representative Peers', *The Scottish Historical Review*, vol. 86 (April 2007)

Jordan, Anne, *Love well the hour: the life of Lady Colin Campbell* (Leicester, 2010)

Kielmansegge, Count Frederick, *Diary of a journey to England in the years 1761–1762* (London, 1902)

Kirkpatrick, R. W., 'Origins and development of the land war in mid-Ulster' in F. S. L. Lyons and R. A. J. Hawkins (eds), *Ireland under the union: varieties of tension* (Oxford, 1980)

Kirwan, John Waters *My life's adventure* (1936)

Lecane, Philip, *Torpedoed! The RMS Leinster disaster* (Cornwall, 2005)

Lodge, J., *The peerage of Ireland*, revised, enlarged and continued to the present time by Mervyn Archdall (7 vols, London, 1789)

MacKnight, Thomas, *Ulster as it is* (2 vols, London, 1896)

Macrory, Patrick, *The siege of Derry* (London, 1980)

Maguire, W. A., *Captain Cohonny: Constantine Maguire of Tempo, 1777–1834* (Belfast, 2002)

Malcomson, A. P. W., 'The Gentle Leviathan: Arthur Hill, second marquess of Downshire, 1753–1801', Peter Roebuck (ed.), *Plantation to Partition: Essays in Ulster History in Honour of J.L. McCracken* (Belfast, 1981)

Malcomson, A. P. W., 'A lost natural leader: John James Hamilton, First Marquess of Abercorn (1756–1818)', *Proceedings of the Royal Irish Academy*, 88C, no. 4 (1988)

Malcomson, A. P. W., 'The politics of "natural right": the Abercorn family and Strabane borough' in G. A. Hayes-McCoy (ed.), *Historical Studies*, x (Galway, 1976)

Malcomson, A. P. W., *John Foster: the politics of the Anglo-Irish Ascendancy* (Belfast, 1978)

Malcomson, A. P. W., *Pursuit of the heiress: aristocratic marriage in Ireland, 1740–1840* (Belfast, 2006)

Malcomson, A. P. W., *Virtues of a wicked earl: the life and legend of William Sydney Clements, 3rd Earl of Leitrim (1806–78)* (Dublin, 2009)

Malcomson, A. P. W., *The Clements archive* (Dublin, 2010)

Marson, Peter, *Belmore: the Lowry Corrys of Castle Coole, 1646–1913* (Belfast, 2007)

Marx , Karl and& Friedrich Engels, *Selected correspondence, 1846–1895* (New York, 1942)

McCreary, Alf, *Titanic Port: an illustrated history of Belfast Harbour* (Booklink, 2010)

McDougall, Margaret Dixon, *The letters of 'Norah' on her tour through Ireland* (Montreal, 1882; reprinted 2004)

McDowell, R. B., *The Church of Ireland, 1869–1969* (London, 1975)

McIntosh, Gillian, *Force of culture: Unionist identities in twentieth-century Ireland* (Cork, 1999)

Metcalfe, W. M., *A history of Paisley, 600–1908* (Paisley, 1909)

Miller, L. E., 'Rameau and the Royal Society of London: new letters and documents' in *Music & Letters*, 66, no. 1 (Jan. 1985)

Monypenny, W. V., and G. E. Buckle, *The life of Benjamin Disraeli* (London, 1929)

Murphy, Desmond, *Derry, Donegal, and modern Ulster: 1790–1921* (Derry, 1981)

Murphy, James H., *Abject loyalty: nationalism and monarchy in Ireland during the reign of Queen Victoria* (Washington, 2001)

Murphy, James H., 'Fashioning the famine Queen' in Peter Gray (ed.), *Victoria's Ireland? Irishness and Britishness, 1837–1901* (Dublin, 2004)

O Dochartaigh, Niall, *From civil rights to armalites: Derry and the birth of the Irish Troubles* (Basingstoke, 2005)

Ohlmeyer, Jane H., *Civil War and Restoration in the three Stuart kingdoms. the political career of Randal MacDonnell, Marquis of Antrim* (Cambridge, 1993)

Ormond, Richard, *Edwin Landseer: the private drawings* (Norwich 2009)

Perceval Maxwell, Michael, *The Scottish migration to Ulster in the reign of James I* (London, 1973)

Percy, Sholto and Reuben, *The Percy anecdotes* (London, 1826)

Potter, Harry, *Edinburgh under siege, 1571–1573* (Stroud, 2003)

Prior, Sir James, *Life of Edmond Malone, editor of Shakspeare* (London, 1860)

Purdue, Olwen, *The Big House in the north of Ireland* (Dublin, 2009)

Rich, Norman, *Friedrich von Holstein: politics and diplomacy in the era of Bismarck and Wilhelm II* (Cambridge, 1965)

Robins, Joseph, *Champagne and silver buckles: the viceregal court at Dublin Castle, 1700–1922* (Dublin, 2001)

Rooney, Dominic, *The life and times of Sir Frederick Hamilton, 1590–1647* (Dublin, 2013)

Ross, John, *Years of my pilgrimage: random reminiscences* (London, 1924)

Rotberg, R. I. and M. F. Shore, *The Founder: Cecil Rhodes and the pursuit of power* (Oxford, 1988)

Rowan, Alistair, *The buildings of Ireland: north west Ulster* (Harmondsworth, 1979)

Rowse, A. L., *The later Churchills* (London, 1958)

Russell, G. W. E., *Half lengths* (London, 1913)

Russell, G. W. E., *Portraits of the seventies* (Dublin, 1916)

Samuel, H. E., 'John Sigismond Cousser in London and Dublin' in *Music & Letters*, 61, no. 2 (Apr. 1980)

Savage, D. C., 'The origins of the Ulster Unionist Party, 1885–6' in *Irish Historical Studies*, xii no. 47, (March 1961)

Shawcross, William, *Queen Elizabeth: the Queen Mother: the official biography* (London, 2009)

Spalding, John, *The history of the troubles and memorable transactions in Scotland from the year 1624 to 1645* (2 vols, Aberdeen, 1792)

Stevenson, David, *Scottish Covenanters and Irish Confederates* (Belfast, 1981)

Turner, Dawson, *Descriptive index of the contents of five manuscript volumes: illustrative of the history of Great Britain, in the library of Dawson Turner* (Sloman, 1851)

Tyerman, Christopher, *A history of Harrow School, 1324–1991* (Oxford, 2000)

Vanderbilt Balsan, Consuelo, *The glitter and the gold* (New York, 1953)

Vickers, Hugo, *Elizabeth, the Queen Mother* (London, 2006)

[Victoria, Queen] *Leaves from the journal of our life in the Highlands, from 1848–1861: To which are prefixed and added extracts from the same journal giving an account of earlier visits to Scotland, and tours in England and Ireland, and yachting excursions*, edited by Sir Arthur Helps (London, 1868)

Vincent, John (ed.), *The Crawford Papers: the journals of David Lindsay, twenty-seventh Earl of Crawford and tenth Earl of Balcarres (1871–1940), during the years 1892 to 1940* (Manchester, 1984)

Walker, B. M., *Parliamentary election results in Ireland, 1801–1922* (Dublin, 1978)

Walker, B. M., *Ulster politics: the formative years, 1868–86* (Belfast, 1989)

Walsh, Patrick, *The making of the Irish Protestant Ascendancy: the life of William Conolly, 1662–1729* (Woodbridge, 2010)

Wraxall, Sir N. W., *Posthumous memoirs of his own time* (London, 1836)

Young, W. R., *Fighters of Derry, their deeds and descendents, being a chronicle of events in Ireland during the revolutionary period, 1688–91* (London, 1932)

Index

Dustjacket photograph and design:
Dunbar Design

Published 2014
by Ulster Historical Foundation
www.ancestryireland.com
www.booksireland.org.uk

© William J. Roulston
ISBN 978-1-909556-22-5

Printed by Nicholson & Bass Ltd.
Design by Dunbar Design

PARTE OF Y BARONE OF STRABANE

Col꞊rane

Tireconel

Riuer of Loughfoyle

Crevcabalan · Clontegorolan
ardkenn
Carngitan · Eremoylon · loybrim
Clagbogc · boynorven
lisconboy · Creagban
bolmallin · benlialla
Cavanocreagh · tulleard · oughto
gortmellan · Sbraghnebrastan · Cloncoose · lacrt
Cullon · ardnegloy · kiclong
dowletter · moyegh · Coolckurry
tavnarvrm · altrusten · loughcnow
teadan · lesduffm · fallasloy · bally olab
tullie · Magberireagh · Cormony · killeria
maghcrim꞊egan · ballybm · grange · altnogalo꞊ · Cooleramony · killogren'bi · Skeagh · gon
Coolonaghcric · tullmckirne · slagh
moamagh · Clogbogall · dromgattin · bailidonogbi · Luneglogber
donalonge · tavnabreodan · magberynclock · Clonckirry · ardogarvan · balliburny
Chagbcor · tavnasolus · b:Mcorrigh · Cloghoguall · b:bugh · nedwsten
gortcucagh · gortmessan · tircornen · ballyarny
Cloagbboy · kankill · Coolcncavil · Calbc · cavanolog
degort

Riuer of Loughfoyle